David Howell
A Pool of Spirituality

A LIFE OF DAVID HOWELL [LLAWDDEN]

ROGER L BROWN

Dedicated to that little band of brethren who, in the 1960s, formed the Evangelical Fellowship in the Church in Wales: Bertie Lewis, formerly Dean of St Davids; Cledan Mears, former Bishop of Bangor; Bill Lewis, now vicar of Gabalfa, and sometime Officer for Evangelism in the Church in Wales; the late Joe Williams, sometime Rector of Cusop; with the assistance of John Stott, Rector-emeritus of All Souls' Church, Langham Place, and of the Hookses, Dale, Pembrokeshire, and then General Secretary of the Evangelical Fellowship of the Anglican Communion.

David Howell (Llawdden)
(by kind permission of The National Library of Wales)

DAVID HOWELL
A POOL OF SPIRITUALITY

A Life of David Howell (Llawdden)

ROGER L. BROWN

GEE & SON (DENBIGH) LTD.

© Roger L. Brown 1998

ISBN 0 7074 0316 2

Published with the financial support of the Welsh Arts Council of Wales.

Printed and Published by
GEE & SON (DENBIGH) LTD.,
CHAPEL STREET, DENBIGH

Contents

PREFACE	vii
BIBLIOGRAPHY	ix
AN INTRODUCTION	1
THE EARLY YEARS	5
THE EARLY YEARS OF MINISTRY	24
VICAR OF CARDIFF 1864-75	41
THE MINISTRY AT ST JOHN'S CARDIFF	69
THE WREXHAM YEARS	118
THE DISESTABLISHMENT CONTROVERSY	157
ARCHIDIACONAL YEARS	187
DEAN OF ST DAVIDS	239
NATIONALITY AND PATRIOTISM	257
THE EVANGELICAL CHURCHMAN	272
CONCLUSION	308
INDEX	313

Preface

This book has been long in writing. If I plead in excuse the demands of a busy parochial life, I need also state that the chapters planned on the Welsh Evangelicals and on the Church and Welsh Nationality have become separate publications: the first, *The Welsh Evangelicals*, was published in 1986, and the second, *In Pursuit of a Welsh Episcopate*, is almost ready for publication.

The historian is meant to be objective. But this advice is almost impossible to achieve. It may be fairer to underline one's own position and let the reader be warned thereafter! I write as an evangelical, who, like David Howell, warms to the Christian love and charity of people of other traditions within the Christian family, while often regretting they may be seriously wrong in some areas of their doctrinal understanding! I trust I can do so with humour and integrity, allowing myself to frequently rearrange my own prejudices!

Over the years I have received much encouragement from Dean Bertie Lewis - a successor of David Howell as dean of St Davids, and Professor R Tudur Jones of Bangor. A considerable number of people have kindly answered queries and indicated other avenues of research. I express my gratitude to the late Canon E T Davies of Usk - who married a grand-daughter of David Howell, and Mrs Grace Thomas of Ipswich, who married one of his grandsons; to the late Mr Gordon Ellis and Mr D Leslie Davies of Wrexham; Bill Hamlin, Bill John and the late Canon E V Davies, of St John's Church, Cardiff; the Revd Dr Brian Lodwick, Canon T J Pritchard, the Revd Michael Semper, and the Revd David Vicars. I am equally obliged to the Archivists and their staffs at Lambeth Palace Library, Clwyd Record Office and the British Library; the Librarians and their staffs at the National Library of Wales, Aberystwyth, University of Wales, Cardiff, and Mr Brynmor Jones of the South Glamorgan Library Service; and to the Secretary-General of the Representative Body of the Church in Wales. and his staff, especially Mr Glyn Ellis. Lord Salisbury has kindly permitted me to quote from the papers of the Third Marquess of Salisbury, housed at Hatfield House, and his librarian, Mr Robin Harcourt-Williams, generously checked some references for me. I am equally grateful to the Wrexham Archives Service for permission to quote from material in its possession, and also for similar permission to quote from D G Lloyd Hughes' history of Pwllheli Church. I would also wish to thank the anonymous readers of my manuscript, who read it on behalf of the Welsh Arts Council, for their useful and helpful suggestions.

Above all, I am indebted to my wife Phyllis, who has borne with this project for much of our married life, and helped translate some of the material.

It may seen somewhat surprising that a life of David Howell was never written until this attempt. This may be because David Jones, vicar of Penmaenmawr, and his close friend, died before he was able to complete this chosen assignment [*Cyfaill Eglwysig*, 1913, p 210], but also, I suspect, because by the mid-1900s Howell's churchmanship was unfashionable, and his ecclesiology discredited by his superiors.

I commenced writing the life of David Howell as I saw him as a key figure in the nineteenth century Church in Wales. As I studied more I realised he had much to say to our contemporary church, especially in the arena of spirituality. But his life too has warmed and enriched my own, so that I no longer think of him as an historical figure but rather as a lively, humorous and warm-hearted colleague and friend in the great Communion of Saints.

Roger L Brown   Welshpool
July 1998

Bibliography
with short titles

MANUSCRIPT MATERIAL
British Library: Gladstone Papers [GP]
Bodleian Library, Oxford, Disraeli Papers
Hatfield House, Papers of the Third Marquess of Salisbury [SP]
Lambeth Palace Library: Benson Papers [BP]
                               Davidson Papers [DP]
                               Temple Papers [TP]
National Library of Wales: Church in Wales Records
                               Letters of Nathan: Ms 987B
                               Letters to Silvan Evans, MS 903B
                               Letters to Eiddon Jones, MS 3295E
                               MS 909B
                               MS 9645E
                               D Parry-Jones MSS
                               Cwrt Mawr MSS
                               Dolaucothi MSS
                               T E Ellis MSS
Representative Body of the Church in Wales, Cardiff: Papers of the Ecclesiastical Commissioners and Queen Anne's Bounty [EC & QAB].
Gloucester Record Office: Dean and Chapter papers.
Ruthin, Clwyd County Record Office, material relating to Wrexham.
Wrexham Public Library, material relating to David Howell and the parish church.

NEWSPAPERS
Bye-gones (Oswestry)
Carnarvon and Denbigh Herald [CDH]

Cardiff and Merthyr Guardian [CMG]
Cardiff Times
Cardiff Weekly Mail
Church & People (CPAS periodical) [C&P]
Church Times
Hansard
News of the Week
North Wales Guardian [NWG]
Record
Weekly Mail
Western Mail [WM]
Wrexham Advertiser
Wrexham Guardian
Yr Haul

BROWN RL, *Irish Scorn, English Pride and the Welsh Tongue* [Cardiff 1987].
   The Followers of Jeroboam [Cardiff 1984].
   The Welsh Evangelicals [Cardiff 1986].
CAMBRENSIS Victor, *The Rise and Decline of Welsh Nonconformity* [London 1912].
CARDIFF, *St John's Parish Magazine* [Parish Magazine].
   Ibid, *Parish Accounts* etc.
CARDIFF, *St Peter's Church, Centenary Brochure.*
CONYBEARE JC, *Essays Ecclesiastical and Social* [London 1855].
DAVIES David, *Reminiscences of my Country and People* [London 1925].
   The Ancient Celtic Church of Wales [London 1910].
DAVIES D T [ed], *Hanes Eglwysi a Phlwyfi Lleyn* [Pwllheli 1910].
DAVIES W Ryle, "Yr Hybarch Archddiacon Howell yn St Margaret, Westminster...", *Traethodydd*, 1890, pp 227-34, 300-7.
DILLISTONE F W, *C H Dodd* [London 1977].
DODD A H, *A History of Wrexham* [Wrexham 1957].
EDWARDS A M Grey, *Reminiscences of an Unknown Man* [1940].
EDWARDS H T, *Wales and the Welsh Church* [London 1889].
ELLIS M, "David Howell, Llawdden", *Haul* 49 [1971] 30-4.
ELLIS Robert, *Living Echoes* [Cardiff 1950].

EVANS David, *Adgofion* [Lampeter 1904].
EVANS Eifion, *The Welsh Revival of 1904* [Port Talbot 1969].
GUIDE to the Church Congress at Cardiff [1889].
GUY J R, *A History and Description of the Mother Church of Cardiff* [Cardiff 1971].
HENNELL Michael, *Sons of the Prophets* [London 1979].
HOWELL David, *A Lecture: The Duty of Charity and Mutual Forbearance in Matters of Religious Belief* [Newport 1856].
A Sermon Preached at Manchester Cathedral on the Eve of St David's Day 1895: Romans 12.18 [Bangor 1895]
"Adgof am Nathan Dyfed", *Geninen*, 19 [1901] 177-80.
Appeal for St David's Cathedral [1902].
Araeth a Draddodwyd ar yr Achlysur o osod i lawr Gareg - Sylfaen Ysgol Alderman Davies [Abertawe 1857].
"Athrawon yr Ysgol Sabothol", *Traethodydd*, 46 [1897] 258-62.
"Emynyddiaeth Gymreig", *Geninen*, 15 [1897] 10-14.
Fitness for Service: A Sermon Preached before the University of Cambridge [Cambridge 1893].
Foreign Mission [offprint, London 1897].
"Gweddi a Bywyd o Dduwiodeb", *Traethodydd*, 97 [1892] 405-11.
"Gwladgarwch y Cymru", *Geninen*, 10 [1892] 145-8, 11 [1893] 77-80.
In Memoriam: Farewell Sermon at St John the Baptist, Cardiff [Cardiff 1875].
Ministerial Life in the Light of 1 Cor. 1X [Bangor nd]
"Peredur", *Geninen*, 17 [1899] 184f.
Prayer as an Aid to the Life of Godliness [offprint from *Rhyl Church Congress Report 1891*].
Religion in the Home: Address to St David's Diocesan Conference [offprint, 1902].
"Rhai o Beryglon Bywyd Gweinidogaethol", *Traethodydd*, 47 [1896] 401-8.
"Speech at Wrexham Eisteddfod", *Y Cymmrodor*, 1 [1877] 48-52.
The Church in Wales and Vernacular Preaching [offprint from *Manchester Church Congress Report 1888*].
"The Corn of Wheat Dying", in JONES J C, *The Welsh Pulpit of Today* [London 1885], pp 214-33.

The Present Work of the Church in Wales [offprint from the *Norwich Church Congress Report 1895*].

The Welsh Church: A Sermon Preached at St Margaret's, Westminster (also known as *The Patriot's Yearning for the Prosperity of Zion*) [London 1890].

"Welsh Hymnology", *Transactions of Liverpool Welsh Society*, 1891-2, pp 79-92.

Women and Missions [London 1900]

Yr Aelwyd [London c 1890s]

HOWELL David: *Unveiling of the Memorial Window at Wrexham Parish Church* [Wrexham 1904].

HOWELL John [Sr], *Colofn y Bardd* [Wrexham 1879].

HOWELL John, "Fy Adgofion am fy Mrawd Llawdden", *Geninen*, 21 [1903] 105-6.

"John Howell, Esq, Pencoed, Llangrallo", *Cylchgrawn*, 19 [1880] 229-32 266-9 303-6 372-4.

HUGHES D Ll, *The History of Pwllheli Church* [1987].

HUGHES H J, *David Howell of Swansea* [Newport 1883].

HUGHES Thomas, *Great Welshmen* [Cardiff 1931].

HUGHES William, *History of the Diocese of Bangor* [SPCK, London 1911].

HUNTER-BLAIR D, *John Patrick, Third Marquess of Bute* [Cardiff 1921].

HUWS Rhys J, "Llawdden", *Geninen*, 21 [1903 St Davids] 1-9.

IDRISWYN, "Y Deon Howell", *Cymru* [OME], 27 [1904] 73-5 113-4 162-4 210-2.

JAMES A W, *St Davids and Dewisland* [Cardiff 1981].

JAMES W & JONES J M, *Cofiant a Pregethau y Parchedig D Saunders* [Abertawe 1894].

JENKINS D, *The Agricultural Community in South-West Wales* [Cardiff 1971].

JOHNES A J, *On the Causes which have Produced Dissent from the Established Church in the Principality of Wales* [3rd edn, London 1870].

JONES David, *The Moral and Religious Condition of Wales* [Bangor 1906].

The Welsh Church and Welsh Nationality [London c 1895].

JONES R Tudur, *Fydd ac Argyfwng Cenedl* [2 vols, Abertawe 1981].

JONES Samuel, "Adgofion am y Diweddar dra Pharchedig D Howell ..", *Cyfaill Eglwysig*, 1913, pp 121-5 144-7 184f 207-10.
JONES T G, *Cofiant Thomas Gee* [Denbigh 1913].
JONES T J, *Cofiant William Evans, Rhymni* [Lampeter nd].
KENNARD E F, *The Remarkable Career of a Well-Known Athlete* [Cardiff 1910].
LERRY George, *Alfred George Edwards* [Oswestry 1939].
LEWIS Henry, *Is Disestablishment Just?* [Conway 1914].
LEWIS J P, *Church Blunder - State Plunder* [London 1913].
LLEWELYN M G, *Sand in the Grass* [London 1943].
LLOYD Canon, "David Howell, Deon Ty Ddewi Gynt", *Haul*, 1932, pp 113-4.
MASTERMAN N, *The Forerunner* [Llandybie 1972].
MAYBERRY J, *I Saw Three Ships* [Cardiff 1988].
MORGAN J V, *A Study in Nationality* [London 1911].
  The Church in Wales in the Light of History [London 1918].
  Welsh Religious Leaders of the Victorian Era [London 1905].
MORGAN K O, *David Lloyd George* [Cardiff 1964].
  Rebirth of a Nation: Wales 1880-1980 [Oxford 1981].
MORGAN R H, *The Disestablishment of the Church in Wales* [Wrexham 1888].
MORGAN R W, *The Church and its Episcopal Corruptions in Wales* [2nd edn, London 1856].
OLLIVANT Alfred, *Visitation Charges to the Diocese of Llandaff*.
OWEN E E, *The Early Life of Bishop Owen* [Llandysul 1958].
PALMER A W, *A History of the Parish Church of Wrexham* [Wrexham 1888].
PHILLIPS Thomas, *The Welsh Revival* [London 1860].
PRICE D T W, *A History of St David's University College, Lampeter II* [Cardiff 1990].
REED J C, *The Church in our City* [Cardiff 1954].
REPORT *of a Meeting in Memory of the late Evan Evans* [Neath 1859].
REPORTS *of the Church Congresses at Manchester* [1888], *Rhyl* [1891], and *Norwich* [1895].
REPORT *of the Royal Commission on the Church of England and other Religious Bodies in Wales* [London 1910-11].
REPORTS *and ABSTRACTS OF REPORTS AND SPEECHES etc of*

the CHURCH PASTORAL-AID SOCIETY [CPAS Report or CPAS Abstract]
REPORTS of the Llandaff Diocesan Church Extension Society.
REPORTS of the Llandaff Diocesan Conferences.
REPORTS of the St Asaph Diocesan Conferences.
REYNOLDS J S, *Canon Christopher* [Abington 1967].
RICHARDS Brinley, *History of the Llynfi Valley* [Cowbridge 1982].
SHARP A, *A Narrative of the Great Revival Work in South Wales 1871* [Cardiff 1871].
SMITH David [ed], *A People and a Proletariat* [London 1980].
STOCK Eugene, *My Recollections* [London 1909].
The History of the Church Missionary Society [London 1899].
SWANSEA Parish Magazine.
THOMAS D R, *History of the Diocese of St Asaph* [2nd edn, 3 vols, Oswestry, 1908-13].
THOMAS M E, *Afiaith yng Ngwent* [Cardiff 1978].
THOMAS W C, *The Church in Wales: Shall we End it or Mend it?* [Birmingham 1893].
VINCENT J E, *Letters from Wales* [London 1889].
THOMAS J M, *Looking Back* [Carmarthen 1979].
WARD J W & COE H A, *Father Jones of Cardiff* [London 1907].
WALLIS-JONES Ll J, *Welsh Characteristics* [London 1898].
WILLIAMS D, "Tra Parchedig Ddeon Howell", *Geninen*, 21 [1903] 151-6, ibid [St David's] 10-16, 22 [1904] 42-3.
WILLIAMS E, *Life and Letters of Rowland Williams* [2 vols, London 1874].
WILLIAMS J, *Notes and Narratives* [Machynlleth 1885].
WRENFORD J T, *Romanising the Church of England* [London 1864].
WREXHAM *Directory of 1886, The* [reprint of 1981].

Introduction

In 1910, Watcyn Wyn, poet and schoolmaster, wrote these lines:

> Cwsg yn dawel, hen bererin,
>   Yn yr hen *Gathedral* mawr;
> Fe fydd plant y mil blynyddoedd
>   I Dy Ddewi'n dod i lawr
> I barchus holi am dy hanes
>   Ac i chwilio am dy fedd,
> A gwrando, fel i glywed adsain
>   Llais yn per gyhoeddi hedd.[1]

[Sleep peacefully, old pilgrim, in the old cathedral. Children of a thousand years will come down to St David's to look for your grave and to ask for your history and listen to a voice proclaiming peace.]

His subject was David Howell, a former dean of St Davids, who is commemorated in that cathedral by a tablet outside the Lady Chapel, which he helped to restore. Watcyn Wyn's words have lost their prophetic tone, and probably few take the trouble to read the inscription on that tablet. His name is hardly known now outside the select circles of Welsh literary and ecclesiastical historians, and yet David Howell was one of the most formative leaders of Welsh-speaking Wales during the latter part of the nineteenth century.

A fo ben, bid bont, is a well known Welsh proverb: he who would be a leader, let him be a bridge. Such a sentiment eminently describes Howell's life. The very circumstances of his birth and upbringing established his role as a bridgebuilder. An early religious upbringing divided between church and chapel, and a

---
[1] *Geninen*, 21 [1903 St D] 57.

youth spent on the linguistic border land of the vale of Glamorgan clearly formulated this bridge-building role. Throughout his life Howell was revered by Christians of all traditions, English and Welsh, even at the height of the disestablishment controversy. His spiritual and evangelical faith was valued by all men of good will, while his quiet influence enabled him to interpret one tradition to another. Dr William Rees (Hiraethog), a noted Congregational minister, is said to have told Archdeacon Griffiths of Neath that a second St David would be needed before reunion between the churches in Wales could take place. Griffiths in return pointed that earnest Nonconformist to the person of David Howell.[2]

Howell was born in the Anglicised vale of Glamorgan but brought up in a Welsh-speaking family. Throughout his life he endeavoured to persuade English monoglots to understand that 'Welshness' was more than just speaking a language, but rather implied a culture and a heritage of inestimable value. He was deeply concerned, too, that the indigenous nature of his chosen church should not be lost in the then all-prevailing policy of anglicisation. His emotional nature, sensitivity, and familiarity with the *gwerin* culture of Wales, made him not only an ardent patriot but a spokesman for his people.

In size so small that he found the pulpit of St Paul's Cathedral much too high for him, this man was a spiritual giant. Rhys Hughes declared that he knew no one so like the old Methodist revivalists as David Howell.[3] Thomas Hughes described him as one who lived in the presence of his Lord.[4] On his death bed he declared that he saw a great revival coming to Wales. This was in 1903. And so it proved to be. In these matters of the spirit he became a spiritual bridge maker; one who made it easier for his fellow men to see Christ. Indeed, he continually pointed men and women in his spoken and written utterances to the saving grace of the Lord Jesus Christ.

His successor as vicar of Wrexham, Canon Fletcher, at the unveiling of a memorial window to him in that church, after noting the disadvantages of his life, particularly his lack of a

---

[2] J V Morgan, *The Church in Wales in the Light of History* [London 1918], p 158.
[3] Rhys J Huws in *Geninen*, 21 [1903 St D] 2.
[4] Thomas Hughes, *Great Welshmen* [Cardiff 1931], p 74.

university education, called him "a most remarkable man, not in the least because of his power of triumphing over difficulties." He continued:

> but by means of innate talent, of extraordinary industry, and by his great powers of eloquence, he triumphed over all these difficulties, and rose, not only to a position of highest dignity in the Church, but to what he himself would have valued far more, a place of the greatest esteem and love in the hearts of his fellow countrymen throughout this Principality.[5]

Today, ninety and more years after his death, David Howell's name is largely forgotten, even though in his lifetime he had an immense influence on the course of events in both the Welsh church and nation. Why should this be? During his lifetime it was said he was not particularly popular with the Welsh clergy. He could preach, said an article in the periodical *Cymru Fydd*, and they could not; "he believes in the power of the gospel; they believe in the charm of ritual; he yearns after spiritual life", but "too many of them are content with the convulsive movements produced by ecclesiastical magnetism; he inclines towards Disestablishment, while they regard it as the modern abomination of desolation."[6] This was a caricature, of course, but clearly a person of Howell's strong views would not be popular in every quarter. But he also met with jealousy from an unexpected quarter, namely from his own and then youthful, inexperienced and irresponsible diocesan, Alfred George Edwards. Howell, throughout his ministerial life, had earnestly pleaded that the indigenous nature of the Welsh Church should be respected by those in authority within it. But Edwards' policy was directly contrary to this, for in order to identify the four dioceses of the Welsh Church with the province of Canterbury, he had to go against Howell's plea and deny the indigenous nature of that Church. At the same time his pugnacious and militant personality made him cast aspersions on the spiritual nature of Welsh Nonconformity. This, of course, was at the height of the disestablishment controversy in Wales, and feelings and tempers

---

[5] *The Memorial Window to the late David Howell in Wrexham Parish Church, Unveiling Ceremony* [1904].
[6] *Cymru Fydd*, II [1899] 322f.

ran high on both sides. Howell's courage and faithfulness in defending his policy against the calumnies of his diocesan, who let it be openly known that he would have stopped Howell's appointment to the archdeaconry of Wrexham had not Bishop Hughes publicly announced it just before his death, was exemplary,[7] and contrasted to a remarkable degree with Edwards' bigotry and rudeness. At the end of the day Edwards forced his *St Asaph policy*, as it came to be called, upon the Church by the sheer force of his personality. Any deviation from it was regarded as akin to disloyalty and rebellion. The end result of this was not only that Howell's name was cast into oblivion, but, even more tragically, Edwards' policy made the Church in Wales more of a political machine than a spiritual body, and contributed much to its religious poverty in our present century.

Although Howell's spiritual influence, godly counsel, and quiet persuasive voice was forgotten in that scramble for political duplicity, the ideas he represented and endorsed are now coming back to the centre of the stage. The Church in Wales today is deeply concerned to stress its indigenous nature and its essential *Welshness,* if only to suggest that it can still form the 'mother church' of a new order of church unity. Thus Howell's life and teaching still speak to us today, and we may well think of him as another Barnabas, "a good man and full of the Holy Spirit."

---

[7] Edwards to Howell, 3 Ap 1893, in *Wrexham Advertiser Supplement,* 8 July 1893.

The Early Years[1]

The age in which David Howell lived and died was an age of reticence. Neither the inner dealings of the soul nor the moral battles of life were to be revealed. It was a convention practised and understood by Howell's obituary writers as well, even though they offer some hint that not all was well in his earlier life. His doings in those days, before what must have been a religious conversion in his early twenties, could not have been unknown to the people amongst whom he lived. But they too shared the same tradition of reticence, and if they knew anything to his discredit, then his subsequent success, if not his religious conversion, cancelled out the misdeeds of the past from memory and recollection.

The age in which Howell was born was also an age of transition. That Welsh part of the vale of Glamorgan, which was his habitat, was losing both its language and its isolation. The language of the hearth would not be the language of David's public ministry in later years. There was cross-fertilisation too in religious matters, as the Welsh Methodist movement had finally seceded from the Established Church in 1811, and young David's family associations fell on both sides of the divide. The rest of his life was an outworking of these tensions and cross currents as they affected the issues of language, nationalism, culture and denomination. These were matters which must have profoundly affected his youth, and which influenced his later course as a reconciler and peacemaker between opposing factions.

---

[1] The main source of this material is the obituary notices in *Geninen* of 1903, especially those of Rhys J Huws [21 (St Davids 1903) 1-9, republished in his *Gweithiau Llenyddol* (Llanelli 1933) pp 71-91], of Howell's brother William [21 (1903) 105f], and D Williams, rector of Llandyrnog [21 (1903) 151-6. St Davids no 10-16]; and the unsigned article on John Howell, his father, in *Cylchgrawn*, 19 (1880) 229-32, 266-9, 303-6, 372-4. See also the articles by Idriswyn in *Cymru* (OME) 27 (1904) 73-5, 43f, 162-4, 210-12.

It was David W Leigh, a godly man, member of a noted evangelical family in south Wales, and then curate of Llangan, who baptised "Dafydd", the eldest son of John and Catherine Howell, in Llangan church on 19 September 1831. Leigh's own evangelical ministry emphasised the spiritual history of that parish. David Jones, who had died twenty-one years earlier, had been rector of that parish for forty-three years, and was one of those men, who, under the Holy Spirit, had forwarded the eighteenth century spiritual revival in Wales. Jones had endeavoured to keep the revival within the pale of the Church, and died, significantly, a year before the final separation. Rhys J Huws stated in a biographical memoir of Howell in *Geninen,* published to commemorate his death, that as a young man, Howell had seen many an old man, even those whose hearts were like hard rocks, weeping profusely whenever the name of David Jones was mentioned. The evangelical ministry of David Jones in this area was still a living tradition in Howell's younger days. Indeed, the Methodist elder, Thomas Dafydd, personified this legend during Howell's father's younger days. Dafydd had travelled as Jones' companion throughout his preaching journeys, heard Howel Harris preach, and attended Daniel Rowland's communion services at Llangeitho.

The death of David Jones in 1810 meant that the Welsh Methodists - who were of the more sturdy calvinistic rather than Wesleyan stock - finally separated from the Church. Although the seeds of that separation had germinated over the years, the actual cause was the ordination, by the Welsh Methodist leaders themselves, of men to the ordained and sacramental ministry of their church. They did so as the Established Church declined to accept "methodist" men for ordination, and apparently preferred breeding and education in its ordination candidates rather than the charisma of the Spirit's annointing. That Church, with its ineffective administrative machinery, its Anglo-Welsh bishops generally unable to appreciate or sympathise with the Welsh temperament, governed, it was believed, by those who wished to force an anglicising policy upon the Welsh Church and nation, could not contain the revival of God's work within it. Yet the life of David Jones would have shown Howell that not only were godly men able to remain within the Church, but were also enabled to exercise a powerful spiritual ministry therein.

David's father, John, represented this other, indigenous Welsh and Methodist culture. At the time of his son's birth he was a reasonably well-off yeoman farmer at Treoes, Llangan. Early in his life he had became one of the heirs of that Welsh revival. On moving to Bryncwtyn in Pencoed he was elected a deacon of Salem Welsh Methodist Church there, and later he became secretary of the Glamorgan monthly meeting. For forty years he served in this capacity at his own expense, often travelling for thirty miles and more to attend its various meetings. He consequently became one of the most influential laymen in his denomination at county level. In his biography of another David Howell, described as of Swansea to distinguish him from others of that name, H J Hughes described David's father as "John Howells, Esq. [sic] of Pencoed", one of "the grave, respectable and faithful men" and "worthy deacons" who enjoyed the friendship of the other Howell. John Howell, he continued, was "an extensive farmer and freeholder, and a man of no mean importance in the part of the county where he resided. ... He was a Christian of established character and widespread influence."[2] A similar tribute comes from Rhys J Huws, who remembered him as a godly man who combined the strength of a strong will with the tenderness of a sensitive heart.[3] The biographers of his son-in-law, David Saunders, a noted Welsh Methodist preacher, inform us that John Howell was a man of good counsel to his denomination and neighours on nearly every matter, one who acted as a lawyer to direct and help, as a judge to end arguments, and as a ruling elder to serve them in holy things.[4]

Apart from being a leading Welsh Methodist, John Howell was also well known in Welsh literary circles. Hughes describes him as a poet who had a rare command of pure and eloquent Welsh. His poetry, all written as *cynghanedd*, was later edited in a volume entitled *Colofn y Bardd*. It was published in 1879 at Wrexham, where his son was vicar, suggesting that the book was seen

---

[2] H J Hughes, *David Howell of Swansea* [Newport 1885], pp 66f.
[3] *Geninen*, 21 (St Davids 1903) 2.
[4] W James and J M Jones, Cofiant a Pregethau Y Parchedig D Saunders [Abertawe 1894], p xxvi.

through the press as an act of filial piety. Included within its pages are an *awdl* to Bruce Knight, dean of Llandaff, of 1845, and a poem on the death of his, John Howell's, wife.[5] He was also an associate editor of the literary magazine Y *Cylchgrawn* between the years 1851-5, and prominent in the Abergavenny eisteddfod movement where he won a number of prizes between 1835-8.[6] This was organised by Sir Benjamin and Lady Hall, and was probably the leading Welsh cultural activity in south Wales at that time. A letter which survives from 1838 relates to a prize which he had won at that eisteddfod, and indicates that his circumstances were not so prosperous then as they later became. In this letter he requested help "towards the cost of coming from the ends of the earth to your honourable meeting, if that is what you are doing for others."[7] However he wrote in the introduction to his collected poems that because his eisteddfodic activities had so interfered with his religious duties, he had determined to consecrate himself to the latter instead.[8] Another witness declared, however, that his youthful excursions into this literary world filled his parents, and their mentor, the elder Thomas Dafydd, with horror. They believed John was abandoning Christianity in favour of some form of pagan druidism, and they also felt that he was mixing with the wrong sort of company. An early desire to be ordained, due to his friendship with an unknown local curate, was discouraged by his parents. You will remain a curate, they told him, all your life, and be little better than a beggar. It took John thirty years before he felt able once more to pick up his bardic pen and attend the occasional eisteddfod, such was the distaste engendered in him at that time against such activities.[9]

Though he later became a reasonably wealthy man, John Howell never paraded his riches. H A Bruce, later Lord Aberdare, thus reported to Gladstone, who as prime minister was endeavouring to find a Welsh-preaching bishop for the vacant see of St Asaph in 1870, and was considering the claims of David

---

[5] John Howell, *Colofn y Bardd* [Wrexham 1879], pp 179f.
[6] M E Thomas, *Afiaith yng Ngwent* [Cardiff 1978], p 63.
[7] NLW MS 13182E, item 130: Bard Coch, 4 Rhag 1838.
[8] Edward Jones, *Enwogion Cymreig 1700-1900* [Caerdydd 1908], p 192; Glyn Ashton in Prys Morgan [ed], *Glamorgan County History*, 6 [Cardiff 1988] 350, notes that Howell's work is technically admirable yet devoid of poetry.
[9] *Cylchgrawn*, 19 [1880] 229-32, 261-8, 303-6.

Howell for that post: "he is the son of a small farmer in Coychurch (the parish where the Bishop of Bangor learnt Welsh) who still, I believe, drives his own cart."[10] The inference of that remark was that curates came from such stock, not bishops. Lady Llanover, the widow of Sir Benjamin Hall, knew better, and on another occasion when Howell was being mentioned for episcopal honours, she wrote to Gladstone in his support, as she wrote for or against likely or unlikely candidates to the then prime minister during every episcopal vacancy in Wales during her later lifetime. She thus wrote that John Howell was looked upon as the Patriarch of the Calvinist Methodists. Though he possessed his own lands, he never attempted to be a squire of high degree but rather lived in "the bosom of his family", keeping the household of a Welsh freehold farmer. The way he had brought up his three children would be an example to any clergyman. He had died some years previously, leaving his residence to his daughter, his farm to his younger son William, and three thousand pounds to his eldest son, David Howell.[11] That sum represented a small fortune in those days.

His mother's indifferent health meant that David was brought up by his mother's mother. Mary Griffiths of Ty'nycaeau influenced him deeply. She was a strong church-woman, of evangelical persuasion, probably due to the influence of David Jones' ministry. To the end of his life her grandson continued to speak and write of the continuing influence over him of those Welsh hymns she had taught him before he was nine years of age. But his grandfather was described as having "wet habits". When he started to take the teenage David to the local taverns, Mary Griffiths felt so concerned that he might be corrupted by strong drink that she persuaded his mother to take him back to the family home at Bryncwtyn. He was then fifteen years of age.

He spent a year with his parents. It was not an easy time, however profitable it appeared to be in hindsight. One has an impression that David found that his father had a heavier hand

---

[10] Bruce to Gladstone, 11 Jan 1870, Gladstone Papers, British Library [GP], Add Ms 44086/78.
[11] Lady Llanover to Gladstone, 14 Jan 1883, GP 44479/121. William remained at Pencoed and farmed there, remaining a loyal member of the Methodist body there until his death.

than his grandmother, and subjected him to restraints which he found irksome. But his father took David and his younger brother to his chapel, asking them theological and scriptural questions on the way, frequently complaining that he was wasting his time in so doing. During the weekdays David worked on his father's farm. A year passed, during which he gradually and then successfully rebelled against this new discipline, so different from his grandparents' home. Persuading his parents to let him return he was received with open arms.

That year with his father had an enormous value in his subsequent life. Within that chapel he made new friends, and heard some of the best preachers of the day. Amongst them were John Jones Talysarn, Henry Rees Liverpool, William Evans Tonyrefail, Owen Thomas and Matthews Ewenni. Some of them were personal friends of his father, and presumably stayed at his house. Consequently, Morien could write that Howell had received his early theological training at the feet of those whom he described as the Gamaliels of the chief denomination of the Principality.[12] Whether Morien's comment was true or not, Howell continued to hear them and others thereafter whenever he had the opportunity, and their influence and style of preaching deeply affected him. Having seen the warmth and piety of Nonconformity at its best, he was therefore unable to deny its spiritual validity and Scriptural character. It seems too that during this year he embarked on a more thorough acquaintance with the Welsh language, moving from a working knowledge to a literary ability within it. One assumes that his father's influence lay behind this development.

There was another profound effect too from that year, for during it, in his father's chapel, he met his future wife, Ann Powell, although neither of them became full members of it. Rather they would have been described as adherents or hearers. Thus Howell would not have attended the society meeting or seiat.

David Howell and Ann Powell were married at St Mary Hill by licence on 13 September 1851. Although he was nineteen and she sixteen, John Griffiths, the vicar, who officiated, described them

---

[12] In the *Western Mail*, 23 Dec 1882, p 3.

both as being of full age, which was obviously incorrect. Her father was a Pencoed farmer, and David's occupation was described in the same way. His address was given as 'Ty'nycaeau' which was his grandmother's home.

The reason for that early marriage is also to be found in the registers of that parish. For on 11 February 1852 is recorded the baptism of their eldest son Taliesin. The same address was given, so the young couple were still living with Mary Griffiths. It may be that the young couple practised the old Welsh custom of 'bundling', or courtship in bed,[13] or maybe not, but it was a marriage which however youthful and inauspicious its beginnings, was a happy one for both parties.

Ann Powell came from a similar background to Howell,[14] but she lacked the advantages which her husband had obtained for himself. This was written by Bishop Ollivant in his letter replying to Gladstone's queries regarding Howell in 1870, the circumstances of which have been noted earlier. The bishop feared that as a bishop's wife she would hardly be able to take and retain her proper place, though Howell himself was by no means "ill mannered or unfit to associate with the gentry of a diocese."[15]

If his wife stood against his claims for high ecclesiastical position - a reflection more of the snobbery of the times than of her intrinsic worth - others discovered the circumstances of his marriage and used them to oppose his candidature for the bishopric of St Asaph in 1889. The 'winner' of that election, Bishop Alfred George Edwards, then used the same circumstances to prevent Howell's candidature for any other Welsh bishopric. Though a few English bishops remonstrated that the sins of ones youth should not effectively bar a man, either Edwards' persuasion or Queen Victoria's scruples prevented Howell from ever achieving episcopal rank.[16]

There was however a credit side to this marriage. It drew the young couple closer to the established Church. One can imagine what the seiat and chapel would have said about this state of

---

[13] Note, for example, Elfyn Scourfield, "Fact Finding in a Welsh Rural Community", *Folk Life*, 1972, pp 64-6.
[14] Bruce to Gladstone, 11 Jan 1870, GP 44086/78.
[15] Ollivant to Gladstone, 14 Jan 1870, GP 44424/97.
[16] See my forthcoming book, *In Pursuit of a Welsh Episcopate*.

affairs, or how John Howell would have felt the disgrace he believed this shot-gun marriage must have brought upon him and his family. The Church in such circumstances was more user-friendly, to quote modern jargon, than the chapel with its strict moral code which sometimes could over-emphasise salvation at the expense of forgiveness, and forget human frailty in the light of Christian privilege. One may assume, too, that marriage and family responsibilities proved a steadying influence on Howell. Until his marriage he must have faced divided loyalties between his grandmother and his parents, but now his responsibilities were quite clear, even though it seems he farmed his grandmother's holding for her.

As David drew closer to the Church he also drew closer to its young vicar, who has already been named as John Griffiths. It would be as well to speak of him now, for his was a formative influence on David's life, and many of his life-long concerns derived from his contact with him. Griffiths was a native of the vale of Aeron in Cardiganshire, where he was born in 1820. Educated at Cardigan Grammar School and St David's College, Lampeter, he became curate of Blaenau in Gwent in 1844, priest in charge of Nantyglo in the following year - this being a huge industrial parish, and in 1847 he was appointed rector of Llansannor and Llangan. He later held these in plurality with St Mary Hill, Howell's parish. Appointed rector of Neath in 1855, Bishop Ollivant selected him to serve as archdeacon of Llandaff in 1877, where he rapidly became the *eminence grise* during the closing years of Ollivant's long episcopate. Griffiths was a great 'pulpit man', a loyal son of the Church, and a patron of all things and institutions Welsh. He thus supported the eisteddfodic movement, was a member of several Welsh language societies, and was one of the founders of University College, Aberystwyth - paradoxically considered to be a Nonconformist institution - and was known far and wide as an earnest temperance speaker. Howell's views on patriotism and language must have owed much to him.

At first David found it difficult to get on with Griffiths, and it is said he opposed him fiercely on several occasions at the parish vestry of St Mary Hill, possibly, said one contemporary, for a bit of fun. But in these disputes, friendly or otherwise, Griffiths noted David's eloquence and persuasion, his courage and ability, and gradually got to know of his literary interests, his humour and interest in people. He determined that as "that boy from Ty'n y caeau is a terror, he must either be restrained or won over". And by that he meant brought to Christian life and even possibly ordained into the ministry of the Church of England. Although the details are not known, the young farmer and husband was brought into that experience of rebirth which must characterise every Christian life, one way or another, and through it he felt called to serve in the ordained ministry. Griffiths' prayer had been abundantly answered. As an obituary note emphasised, young Howell could not have been said to have been religious in his younger days; but he was brought to a serious state of mind through the ministry of John Griffiths.[17]

There were two obstacles to this chosen path, apart from the moral one, which appears to have either been concealed or revealed and forgiven. Firstly, the young David had no money of his own, and money was required to train for that ministry and support his family. And, secondly, Howell had received nothing more than a mere elementary education, so that a lengthy course of preparatory schooling would be necessary. His father, of course, was reasonably well-off, but there had already been a dispute between him and David on a similar issue. His father wished his eldest son to take over a farm of his own, and was probably willing to provide the capital required. But the son wanted a bond of three hundred pounds from his father in order to give security for a job in the customs and exise. It was refused. However the vicar approached the father and informed him that his son should be ordained. John Howell was indignant. This was not because of his Methodist creed, for until the early 1860s and even beyond Church and Methodism generally got on very well together. The services were arranged at different times so as not to clash, and members of the one frequently attended the services of the other. Welsh Methodism had also given many of her sons to the ministry of the Church, not because they believed the Church to possess a more apostolic ministry, but simply because at that time that Church alone had a full time stipendiary ministry. Nonconformist preachers were required to support themselves by

[17] *Record*, 23 Jan 1903, p 79.

their own exertions until the latter part of the century. Rather John Howell's indignation concerned the spiritual state of his son. He accused Griffiths of wanting to put a "graceless man" into the pulpit, and declared that he would prefer his son to sweep the streets rather than preach the Gospel without grace in his heart. No, he would not support his son, financially or in any other way, in such a venture. As John Griffiths' character was that of a godly man it is difficult to believe that he would have encouraged an unconverted man to consider ordination, and it may well be that John Howell was unaware of the quiet influences at work in his son which Griffiths was privileged to see and develop.

Thankfully David's mother agreed with Griffiths, and gave all she could afford for his support. His grandmother also believed in him, and gave him her marriage dowry for his maintenance. Her death in 1852 profoundly affected him. In the end, with such persuasion and example, John Howell eventually if reluctantly agreed to allow his son to enter the ministry and promised to support him financially during his training. It was thus settled that David should attend the Eagle Academy in Cowbridge, conducted by William Lewis, a strict disciplinarian, in order to obtain an elementary knowledge of the classics. This was in 1851-2, the year after Bishop Ollivant had withdrawn his licence for Cowbridge Grammar School to act as a divinity school, training men for the ministry of the Church and preparing them for the bishop's examination prior to their ordination. Ollivant believed that it was better for men to go to a proper institution such as St David's College, Lampeter, for their training, although at the time there was much criticism of that college for its neglect of the Welsh language and literature.

At the age of twenty, Howell must have felt rather out of place sitting at a school desk learning his classics with youngsters half his age. It should be mentioned that there is no record of his attending any other school than a dame school. From Cowbridge he transferred to a Merthyr preparatory college or private grammar school, possibly the one at Vaynor or Cefn y Coed, which was kept by a former curate of Vaynor, Richard Jenkyn, described as "an excellent Welsh classic."[18] The work of this

[18] WM, 21 Jan 1903, p 4.

school was to prepare men for entry into the Abergavenny divinity school, still accepted by Ollivant, with some misgivings, as a valid place for training men for ordination in his diocese, who were unable to obtain a university qualification, either for want of money or through lack of education. As the Abergavenny school had an extremely difficult entrance examination, the Merthyr school had the reputation of being an intensive cramming establishment. At this time Cefn y Coed had an active Unitarian chapel, and it appears that while he was there Howell read the Unitarian journal, *Yr Ymofynydd*. His reading of it, it is said, gave him a life long hatred of theological and denominational arguments. He thus refused, at a later stage, to assist the church controversialist, Brutus, editor of the Anglican *Yr Haul*, in his attacks on the public figures of the Nonconformist denominations, though he was strongly urged to do so by his friends.

Though Howell always regretted that Griffiths had not advised his parents to send him to one of the ancient universities, he probably received a more thorough and practical training at Abergavenny than he would have obtained elsewhere, though the school, as we note later, had its limitations. In his *Charge* of 1866 Bishop Ollivant explained that the Abergavenny school was used almost exclusively by Welsh-speaking candidates, and he felt therefore that the college was not able to give men an adequate knowledge of English, or help with a more general education. He much regretted that it only offered a two year course, and as a result became more popular than the three year Lampeter course. The principal reason for this was that instead of having to find an additional one hundred pounds for that third year at Lampeter, an Abergavenny man was already by then in receipt of an income from his first curacy. The *Charge* of 1866 in fact prepared the ground for the closure of the school, as Canon Williams, its headmaster, had recently died, and Ollivant had already before his death reduced the number of his pupils to twelve.[19] A protest against its closure appeared in the *Cardiff and Merthyr Guardian* in the form of a letter from one Leoline Jenkins. The school's

---

[19] Alfred Ollivant, *Visitation Charge to the Diocese of Llandaff 1866* [London 1866], pp 5-8.

demise would prevent numerous men from entering the ministry of the Church, he wrote, especially at a time when all the Welsh dioceses were crying out for Welsh-speaking men. Many Nonconformists had entered the Church's ministry as a result of the short cut provided by this college, and there was no other body which could supply what it had previously offered. Jenkins also provided a list of the outstanding men of the Welsh Church who had been trained there. It included the names of William Morgan, Ystradyfodwg, Thomas Walters, Ystradynlais, and David Howell, Cardiff.[20]

Howell was a student at Abergavenny from February 1853 until August 1855. He brought his wife and two sons to live with him at Somerset Cottage in that town, and here his third child and first daughter Catherine was born. It is clear he studied well and hard, working though such books as Butler and Hooker. Writing to Thomas Stephens of Merthyr in the September of 1855 Howell wrote: "I am and have been for the last three months, reading for my life as it were, pouring over my books for as many as twelve or fifteen hours every day, in anticipation of the ordeal I shall have to undergo six months hence."[21] By this he meant the examination by the bishop's chaplains which preceded every ordination. This could mean that a candidate might be rejected on the eve of that ordination, though many bishops by this time were moving towards a system which offered a better preparation for ordination than one which encouraged the ordinands to be more concerned about passing an examination than in asking for God's anointing upon their future ministry.

In later years Howell wrote of the deficiencies of the kind of theological training he had received at Abergavenny:

> I myself, for instance, was ordained to an important parish, and made to prepare three sermons a week, in Welsh and English, without having ever written a sermon in my life, or ever addressed a public audience, or ever knelt at a sick bedside, or ever performed any religious function outside of my own family. Now, fancy putting a person in pastoral charge of a district of many hundreds of people without having been taught the very rudiments of his

---

[20] CMG, 2 Mar 1866, p 8.
[21] Howell to Stephens, 6 Aug 1855, NLW MS 964E, f 130.

vocation! Who would trust his life to a medical student who had never witnessed an operation, and who had never written or dispensed a prescription, who had never felt a pulse, and who had never formed a diagnosis of any disease, but had simply attended certain courses of medical lectures?[22]

He was not alone in his feelings about the deficiencies of the training he had received at Abergavenny. H A Bruce reported of him in 1870 that "he cannot have over a modicum of learning - for his education was begun and completed in the small divinity school at Abergavenny, - a two year course."[23] Ollivant wrote of Howell on the same occasion that "he is a sensible man but cannot be a man of learning, for his professional education was confined to the very inferior advantages of a two years course at the Abergavenny Grammar School which was conducted solely by the Rev. T Williams, a very excellent person, but a man of no attainments. I should have said 'theological' than 'grammar' school, for such was its character, at least of late years."[24] But even so the school provided a more thorough training for a Welsh-speaking candidate than any Oxford or Cambridge course could have provided at that time.

We are fortunate to have some personal glimpses of Howell during this period of his life. These are found in his correspondence with Jonathan Reynolds, which has fortunately survived, and whose obituary was written by Howell.[25] The correspondence is mainly written in Welsh. Reynolds, whose bardic name was Nathan Dyfed, was a Caernarvonshire man who had moved to Merthyr in 1835. Here he had set up as a coachbuilder and wheelwright, but his real importance lay in his literary activities. He was secretary of the local Cymreigyddion Society, a noted eisteddfodwr, and edited the Welsh columns of several local newspapers. Howell wrote he had known him since 1847, but their friendship had been cemented by their

---

[22] *Report of the St Asaph Diocesan Conference*, 1885, p 17.
[23] Bruce to Gladstone, 11 Jan 1870, GP 44086/78.
[24] Ollivant to Gladstone, 14 Jan 1870, GP 44424/97.
[25] NLW MS 987B: David Howell, "Adgof am Nathan Dyfed", *Geninen*, 19 [1901] 177-80. Another obituary of Nathan Dyfed by Watcyn Wyn is to be found in *Geninen*, 12 (1894) 31-3. See also Huw Williams, "Jonathan Reynolds, Nathan Dyfed", in *Merthyr Historian*, 6 [1992] 85-95.

participation in the great Abergavenny eisteddfod of 1848. Nathan's chief ability, suggested Howell, lay in his letter writing, which was amusing, original, playful yet trenchant. Unfortunately Nathan's side of the correspondence has not survived, but Howell's letters too have the same characteristics about them, often being enriched by shafts of humour: "have almost no time to piss", "Son of Belial, your negligence is enough to make a man swear".[26] Concern is expressed for the poverty of Nathan, his family and other local bards. There had been some trouble at Merthyr, for Howell writes about "the vile conspiracy of the petty priests of Merthyr, but thank God and Dewi, I have by now friends and supporters among the Levites who can blow with one breath", while he is thankful he can condemn "the dirty and jealous cowards to eternal nothingness." He would like to come and see Nathan, but he would never visit Merthyr again.[27] It is probable that this was some literary conflict, for writing from 'Fenni' he mentions "the devils in Merthyr and the area have tried to destroy me but cannot. They caused me to give up my office as editor of the *Star of Gwent* but this morning I received a diamond ring from a nobleman (MH) connected with the Star as a recognition of my services. The gift, apart from its worth, is an honour not possessed by my cowardly opponents. Dirt, dirt to them."[28] The nobleman was probably Sir Benjamin Hall, but the whole affair appears to have hurt Howell considerably.

The reference to the *Star of Gwent* is a reflection of David Howell's considerable literary activities throughout this period. The financial rewards, though small, must have helped a meagre budget and the heavy expenses of family life. He was probably the paper's Welsh editor, and he also appears to have acted in a similar capacity with the other Monmouthshire local paper, the *Merlin*. Writing again to Nathan, Howell asks him, "let me have legends, Biographical and Historical Sketches for the Merlin. The two columns [of] Welsh matters .... are full with me every week." Nathan was asked to supply *englynion*: "hurry with it", Howell begs, write it in time, "not as usual the night before."[29] Watcyn

---

[26] Ibid, ff 449 and 237: 21 Oct 1851 and undated. Translated.
[27] Ibid, ff 383, 327: 16 June 1853, and undated. Translated.
[28] Ibid, f 317: undated. Translated.
[29] Ibid, ff 327, 239, and cf 275, 361. All undated save last, 24 Ap 1853. Translated.

Wyn reported that he was submitting poetry to every magazine in existence in Wales whatever its denominational allegiance.[30] His bardic name, *Llawdden,* probably dates from this period, and Howell writes that throughout this time he sat at the feet of *Myfyr,* - Evan Davies, the old watchmaker druid of Pontypool - as his Gamaliel.[31] A check list of Howell's signed articles and writings in the Welsh Church periodical, *Yr Haul,* during the years 1851-4, reveals poems on such items as the grave of the poor man, Dives and Lazarus - warning against a literal interpretation, the Welsh sailor's farewell, one praising Bishop Thirlwall for learning Welsh, another welcoming the Revd Thomas M Davies to his new parish. His essays, and some ran as a series over a number of months, were on such topics as the south Wales coalfield - a twelve part serial, the usefulness of flannel, on the health of the people, the comedy of the penny letter, antiquities of Llanilid, the duty of the Welsh to better themselves in the arts and sciences, popular pastimes and their tendencies, the worthlessness of earthly things, and how workmen should care for themselves.[32] Other poetry of the same period appeared in David Rees' *Diwygiwr* of 1851 - on Miskin Castle, Ieuan Gwynedd's *Cymraeg* of the following year, and a poem relating to Bishop Thirlwall of St Davids was submitted to and published in the proceedings of the Aeron Afan eisteddfod of 1853.[33]

Like most of the literary figures in the Wales of his day Llawdden - to give Howell his bardic name - competed and took part in the various local eisteddfodau. Watcyn Wyn quotes a friend who remembers seeing Howell at the Pontypridd eisteddfod of 1851 dressed as a comfortable farmer of that period.[34] Not only did he take part but he also endeavoured to persuade other prominent literary figures, such as Ebenezer Thomas (Eben Fardd) to enter the Abergavenny eisteddfod.[35] By Howell's time the death of Thomas Price - Carnhuanawc - had

[30] *Y Geninen,* 21 [St Davids 1903] 14.
[31] Writing to Dewi Hanan, 11 Dec 1883, in NLW MS 6245B.
[32] *Yr Haul,* poetry, II [1851] 275f, IV [1853] 91, V [1854] 152, 217, 22-6, 395f, VI [1855] 45.
[33] Aeron Afan Eisteddfod 1853 [Carmarthen 1855], pp 210-13. His English translation of Iolo's *Song to the Glamorgan Volunteers* appeared in *Geninen,* 7 [1889] 198-9.
[34] *Geninen,* 21 [St Davids 103] 13.
[35] NLW Cwrt Mawr MS 77B, f 107: Howell to Eben Fardd, 30 Ap 1853.

robbed this particular eisteddfod of its leading figure, and the increase of the English language in Gwent was to cause its eventual decline.[36] At one particular eisteddfod he met, for example, such figures as Joshua Hughes, later bishop of St Asaph - the first Welsh-speaking bishop of a Welsh diocese for one hundred and fifty years, David James, John Williams (Ab Ithel), both leading Welsh literary clerics, and Baron Bunsen, a friend of Gladstone, brother-in-law to Lady Llanover and for some time Prussian ambassador to the court of St James. It was a mixture of literary activities, cultural exchanges, Iolo worship, and prizes for Welsh woollens and stockings![37] Howell won a number of prizes at these Abergavenny eisteddfodau for such items as an essay on the history of Talley Abbey,[38] another essay on the hand of God in the history of the prophets - for which he received a prize of three guineas worth of Clarke's Commentaries, and for some *englynion*, "The Coming of Christianity to Britain", described by the adjudicator as "very excellent and almost perfect."[39] There had been some notoriety at the 1854 Bridgend eisteddfod when Llawdden had gained both the first and second prizes for an ode on the recent opening of the South Wales Railway. This he appears to have later published as a pamphlet, writing to Robert Ellis (Cynddelw) asking him to sell some copies for him.[40]

His letters to Nathan refer to many essay competitions, for which Howell asked for his advice. Various subjects are mentioned, such as the advantages of a plentiful supply of water for the working classes of Morriston - for a two guinea prize, and another on the uses of Welsh wool.[41] Thomas Stephens also persuaded him to make a translation of *Coelbren y Bardd*, first published in 1840, during 1853, and this may also have been for an eisteddfod entry.[42] Many of these essays were probably

---

[36] Thomas, *Afiaith yng Ngwent*, p 144.
[37] See the programmes and papers, for example, in NLW MS 13185E, ff 19 and 115.
[38] An English translation is in NLW MS 12364D, ff 378-89.
[39] In his letters to Nathan, NLW MS 987B, ff 391 and 347: 18 May 1852 and 27 Oct 1853. Translated.
[40] NLW MS 10221D, f 127. Howell to an unknown correspondent. Undated. Translated.
[41] NLW MS 987B, ff 351 and 303: Howell to Nathan, 19 July 1854 and one undated. Translated.
[42] It is found in NLW Cwrt Mawr Ms 320.

published in *Yr Haul* as mentioned earlier. But the glory faded. By the time of his leaving Abergavenny Llawdden swore, "I've given up eisteddfodau for ever. I have enemies thirsting for my blood."[43]

One notes, too, in his letters to Thomas Stephens of Merthyr, a considerable interest in the Welsh literary scene. Stephens was one of the foremost literary critics of his day in Wales, and Howell probably met him whilst a student in that town. Writing of John Williams (Ab Ithel), "the first Welsh scholar of his day", Howell suggested that his book on Gomer had made him "as another of those of our countrymen who by their examples and prejudiced notions of the glories of our nation have made us a laughing stock of the literary world." He felt that the book was all "bosh", a judgment which was well in advance of the Welsh literary scene. Other such examples of his interests could be quoted.[44]

These years saw a burst of literary activity which was never to be repeated in his lifetime. Howell was to write later that during this time, presumably before his ordination, he wrote about one third of each issue of *Yr Haul*, and was also connected with other periodicals, until these activities were stopped by Bishop Ollivant.[45] It may have been his need for money which prompted him to enter so many competitions, as well as his thirst for knowledge and a desire to make up for the lost ground of his youth. This, of course, was at a time when he was fully engaged in his studies for the ministry: "day and night I am devouring Greek and Latin - a month tomorrow I face the trial", or "I must in the meantime read for my life", are not infrequent expressions in his letters to Nathan.[46] If he could barely afford to insure his life for three hundred pounds, "lest Ann and the children should starve when I die", in his next letter to Nathan he had to ask him to sell some books as he needed the money to pay Mr Rees -

---

[43] To Nathan, NLW MS 987B, f 255: 6 July 1855. Translated.
[44] NLW MS 964E, ff 127 and 130: Howell to Thomas Stephens, Nov 1854 and Aug 1855.
[45] Writing to "Silvan" (probably Daniel Silvan Evans), 23 Dec 1896. NLW Cwrt Mawr MS 903B, no 46. Apart from the signed articles there were probably a considerable number of anonymous and unsigned articles from his pen, as is the wont of many editors of such periodicals.
[46] Eg, NLW MS 987B, f 227: Howell to Nathan, 21 Aug 1855. Translated.

possibly a doctor, as his wife was seriously ill at that time. "Sorry I have not paid you my debts earlier", he continued, "but every penny was needed though we have the necessities of life without any comfort. I am thankful for this as I know that hundreds of better men than myself have a narrow table and an empty cupboard." But he was later able to offer Nathan about ten or fifteen pounds which he had in the bank if it would be a help to him "in his dire straits", and to buy an overcoat for 'Ieuan' to hide his old one. He also offered to borrow twenty pounds, on the strength of the security of his life policy of one hundred pounds, in order to assist another "dear friend".[47] Clearly, however generous he was to his friends, every penny counted in that household, and his prize money and the small income from his literary activities must have been a useful bonus to his resources.

His father, John Howell, also took note of this extended literary activity, and at his son's ordination in 1858 offered him some useful advice. The claims of the ministry, he argued, were more than enough for him, and he added that his own exceptional love of writing poetry had almost cost him his personal religion. This was advice that Llawdden appears to have taken to heart. During the early part of 1855 Howell was offered a title, that is a curacy allowing him to be ordained, under his old vicar, John Griffiths, who had recently been appointed rector of Neath. He wrote that he would soon be "an apprentice-priest."[48] Those few months before his ordination saw a constant anxiety about leasing a home in Neath for himself and his family at the right price, and obtaining the furniture required for it. The house needed to have two front rooms and two back, plus kitchen, and four bedrooms, but for a long time he was unable to find one at an annual rent of less than twenty pounds, including taxes. Eventually one was found, which answered his requirements, in Queen Street, at a rental of eighteen pounds. The furniture was the next problem. Nathan was continually asked to find such items as bookcases, chairs, chest of drawers and tables. Howell's father later came to the rescue, a month too late. The three pound cost of removing

---

[47] Ibid, ff 303, 305, 307, 271: Howell to Nathan, undated, but from Abergavenny. Translated.
[48] Ibid, f 341: Howell to Nathan. Undated. Translated.

their goods from Abergavenny was prohibitive, and Nathan was asked if he had an acquaintance who might do it cheaper.[49] The first letter to Nathan from Neath after his ordination indicated that all his spare cash had gone on these costs and the expenses of his ordination, for he had to pay legal fees to both the chancellor and the registrar of the diocese. "Am living from hand to mouth" was his comment.[50]

David Howell was made deacon at Llandaff Cathedral on 23 September 1855. His fellow ordinands were two literates, that is men without a university education, from Lampeter, and three other literates like himself.[51] Lady Llanover states that he was commended on his attainments by the bishop's examining chaplain as a result of his examination for deacon's orders.[52] This is confirmed by Ollivant's comment in his Diocesan book. He noted that Howell had been made deacon but had not been subjected to the five year rule he often required of 'literate' men, declining to ordain them priest until a five year period of further study had been successfully accomplished. Ollivant also noted that Howell's curacy was in order to provide a "pastoral visitation" and ministry to the benefit of the Welsh families in Neath, and the stipend was five pounds per annum, which hopefully related to a diocesan grant rather than the actual amount.

Howell must have come to his ordination with a deep sense of humility and gratitude. Gratitude for the many who had influenced him for his good: his father for his religious and cultural influences; his grandmother with her love for the Church and her care of him in his unregenerate days; his vicar for leading him to seek Christ for his salvation and for sharing with him his concern for their nation and their Church's evangelical heritage, and for his wife who had valiantly and quietly stood by him in many difficulties and hardships. But above all there was that gratitude to God who had led him by His grace along that chosen path. These legacies Howell furthered and enhanced throughout the remainder of his life.

---

[49] Ibid, ff 207, 211, 222f, 225, 227, 229: Howell to Nathan, 2 & 10 Oct 1855, 16 & 30 July 1855, 21 Aug, 3 Sept 1855. Translated.
[50] Ibid f 293: Howell to Nathan. Undated. Translated.
[51] *Yr Haul*, 6 (1855) 363.
[52] Lady Llanover to Gladstone, 25 Dec 1882, GP 44478/234.

The Early Years of Ministry

His ordination at Llandaff over, Howell received the bishop's licence to serve as assistant curate of the parish of Neath with Llantwit. Ollivant made it clear that he had been ordained "solely for the pastoral visitation" of the Welsh families of that parish. His stipend was ninety pounds per annum, and out of this sum he was required to find his own home. As we have noted, his rector was his previous vicar and mentor, John Griffiths, who had been appointed to Neath in 1855. Howell was priested in the following year.[1] The Llandaff Church Extension Society had given one of its first grants to Neath in 1852. This was of sixty pounds and was towards the cost of providing a Welsh clergyman in that parish, utilising a licensed mission room made available for these Welsh services at Melincryddan. After some mishaps a good Welsh congregation had been built up. Many people who had joined the Nonconformists because of the lack of a Welsh church in Neath now rejoined the Church flock.[2] But the Welsh cause appears to have fallen on hard times and Griffiths had to start this work once again. To assist him in this work he received grants from both the Llandaff Diocesan Society[3] and also from the evangelical Church Pastoral-Aid Society.[4] Both grants were given specifically for a Welsh-speaking ministry.

It was this Welsh mission room cum-church which Howell served, and under his leadership the work prospered, and a consistent ministry to the Welsh population of the parish began. Half the population of the parish was Welsh, and Griffiths said of

---

[1] Church in Wales records, NLW LL/0/1007.
[2] *First Report of the Llandaff Diocesan Church Extension Society, 1852*, pp 7f.
[3] Ibid, 5th Report, 1856, p 7, and 8th Report, 1859, p 7.
[4] *Church Pastoral-Aid Society Report*, 1904, p 38; *Church and People*, 3 [1891] 81. *Church Pastoral-Aid Society Abstract of Report and Speeches etc*, 1873, p 17, and 1884, p 19. A grant from the Ecclesiastical Commissioners was made available in 1863. The financial circumstances of the commissioners had prevented grants for assistant clergy being made before that date.

them, with reference to Howell's appointment, that for more than half a century they had been "left destitute of means of worshipping God in the language understood and appreciated by them."[5] But this work was not without opposition, according to a report in the pages of *Yr Haul*, the Welsh Church periodical, although neither Howell nor Griffiths' names are mentioned in it. Under the heading of "A Report about the Established Church in Neath", the paper reported that the Church had faced lots of storms and the poison of Nonconformists who had tried to harm the work but whose power had proved to be like wolves in chains. It was as Joseph had said, "though they intended evil against me, God has destined it for good." As a result of these attacks a spirit of unity, love and co-operation had developed within the church. For many years, the report went on, the church in Neath had been declining, but now things had improved, so that there were three different places of worship, each with two services and well attended. There were also plans to build a new church seating between eight and nine hundred people. Although there were four Sunday schools there was still room for more progress.[6] The revival of the church in Neath under Griffiths had clearly aroused some Nonconformist opposition, especially as he had managed to bring back into the churchfold former church people who had worshipped with the dissenters because of the absence of Welsh or a lack of spirituality in their own church.

Little else is known of Howell's ministry at Neath. A Welsh sermon which he preached on the occasion of the laying of the foundation stone of Alderman Davies' school in 1857 was published the same year.[7] His involvement in the temperance movement is noted in a report of a memorial meeting to one Evan Evans, a temperance leader in that town.[8] It is clear that John Griffiths was more than pleased with his ministry, for he declared of Howell, "[m]y junior in years, but my senior in point of talent."[9] Howell himself wrote to Nathan of those early days of his ministry there, in November 1855: "I am fairly successful in

[5] *Church Pastoral-Aid Society: Abstract of Report and Speeches etc*, 1884, p 19.
[6] *Yr Haul*, 8 [1856] 226f. It is signed *Durtur*. Translated.
[7] David Howell, *Araeth a dreddodwyd ar yr achlysur o osod i lawr gareg-sylfner Ysgol Alderman Davies* [Abertawe 1857].
[8] *Report of a Meeting in Memory of the late Evan Evans* [Neath 1859], pp11f.
[9] J Williams, *Notes and Narratives* [Machynlleth 1885], p 77.

my ministry. I am a favourite with the poor and acceptable to all classes of society."¹⁰ A more barbed comment came from Griffiths' successor as rector of Neath, A F Evans, who was a Tractarian through and through. Writing after Howell's death, he noted that there were many still alive who remembered his first sermon at Melincryddan, which showed indications of that intense emotionalism "which was both his strength and weakness."¹¹

Two years passed in Neath, and in 1857 Howell was appointed the Church Pastoral-Aid Society's travelling secretary for Wales. Wyndham Jones had been the first stipendiary Welsh secretary of this London based organisation, in 1847, and he was followed by Thomas Walters from 1853-7. It may be that for the first year his was a part-time appointment, which he combined with his curacy at Neath, but we cannot be sure because the records of the society did not survive the bombing of its Fleet Street premises in 1941. By April 1859 his address was given as Brynteg Villa, Swansea,¹² and he probably found Swansea to be a more convenient centre for his work than Neath.

The Church Pastoral-Aid Society had been founded in 1836 to assist the home mission work of the Church of England. One of its primary ways of assisting this work was by making grants of money available for the stipends of curates and lay workers working in necessitous parishes. It was founded as, and still remains, a strongly evangelical society. Howell's work was to represent this society throughout the four Welsh dioceses, thus indicating the strength of evangelical life in the Church in Wales at that time.¹³ This was a period described by J V Morgan as "the Pentecostal period in the history of the Welsh Church in Wales."¹⁴ Men such as Hughes of Llandovery - later bishop of St Asaph, Richards of Caerwys, Griffiths of Llandeilo, Parry of Llywel, Griffith of Merthyr, as well as Howell's own rector, were some of the evangelical leaders of the Welsh Church. They were

---

¹⁰ Letters to Nathan, NLW MS 987B, f 219: Howell to Nathan, 23 Nov 1855.
¹¹ WM, 19 Jan 1903, p 6.
¹² *Report of a Meeting*, quotes Howell's letter on p 11.
¹³ For a history of the Society's work in Wales see my *The Welsh Evangelicals* [Cardiff 1986].
¹⁴ J V Morgan, *Welsh Religious Leaders of the Victorian Era* [London 1905], p 106.

supported in turn by a large number of the indigenous Welsh clergy, especially those who originated from west Wales, many of whom served in the industrial valleys of south Wales. The majority of these men were active supporters of the Church Pastoral-Aid Society. In 1895, for example, forty-three per cent of the inhabitants of the diocese of Llandaff, which then included Gwent, lived in the twenty-three parishes of that diocese whose incumbents were grant-aided by the society. The society was committed also to a bilingual policy in Wales, and recognised that this policy required for its fulfillment, parish by parish, additional churches, services and clergy. It was thus prepared to consider a bilingual parish with a population of three thousand as equal to an English speaking one of five thousand for the purposes of awarding grants.[15]

It was this society, to quote the words of John Griffiths:

> that really fanned the well-nigh dying embers of the Church on the hills and in the crowded valleys of the southern portion of the Principality. It was a time too when a band of powerful Welsh preachers went forth - many of them from places assisted by the Church Pastoral-Aid Society - men whose hearts were fired by the love of souls, men of unusual gifts and eloquence; these men, like flying angels, went occasionally abroad through the country districts of the land and preached to eager thousands the everlasting Gospel.
>
> They inspired the country parson with new desires; they rescued the old Church from the disrepute which had long lain on her, of having no men who could exercise the weapon of preaching to any creditable extent.

At the annual Exeter Hall meeting of the Society in 1884 Griffiths also spoke from the heart as to its value to him and to his own Church:

> The hand of sympathy was by her extended to the overburdened minister. There was placed by his side a companion and fellow-labourer. His energies had a new life imparted to them. He felt armed with a power he had never before experienced, and there opened out opportunities for successful and extended labour. The

---

[15] Brown, *The Welsh Evangelicals*, pp 84, 144; and *CPAS Abstract*, 1861, p 10.

grants made by the society were really life from death. A breath fell upon the well-nigh expiring embers, and fanned them into a flame. The Church was thus enabled to appear in her proper character, as a Church deeming it to be her duty to deal, as far as her power enabled her, with all the people. ...

The grand old historical Church appeared to be animated with a new life. Her voice was heard proclaiming the clear Evangelical doctrines of her Creeds and Articles. Christ dying for man's sins and rising for man's justification, was the theme of her pulpits. The supremacy of God's Word, and the testimony of Jesus, for which her Martyrs died, were her constant utterances. It was felt that public confidence was gradually, though slowly, being recovered, and her once-deserted fold became the home of thousands. All this time, be it remembered, her strongest aid came from the society, which you cherish, and whose interests you are here this day to uphold.[16]

One wonders if Griffiths had Howell and others of his curates in mind when he wrote and spoke these words.

David Howell's name became widely known through his work for the society, and he was soon recognised as an outstanding preacher and platform speaker. He travelled the country from end to end,[17] and was soon familiarly known by the title "Llawdden, Pastoral-Aid." It was said of him that during those days he placed the Society's claims before his countrymen in a manner unknown to them before.[18] Canon Lloyd of Aberystwyth remembered as a boy listening to him preach at his home church on behalf of the society, on the text Luke 13, verses 6-9. This related to the figtree, and the way Howell emphasised the words "let it alone this year" remained with him for the rest of his life. It was one of the most powerful sermons ever heard from that pulpit.[19] Robert Isaac Jones (Alltud Eifion) related similar stories. When Howell first came to the north, he preached at Penrhyndeudraeth. The crowds saw a small, serene, dark, and young-looking man. Nobody would forget what he said, wrote Jones, adding that he would remember it to his dying day. At

---

[16] Church and People, 3 [1891] 34: CPAS Abstract, 1884, p 20. Until the 20th century an incumbent was personally responsible for finding the stipends of his assistant clergy.
[17] See *CPAS Report*, 1904, p 38.
[18] WM, 16 Jan 1903, p 5.
[19] *Yr Haul*, 1932, p 113; *Cyfaill Eglwysig*, 1903, pp 60, 93.

Llanbeblig the influence of his sermon remained in that church for years, and its vicar, Canon Thomas, remarked that "this boy" was God's spiritual gift to the Church in Wales. Though Howell frequently attended the monthly preaching meetings, held throughout Wales by the evangelical clergy, diocese by diocese, Mary Ellis suggests that he disliked them because they emphasised too much the 'big' preachers.[20] This may have been the case, for Howell was well aware how nonconformity had stressed the great preachers at the expense of the day-to-day pastoral ministry. However, unlike Bishop Thirlwall of St Davids, who disliked these clerical meetings as he believed they depreciated the liturgy of the Church, Howell was aware of their spiritual force and power. At the end of his life, when these meetings had declined, he longed for their revival, arguing that their aim should be to raise the standard of the Church's preaching, in order that it might resemble the best of Nonconformist preaching. And he also wished that all should learn to preach as some could.[21]

By the time of the 1859 revival the name of David Howell was widely known throughout Wales. This revival came as a powerful and extraordinary spiritual impetus which swept throughout Wales. Sweeping aside barriers, the Holy Spirit led church and chapel to unite for prayer meetings, which prayed expectantly for this work of revival. It affected the Anglican church too, and there was a vast increase in the number of communicants in the Welsh churches of Aberystwyth, Aberaeron, Lampeter, Llandeilo, Ffestiniog in north Wales, amongst many others. In every case these parishes were in the hands of evangelical men, who themselves were revitalised and renewed by this outpouring of spiritual life. Regretfully little is known of David Howell's part in this revival, although it is known that he was greatly used of God during it to encourage and to assist this work of spiritual renewal. Two pictures, thankfully, remain. One is from the hand of Archdeacon David Evans, of St Asaph, who remembering his Cardiganshire childhood, wrote that Howell preached at

[20] In *Y Haul*, 49 [1971] 31.
[21] Howell never wanted to minimise the pastoral work of the Church, though he wished to have itinerant preachers appointed [David Howell, *The Church in Wales and Vernacular Preaching: reprinted from the Report of the Manchester Church Congress, 1888*, pp 5f].

Llanrhystud during this time with such great strength and power that thirty-eight were added to the roll of communicants in that parish. Thomas Phillips, in his book, *The Welsh Revival*, published in 1860, indicates how Howell was used in one particular instance in helping a dissolute young man to come to spiritual reality.[22] This image of Howell as a preacher of force and power during this time remained in the memory of people for many years. In 1897 the *Record* wrote of this period of his life that "he became well and widely known in the Principality as a preacher of exceptional power at a time when a great revival was sweeping over that country. His sermons at this time created a profound impression. Crowded and overcrowded churches awaited him wherever he went, and there are many who to this day retain a vivid recollection of his powerful discourses."[23] The same paper, in his obituary, noted that during that revival Howell's "ministry was conspicuously proved of God in the conversion of sinners."[24]

These years with the Church Pastoral-Aid Society made Howell a man of note and conviction, and gave him an English as well as a Welsh reputation. It was later noted that it had given him a substantial insight into the work of the Church within the four Welsh dioceses.[25] But the strain of such constant travels and continual preaching engagements was too much, and his health broke down twice. A London specialist whom he consulted suggested that the cause of this breakdown was his habit of leaving his bags at the railway station and walking five or six miles to the church where he was due to preach, often not allowing himself a cup of tea before preaching, let alone any more substantial refreshment. Most great speakers, the specialist pointed out, rested for twelve hours before making a major speech, declining to undertake any strenuous activity.[26]

By this time it was clear that Howell could not continue this pace of work, which must have caused much disruption in his family life. He thus accepted the parish of Pwllheli in

---

[22] Thomas Phillips, *The Welsh Revival* [London 1860], pp 90f; Brown, *The Welsh Evangelicals*, pp 148-50.
[23] *Record*, 2 Ap 1897, p 321.
[24] Ibid, 23 Jan 1903, p 79.
[25] WM, 30 Mar 1897, p 4.
[26] *Geninen*, 21 [1903] 155.

Caernarvonshire offered him by Bishop Campbell of Bangor. Campbell would have known him not only through his CPAS connections, - for the bishop was one of its vice-patrons, had preached before it at its annual meeting in 1860, and had been grant-aided by the society in his Merthyr incumbency - but also as he had been rector of Merthyr during the year Howell was at school there. It may also be possible that the bishop knew his family, for H A Bruce's comment, already quoted, was that Campbell had spent some time learning Welsh in Howell's home parish. This move to Pwllheli did not affect Howell's interest in the society, and for the rest of his life he continued to support it. On his appointment as dean of St Davids the society's magazine *Church and People* commented that he had been associated with the Church Pastoral-Aid Society "for many long years; and in the pulpit, on the platform, and in the press he has pleaded by voice and pen frequently and fervently on our behalf." A later tribute read, "[n]one who heard him on the Society's platform here in Exeter Hall will ever forget his fervent invocation of the Holy Spirit that He would descend upon the Church in Wales."[27] And Howell was well aware that one way in which the Holy Spirit would work would be through such societies as the one he had served so conspicuously and successfully.

Pwllheli in fact comprised two parishes united together, those of Llannor and Deneio, and there was also the church of St Peter in the town itself which had been opened in 1834. The living was valued at £195 per annum in 1853, so that it represented hard work for little reward. Its population was then about three and a half thousand. The new vicar's immediate predecessors were Thomas Jones, 1849-60, a native of Llanbadarn Fawr, who was well known as the author or compiler of a much used Welsh Church hymn tune and chant book, and Benjamin Morgan, whose brief stay of a few months duration was ended through his being unsettled by the death of a daughter from scarlet-fever. Thomas Jones had laboured hard in the parish. The church buildings had been repaired, the cemetery enlarged and a new vicarage, Ty Gwyrdd, purchased in 1852. From plans still remaining in the

---

[27] CPAS *Church and People*, 9 [1897] 41; *CPAS Report 1904*, p 38.

papers of the Queen Anne's Bounty, a church charity which gave a grant towards its cost,[28] the building, whose site is now occupied by Woolworth's store, had been erected for a local solicitor of the town, David Williams, later a member of parliament. An archway from the street led to a courtyard with stables and coach-house, while the four stories of the building contained on the ground floor the kitchen with its extensive offices, study, dining room and small parlour; the drawing room, best bedroom and its dressing room, together with a water closet, were on the first floor, and there were four more bedrooms and a dressing room on the second floor with attic rooms above. One wonders how Howell and his wife not only furnished this house, but managed to maintain it, on the income of that benefice.

But however much the parish had been enriched architecturally, one has the distinct impression that it had been neglected spiritually, and that Howell was offered it on the assumption that he was the man to bring new life and vitality to it. One indication of its condition is given in the 1863 report of Her Majesty's Inspector into the National School. He wrote that the population was "peculiarly poor, dirty, ill-clad, and ignorant, and the only means of regulating will be found in a vigorous infant institution."[29] The bishop had strongly urged Howell to accept this parish, and accordingly he was instituted to it on 17 February 1861, becoming one of the few evangelicals in that slightly high-church diocese. There was, it appears, some bitterness amongst the clergy of that diocese that he had been brought in from another diocese, and even worse, had served in his bishop's former diocese.[30] But such comments would not have hurt Howell. His sense of providence would suggest to him that God had called him to that parish, rather than the bishop. One of his first appointments there was to preach before the Eifionydd Deanery clerical meeting. His text was Heb. 10 verse 38, which he expounded with great eloquence, it was reported, touching the hearts of the listeners.[31] It was a good start, and soon he was to

[28] Now in the possession of the Representative Body of the Church in Wales.
[29] CWR, SA/MB/56. The report is signed by both Howell, and J A Jackson, the schoolmaster. There are occasional entries in the school log-book indicating that Howell and his wife, both together or individually, visited the school.
[30] D Ll Hughes, *The History of Pwllheli Church* [1987], p 23.
[31] *Yr Haul*, 5 [1861] 377f.

touch the lives and hearts of his parishioners, and to make Pwllheli the spiritual centre for a wide area.

At first it was said that he worked harder here than anywhere else, but found little fruit from his toil. Puzzled and concerned, he asked a Welsh methodist deacon why his ministry was not succeeding. An answer was made in this way: every parson is regarded as a bad man until he proves himself good, and every Nonconformist minister is said to be good until he proves himself otherwise. The speaker continued by saying that they were still only just changing their opinion of him. He then questioned the new vicar: "Have you been on your knees asking the Lord to adopt your ministry to the people's condition or to turn their hearts to your ministry? It won't come right without this." This, confessed Howell later, was the best advice he had ever received. He never forgot it, stating that he was more and more convinced as his life progressed that only those who spent time on their knees could be the chosen instruments of God.[32]

The result of this conversation may best be summed up in the words of D Ll Hughes, who writes of Howell's ministry in this parish in his history of Pwllheli church:

> According to the Rev. Samuel Jones, once vicar of Llandrygarn in Anglesey, who was brought up at St. Peter's during the 1850s and the 1860s, no better appointment [than that of Howell] could have been contemplated....
>
> Without delay he set about organising church services in such a way that they would become central to life, both lay and spiritual; his inspirational hand could be seen in all spheres. Before he went to Pwllheli only two services were held on a Sunday, one in Welsh in the morning and one in English at night, apart, of course, from the Sunday School. His first impression was that there were in fact two churches under the same roof in the town, no doubt representing two cultures. The vicar's early reaction was to separate them and, hearing that the Baptists, who were getting ready to move into their new chapel at Tabernacle, could see no further use for their old Chapel, Bethel, North Street, he inaugurated plans to acquire it for non-Welsh church services. But many of his flock expressed their concern about the great danger to

---

[32] From *Geninen*, 21 [1903] 155f.

the unity of the Church if such a step was taken and said that they preferred to work together and to co-operate in order to preserve it. The vicar gave in to their entreaties.

He arranged four services on Sundays, two in Welsh and two in English, and concentrated his early efforts on developing the influence and strength of the Sunday School, gathering a numerically strong school, Welsh and English, at St. Peter's and holding another at the church in the cemetery. He inaugurated a communicants' meeting on Monday evenings, had choir practice on Tuesdays and a Confirmation class on Wednesdays. On Thursday evenings he preached in Welsh and on Fridays in English and held a weekly service in the workhouse. Special services were held on Holy Days.

As if that programme was not enough in itself - he also had services at Llannor - the vicar had a weekly class, open to the clergy and to laymen, where the Collects of the church were discussed. One man who was greatly influenced by those discussions was the headmaster of the National School, J A Jackson, who sought Holy Orders as a result and, before his untimely death brought it to an abrupt end, had embarked on a very promising career as Inspector of Schools in the Diocese of St Asaph.

Through the force of his personality, his unflagging labours and his exceptional ability effectively to communicate, the Rev. David Howell saw his Welsh congregation doubling in size; many Welsh speakers also went to hear his English sermons as well. He was respected by all, church and chapelgoers alike. His eloquent articulation in Welsh set a standard for all to follow. He succeeded in nurturing a very close relationship between Church and Chapel in the town but there is always someone to prove that prejudice can outstrip commonsense. When Salem Calvinistic Chapel was opened in 1864 Vicar Howell and his curate attended the inaugural services, a fact which did not pass unnoticed by one Churchman who saw fit to vent his misgivings in the press.

While mentioning that chapel it is worth relating the vicar's reaction when the owner of the land on which it was to be built, Lord Newborough, approached him in order to ascertain whether he had any objections, since the new chapel would be within a stone's throw from the church. The Rev. David Howell replied that he had no objection whatsoever, all that he needed was sufficient room to open the church door.

In his three years at Pwllheli the Rev. Howell [sic] brought St Peter's great prominence, and an indication of his abiding influence appears in an issue of Yr Haul, a church periodical, in 1934 in an article which asserts that the memory of his indefatigable efforts was still very much alive in Pwllheli. When it is recalled that the vicar had left the town some 70 years before, and had been dead for 30 years, a more fitting tribute could hardly be found.[33]

The article mentioned above, by Canon Lloyd, notes how Howell used those meetings which studied the collects, almost as a kind of seiat, or experience meeting. Always anxious that people should know the meaning of prayers consecrated by centuries of use, he was even more anxious that the thoughts and aspirations conveyed by them should be experienced by his hearers. Thus he used these occasions to speak publicly about matters relating to church life and to remind people about the deeper spiritual issues which lay behind them. In addition Howell encouraged his laypeople to speak publicly on questions connected with church life and work.[34]

An unsigned and undated report on the spiritual life of the larger towns in Wales, dated around 1865-70, suggested of Pwllheli that while there was a friendly feeling in the town towards the Church, and its previous clergy had been able and consistent men, it was not until Howell's arrival that the clergy became "active visitors of the parishioners". While his sermons displayed a "fervid and somewhat romantic imagination", and combined a "warm impulsive eloquence" with "a winning and pleasing manner", Howell was what was much more important, a laborious pastor. Always in his parish, at work from morning to night visiting his parishioners, consoling the sick and unfortunate, admonishing the reckless and criminal, contributing towards the necessities of the poor, he not only preached the "everlasting Gospel from the pulpit, but from door to door."[35] Richard Baxter's *Reformed Pastor* may well have been the model of Howell's ministry.

---

[33] Hughes, *Pwllheli Church*, pp 23f, quoting the articles by Samuel Jones in *Cyfaill Eglwysig*, 1913, pp 121-5, 144-7, 184f, 207-10. See also D T Davies [ed], *Hanes Eglwysi a Phlwyfi Lleyn* [Pwllheli 1910], pp 230-45; D G Lloyd Hughes, *Pwllheli* [Llandysul 1991], pp 271-3; William Hughes, *A Short Memoir of the Rev J A Jackson* [Rhyl 1877] p 11.
[34] *Haul*, 1932, pp 113f.
[35] NLW MS 43163, cit Pwllheli.

David Williams, however, in his article on Howell, is more disparaging about his ministry at Pwllheli. These were hard years of labour, he wrote, during which Howell engaged in prayer that his might be a fit ministry and that the souls of his people might be saved. But he saw little obvious success or growth as he tried to defeat the old prejudices and lay new foundations.[36] His successors, however, appear to have reaped the benefit of his diligence and prayers.

It is not surprising that Howell found little time to involve himself in the life of the diocese of Bangor. Nevertheless he appears to have been a member of the diocesan tract committee, along with J C Vincent and Morris Williams (Nicander), one the member of an influential clerical county family, and the other one of the leaders of the Tractarian revival in the country![37]

One of his curates, and his near contemporary, was Henry Jones (1832-93). Born at Manordeifi, the son of an Independent minister, Jones himself served that denomination as a minister at Ammanford from 1852 until his ordination into the Church's ministry. He served his title under Howell at Pwllheli until he left in 1864, being appointed to his home parish as vicar in 1877.[38] Howell would certainly have appreciated a man with such a background, and might well have encouraged him to be ordained.

Howell's two closest friends during these years at Pwllheli were Canon Robert Williams of Llanfaelog (who, it is said, suggested his name to Campbell for the parish)[39], and Canon Eliezer Williams of Llangefni, Anglesey. Both were strong evangelical men. Yet they became more than a little concerned about their younger friend's orthodoxy. Their concern seems to have come about in this way. For many years Howell had been disturbed by what he later described as "the superficial flimsy trash so copiously supplied during late years under the name of Welsh Theological literature." But he knew that he did not possess "the learning and ability required to grapple with so great a subject.[40]

[36] David Williams in *Geninen*, 22 [St Davids 1904] 42.
[37] From a note about this committee on the backcover of David Jones, *Eglwys Crist* [Carmarthen 1864].
[38] R Tudur Jones, *Fydd ac Argyfwng Cenedl* [Abertawe 1981], I 159.
[39] Samuel Jones in *Cyfaill Eglwysig*, 1913, p 122.
[40] Howell writing to Thomas Stephens, NLW MS 9645E, f 131: 28 May, addressed from Neath.

In order to remedy this deficiency Howell wrote to Rowland Williams, then vice-principal of St David's College, Lampeter, and a fellow of King's College, Cambridge, asking him to supply a list of books which would assist his reading. This was in 1860, and it was a bold step for him to do, for in the February of that same year the book *Essays and Reviews* had appeared, to which Williams was a contributor. Another contributor was Frederick Temple, later archbishop of Canterbury. The book, and in particular Williams' article, popularised the more advanced German theology of its day, in the same way as Bishop John Robinson's book, *Honest To God*, did so for a more recent generation. Rowland Williams was regarded as the villain of the piece, and thus became the scapegoat for the introduction of sceptical thought into the doctrinal aridity of the then church. A vast evangelical outcry resulted. In Wales this was manifested in demands that Williams be dismissed from his post as a theological teacher at Lampeter, and by an onslaught directed against him by his diocesan, Thirlwall, in one of his celebrated Charges. Here again we may note the catholicity of Howell, and his refusal to accept the decisions of the crowd, even if these came from his own evangelical constituency.

Rowland Williams replied in a long letter, dated from St David's College in the June of 1860. He wrote as follows in his introduction:

> My dear Sir, - It would have been easier to comply with your gratifying request if I had known something more than you tell me of your past reading. But, knowing you to be eloquent, I will presume you to be thoughtful, and take for granted that you wish to remain within the circle of the hereditary theology of our Church, which affords the greatest range for usefulness in this country, while yet you may be willing to have some acquaintance with the mental experiences of our own age.
>
> Shall I begin by bidding you to lay a foundation of Pearson, Butler, Hooker; or shall I assume that you know such books well already, and speak only of newer ones? It may be best to proceed by divisions, under certain heads, and mention some of old and new. In all cases I would have every one read the *old authors first*, and then, by their light, proceed to estimate the new, so as to have neither an ignorant admiration of the latter, nor an equally ignorant contempt for them.

A lengthy list follows, in which Williams sets out the merits and demerits of each book recommended. In the section on dogmatic theology, to give one example, he suggested Pearson on the Creed, Bishop Bull's works in Latin, "[c]ompare with him Davenant on *Justification*. See this controversy renewed in our time by Dr. Newman, in his *Letters on Justification*, and Julius Hare in his Sermons *(and their notes)*, in the *Victory of Faith*." After recommending some distinctive books on Anglicanism and others on "science in connection with religion" and a few on comparative theology, he concluded:

> Nothing pleases me more than to see thoughtfulness and study go hand in hand with piety. You may live to see evil days for all who speak the truth in simplicity; but it is better to walk in the light than in darkness, and to follow Him who bare witness to the Truth, rather than to court safety by ignorance. I wish you every prosperity in your work and study... [41]

It may have been the knowledge of this correspondence with one who was widely regarded as undermining the truths of the Christian faith that upset Howell's friends, or perhaps his reading of some of the books Williams had recommended. He satisfied them, however, as to his orthodoxy by quoting in his defence such writers as Hooker, Simeon, Venn and Romaine (the first alone having been recommended by Williams, thus indicating a wider reading again). He added, "I am no Methodist or Papist but a Churchman.... I find no sacerdotalism in the New Testament and Book of Common Prayer, but I accept and use the liturgy in all its fullness."[42] Thereafter Howell always held that his theological position was that of the Book of Common Prayer as historically understood by the Reformers and the Anglican divines.

Another fruit of this reading is to be found in the starting of a new periodical which he pioneered and edited, *Cyfaill Eglwysig*. He continued to edit this for a number of years until his old friend, Canon Evans of Rhymni, took it over from him. The Sundays it appeared in his Sunday Schools were said to be red-letter days.

---

[41] E Williams, *Life and Letters of Rowland Williams* [London 1874], II 85-90.
[42] *Geninen*, 21 [1903] 156f.

In early January 1864 it was announced that Howell had been appointed to the vicarage of St John's, Cardiff, by the Dean and Chapter of Gloucester. They were looking for a Welsh-speaking man who could impart new spiritual life into that long neglected parish. Howell's track record at Pwllheli was impressive, even in the three short years of his ministry there. It had brought new life to that parish, and it seems to himself as well. After some hard and demanding years with the Church Pastoral-Aid Society Howell was able to relax a little at Pwllheli and clearly received a renewal of God's vision for him, even in the midst of his parochial burdens. Here too he learnt another lesson that not only remained with him for the rest of his life, but provides a clue to the origin of the powerful and spiritual impact of his ministry. This was that prayer was the essence and mainstream of spiritual life and pastoral opportunity. And we may note too that this sense of prayer anchored him to spiritual reality so that he was able to launch out into a deeper examination of theology, and of accepting fellowship with Christians of different traditions. His years were few in that parish, but his experience there was vital for an understanding and appreciation of the remaining and more powerful years of his life.

Samuel Jones noted how both Howell and his parishioners had tears in their eyes as he climbed into the wagon that took him and his family to Caernarfon to catch the train for Cardiff. Another wrote that both church-people and dissenters exhibited a depth of feeling on this occasion that few could imagine or appreciate. The town was in tears. Strong men wept, and the old stage coach was followed until it was well out of sight. They would miss a face Jones described as dark and beautiful, shining with joy and contentment, and one who was the life and soul of whatever society he was in. And they would remember his sermons, forty-five minutes long, delivered from memory but with the aid of his full script if necessary, and delivered in such a way that no one could take notes as they were too busy listening. There was gratitude too, for a wise and gracious pastoral ministry, given as much to the leaders of the town as to the inhabitants of the workhouse.[43]

[43] *Cyfaill Eglwysig*, 1913, pp 259, 124, 145; MS 43163.

He was succeeded at Pwllheli by Daniel Jones, who had been Bishop Campbell's former curate at Merthyr. He too had previously been an Independent minister and was probably well known to Howell. When Campbell had been appointed bishop of Bangor in 1859 he and Jones had gone on an incognito walking tour of his new diocese. In one church they inquired where the heating apparatus was situated. The clerk pointed to the pulpit. They found many such parishes where the congregation was warmed by the Word of God faithfully expounded and delivered rather than by artificial heat. Both Howell and his successor, who did not live long after his appointment, fitted into this tradition, and while Jones was equally able to draw immense crowds to listen to his preaching, he did so as an itinerant preacher rather than as pastor of a parish. One wrote of him that he was no exception to the rule that former Nonconformist ministers did not make successful parsons. This was because he spent too much time outside his parish and too little inside, nor did he possess the mastery of the English tongue which Howell had acquired.[44]

---

[44] William Hughes, *History of the Diocese of Bangor* [SPCK, London 1911], pp 127f. It appears that under Jones the attendances dropped, but Jones' claim that the numbers had been higher during Howell's ministry only because of a split in the Calvinistic Methodist chapel was regarded as unfounded by the contributor to the report in MS 43163. Though he accepted that for some time the congregation had been supplemented by "quarrelsome Methodist brethren", they had left for their own cause, Tabernacle, before Howell had left the parish. At that time the numbers attending the morning services had increased since the beginning of Howell's ministry from 30-60 English to 160-170, and from 40-50 Welsh to 100-120. In addition the Sunday School had increased from 30 to 230. A story told against Jones by this writer was that at a clerical meeting in south Wales a clergyman preached on the duties of pastoral ministry, emphasising that a clergyman should constantly reside in his parish and devote himself to a pastoral ministry. The devil, he added, was an excellent priest, always in his parish. Afterwards, at the luncheon, Canon Jenkins of Dowlais asked "who of us is most unlike the devil?", to answer, "Jones of Pwllheli, because he is never in his parish."

Vicar of Cardiff 1864-75

David Howell was appointed vicar of St John's Church, Cardiff, in 1864. In this chapter we examine the position of the church in Cardiff at that time, and note the various issues which were to come into prominence during his years of ministry in that town. At the time of his appointment the town of Cardiff had grown, in sixty years, from a large village with a population of one thousand eight hundred, to one of thirty-six thousand people. The boundaries of the parish were far from clear, however, and they were last "walked" in the time-honoured way in April 1830.[1]

Such a rapid increase brought with it all kinds of moral pressures as one would expect, particularly those associated with a major seaport and expanding industrial area. A conference of Cardiff Nonconformists, led by Dr Edwards of Pontypool Baptist College, met in 1869 to consider the religious condition of the town. One Thomas White stated:

> They had 336 houses in their midst licensed for the sale of beer and spirits - 188 of which were licensed to sell beer alone. In his calculation he regarded Roath and Canton as part of the town, which comprised about 7,000 houses. These licensed houses were in the proportion of 1 to every 22 houses, or of 1 to every 160 of the people. The houses looked upon by the police as houses of bad character were 286 - which number, he thought, might possibly include some of the licensed houses - and this was in proportion to 1 house in every 26 bearing such a stigma. The brothels numbered 125 - known as such to the police. This was at the ratio of 1 to every 61 houses, or of 1 to every 432 of the people. It should be known that some of the men who owned these hells were men who attended places of worship - men claiming a respectable name and holding a high position.... The number of thieves known to the

---

[1] CMG, 16 Mar 1866, p 8.

police were, under 16 years of age, 46, and over that age, 63 - total 109. Then came one of their worst evils - that of prostitution. The numbers he would give were those known to the police, but there was too much reason to fear that there were dozens, nay, hundreds, besides. Of prostitutes there were under 16 years of age, 25, and over that age 546. These were in the proportion of 1 to 94 of the population.

White also revealed that one in every forty four of the population had been convicted by the magistrates of common assault or of being drunken and disorderly in the previous year, though he allowed that many of those charged were the same persons "time after time." One in every 371 of the population was regarded as a habitual drunkard. Estimating the population as being 54,000 in 1869, he suggested the number of those able to attend "protestant" worship as 26,898, for whom there was provision for all but a thousand in the various churches and chapels of the town. These had a membership of 6,012 and an attendance of 15,680, which meant over 10,710 did not attend any place of worship. In a canvass of parts of the town it had been discovered that out of 765 houses, occupied by 1609 families, only 308 families had one member or more who attended a place of worship, suggesting that in a small district of twenty-one streets over five thousand people did not so attend.

Such people, it was stressed, had "souls equally valuable and equally eternal as their own". Mr Tilly, a noted minister of the town, argued that it was their duty, on the ground of sheer humanity, to remove the immorality around them, and to proclaim that only by the cross of Christ could man be delivered from his moral degradation. The command of God, and their own experience of God's saving power and love, must compel them to be missionaries to those living around them.[2]

There is adequate testimony to the truth of these assertions. The sanitary surveys of the town as well as the photographs of the courtyards around the Hayes and other such areas reveal all too clearly the poverty and destitution in which many families were forced to live. E F Kennard in his biography also notes the

---

[2] *Cardiff Times*, 12 June 1869, p 8.

violence in the Cardiff of his youth, the 1860s, adding that Custom House Square and Charlotte Street were dens of iniquity.[3]

* * * *

The Church of England in the town was almost silent about the problems in its midst. Howell's predecessor as vicar, John Webb, had been appointed to the parish in 1822, when it was still joined in plurality with St Mary's parish, whose church had been damaged in the great flood of 1609 and allowed to fall into decay.[4] The official decree of consolidation was made as late as 1808, but St Mary's was revived as a separate parish in 1844. Webb was appointed by the then patrons, the dean and chapter of Gloucester, possibly having served as one of the junior clergy linked with the cathedral, but he was also rector of Tretire near Ross, in the diocese of Hereford, which he received in 1812, and where he generally resided. In old age he appears to have retired to the coastal area of Swansea. His work at Cardiff was done by deputy, although double duty (two services a Sunday) and a monthly celebration of the sacrament were duly performed. Thus the leadership needed to take what had been a small town parish into the new age of progress and to face all the problems this caused, was totally lacking. As the vicar had a freehold in law and acted within the law regarding his pluralities, nothing could be done to alleviate this position of spiritual and moral stagnation, until he choose to resign or died.

The diocese clearly felt considerably embarrassed by this state of affairs, especially as the town church of Cardiff was regarded as one of its major churches. When Webb was induced to resign on account of old age, but possibly through moral pressure exerted by the bishop, the local paper summed up what must have been the feelings of the diocese, as well as the town, after his forty years' non-residence:

> The many grave disadvantages of such a course must have been keenly felt by the parishioners; and they must assuredly have presented themselves to the Vicar's mind. Socially, aesthetically,

[3] E F Kennard, *The Remarkable Career of a Well-Known Athlete* [Cardiff 1910], pp 98f.
[4] J R Guy, *A History and Description of the Mother Church of Cardiff* [Cardiff 1971], pp 28f.

and spiritually, the flock must have "suffered loss". So far, therefore, from entertaining regret at the step the Vicar has thought proper to take, they must rather feel thankful that the shepherd who did not preside over, watch and tend his charge, should be removed from the nominal responsibility of the same.

A curate lacked the responsibility needed to make the changes required, but, added the editor, "[t]hat congregations are held together at all under such adverse circumstances only evince the tenacity with which they cling to the doctrines and discipline of the Church, and the powerful spiritual influence she wields over the minds, consciences and conduct of her members."

Webb's non-residence was made all the more deplorable by the fact that immediately before his appointment a meeting of parishioners, "[i]mpressed with the serious disadvantages that would accrue from a non-resident or inefficient clergymen", resolved that the new man appointed by the dean and chapter of Gloucester should not only be concerned by precept and example to maintain the doctrines of the Church, but should also realise that as the value of the living depended upon the Easter offerings, or voluntary contributions, of the inhabitants, full residence was required. The dean and chapter were implored to ensure that no person should be appointed without due consideration and that the new man should be capable of performing the duties of the parish with honour to himself and advantage to the parishioners. Such were their words and wishes, but Webb's appointment failed to fulfill them, and Webb simply left the parish in the state into which it had fallen by the early 1820s for a further forty years.

If such an expedient was required then, argued the editor, it was far more required now. The parish had grown extensively and its spiritual needs were equally urgent. But there was another argument which needed to be pressed, which was not so relevant as on the previous occasion. This was that Dissent was "ready to carp at anything savouring of abuse in the Church", and any scandal would form "a specious pretext for all kinds of invidious and insidious attacks" upon it.

An energetic replacement was required, especially as the value of the living still depended on the Easter offering, which had dwindled down to fifty pounds. He continued:

There is little reason to doubt, however, that with an energetic Vicar, who could devote himself to the faithful discharge of his sacred trust, the emolument thus derived would be increased fourfold. The parishioners would then feel it an incumbent duty that they should comply with the Apostolic injunction, "They who minister at the altar, should live by the altar."[5]

Clearly, Mr Webb had failed in his sacred trust, and left a legacy of bitterness and apathy in the cure he had declined to serve in person.

For much of this time Thomas Stacey served as curate of St John's, Cardiff, as Webb's deputy. Born in 1796, apparently a Welsh speaker, educated at Jesus College, Oxford, Stacey served curacies at Cowbridge and Penarth, until in 1827 he was appointed rector of Gelligaer, and vicar of Roath in the following year. Both these preferments were obtained through his friendship with Lord Bute, an evangelical, who did not lightly distribute his considerable patronage. Finding, however, that the "bleak climate of the inhospitable mountain regions" affected his delicate health, he succeeded one Henry Elliott Graham as curate of St John's.[6] This was in 1835, and he remained as curate until 1861, still retaining his parish of Gelligaer, though resigning Roath in the 1840s. Bishop Copleston, his former tutor who became his lifelong friend, made him rural dean of Cardiff and in 1845 appointed him precentor of the cathedral. Stacey thus became one of the most important clerics in the diocese. Furthermore his social position enhanced by his appointment as a magistrate and his elevation as a deputy-lieutenant meant that he was a man to be reckoned with in the Glamorgan of his day.

By the standards of his generation, although not of a subsequent reforming one, Stacey was a conscientious and successful clergyman. With "his great purity of character and earnestness of purpose" he took a leading part in the establishment of National

---

[5] CMG, 16 Oct 1863, p 5.
[6] WM, 22 April 1872, p 3. A writer in the *Bristol Times* [quoted in CMG, 28 December 1849, p 4], severely criticised Stacey for paying some Cambrian curate to serve Gelligaer, "whose moderate wants are supplied by a leak and a Welsh rabbit", half the sum he received for serving Cardiff. He also suggested that his preaching style was mistaken, while he over-dramatised the reading of the liturgy. According to the Ecclesiastical Commissioners' files for the parish of Cardiff Stacey received a stipend of £150 per annum for serving as curate, and had been appointed in 1832.

Schools in Cardiff and in the foundation of the Royal Infirmary, while he publicly supported the leading church organisations of his day: the evangelical Church Pastoral-Aid Society, and the Seamen's Mission. If he was to be judged as a preacher in an age which valued preaching, Stacey scored heavily: "As a preacher he was eloquent and impressive, commanding the attention of crowded congregations; and being gifted with a sonorous voice, he filled the church clearly and easily, so that he was justly held to be one of the most accomplished pulpit orators of his day."

Lady Dunraven, to whose husband Stacey had been a private chaplain, appointed him to the rectory of Coity in 1861, and in that same year his fellow clergy elected him as a proctor in convocation - a position in which he was succeeded by his son-in-law, Charles R Knight, of Tythegstone Court. He thus retired from his Cardiff curacy, and served Coity personally, until increasing ill health caused him to serve the parish by the use of curates. He died in 1871, deeply mourned as a benevolent and sympathetic man and a gracious friend to many.[7]

St John's Church, then as now in the centre of the town, was a medieval foundation. Its tower, built in 1443 by the Nevill family, is still a notable architectural landmark. This medieval church now served a population undreamed of when it was built, with the result that galleries had had to be built in the church itself to accommodate the growing number who attended its services. The staircases to these galleries, which were outside the building, were of such a character that no respectable person could ascend them,[8] while the galleries had been built so close to the ceiling that the heat from the gas lamps produced a "most oppressive" atmosphere there. The choir sat in the gallery, and as the organist noted, singing under such circumstances required no ordinary amount of courage as well as a great love of music.[9] The organ,

---

[7] WM, 22 Ap 1872, p 3. See also the reports of presentations made to him on leaving Cardiff, noting his pastoral ministry and his acts of kindness and sympathy. Stacey, however, replied that he felt that his feebleness of recent years had meant that he had given an "incompetent supervision" to the "arduous and important requirements of so largely populated a parish as this" [CMG, 5 Oct 1861, p 5; 12 Oct 1861, p 12].
[8] CMG, 21 Ap 1865, p 8.
[9] CMG, 11 Sept 1869, p 6. In 1861 the boys of the choir, whose "harshness of voice and rudeness of articulation offended those who could distinguish music from noise" were replaced, to the admiration of the congregation, by three or four ladies [CMG, 7 Dec 1861, p 5].

also in the gallery, obstructed the exits from it, causing fear in many that if those in the gallery tried to get out quickly, panic would soon result. Furthermore a false plaster ceiling had been built, probably at the same time as the galleries were installed, and this not only darkened the church but also hid what one architect, Mr Robinson, described as "the most beautifully finished oak roof". Not surprisingly he recommended that these ceilings and galleries, of "execrable taste", should be removed.[10] A similar plan had been suggested a little earlier, when it was proposed to move the position of the organ, thus opening up the west windows of the church, and build new galleries and staircases.[11] The diocesan architect, John Prichard, writing in 1885, noted the same problems. The galleries had done more to darken and disfigure the church than anything else, and had distorted "the original beautiful conception" of the interior; though regretfully, he reported, they needed to be retained.[12] The interior stone work was encased in coats of plaster, and the columns were covered with thick coats of paint.[13] It is not surprising that year by year considerable monies had to be found for repairs to the church fabric, although many gifts were given to enhance the building as a place of worship.[14] Even worse the pulpit and reading desk had been built up against the organ gallery, with the result that the pews in the chancel were at the "remotest end" from the officiant, and most of the congregation had their backs to the communion table.[15] This may have changed by the time of Howell's arrival in Cardiff.

[10] CMG, 27 Ap 1866, p 5.
[11] CMG, 20 Ap 1866, p 7; cf CMG, 11 Nov 1864, p 8. A proposal in 1867 by the Stacey brothers to give a stained glass west window in memory of their uncle, Edward Priest Richards, provided the western gallery containing the organ was demolished, was not pursued [CMG, 28 Dec 1867, p 5].
[12] *Transactions of the Cardiff Naturalists Society*, 27 (1885) 140f. The church was eventually restored in 1886-7 to make it ready for the Church Congress' visit to Cardiff in October 1887. It appears that until then the church had no central aisle, and a contributor to *The Illustrated Church Congress Handbook* of 1889, edited by C Mackeson, alleges that the old church needed artificial lighting save on the brightest of days [p 30]. In this restoration the galleries were removed, a new nave roof built together with two new aisles and a vestry, the bells recast, and a surpliced choir introduced into the newly furbished chancel. Canon Thompson, its then vicar, is said to have refused a colonial bishopric in order to see this work through [WM, 18 Feb 1889, p 3]. An earlier restoration had taken place in 1877 [WM, 17 July 1877, p 4].
[13] *Guide to the Church Congress at Cardiff* [1889], p 32.
[14] see CMG, 20 April 1866, p 5, and 25 June 1870, p 8: £80 for the tower. In 1851 £1,200 had been spent on repairs [CMG, 27 Dec 1851, p 3].
[15] CMG, 28 December 1849, p 4, quoting the *Bristol Times*.

Clearly St John's Church had become a preaching auditorium, but the situation was exacerbated by two further issues. The first was that most of the pews in the interior of the church were appropriated to individuals and families, who sometimes locked their pews, so that even if they were not in use, they were not available for use by others. During the 1850s and early 1860s this was a source of considerable criticism. Those who paid the church rates felt it was wrong that people who lived in other parishes were able to retain their pews in St John's Church, with the result that many would-be attenders were forced to worship at other churches or even Nonconformist chapels. It was said that when the wardens reallocated the pews in 1852 they could have allocated twice as many as were available. This reallocation had the additional advantage of enabling the wardens to obtain a greater measure of control over the pews than beforehand, and permitted them to introduce pew rents at a later date. A report to the Ecclesiastical Commissioners of 1864 pointed out that of the eleven hundred seats in the church, only four hundred were free, and these were the ones in the galleries. As part of the income from the pew rents formed an essential part of the income of the church, having been substituted for the church rate in 1862, it was difficult to do without them, or to find an alternative and acceptable method of raising money for church purposes. The pew rents were ten shillings per annum for those in the centre and chancel - there was no surpliced choir and the choir sat in the galleries, and seven shillings for those elsewhere. Some annoyance was expressed that the cost was the same for a small or large pew. In 1865 a sum of £149 was obtained in this way, although in the previous year it was but £133. One of Howell's first actions was to insist that those in arrears with their pew rents would lose their rights and their pews would be let to others instead. He later required the pews to be reallocated on an annual basis at the option of the wardens, thus allowing a better distribution of available seats, so that one pew would no longer be occupied by one or two people only. It is not surprising, however, that some regarded this move as an "obnoxious insult" which prevented them from retaining the seats they had held for many years.[16]

[16] CMG, 28 Aug 1847, p 3; 31 Mar 1849, p 3; 21 Feb 1852, p 4; 28 Feb 1852, p 3; 20 Ap 1866, p 7; 6 Ap 1866, p 7; 26 Ap 1867, p6; 3 May 1867 p 5. Ecclesiastical law stated that all pews built without a private faculty were at the disposal of the wardens. The legality of pew rents under these circumstances was questionable.

There were some pews, however, which were exempt from even these requirements. A few people, it appears, had obtained, or inherited, seats for which a faculty had been granted, and these were regarded as private property. Lord Bute, for example, claimed a large pew in the Alderman's aisle, for which he paid no rent, although it had been let out by him for one pound per annum for forty-two years.[17] Another pew, or pews, were owned by the Corporation. Constant complaints were made that they were only used once a month, and stood empty while the galleries were crowded.[18] This situation was not unusual: at Swansea, for example, half the church was completely empty, while half was overcrowded.[19]

The second issue was that Howell filled the church to an extent that Stacey had never done. The popularity of his preaching drew large congregations which crowded into the galleries, making even more obvious their lack of adequate room and ventilation. Indeed a crowded congregational meeting requested that a better system of ventilation be installed in the church as a result.[20] During 1865 a journalist from the *Cardiff and Merthyr Guardian* attended the various Cardiff churches and reported his impressions in a series entitled "Our Churches". Attending St Mary's Church in Butetown he contrasted it with St John's. Few of the St Mary's pews were cushioned, although the object of the worship there appeared to be "to please and instruct" the hearers, and to induce them to join heartily in the service with plain tunes and chants, designed for congregational rather than choir use. By contrast, St John's pews, he noted, were elegantly cushioned, indicating that the congregation belonged to the middle and upper classes. The choir and the organ were at the west end of the gallery, while the matting down the aisle indicated a large congregation, of one thousand plus. Noting the gas lighting he naively commented that "physical comforts were not altogether neglected in this place."[21] He clearly implied that at St John's the

---

[17] CMG, 30 Nov 1865, p 5. Even worse, he only gave £5 per annum to the organ fund. See also Henry Webster's comment, CMG, 28 Aug 1847, p 3.
[18] CMG, 6 Ap 1866, p 7. An attempt was made to persuade the Corporation to contribute to the costs of the church in return for this pew [CMG, 26 Ap 1867, p 6].
[19] WM, 3 July 1869, p 5; 5 July, p 2; 31 July, p 8.
[20] CMG, 27 Oct 1865, p 5.
[21] CMG, 13 Jan 1865, p 8; 6 Jan 1865, p 5.

worshippers listened rather than participated in the services. Large congregations at that time caused other problems. In 1869 the church had to be "cleansed" at the cost of seventy pounds, having been infested with insects which the local paper reported could not be mentioned by name in polite society, but "usually designation by the musical symbols of F sharp and B flat."[22]

The church clock was in the tower, and when it was lighted by gas for the first time it was the "source of great attraction". At the same time a uniformity of time was introduced between the various public clocks in Cardiff, at the Post Office and station, so that the inconvenience of being a minute late would be avoided: Greenwich mean time now being regarded as standard, instead of the local time which was a little behind. The church was never successful in persuading the town council to take over the maintenance of the clock and this became the source of no little feud between the vestry and the corporation.[23]

If the papers picked up the difficulties inherent in the church's architectural features, these features nevertheless provided some comfort to those who decorated the church at Easter and Christmas time. This was a great Victorian innovation much publicised by the newspapers, which devoted columns to these decorations, church by church. In December 1864, for example, St John's Church had a greater extent of these decorations than the other churches of the town, as befitting its leading position. The galleries were festooned with seasonal berries and greenery, and the font, pulpit and reading desk decorated, while "mottoes" abounded in and around the windows.[24] Howell discouraged this activity, it seems, so that by 1869 St John's had lost its premier position. Indeed, the local paper's columns reported at Easter 1866 that a fine balance had been achieved between "extensive decorations and superstitious symbolism" as befitting the "sturdy protestant tendencies of the congregation, and the earnest simplicity and evangelical doctrine of our respected vicar."[25]

St Andrew's Church - now Eglwys Dewi Sant - had only just been built in the fashionable suburb of Tredegarville when Howell

[22] CMG, 28 Aug 1869, p 5.
[23] CMG, 5 Aug 1864, p 5.
[24] CMG, 30 Dec 1864, p 5.
[25] CMG, 20 Ap 1866, p 5; cf 2 Jan 1869, p 5.

arrived. Designed by Prichard and Seddon it was built in such a way that a large congregation - of nearly six hundred - could be seated under a single span. If the lack of accommodation at St John's was the justification for its building, it was also hoped that it might be a more "fashionable" church than the parish church. Stacey had obtained the land from the Bute estate, and was instrumental in its building, taking part in the laying of its foundation stone in June 1860, an activity which was shared by the Cardiff masonic body. Unfortunately a series of disputes between the vestry and the architects about the amount of money required for its building took place, the parishioners having anticipated a cost of about £4,000, which was exceeded long before the building had been completed. Consequently the architects were "paid off" when the building work had reached the clerestory level, and it was only completed by 1863 in a very inferior manner. Even this would not have happened had it not been for the liberality of one of the contractors.[26] A newspaper report thus commented on the plainness of the chancel, the furniture being bare of ornamentation, with a harmonium rather than an organ, and the plain brick walls of the interior. It concluded: "There is an evident mark of want of funds in the fitting up of the interior".[27] The church was to provide further headaches for Howell in the years to come.

In order to accommodate the rising dockland population, and possibly to establish at least one church in Cardiff which would be evangelical in tone, the second Marquess of Bute built St Mary's Church, in Butetown, in 1843. Its foundation stone was laid in 1840, when the local freemasons, who appeared to like these affairs, came and inspected the foundations: their regalia, reported the local newspaper, contrasting with the more sombre dress of the clergy and gentlemen present.[28] Wordsworth was even persuaded to write a rather indifferent poem to celebrate its opening. The new church was able to seat eighteen hundred people. Its pews - many rented to the wealthy merchants who then resided in this

[26] *Guide to the Church Congress at Cardiff* [1889], pp 34f; CMG, 5 Dec 1857, p 5; 5 Jan 1861, p 5; 7 Mar 1863, p 5; 21 Mar 1863, p 6; 13 Ap 1865, p 8; 1 Sept 1865, p 5. Webb was present at the consecration, when the offertory of £60 was the subject of some scorn for its paucity.
[27] CMG, 20 Jan 1865, p 8.
[28] CMG, 11 July 1840, p 2.

area - covered the interior almost up to the apse, and there were galleries around on three sides. A huge three-decker pulpit stood in the middle, almost obstructing from view the small altar covered with a red cloth in the apse. This arrangement was altered in 1878 under the influence of the Tractarian revival.

The first vicar of St Mary's was our old friend, John Webb, simply because he was vicar of the united benefice. His curate was J C Campbell, equally a pluralist, for he was vicar of Roath, and later became bishop of Bangor. But Webb resigned in 1844, presenting the church with its communion plate as his parting gift. Bute accordingly presented William Leigh Morgan, then vicar of Bedwellte, a member of the powerful and evangelical Leigh family, to the benefice. His uncle was the man who baptised Howell. Morgan was later to become the domestic chaplain of Lord Bute's widow and also rural dean of Cardiff.

Morgan's ministry and its rather tragic sequel need to be noted, for they had a vast influence on the church life in Cardiff of Howell's day. Certainly, the Marquess' wish for an evangelical centre in Cardiff through Morgan was amply justified. St Mary's parish became a noted evangelical parish, and Morgan became known as one of the more celebrated preachers of the now reviving Church of England in Wales.[29]

Church building continued. An iron mission church, nearer the docks than St Mary's, was opened in 1855, and in the following year All Saint's, Tyndall Street, was opened as a Welsh church for the town. Church schools were also built. Morgan's services at St Mary's were clearly designed for working-class people, congregational singing, as already noted, being encouraged for this purpose, even though at times police constables had to be stationed in the galleries to keep order. Mother's meetings were established as well as Sunday Schools, and an extensive pastoral visitation of the parish carried out year by year.[30] He was thus able to state in 1859 that while he had a congregation of between fourteen and fifteen hundred at St Mary's, yet there were thousands of people living near the church, visited by his Scripture

---

[29] See Guy, *The Mother Church of Cardiff*, pp 37-9.
[30] CMG, 13 Jan 1865, p 8: letters of *Veritas* in CMG, 1 Jan 1870, p 5, and *A Churchman* in CMG, 16 Jan 1869, p 5.

reader and tract distributors, who still "continued to disregard the things which belonged to their everlasting peace."[31] But Morgan's most noted ministry, apart from his parochial work, lay among the seamen. Noting the problems associated with seamen and the way in which they were exploited - in 1864 he commented that over eight years seventy-one seamen had been drowned in the docks, some through drunkenness, but others had been murdered - he obtained through the instrumentality of Lord Bute an old wooden-walled ship, HMS *Thisbe*. This ship became the centre of his work amongst seamen. A chapel was built on its deck, and a curate of the parish was delegated to serve full-time as chaplain to the seamen. A lay-reader was also appointed to hold services on board visiting ships. In 1864 it was reported that in four months 2,455 seamen had come to services on the *Thisbe* - averaging 120 at the afternoon service and 70 during the evening - and 928 had come to read periodicals provided in its reading room.[32] Seeing a seaman with smallpox driven from door to door, with no-one prepared to take him in, Morgan resolved to obtain a hospital ship. This was the origin of the *Hamadryad*. By 1870 Morgan had obtained a seaman's hostel which was able to accommodate between sixty and seventy men, and he also provided a banking service for their money, instead of it being spent in drink and "passion".[33]

By his evangelical ministry and practical concern, Morgan rapidly became the active leader of church life in Cardiff. His involvement in the local auxiliaries of the Church Pastoral-Aid Society and Church Missionary Society was substantial, and he was even involved in the work of the non-evangelical Curates' Aid Society and the Assistant Curates' Society.[34]

After a noted ministry in St Mary's parish Morgan accepted the pre-retirement post of the rural vale parish of Llanmaes. This was in 1871. A presentation was made to him in which it was stated:

---

[31] CMG, 26 Nov 1859, p 6.
[32] CMG, 4 Mar 1864, p 6.
[33] CMG, 21 Mar 1868, p 6: John Mayberry in *I saw Three Ships* [Cardiff 1988], suggests that the founder of this work was Dr H J Paine, medical officer of health for Cardiff, but he makes no mention of Morgan's work in his booklet.
[34] CMG, 23 Nov 1867, p 5.

> Rev. and Dear Sir, - We, the undersigned, on behalf of the congregation of St Mary's Church and subscribers generally, desire to express our heartfelt regret at the severance of the tie which has so long existed between us; and in doing so wish to bear our testimony to the faithfulness with which you have exercised the duties of your pastoral office during the 28 years you have been amongst us.
>
> We feel that the Gospel of Christ has been preached by you in all its purity and simplicity, with an earnestness which showed your extreme anxiety for the souls of your people, and you have exemplified the same by the consistency of your daily life.
>
> We appreciate most highly the patient perseverance and energy which you have exhibited in the management of the various institutions and charities which owe to you their origin. You found us destitute of many appliances for the advancement of the religious and moral welfare of the poorer inhabitants of the parish, and you leave us with large, flourishing, and efficient day and Sunday schools, Bible classes, clothing clubs and many other kindred societies.

The framed address went onto speak of his wife's "invaluable and untiring assistance". In his reply Morgan noted how the parish had changed over the years of his ministry.

> You have assisted me liberally in maintaining the church, parish, and other charities, and enabled me to deliver them into the hands of my successor unburdened with debt. The schools, which were the heaviest charge, have a large balance in their favour. Upon my part, I know of many deficiencies, faults, and failings in duty. I can honestly say, however, that I tried to do my best, but, oh, how far was that from which I could have wished it had been! ... As to the all-important matter of preaching the truth of the everlasting Gospel, I have not shunned to declare unto you all the counsel of God, but have warned everyone night and day. As far as I have known the truth, I have conveyed it sincerely to each of you without respect of persons. In this portion of my ministerial labours I have always felt my constant need of Divine grace and of your earnest prayers. I have no doubt but that both have been freely given. If I have felt my infirmities and failing in my parochial ministrations, how much more have I felt them in my labours among the great congregations? To give those up was a great trial to me, as to perform them was my great pleasure....[35]

---

[35] CMG, 13 Jan 1872, p 6.

Morgan was also vicar of Roath, then a country parish in which resided many wealthy families. If the people of St Mary's were complimentary about his ministry, there was a different order of things at Roath, for there were complaints that he neglected this parish, leaving its work in the hands of a curate and appointing wardens without holding a vestry meeting. His answer to the latter was severe though polite: he had always so appointed and would continue to do so, and if his parishioners there wanted a remedy they could apply to the courts. For himself, he felt he was legally obliged to continue his former practices. The paper reporting this accused him of flinging the law at his parishioners. This was his last year as vicar of Roath, and possibly this incident helped persuade him to resign his two Cardiff parishes and seek a quieter field of ministry.[36] There had been an earlier dispute between Morgan and a curate, Thomas Clapp. Mr Clapp accused Morgan of allowing him, as curate, to shoulder the costs and problems of the National School at Roath himself, and when he resigned, of refusing to repay him the fifty pounds owed him on this and possibly other accounts.[37] The truth of this matter is not known. It must be said that such behaviour was highly uncharacteristic of Morgan if these facts were true.

On the credit side Morgan not only established a mission on the East Moors, then part of the parish, he was also responsible for rebuilding the parish church at Roath in 1870, albeit with Bute money. Some years earlier a reporter attended a service there, and wrote about the small low building, a chancel covered in seats, with a small children's choir, and "[a] relic of the past ages", an old and neglected clerk assisting in the service. This clerk was responding "to the clergyman in the good old English style while reading the psalms" - that is, they read the verses alternatively, the congregation probably repeating them after the clerk. Furthermore, the sermon was preached without the clergyman retiring to replace the surplice for the gown.[38] The latter, although regarded as a low church practice, was never customary in south Wales. It may well be that Morgan concentrated on St Mary's

---

[36] CMG, 22 Ap 1871, p 5; 29 Ap, p 5.
[37] CMG, 8 Sept 1865, p 5.
[38] CMG, 10 Feb 1865, p 8.

church, and was possibly wrong to retain Roath along with his main parish. The consequence was that his Roath parishioners greeted his resignation with delight, even if it meant the appointment of a Tractarian, Father Puller, to the parish, as it allowed them a vicar of their own.[39]

Leigh Morgan resigned St Mary's parish in August 1871, and the Bute trustees, appointed to act as the third marquess had become a Roman-Catholic (all of whom were men sympathetic to anglo-catholicism), appointed a man of very different temperament and churchmanship as his successor. This was Griffith Arthur Jones, who was then the forty-five year old vicar of Llanegryn, Merionethshire, into which parish he had introduced the ritualistic trappings and teachings associated with the second and degenerate stage of the Tractarian revival. It was not an appointment welcomed by the parishioners of St Mary's, for they had petitioned the senior trustee, Canon Jenkins of Aberdare, for the appointment of a former curate of St Mary's, D Parker Morgan, then vicar of Aberafan and Baglan, to the parish.[40] Morgan was regarded as a powerful evangelical preacher.[41]

What the parishioners feared in the appointment of such a Tractarian occurred. Various ceremonies, altar lights, eucharistic vestments, incense and other such practices were gradually introduced. It was these which caused the upsets, for generally speaking what is seen is often regarded as being more important than what is heard, and what was seen in St Mary's at this time appeared to many to be barefaced popery. Though John Guy suggests in his history of St Mary's that Jones did not rush matters, not introducing vestments for ten years and retaining Morgan's black gown in the pulpit, this assertion is not supported by the available evidence, for the teaching went hand in hand with the outward symbolism.[42] Furthermore in the June after his arrival consistory court proceedings were instituted against Jones for introducing unauthorised church furnishings and making

---

[39] J W Ward and H A Coe, *Father Jones of Cardiff* [London 1907], p 34.
[40] CMG, 16 Sept 1871, p 5. He died as rector of a parish in New York USA.
[41] CMG, 1 Jan 1870, p 5.
[42] Guy, *The Mother Church of Cardiff*, p 45.

unauthorised alterations.⁴³ These allegations were clarified by a memorial organised in that same year for making a separate ecclesiastical district out of St Mary's parish. It made clear that the desire for such separation had been caused by Jones introducing certain forms and ceremonies "such as kneeling before the altar in private prayer before offering the bread and wine to the communicants at Holy Communion, and other ritualistic tendencies."⁴⁴ A letter in the *Western Mail* some years later accused Jones of teaching transubstantiation, mariology, good works and baptismal regeneration, as well as introducing the High Church inspired *Hymns Ancient and Modern*.⁴⁵ Some of the trappings may have been missing, but the field-work was well in place. Undoubtedly the fact that Jones was known as a Tractarian was sufficient to cause tempers to rise. If a few hated his theological position, many more preferred to remain under an evangelical ministry, and this was clearly not to be had at St Mary's, where Jones claimed that he allowed the prayer meeting to die a natural death.

Further annoyance was caused by Jones' dismissal of J W Osman, the popular curate of the daughter or iron church. It was generally believed that this was because Osman had shown no leanings "towards ritualistic or other objectionable forms." Nevertheless a new incumbent had the right to give notice to the existing curates of the parish. Father Jones was reminded by the editor of the local newspaper that in Cardiff, whatever his preconceived notions may have been, the clergy as a rule treated their parishioners and neighbours with kindness and respect.⁴⁶

Though Jones protested to Bishop Ollivant that he had been bitterly opposed in this and other parishes and accused of a want of judgment and of Christian charity,⁴⁷ it has to be argued that he displayed a want of tact and good sense in imposing distasteful practices, teachings and ceremonies on an articulate and well-taught congregation. The result was that a branch of the anti-

---

⁴³ CMG, 28 June 1873, p 5: 12 July, p 5; 15 Nov, p 5. These were the repositioning of the pulpit, removing the organ from the gallery to the chancel, and introducing free pews. The court hoped a compromise could be reached.
⁴⁴ CMG, 17 Oct 1872, p 5.
⁴⁵ WM, 9 Ap 1875, p 7.
⁴⁶ CMG, 1 June 1872, p 5; 24 Aug, p 5. He was later rector of Llanarth, Gwent.
⁴⁷ *Cardiff Weekly Mail*, 19 June 1875, p 4.

Tractarian Church Association was formed in Cardiff,[48] and the congregation split three ways.[49]

Some of the congregation remained with Father Jones, though he boasted that he had lost most of the congregation of Morgan's time, which comprised four hundred Sunday communicants and a church nearly full for the other services. These large congregations, said Jones' biographers, had "to a great extent left", having found, in the words of a letter of 1872, that the illegal ceremonies used at the Holy Communion and other services were "utterly at variance with the simple character of the worship to which they had been for many years accustomed."[50]

Another group linked up with the Free Church of England, and eventually established St Paul's Free Church, thus fulfilling the prophecy of W J Conybeare in his essay in the Edinburgh Review:

> [T]he chief mischief done by the Tractarians is that they alienate these classes [the middle and lower] from the Establishment. The accession of a Tractarian rector is always followed by the overcrowding of old conventicles, and the erection of new ones. The clergyman who has thus succeeded in driving half his hearers into Dissent, seems often rather pleased than otherwise at his achievement. He congratulates himself that he has winnowed the corn, and fairly separated the chaff from the wheat. "I have only twenty people now who come to church," said a country rector - "but they are all sound churchmen." Moreover, such a priest feels his labours lessened by the desertion, as he is not bound to take charge of his schismatical parishioners, and gives himself no farther trouble about them ...[51]

This Free Church had considerable success in Cardiff, especially as its lay leaders, Messrs H Fothergill and H North, had been leading members of St Mary's Church, North having been chairman of the presentation to Canon Morgan. He made a public protest against Father Jones' ministry, alleging that had he followed Jones years ago he would have been, with him, a

---

[48] CMG, 1 June 1872, p 5.
[49] The information which follows is partly drawn from J C Reed, *The Church in our City* [Cardiff 1954], p 67, and Guy's *The Mother Church of Cardiff*, p 45.
[50] *Father Jones of Cardiff*, p 35: CMG, 24 Aug 1872, p 5.
[51] J C Conybeare, *Essays Ecclesiastical and Social* [London 1855], p 134.

member of the Church of Rome.⁵² The congregation first met at the Town Hall, and then for some years at premises in Crown Court, off Duke Street. A grand bazaar in 1875 raised £250 for their building fund and fifteen hundred people attended it. Under the ministry of Philip Norton their cause gained momentum. If Norton was accused by Father Jones and his supporters of not being an ordained clergyman, the Free Church members retorted that Lord Erbury had stated that the Free Church of England was essentially at one with the evangelical portion of the Established Church. Neither did they stop there. Claiming they were prepared to meet the spiritual needs of the parish of St Mary's, which clearly Jones was not, they requested a vestry meeting to be convened in order to put forward their request to purchase land on which to built their new church. The request was denied, but the congregation successfully built its own church, known as St Paul's.⁵³ Norton, who had been ordained as a minister of the Countess of Huntingdon's Connection, eventually joined the Church of England, and was ordained in 1879 by the bishop of Worcester.⁵⁴ Without his leadership the cause floundered, and eventually died out. Father Jones, ironically, purchased the disused church and it later became a daughter church of his parish, being re-dedicated to St Michael.

A third group wished to remain within the Church of England, but not within the parish of St Mary's. In October 1872 they drew up a memorial to the bishop signed by 2,764 adult residents of the parish, requesting the formation of an ecclesiastical district out of the parish of St Mary's, based on that area of the parish near the pierhead. They indicated as their reasons for this request the size of St Mary's parish, their distance from the parish church, and the dislike of the forms and ceremonies introduced into that church by Father Jones.⁵⁵ In their protest they clearly had the sympathetic ear of Bishop Ollivant. All kinds of objections were raised by Father Jones which delayed the formation of this district, such as the extent of the boundaries and whether the National

---

[52] CMG, 21 Dec 1872, p 5 (the original is now missing).
[53] WM, 11 Ap 1874, p 8; 16 May 1874, p 6; 18 June 1874, p 6; 26 June 1874, p 7; 11 July 1874, p 7; 18 Sept 1874, p 5; 20 Mar 1875, p 8.
[54] Lambeth Palace Library, Benson Papers, 37/304f, 330f.
[55] CMG, 24 Aug 1872, p 5; 17 Oct 1872, p 5.

Schools should remain with St Mary's or go into the new district. Eventually these remained with St Mary's, but the Bute Trustees, sympathetic to the vicar they had appointed, demanded and obtained £2,000 for the site on which St Stephen's iron-church was built in 1877. The bishop rightly appointed an evangelical to the parish, which became a separate parish under the Peel Act in 1888, and for many years it remained the only evangelical church in the Cardiff area.[56]

It is not surprising that Father Jones had to put up with a great deal of well-deserved hostility, especially at the annual vestry meetings which were open to the whole parish, and were a civil as well as an ecclesiastical affair in those days. This meeting elected the wardens and fixed the various parochial rates for the year. In 1875, for example, it elected a Nonconformist as people's warden of the parish, and when the vicar and his supporters left the meeting, for the civil business to be concluded, the newly elected warden proposed a vote of censure on Jones which was carried with acclaim. One of Jones' supporters, describing the same meeting, accused the "Protestant party" of Messrs Richard Cory (its chief), Pullen, Hodge and Buckingham, of "bull-baiting" the vicar, and especially with the charge that he, as a pseudo-Jesuit, had endeavoured to subvert the principles of the Reformation "by wickedly lighting up a dark part of the church with candles."[57] Father Jones argued that he never considered that the vestry meeting had any true relation to the Church of St Mary's, although he with others "always felt keen indignation as Churchmen at a state of things which permitted a yearly annoyance to our Vicar, and shame as inhabitants of Cardiff at the scandalous scenes which have hitherto been a disgrace to the town..." He hoped that "even the Dissenters will in time see that as they have perfect liberty to manage their own religious affairs, so it is unfair as it is unchristian to attempt by unwarrantable interference to hinder the work of the clergy of a Church whose doctrines they do not hold and whose Services they cannot therefore be expected to understand."[58] By the time this was

[56] WM, 25 Mar 1874, p 4; 31 July 1874, p 4.
[57] WM, 1 Ap 1875, p 6.
[58] *Father Jones of Cardiff*, pp 38f. He was writing in the third person in his parish magazine.

written, 1878, the resentment and bitterness had died down to a certain extent.

These and other matters brought home to many Cardiff people what John Griffith, rector of Merthyr, and many others had been shouting about over the years. Griffith had organised the great anti-ritualistic rally at Newport in 1868. Some of the more prominent evangelical clergy of the diocese also took part in this, amongst them Wrenford of Newport, Griffiths of Neath, James of Panteg, Bury Capel, Canon Hawkins of St Woollos, and Chancellor Williams. Howell, however, did not take part. Bishop Ollivant, anxious to retain the peace of his diocese, accused Griffith of stirring up trouble, but he, regarded by many as the un-mitred bishop of Llandaff, was well able to defend himself.[59] This meeting had closely followed another controversy in which Griffith had been involved. This regarded the annual meeting of the Llandaff Diocesan Choral Association. Bishop Ollivant's remarks at this meeting about the previous meeting at Maindee, Newport, and the ritualism permitted there, were widely circulated by Griffith. He accordingly claimed that the bishop disapproved "of these puerile imitations of Popery, these lifting up of crosses, carrying banners, and walking in surplices", as well as candles lit at noon, and regretted that the bishop had allowed the matter to be shelved. The secretaries of the association alleged in reply that much of the bishop's address had been taken up instead by the "expression of his abhorrence of newspaper controversy on such subjects."[60]

Wrenford had already preached and published a sermon in 1864 whose title was *Romanising the Church of England*. In this he accused the Tractarians of stretching the language of the Prayer-Book and the Thirty-Nine Articles to bear a Roman meaning; of introducing medievalism into the church; favouring chairs instead of pews; putting crosses on everything "plain or coloured"; encouraging images, crossings and bowings; observing saints' days; singing Gregorian chants and Roman hymns; practising monkery and confessionals. Asking if such men who

[59] CMG, 14 Mar 1868, P 5. See also Wilton D Wills, "The Revd John Griffith and the Revival of the Established Church in Nineteenth Century Glamorgan", *Morgannwg*, 13 (1969) 96-7.
[60] CMG, 8 Feb 1868, pp 4f; 15 Feb 1868, p 8.

introduced these things could be regarded as brethren, friends or foes, he reiterated that one must not remain silent while these men endeavour to bring the church back to popery.[61]

Griffith continued his attack. In his sermon at the opening of Llanhetty Church, Buckland, he declared that he had no objection to such matters as surpliced choirs, genuflexions, turning to the east, processions, and so forth, but asked what was their value compared to the great commission of preaching the Gospel and in making the society of their day a better place in which to live? Did such things promote holiness, purity and peacefulness?[62] Clearly they did not, for he repeated the same charges in 1874 at another great anti-ritual rally at Manchester. Here his sarcasm and bitterness had full rein, from women giving up their souls to the custody of a priest in the confessional, to the burlesque imitation of Roman services. Though the bishop of Manchester censured Griffith and the vicar of the parish in which the meeting took place, the editor of the *Western Mail* took Griffith's side, indicating the extent to which his views were generally held within the Church. He may be blunt, but he is sincere, was his comment.[63]

Howell was thus thrust into the centre of an ever growing storm about Tractarianism within the Church, and during his time at Cardiff that storm burst with fury. His every move would be watched and every word he said on this subject remembered, especially by those who feared these romanising influences.

Howell, however, pursued a policy of moderation, unlike his contemporary at Merthyr. None could doubt where his sympathies lay, but the pressure of his parochial life and his concern to see good in every aspect of life prevented him from publicly opposing Father Jones. Thus the Church Association, a Protestant body with a local branch in Cardiff, regretted the lack of co-operation in its work by the local clergy, and this at a time, 1873, when there was an even greater responsibility to protest at the attempt to introduce Roman dogma into the Protestant church. At Swansea the situation was quite different, for here the

---

[61] J T Wrenford, *Romanising the Church of England* [London 1864].
[62] CMG, 9 Nov 1872, p 6; cf his attack on ritualism at Swansea, WM, 13 June 1874, p 5, and on Gladstone, WM, 13 Oct 1874, p 7.
[63] WM, 14 July 1874, p 4 & 6; 3 June 1874, p 4; 21 July 1874, p 4.

vicar of Swansea, Squire, had addressed the local association.[64] Even more significantly, both Father Jones and Father Puller of Roath appeared on the platform at the inaugural meeting of Howell's testimonial fund when he was about to leave Cardiff.[65]

Equally interesting is that Howell intervened to assist St Peter's Roman Catholic Church in obtaining land from the Tredegar estate. Father Signini, the parish priest, was convinced that the estate was withholding land the church required for making a road to its west end on purely religious grounds. The poor father, who had been badly deceived about the planning of the site, wrote to Howell, who persuaded the Tredegar agent to allow the church to have the land it needed on fair terms. It was a situation which showed Howell at his best and some of the city fathers and land agents at their worst.[66]

* * * *

Another problem which was to involve Howell was the emotive one of the provision of a church for the Welsh-speaking population of Cardiff. By the 1840s the Welsh coastal trade and the opening of the docks had brought many Welsh-speaking people to Cardiff. Stacey at St John's had no wish to accommodate these people, but Morgan at St Mary's, equally a Welsh speaker, realised that without a Welsh church many churchpeople would be lost to the twelve or thirteen Welsh chapels in the town. Morgan thus started services in the Welsh language which led directly to the opening of All Saints' Church, Tyndall Street, as the Welsh Church, in 1856. Until 1867 it was served by curates linked with St Mary's Church, but in that year it became a separate ecclesiastical district with its own vicar. But this move was taken in order to provide an endowment for its clergyman as the Welsh work was poorly supported financially. As a parish church All Saints' was required to hold bilingual services, but a subsequent vicar, Richard Goyne, a Cornishman who had learnt Welsh as a second language, endeavoured, unsuccessfully, to

[64] CMG, 16 Aug 1873, p 5.
[65] WM, 12 Feb 1875, p 4. Many Nonconformists also contributed to the fund, at a time when the disestablishment battle was commencing.
[66] *St Peter's Church, Cardiff, Centenary Brochure*, unpaged.

end the Welsh services there and to substitute another building, in a more convenient location, for the parish church, allowing the Roman Catholics to purchase the original church for their own use. The move was supported by the local Cardiff clergy, it was claimed, for they would have been aware of the difficulties of this parish in both a bilingual and geographical sense. A new vicar, Charles Jones, a fine Welsh speaker, also realised these difficulties, and finding the Welsh services there so badly supported, closed them down. The Welsh press made the position of this church, the only church for the Welsh inhabitants of the leading town in Wales, into a cause célèbre, but however much the moral argument was on their side, the legal position was quite clear, that All Saints, as a parish church, was required to serve its parishioners first, and they, as both vicar and bishop agreed, would be better served by services conducted in the English language rather than in Welsh.[67]

Thus after 1875 there was no ecclesiastical provision for Welsh services in Cardiff, and though the Welsh speakers frequently petitioned for them, they were unsuccessful. It seems a pity, wrote James Davies to Bishop Ollivant, that those who have been brought up from their cradle within the Church should have no church in which to worship God in their own language in a large town such as Cardiff. Ollivant replied, generally, that most Welsh people spoke English in any case - which rather missed the point, for he never seems to have realised that Welsh people preferred spiritual truth to be imparted in their mother tongue. He even seemed unaware that by the 1880s Cardiff contained around sixteen thousand Welsh-speaking people.

It appears that Howell alleviated this position by obtaining funds from Lady Llanover to provide for some Welsh services the matriarchal figure of all things Welsh. If in 1870 Ollivant could write to Gladstone to suggest that all Howell's ministrations were in English, and that he had had no opportunity of hearing him speak or preach in Welsh,[68] the *Western Mail* was able to report four years later a Welsh harvest service held in St John's

---

[67] The lengthy dispute, which involved parliamentary bills, will be found chronicled in my pamphlet, *Irish Scorn, English Pride and the Welsh Tongue* [Cardiff 1987].
[68] Ollivant to Gladstone, 14 Jan 1870, British Library, Gladstone Papers, Addit Ms 44424/97.

schoolroom.⁶⁹ After his departure Howell had to placate Lady Llanover's wrath that his successor, Charles James Thompson, had discontinued the Welsh services through want of resources, while the Welsh curate he had appointed failed to satisfy her ladyship's exacting standards of proficiency in Welsh.⁷⁰ This embarrassment of not having a Welsh church in Cardiff, which became acute in the 1880s during the early stages of the disestablishment campaign, was resolved in 1886-7 when Eglwys Dewi Sant was built in Howard Gardens, but this was long after Howell's time in Cardiff, and when the subject had became one of even more passionate concern.

* * * *

By the early 1860s there was another area of disquiet. The Nonconformists, after their celebrated gathering at Swansea to commemorate the bicentenary of the great ejection of 1662, resolved to take the offensive against the established Church and agitate for its disestablishment. They did so on the grounds that the Church-State link prevented the Church from exercising a spiritual role within society, but at a later stage it became more a question of bitterness and revenge rather than the liberation it was claimed to be. Irish disestablishment was the first item on the agenda, and Gladstone pursued this on the grounds of justice and common sense, as the Irish Church was in a minority in Ireland and had a privileged position which could not be justified. Church leaders saw it as religious spoliation, and feared that it was the prelude for further attacks on the Church, especially in Wales, where the situation between Nonconformity and the Church was analogous to the Irish one.

The Irish disestablishment question came before Parliament in 1868, and there were many meetings for and against it organised in Cardiff.⁷¹ Howell came in for some criticism himself, for he allowed the Constitutional Association, which supported the Church, to use the National or Church school, for a meeting.

---

⁶⁹ WM, 23 Oct 1874, p 7.
⁷⁰ David Howell to Lady Llanover, 9 Sept & 3 Nov 1875, NLW, D Parry Jones papers, 1979; printed letter of Lady Llanover to C J Thompson, Lambeth Palace Library, Benson papers, 39/245-7.
⁷¹ CMG, 3 Oct 1868, p 6; 10 Oct 1868, p 8; 14 Nov 1868, p 5f.

Many Nonconformists, who had subscribed to the cost of this school in spite of its church association, protested at this use. Howell argued that the meetings were not for political ends, rather they were for the defence of the Irish Church. He also pointed out that he found no fault with those who had allowed their chapels and the British schoolrooms to be used for meetings of the Liberation Society - a pressure group founded to promote the disestablishment of the Church - but merely claimed the same liberty of action for himself.[72]

A branch of the Church of England Defence Association was formed in Cardiff in 1873,[73] by which time the whole position had become one of increasing hostility and entrenched positions. Nevertheless Howell endeavoured to maintain good relationships with Nonconformists, and many of them appreciated his spiritual ministry and contributed willingly to his testimonial fund.

The vicar of a parish had not only his ecclesiastical duties to perform, he also acted as chairman of the parish vestry, as noted earlier in relation to St Mary's Church. This body, comprising all the ratepayers in a parish, had the power to elect one of the churchwardens[74] - the incumbent nominated the other - and to oversee the levying and collection of the various parochial rates. The church rate, used for the upkeep of the church, its fabric and the incidentals of worship, had only just been abolished when Howell arrived in the parish, after a long series of Nonconformist protests regarding its injustice. The vestry meeting called to abolish it, and to hold a poll for a new assistant overseer of the poor, was chaired by the curate, and was so crowded that it had to be adjourned to the town hall. It was a stormy meeting.[75] Pew-

---

[72] CMG, 5 Sept 1868, p 5; cf p 8, where it is said as a result of the Irish disestablishment Howell was driven to support the conservative party, having refused to act in any political sense for the previous seventeen years.

[73] CMG, 18 Oct 1873, p 5.

[74] The churchwardens were not required to be churchmen, though Canon Morgan always tried to ensure that communicants were elected as wardens at St Mary's, where the church was maintained by a church rate until 1865 at least [CMG, 21 Ap 1865, p 8]. A man could be fined for non-acceptance of the office of warden.

[75] CMG, 12 Feb 1864, p 5. Since the late 1840s John Batchelor and other Nonconformists had proposed that the church rate should be replaced by a voluntary rate, or questioned whether the organist's salary was a proper payment from these rates. By the 1850s the wardens were finding it more and more difficult to collect these rates, even from churchpeople, let alone Nonconformists. One Mr Duncan was typical

continued on next page

rents, subscriptions and voluntary contributions took its place,[76] for the offertory at the communion service was designated for the poor, and few clergy had the audacity to propose that a collection for church purposes should be taken at every service. The incumbent's stipend generally came from sources independent of the parish vestry, such as tithes, rent-charges, endowments and the like, though a few town parishes, such as St Mary's, depended on pew rents as part of the income of their incumbent.

Howell's first vestry heard him state that he did not wish to appoint the retiring people's warden as his own warden, for this would place the entire management of the church in the hands of the parishioners. Such appointments could - and frequently did - lead to difficulties when parishioners were not well affected towards the incumbent, and if the churchwardens were not zealous in the discharge of their office.[77] Most parishes found it difficult to obtain people willing to act as wardens, mainly because of the responsibility and work involved in that role, which had a civil as well as an ecclesiastical importance at that time, and Cardiff all the more so because of the exacting standards Howell required from his wardens. Speaking at his Easter vestry of 1866 he indicated that the most essential qualification was that of being a communicant member of the church, one with a warm, earnest and sincere attachment to the Church, and with a zealous desire to promote her prosperity and welfare. Next to this he placed the requirement that a man be one who through his length of residence, position and character, could command the respect and confidence of his fellow parishioners.[78]

* * * *

continued from page 66
of many. He objected to pay because he was unable to obtain a seat at St John's and instead had to pay rent for a pew in another church. In 1862, for example, only £130 was collected out of a possible £400. By this date the wardens were declining to enforce payment, and virtually collecting a voluntary rate in all but name. The sums collected were never sufficient for the requirements, and the system was compounded by the custom of allowing arrears to accrue which had to be paid out of the following year's income [CMG, 15 Jan 1848, p 4; 10 June 1848, p 3; 2 June 1854, p 3; 11 Aug 1860, p 6; 10 Aug 1861, p 8; 5 Oct 1861, p 3; 30 Aug 1862, p 5; 4 Sept 1862, p 5].
[76] As Archdeacon Blosse noted at his visitation [CMG 4 June 1870, p 6]. Pew rents had been proposed as a solution to the church rates question at a much earlier date [CMG, 13 Sept 1862, p 5; 24 July 1863, p 5].
[77] CMG, 21 Ap 1865, p 8, as happened at St Mary's.
[78] CMG, 6 Ap 1866, p 7.

When Howell was appointed to St John's in 1864 the town was almost a frontier post. The church in his parish was in one sense fairly successful, its congregations were large and its finances in a reasonable state, but a want of clear and decisive leadership over four decades had meant that - in words addressed to another church, it "was neither hot nor cold". Spiritually it was complacent. Pastorally it ignored the social demands of the parish it served. The active spiritual leadership of the town had been taken over by Leigh Morgan of St Mary's, but that church was to be torn apart by controversy when he left, and that controversy, relating to its wider rather than local issues, was disturbing the peace of the Church long before. The issues of nationality and disestablishment were equally in the local arena, although again they were to be magnified during Howell's ministry. And there was always the possibility that those who above all should be supporting his ministry, namely the wardens, could be elected by, and representing, those who were diametrically opposed to that ministry.

Howell thus entered a parish which needed a thorough shaking up, spiritually and pastorally, and his ministry took place in a town and within a church community which was to be torn asunder by ritualistic and linguistic disputes. In him, however, the man and the need of the day was well matched, and his ministry at St John's proved to be one of the success stories of the Victorian church in Wales, although he himself, more modestly, saw himself as a pioneer for other and more capable men.[79]

---

[79] CWR, SA/DR/50, fol 142.

The Ministry at St John's, Cardiff

David Howell was appointed to the parish of St John's Cardiff by the dean and chapter of Gloucester Cathedral, its patrons. The chapter had recognised the need for a strong and vigorous man, who would be able to re-establish the church in that rapidly expanding parish. On several occasions Lady Llanover referred to Howell's appointment to St John's, although as the papers relating to it are not to be found in the archives of the dean and chapter, her claim to have influenced it cannot be clarified.[1] Indeed, her ladyship took the credit for Howell's appointment, stating that it was upon her representations that the dean of Gloucester, Henry Law, a well known evangelical leader and writer, made it a point of conscience to appoint a well qualified Welsh-speaking clergyman to Cardiff. To ensure this he gave up his own turn at the next vacancy to the chapter, exchanging it for the sole right of nominating to this parish, so that Howell's appointment was strictly by the dean rather than by the chapter of the cathedral.[2] It was later said that there were many candidates for the position, many of them backed by people in high positions, and that considerable pressure was brought to bear on the dean regarding certain of these candidates. There was also a petition signed by a considerable number of the congregation of the parish, including the churchwardens, on behalf of the its then curate, Mr Pierpoint. He had presided over the parish as Webb's deputy for over two years, and given "much satisfaction"; the congregation had considerably increased and the number of communicants trebled. The petition continued to add further points in his favour:

---

[1] The papers relating to the appointment of Howell's successor are at the Gloucester Record Office, Dean and Chapter records, D936 C15. They reveal a large number of applicants.

We must be permitted to observe that the parish is essentially English, and in our opinion there is not a single member of the congregation who does not understand that language.

The parish church is an antient [sic] structure, not lofty, surrounded by an old fashioned roomy gallery. A clergyman with a weak voice could not be heard at all in many parts of the building, whilst the clear sonorous voice of Mr Pierpoint is distinctly audible in every part.

Further, Mr Pierpoint is most ably assisted in his ministerial duties by his wife, which is a circumstance of vast importance in a parish containing so large a proportion of poor.

Though there were only sixty-five signatures, the petitioners were convinced that had there been time every member of the congregation would have signed it.[3] As the *Wrexham Guardian* put it many years later, the petition on behalf of a "most unsuitable person", and all the individual requests, were of no avail, for the dean resolved to be influenced only by the considerations of public interest.[4]

Lady Llanover also had to win the approval of the bishop of Llandaff in order to secure Howell's appointment to the parish. Writing to Gladstone in 1870, during the prime minister's search for a Welsh bishop for the vacant diocese of St Asaph, H A Bruce enclosed a letter which stated that when Ollivant discovered that the dean and chapter were about to appoint Howell to Cardiff, the bishop wrote "letters of strong expostulation", mainly on account of Howell and his wife's social position, or rather lack of it. But he added, "Lady Llanover carried the day." His correspondent noted too that Howell's religious views were narrow but their narrowness had commended him to the evangelical dean of Gloucester.[5] At the same time Ollivant wrote further of Howell's appointment:

---

[2] Lady Llanover to Gladstone, 25 Dec 1882, British Library, GP, Addit Ms 44478/203.
[3] Contained in the dean and chapter records, D936 C/3. The wardens were W Woods, governor of the prison, and J E Williams, and other signatories included John W Vachell, William Thomas the parish clerk and Edmund Rees, the parish sexton. Pierpoint resigned his curacy when he was aware of Howell's appointment [CMG, 19 Feb 1864, p 5].
[4] *Wrexham Guardian*, 6 Feb 1875, p 8.
[5] Bruce to Gladstone, 11 Jan 1870, GP, 44086/78.

When the vicarage of St John's Cardiff was vacant, I thought his appointment was the wrong step because it was throwing away his Welsh tongue, which the Church in Wales might have profited by, and I thought that his social position and that of Mrs Howell would prevent him from getting that influence over the educated portion of his parishioners, which a graduate of an English University might be expected to gain. But I am bound to say that he has so conducted himself as to secure, to the best of my belief, universal respect.[6]

Howell's appointment to the parish was announced in February, and though it led to the almost immediate resignation of Mr Pierpoint, it was greeted by others with "gratification" as Howell had already won much local fame as "a powerful and eloquent preacher". The local newspaper reporting this mentioned that he was due to preach at St Andrew's church on the following Sunday, and assumed he would attract a large congregation, even if some came for the sake of curiosity.[7] And this was the case, for the paper reported that the unusually large congregation augmented "the much needed contributions" by an additional thirteen pounds, while Howell's morning "discourse" was regarded as

> remarkable for its simplicity of doctrine and total absence of theological difficulties; he besought his hearers with all the earnestness of 'a dying man speaking to dying men' to satisfy themselves whether 'Christ crucified' was to their minds a thing belonging to the history of the past, or a living faith necessary for the salvation of immortal souls? A deep humility of tone and bearing in the style of delivery, gave additional importance at times to impassioned eloquence as the preacher dwelt with force upon the weekly labours of the ministry, and the probable effects of the Apostolic preaching upon two classes of hearers.[8]

Such earnest preaching was to be the hallmark of Howell's ministry at Cardiff.

David Howell "read himself in" - by reading the Thirty-Nine Articles - as vicar of St John's on a May morning in 1864, stating

[6] Ollivant to Gladstone, 14 Jan 1870, GP, 44424/97.
[7] CMG, 19 Feb 1864, p 5.
[8] CMG, 26 Feb 1864, p 5.

in his sermon that it was force of conviction that had brought him into the Church of England as "the arena of his discipleship".[9] It appears however that he had preached himself in with what the local paper termed his *initiatory* sermon at the parish church "to a full and attentive congregation" in the March of that year.[10] Writing at the close of his ministry in this parish he remembered these early days:

> Most vividly do I remember that, to me, ever memorable Sabbath morning when I first stood in this pulpit as an ambassador for Christ. A stranger to most of you, labouring under many disadvantages, trembling under a sense of the magnitude of the work I had undertaken, with many prejudices to conquer, and many difficulties to overcome.[11]

It was an enormous contrast to Pwllheli, and he was to find himself so burdened with work that, as he wrote to J Ceiriog Hughes (the poet), "often I wish I could add a day or two to the week."[12]

The principles which underlay Howell's approach to his pastoral and spiritual work in the parish were noted in a tribute to him at the close of his ministry there:

> When Mr Howell commenced his labours at Cardiff, the congregation was select and respectable. Its gentilities had not been disturbed by rude or harsh utterances from the pulpit. No innovations had taken place. Order and decorum prevailed. The doctrine was moderate, and such as could not offend sensitive ears. Those points which excite rancour amongst the parties who divide the Church into its present well-defined sections were not insisted on. But such as the congregation was, so it had been for thirty years and more. The town increased in population and wealth, chapels and congregations increased, but the church stood still. It is true that after years of begging, and appeals to unwilling charity, the church of St Andrew's had been finished - not indeed according to the elegance of its original design, but still finished, and open for

---

[9] CMG, 13 May 1864, p 5.
[10] CMG, 25 Mar 1864, p 5.
[11] *In Memoriam. The Farewell Sermon of the Rev. David Howell at the Parish Church of St John the Baptist, Cardiff* [Cardiff 1875], p 2.
[12] Howell to J Ceiriog Hughes, 4 July, dated from Cardiff, NLW MS 10183D/66.

the celebration of divine worship. The services in the parish had doubled in number; for, in addition to two at St John's, there were two at St Andrew's. And to the credit of the times be it stated, that there were two Church schools and a little more than 200 scholars. This tameness and apathy were not congenial to Mr Howell. Had such a state of things existed even in his little parish of Pwllheli, his three years' residence there would have been intolerable. He determined to initiate a new regime. In spite of lukewarmness and opposition, he resolved to be true to his Master and his mission. His powerful preaching awakened the profoundest attention of his hearers. They were reminded of their short-comings in a way to which they had been unaccustomed. The solemn verities of our most holy religion were clearly unfolded. The punishment which awaits sin was faithfully pointed out. But while the preacher did not scruple to unmask "the terrors of the law," his more congenial duty was to dwell on the doctrine of the Atonement, and to commend that grace which the New Testament so clearly offers. Here was an anxious, earnest, man, deeply impressed with a sense of his own responsibility, and affectionately solicitous of the interests of those he addressed. His pleadings were as though he pleaded for life - "with tears, with pathetic gestures, and burning words". ...

The powerful and intensely earnest preaching of such a man as the new vicar could not long fail to produce effect. The churches both became crowded, and new life was apparent everywhere. Possessed of new energy and power, the Church became more effective in her ministrations, and the results were clearly perceptible without. Fresh charities were awakened, and dormant faculties were quickened into life. Neither was the effect spasmodic, nor were its results temporary. Time would fail us to describe the new agencies which the restless energy of the vicar called into existence. Suffice it to state that in lieu of apathetic and thin congregations, enthusiastic and crowded assemblies meet together to pray and praise. Instead of two or four weekly services, there are thirteen; in the place of two schools, there are six; the children attending these number 1,755, as against 200; there are 1,821 children attending the Sunday schools; and there are five curates and one scripture reader actively engaged in the work of the parish. This, we think, is enough to show that Mr Howell has proved himself a thorough working and a successful parish priest.[13]

[13] *Weekly Mail*, 6 Feb 1875, p 10.

The editor was clearly right to pinpoint Howell's evangelical preaching as the reason for the "success" of his ministry, although as Howell would have pointed out, this was the work of the Holy Spirit more than of himself, in convincing people through his faithful preaching of the need for repentance and faith and reminding them about the responsibilities of Christian life and witness. But that preaching was also backed up by his concern for pastoral work amongst his congregation and parish. As he preached from the pulpit, so he proclaimed in the homes of his people, and so he lived in his daily life.

In his earlier days much criticism was voiced about the length of his sermons, and some complained too that he had attracted a host of camp followers to his pulpit ministry. Having preached the same sermon for the Church Pastoral-Aid Society at Cardiff as he had used at Bristol, one correspondent noted "the very objectionable practice of some persons who follow the Vicar from one church to another". But what was worse was that his forty-five minute sermons were too long for people to listen to with profit, "not a fourth of what he says, good as it is, can be carried away by any ordinary memory." The Queen's example of giving an eighteen minute sand glass to the Savoy Chapel was commended with a clear hint that that was sufficient time for Howell as well. Indeed, this writer suggested that if the parish wardens could obtain a thirty minute glass it would save the vicar much physical wear and tear and cause no dissatisfaction to his large congregations if he closed when the sand ran out! The editor too added his own comments. Nothing was more calculated to empty a church or to give an impetus to dissent "than the lengthy sermons which some clergymen will insist upon inflicting, week after week, upon their congregations. A short sermon movement is absolutely essential in many parishes of the United Kingdom".[14] The same complaint was repeated by a member of St Andrew's Church in the following year. Forty-five minute sermons were too long, even if Howell was able to hold the attention of people for longer than most clergy, with sermons that were good "from end to end".[15] It was these sermons,

[14] CMG, 7 Dec 1867, p 4.
[15] CMG, 1 Feb 1868, p 5.

however, which changed people's lives, and there is no evidence to suggest that Howell modified his practice in later years. Rather he trained his congregation to listen to and to act upon the Word of God. The evidence is to the contrary of these letters, for Howell's preaching drew large congregations. This is noted time and time again in the press. His sermons on the Second Advent in 1864 were "listened to with marked attention by very crowded congregations"; St John's church since his coming had been "crowded to excess," and scores of people had been unable even to find standing room, especially as seats had been placed in the aisles.[16] But one of Stacey's friends wrote on a more sour note. Agreeing that St John's Church had never been so well filled since "the days of the excellent Precentor Stacey", he alleged that Howell's congregation consisted mainly of strangers from all the Nonconformist congregations in Cardiff. The proof of an evangelical ministry was not to be found in crowded congregations. Rather it was to be judged by the same congregation appearing week by week, and the services of the church being performed in accordance with the rubrics of the Prayer-Book. Instead, he virtually accused Howell of disregarding church forms and ceremonies, ignoring fasts and festivals, and allowing private judgment to wilfully and purposefully break the Church's ordinances.[17] It appears that a deputation wanted the bishop to take formal notice of these so-called "abuses", but without success.[18]

These comments were not altogether untrue, for Howell endeavoured to introduce congregational singing into St John's, to the dismay of many of the traditionalists who preferred the choral services sung exclusively by the choir. His changes, retorted one of their number, meant that instead of performing the worship to the best of their abilities, they were being performed to the worst of them. However, he added, this was true of all the Cardiff churches.[19] This debate took place against a backcloth of annoyance over the state of the church organ and choir, and one

[16] CMG, 2 Dec 1864, p 5: 11 Nov, p 8. He was described here as the Spurgeon of the Welsh Church pulpit, though without his eccentricities.
[17] CMG, 25 Nov 1864, p 8.
[18] *Report of the Llandaff Diocesan Conference*, 1905, p 91.
[19] CMG, 27 Sept 1867, p 8.

gets the impression that church music was a most important matter to the church people of Cardiff at that time. A new organ was needed - and a new position for it, away from the galleries. A paid choir was a necessity. The chants and hymns were sung too slowly causing the music to flatten, and the organist was introducing too many new tunes.[20] Some of these complaints surfaced at the 1867 vestry meeting when one Mr Alexander and others complained that the music was not equal to that of other churches in the area. Some suggested that a committee should be appointed to examine these complaints. The new innovation of singing the psalms, said one, was extremely unpopular, and never known in other churches. Mr Grover told the meeting he was so dissatisfied that he attended St Mary's for a time, but was reminded that instead of one anthem he would find two! But it was pointed out that the money was not available for a professional choir, and the organist supported Howell's wish to have good congregational singing. This was backed up by others too, some stating that the singing at St John's was better than that in many London churches.[21]

A further controversy flared up in September 1869 when the criticisms were answered with a vivid description of the problems facing organist and choir. Fred Atkins the organist, responding to letters of criticism in the local press, complained it was hard to do anything with an out of tune organ, with its bellows full of holes, stops running into one another, and built in the reign of George II. It was capable of "little more than some monotonous qualities of tone from beginning to end." The choir was stuck in the gallery singing into people's backs, and the scanty headroom there diminished their musical effect. And as the congregation joined heartily in the singing, the choir was not really heard. Their proper place was the chancel, and until the choir and organ were removed there little improvement could take place. Because of the lack of finances, economy had to be the order of the day. Instead of an annual tuning, the organ was tuned once every four years. Their choir was the only local choir which did not receive a picnic or some entertainment as a thank-you for their voluntary

---

[20] CMG, 3 May 1867, p 5; 6 Sept 1867, p 8; 20 Sept 1867, p 8; 21 Ap 1865, p 8; 6 Ap 1872, p 6. One correspondent even suggested the use of plainsong.
[21] CMG, 26 Ap 1867, p 6.

labours.²² Such were the difficulties. But at least Howell managed to make the services congregational ones, which well matched his desire for the active involvement of all within the life and worship of the parish.

The musical position at St Andrew's was even more difficult. There a row developed as Howell endeavoured to establish congregational singing. The harmonium was lent, it appears, by the choirmaster, Mr Gawn, who, complaining that Howell's policy meant that "the drone of a conventicle" was supplanting "the cheerful sound of praise", demanded either he was paid for it or he would take it back.²³ Singing, Gawn argued, was as important as prayer itself, and any attempt to introduce strictly congregational singing, unaided by the assistance of a regularly trained choir, would be a lamentable failure and a perfect mockery of public worship and devotion. He claimed, too, the support of the congregation. Howell replied stating that he never meant congregational singing on its own without a choir, and felt that Gawn's protest was unjustified. He had written to Howell, for example, that "his labours had been attended with results so distasteful to you, so unsatisfactory to the congregation, and so unprofitable to myself ..." that he had no option but to resign.²⁴ The situation was complicated by the desire to purchase a pipe organ. Though Howell had canvassed the congregation, and obtained promises of £150 against an estimated cost of £400,²⁵ the slow progress in obtaining this organ, and the state of hostility shown to Howell by Gawn and others in the choir, resulted in several well publicised rows, the resignation of various organists and the withdrawal of the choir.²⁶ These events may have been fortuitous, for Howell's preaching and the congregational nature of the worship meant that by 1871 the vestry had to be informed that twenty applications for seats made that year could not be

[22] CMG, 11 Sept 1869, p 6.
[23] CMG, 2 Sept 1864, p 5; 25 Mar 1864, p 5. Howell appears to have wanted congregational rather than choral singing from the first.
[24] CMG, 9 Sept 1864, p 5.
[25] CMG, 10 Feb 1865, p 5.
[26] CMG, 16 Sept 1864, p 5; 23 Sept 1864, p 5. The new organ was in place by early 1866, aided by a gift from the Bute trustees, E P Richards and H Jones of Canton, who gave £50 each. It was then stated that the church needed an elegant reredos and a stained glass east window [CMG,, 6 Ap 1866, p 7; and see 23 Aug 1867, p 5].

granted through lack of room, while there was a corresponding increase in the amount of the voluntary offerings.[27]

The marks of an evangelical ministry were seen too in the daily services of the church. There was a daily service at St John's at 8.00am, and at St Andrew's services at 11.00am on Wednesdays and Fridays, with evening services on Wednesday and Friday at the two churches respectively. In these the shorter forms of service permitted by convocation were used, that is, the old order of Matins, Litany and Ante-Communion, was not followed. There were also Sunday morning prayer meetings, and evening communions. Cottage services were also held during weekdays, while a communicants' guild held a monthly sacramental lecture. These were apart from the round of Bible classes and monthly Sunday School conferences. An article in the June 1870 parish magazine urged people to attend the daily services of the church. Here those facing life's sufferings and sorrows could find peace, and a devout attendance at the daily services would make the Sunday service overflow with blessings.[28]

Howell's pastoral ministry, which enabled him to apply to individual lives the message he preached from his pulpit, might be best summed up in the words he addressed to his congregation on 18 April 1875, his last and farewell sermon as vicar. He was "listened to with an almost perfect intensity of interest, and in the most pathetic portion of the sermon scarcely a dry eye was to be seen throughout the immense congregation". In it Howell reveals his intense desire that all those under his spiritual charge should be mature Christians and lead holy and godly lives. He stated:

> Few things, my brethren, in this world are more deeply solemn and affecting than the act of separation between a Christian minister and the souls committed to his charge; when for the last time the long familiar voice sounds in their ears, and they are met together as pastor and people ere they meet in judgement at the bar of Almighty God. Such an occasion demands most severe self-searching on both sides. Every heart should be laid bare before God; the secret chambers of every soul should be laid open before the eye of Him "from whom no secrets are hid."...

[27] CMG, 15 Ap 1871, p 6. The financial position of St Andrew's Church meant that special preaching services, designed to raise money, were held for a number of years [CMG, 24 July 1863, p 5, is the account of one].
[28] St John's Parish Magazine, issues of June 1870 and Oct 1872.

The Christian ministry, if viewed only in its secondary aspects, carries with it influences of the very utmost importance, even to the temporal welfare of men. As the friend, the counsellor, and the comforter of his flock, a faithful minister is of no small service to the people of his charge. As the promoter of education, as the helper of the poor, as the adviser of the perplexed, as a reconciler of differences, he serves many important ends; but the supreme end and object of his mission is the salvation of the souls of his people; and where this is not attained, the Christian ministry falls short of its grand purpose. Large congregations, an attached people, many benevolent agencies at work, activity, liberality, and zeal on the part of church members, these (and such as these) are tokens of good, and afford reasons of devout thankfulness; but in themselves, observe, they are not the certain evidence of a fruitful ministry. No, my brethren, nothing short of "fruits unto holiness" - nothing short of souls, "converted from the error of their ways", "washed, justified, sanctified in the name of the Lord Jesus, and by the spirit of our God" - human lives radically changed, "old things passed away, and all things become new" - this, and nothing else, than this, can be regarded as the true test of a successful ministry. And, therefore, it is that the question comes to my heart to-day with such oppressive solemnity, have these results been produced? Have the ministrations of eleven years borne fruit, adequate fruit, in souls "turned from darkness to light, and from the power of Satan unto God"? This question can only be answered by the issues of the Judgement Day....

And this, my brethren, is my heart's desire on your behalf. May you ever strive after higher attainments in spiritual things. May you ever aim at a closer conformity to the image of Him who is the type and pattern of what His followers ought to be. And may you never rest satisfied with anything short of the clear and emphatic testimony of the Spirit of God "bearing witness with your spirits that you are the children of God."[29]

The same concern is found in his 1869 address to the parish in the printed volume of parish accounts. After noting the progress made in the parish and its schools he asked:

> What shall we say of *ourselves*? Have we personally and individually advanced in holiness? Are we more meet for the inheritance of the saints in light? You know your own besetting sins,

---

[29] *In Memoriam*, pp 1-3.

have you, or have you not, made any decided steps towards overcoming them? Has the grace of God enabled you to overcome the evil appetite within you? Are you as far from Christian perfection now as when I came amongst you five years ago? In the general bias of your souls, in your tempers, dispositions, home life, social enjoyments, and daily associations, have you the mind which was in Christ Jesus? May God grant that you may press this matter home more and more earnestly to your hearts and consciences, knowing that true religion will be progressive, and that herein is our Father glorified, that ye bear much fruit?[30]

This was the content of his pastoral visitation of his flock, pressing home this message of grace and the need for holiness. This pastoral care is illustrated by a story told by J V Morgan. Seen struggling one wretched night in abysmal weather, Howell was asked what he was doing. Pointing to a house in the distance, he replied, "I am going to see a navvy who lives in that house and who is dying." Urged to go another day rather than risk his life from being out in a night like that, he retorted, "no storm would stop me when there is a soul to be saved."[31] It was this pastoral work which grounded his preaching into a living reality. "His greatness", said one report, "consists in his intense love of parochial labour. With him the work of his parish is a necessity which knows no law but that of attention, and attention ... He is wrapped up in his parish, as his parish is wrapped up in him; and to say that his work is a labour of love is to bestow faint praise."[32]

Writing in his parish report of 1869 Howell asked people to inform him of the names of those who were sick, for it was the great strength of the Church of England that its ministers in every parish were able to be the connecting link between rich and poor, and the organ of mutual assistance and friendly feeling between them. But the size of his parish meant that he did not always know those who were sick, and he frequently called on people only to discover they had been ill for some time, without having been able to offer them "the consolations of the Gospel". His prayer on these occasions was that his "humble labours" might bring a blessing to those "who are placed under my charge - not

[30] CMG, 22 May 1869, p 5.
[31] J V Morgan, *Welsh Religious Leaders in the Victorian Era* [London 1905], p 119.
[32] *Weekly Mail*, 7 Nov 1874, p 10.

only that we may live on friendly terms while we are together on earth, but that my preaching and exertions may be rendered the blessed means of winning souls to Christ and drawing you, my friends and parishioners, nearer to Heaven."[33]

This ministry to the sick, irrespective of class or denomination, was noted especially at the testimonial meeting which took place when he was about to leave the parish. One Mr Stephens paid particular attention to Howell's concern here, and noted that "he had heard scores of people speak of the comfort which ... [he] had afforded to those leaving the world by his ministrations." He made specific reference to the fact that Howell had not confined these "ministrations" to the rich. "He had gone among all classes. He knew one poor man who said that when Mr Howell entered the room he always felt as if his actual bodily suffering became less", for he always offered up "his earnest prayers with them". Dr Taylor noted at the same meeting how Howell had spared himself no rest in this work, even giving up part of a holiday to return to comfort a person "who could not be comforted by anyone else". Nor had he confined himself to any particular group in his parish, but had attended persons of all sects, creeds and denominations.[34]

Though H A Bruce wrote to Gladstone that Howell's social position was low, alleging that "he and his wife are not seen in the society of even the upper middle class at Cardiff",[35] this was more a reflection on the work of his predecessors than on Howell, for they gave most of their time to this class of society. Howell, however, regarded his ministry to the poor and underprivileged as one of the more important aspects of his pastoral work. Not only did he visit them in their homes, especially when they were sick or dying, he also made sure that some provision was made for their physical relief. One of his first acts was to start a Christmas dinner for the poor of the parish, who were invited irrespective of creed or race. "Thou that makest a feast, call the poor, the maimed, the lame and the blind, and thou shalt be blessed", was the motto he quoted to his parishioners as he begged their assistance and their finances for this work. In 1870 over four hundred sat down to a

[33] Quoted in CMG, 22 May 1869, p 5.
[34] WM, 12 Feb 1875, p 4.
[35] Bruce to Gladstone, 14 Jan 1870, GP 44086/78.

meal in the Crockherbtown schoolroom, of roast beef and plum pudding, and in addition fifty were served in their own homes. A meal of roast goose was also provided for the poor and sick communicants of his parish.

The same appeal also covered the provision of cheap dinners for the poor held three times weekly, on Tuesdays, Thursdays and Saturdays, during the winter months. All were served who could pay one penny towards the cost - they cost twopence each - and books containing five shillings worth of tickets were sold to members of the congregation for them to distribute free of charge to those known to them. During the winter of 1870-1 over three thousand such meals were served.[36]

In addition the usual clothing clubs, saving banks, maternal charities and mother's meetings were held, the costs of some being defrayed by "entertainments". One of these, held in 1875, included slides on canvas of views of London and the dangers of the sea, together with "suitable vocal and instrumental music". A coffee stall is mentioned as part of the temperance work of the parish, while in the 1870s Howell supported a local association founded to prevent the Sunday liquor trade. He well knew, he wrote, that the better class of publican was glad to close on a Sunday.[37] His interest in the working classes was sufficiently established for him to be asked to arbitrate on behalf of the Cardiff building masons who wanted an increase in their hourly rate. He secured that for them too.[38]

The parish magazine was clearly regarded as an extension of his pastoral ministry, and designed to be read in every home of his parish. Writing in its first issue of January 1870, Howell said that he had introduced it in order to provide cheap literature "on the side of morality", bearing in mind that much of the cheap literature of his day was on the other side, and whose influence sent scores of boys to prison every year. The inset *Home Words* was included from the following year. Articles on the life of a Christian family, the benefits of giving out Christian tracts to

---

[36] CMG, 11 Dec 1869, p 5; 31 Dec 1870, p 6; 7 Jan 1871, p 5; 9 Dec 1871, p 5; *Parish Magazine* for March 1870 and Feb 1871. Canon Morgan did the same thing at St Mary's.
[37] CMG, 22 Feb 1873, p 5; WM, 1 Jan 1875, p 7; *Parish Accounts* for 1877.
[38] CMG, 10 May 1873, p 5.

working class families, on the observance of the Sabbath, almsgiving, the sacraments and various aspects of Christian doctrine duly appeared, as did such matters as ritualism, disestablishment, and the conversion of the Marquess of Bute to Rome, "laying a large part of his wealth at her feet."[39]

By his preaching and pastoral care Howell had established a large and active congregation, but he still realised that more was needed to fulfil the great commission given by Christ to his Church: to go and make disciples. True, the number of his confirmation candidates was impressive, one hundred and fifty being confirmed in 1865, due, one assumes. to Howell's perseverance and energy.[40] But he knew full well that even such a large number was small compared to the population and needs of his parish. Help was at hand. It came through two great missions to Cardiff, both of which helped to consolidate his pastoral work and preaching ministry.

The first mission was an interdenominational one of 1866 arranged by the Cardiff Local Missionary Association and addressed to the whole town.[41] Its leaders were Howell, Vincent Saulez, vicar of Canton, and Alfred Tilly, a prominent Nonconformist minister. There were many, argued Howell, though living in the shadow of a church or chapel, who remained in a state of "perfect heathenism", who were unthought of, unsought for and unsaved. It was a melancholy fact that while they were spending vast sums on mission abroad, there had been no proportionate effort "to chase away heathenism at home ..." The mission thus endeavoured to remind such people of Christ and his love for them. Eleven thousand people attended the fourteen open air meetings; nine thousand home visits had been made; eighteen thousand tracts distributed, with the result that forty-four people had been "hopefully" converted, twenty-seven restored to church membership, and twenty-three induced to sign the pledge.[42]

---

[39] Files of the magazine are at Cardiff Central Library.
[40] CMG, 1 Sept 1865, p 5.
[41] CMG, 14 July 1865, p 7.
[42] CMG, 1 June 1866, p 7.

The second mission was organised by the Cardiff clergy during the Lent of 1871, and probably gained from the experience of the former. Writing in his April 1871 parish magazine Howell stated:

> For many years the conviction has been gradually forcing itself on the minds of earnest men that the ordinary Services and Ministrations of the Church were insufficient to cope with the rapidly growing wickedness, and irreligious tendencies of the age. A great need of some supplementary agency has long been keenly felt. ... Mission Services have been conducted by individual Clergymen in different parts of the country for many years past, and one of the missioners who has just left us has been engaged in this work for 30 years. It was not however until the end of the year 1869 that any intensive and united effort was made to break down the strongholds of sin, ignorance, indifference, and unbelief. Just before the season of Advent, 1869, a Mission was undertaken in many of the London Parishes; a band of holy and earnest men were engaged in the work; the Churches were crowded by attentive listeners, and deep and lasting impressions were made. The results here more than justified the expectations of the most sanguine, and convinced the most prejudiced that "Missions" undertaken with the single aim of the conversion of sinners, and the glory of God, are sure to receive the blessing of the Holy Spirit.

One of the men involved in this great London mission was the Revd C W Furse, vicar of Staines, who made a deep impression as the missioner appointed to St John's parish, especially amongst the working classes. For several weeks before the mission began, Howell recollected, "we used to meet together to pray for an outpouring of the Holy Spirit upon the work, and to prepare our minds for the reception of the truth which would be addressed to us by those who would come to us as Ambassadors for Christ; you will remember too, that in private as well as in public the subject occupied much of our prayers."

Such prayers by those in Cardiff and those throughout the country who prayed for this mission were abundantly answered. It was termed a mid-Lent mission. A Bible class held after the evening service at the cathedral in the prebendal house was soon over-crowded. Special weekday services were held at St John's Church, and these were addressed by such well known missioners as Robert Aitken of Pendeen, his son W Hay Aitken of Christ

Church, Everton, and William Haslam, a man who had been converted in his own pulpit by his own sermon! The after-meetings were held in the schoolroom, and were crowded by anxious enquirers night after night, one lasting until midnight. At the same time, it appears, prayer meetings took place in the church. Altogether seventeen churches were involved, while other mission services were held at Roath, St Mary's, St Andrew's and at Tongwynlais. Nonconformists joined in the work as well as church-people. Wrenford of Newport, Griffiths of Neath, Evans of Rhymney, Griffiths of Machynlleth, and Jenkins of Dowlais, all prominent evangelical men, also acted as missioners, as did James Malcolmson and Richard Twigg, vicar of St James', Wednesbury, who with Furse were prominent in this work of mission in England. However, Alexander Sharp in his booklet commemorating this work, suggests that the most substantial results of the mission were within Howell's own congregations.[43]

Undoubtedly this was due to two interconnected facts. The first was the amount of preparation and prayer given to this work by Howell and his colleagues. In his March 1871 parish magazine he wrote as follows to his parishioners:

> READER - You are earnestly and affectionately urged to attend the Mission Services. Whoever and whatever you are, the Mission is a message from God to *you*. If you are unconverted, it may be the turning point in your destiny - *the last means* God will use to bring you to repentance. If you are a true follower of Christ, it will be the means, under the Divine blessing, of quickening and stimulating you to increased zeal, self-sacrifice, and Christian devotedness, with more earnest efforts after higher degrees of personal holiness. *Fix your thoughts* on the Mission, in order that it may engage your lively interest. Put the subject frequently before your friends and neighbours in its true light, namely, as a special effort to promote the salvation of souls with a single eye to the glory of God. STRIVE to bring *others* with you. Think of those among your acquaintances who are careless of their souls, plead for them earnestly in prayer, and afterwards do all you can to persuade them to accompany you to the Mission Services. Make a point of attending, if possible, EVERY Service - come as you are, in your working dress; God looks

---

[43] A Sharp, *A Narrative of the Great Revival Work in South Wales 1871* [Cardiff 1871], pp 17-19.

at the state of the heart, not the clothing of the body. Be not offended at anything that may not altogether approve itself to your judgement; there are "diversities of gifts" and "diversities of operations; but it is the same God which worketh all in all." Purge your mind of all prejudice; and *enter heartily and devoutly into the Services*. Come *expecting* a blessing. Think how rich and assuring are God's promises! "Ye shall seek me, and find me, when ye shall search for me with all your hearts." "And it shall come to pass that, before they call, I will answer; and while they are yet speaking, I will hear." "All things, whatsoever ye shall ask in prayer, believing, ye shall receive." The truth of these promises has been proved and experienced in ten thousand instances; will you not share in their contents? Should it be absolutely impossible for you, through sickness, or any other unavoidable cause, to be present at all the Services, you can still help forward the great work by lifting up your heart to God, and wrestling mentally with Him for the promised blessing. I beseech you to give this matter your most earnest consideration. The highest welfare of Cardiff is involved in the spiritual success of the Mission, and that success depends, under God, on united, frequent, fervent, and persevering Prayer, in the all-prevailing NAME OF JESUS CHRIST. READER I ENTREAT YOUR PRAYERS.

The second reason was that God so honoured these preparations, that it became clear a second week of mission was required. The result was that at St Andrew's Church one hundred and twenty communicants presented themselves at the altar, and there was an equally large increase at St John's.[44] The number of communicants was then regarded as the best measure of renewed spiritual life. At that service, reported the April parish magazine, "322 persons partook of the Holy Communion".

> The Service was one never to be forgotten, it was characterized by great earnestness, and deep emotion, and perhaps the most impressive feature of all was the hearty and soul-stirring manner in which the whole of the congregation sang the *Te Deum* at the close of the Service, just before the blessing was given.

One of the missioners, James Malcolmson, wrote in that same magazine that he was "thankful to God ... to hear from you that

---

[44] See CMG, 18 Mar 1871, p 5; 25 Mar 1871, pp 4f; and the April 1871 parish magazine.

it [the mission] has been characterised by a rich and an abundant blessing, and that the interest had been fully sustained until the end, or rather shall I not say the beginning of the real work of the ingathering and building up of souls in our most holy Faith." For St John's Church the work of mission was a real answer to prayer "for the revival of the Church of England and especially in St John's Church", while one lasting result, apart from renewed lives, was a Sunday morning prayer meeting at 7.30am which was attended by over two hundred people. It was said that the results of the mission were still discernible twenty years later, while a profound impression was made on the town itself.[45]

* * * *

There were two National Schools in existence when Howell arrived in the parish, although their viability was precarious from a financial point of view. Such schools depended as much on government grants as they did from the generosity of the parishioners, which often meant the incumbent. They were subject to the requirements of Her Majesty's inspectors, who could demand additional accommodation and other alterations to the school buildings, as well as determining the amount of grant-aid available according to the results of a school examination. But these schools were generally regarded as a powerful aid to the Church in its mission to and work for the nation. Not only did they teach the youngsters attending them the three "R's", they also imparted church teaching, and many vicars, who acted as the school managers, required the children to attend Church services on Sundays. For hard-pressed parishes, facing an enormous increase in population, they also offered another opportunity. These schools, built with grant-aid, church funds and public subscriptions, could also be used on Sundays for Sunday School work or for public worship, if so licensed by the bishop, and thus had a dual use.

The Crockherbtown school had been built in 1818, and in spite of the rapid increase in population, had never been extended. The

---

[45] Sharp, *A Narrative*, pp 18f; Roger L Brown, *Reviving the Clergy, Renewing the Laity: Archbishop Benson's Mission in Wales* [Welshpool 1994], pp 13f.

result was that in 1867 the inspectors required accommodation to be provided for 238 boys and 200 girls, utilising the existing school for boys, and building a new girls' school, at an estimated cost of £1,900.[46] A site was given in Cathays by the Marquess of Bute, together with £300,[47] and it appears that David Howell made himself personally liable for considerable sums of money in order to further this particular work. He later did the same for another school at Tredegarville. By the time of his departure he was still owed £577 of this money.[48] The Ecclesiastical Commissioners had been asked to help with the costs of the Cathays School, as, having taken over the revenues of the dean and chapter of Gloucester, they were in effect the rectors of the parish. The commissioners were thus empowered to respect these so-called "local interests" and were enabled to use their funds to further the work of the church in these particular parishes. There was much disquiet when they declined to help with the Cathays school, especially as Howell pointed out that many parishioners had declined to assist the parochial agencies - as he termed them - on the grounds that the only persons deriving advantages from the ecclesiastical revenues of the parish "do nothing for the promotion of its welfare". The patrons, namely the dean and chapter, "who might otherwise be expected to assist me in my labours, declare that the means to do so are in the hands of the commissioners..." But in spite of repeated applications to this body, even though it was painful to his feelings to press this matter, he was unable to obtain a grant from them.[49]

The schools were always in debt and there was continual concern that few parishioners subscribed to their cost. This was in spite of Howell's frequent assertion that Church schools not only served the best interests and welfare of the community, ("knowledge without religion is power without principle",[50]) but also saved the ratepayers considerable sums of money. He noted too, in their support, that while he had 1,700 children in his

[46] CMG, 14 June 1867, p 5; 6 Sept 1867, p 5.
[47] CMG, 19 July 1867, p 5.
[48] *St John's Parish Statement* for 1877; Howell to Lady Llanover, 9 Sept 1875, in D Parry Jones Papers 1979, NLW.
[49] David Howell to the Ecclesiastical Commissioners, 11 Mar 1868, in the EC file for the parish held by the Representative Body of the Church in Wales, Cardiff.
[50] From a handbill appealing for funds for the new Cathays School in 1867-8 in the Ecclesiastical Commission's files for St John's Parish.

schools, from the Church, Nonconformist and Roman Catholic communities, "the religious difficulty" had never arisen in them, and that "not a single complaint has ever been made in regard to the religious instruction given". Howell, at least, had refused to allow his schools to become a proselytising agency of the Church.[51]

The situation became a little tense after 1870, however, when many Nonconformists believed that as a result of Forster's Education Act in that year, church schools were teaching "church religion" "on the rates". In fact, Howell explained, this was not so, for the church teaching was carried on at the beginning or at the end of the day, and was optional. Thus it was not part of the schooling for which fees were paid: the local School Board, set up under this act, having the power to pay the school fees of the children of 'indigent parents'. An impending election for membership of this Board set the Nonconformists clamouring that if all five church candidates were elected they could compel unwilling ratepayers to pay for sectarian teaching. Howell replied to this piece of "tub thumping" that this was not the case, and the church candidates were simply concerned to safeguard the principle of the Act that the poor man had the right to educate his children in his own beliefs Christian or secular, as well as to obtain efficient elementary education.[52]

It is hardly surprising that the finances of the schools were always a headache. Annual sermons, preached on behalf of this work, when a retiring collection was taken, produced very little. Seventeen pounds were so collected from St John's in 1865, when the debt on the infants' school amounted to £200, though it was said the collection would have been more had the weather been more favourable.[53] In 1873, when there were 1,707 children attending them, the schools cost £1,542 per annum, and money was so short that some teachers' salaries for the previous quarter were still outstanding.[54] A new infants' school was required in the following year, for 250 children, costing £1,100, but Howell had

---

[51] *Parish Magazine* February 1874.
[52] WM, 12 Jan 1875, p 4.
[53] CMG, 3 Nov 1865, p 5; cf 4 Oct 1867, p 5.
[54] CMG, 1 Nov 1873, p 5.

to inform his congregation that the Education Department no longer provided building grants. He believed, however, that the Church could still supply this school accommodation more cheaply than the Cardiff School Board, established under Forster's Act of 1870, and challenged his parishioners to find the money required.[55]

These buildings were available for Sunday School purposes as well, and in 1867 it was reported that the two school rooms and the infants' school were used in this way each Sunday, with "some hundreds of scholars".[56] In the previous year Howell received a presentation "timepiece" from the Sunday school teachers, who were clearly impressed with his concern for their work, as well as his practical involvement in it. They noted his "willingness and self denial exhibited ... each Sabbath in succession, and the extreme kindness and gentleness which has lent a charm to every word, claim alike our love and respect."[57] An "adult Sunday school" is also mentioned in 1869.[58] Howell managed to obtain "a limelight apparatus" for the use of the Sunday School and with it showed "Scripture views" and illustrations from *Pilgrim's Progress*, to the great delight of the youngsters. It cost fifty pounds, a massive sum for those days.[59] An annual Sunday School festival took place to which the Whitsun offerings were devoted, though they were never sufficient, while on one occasion the Sunday School held an oratorio on the life of Christ, specifically adopted for its use. And there was, of course, the annual outing to Penarth, by steam packet, with the attendance of the church drum and fife band.[60]

Sunday services were also held at these schools, which were licensed for public worship by the bishop. A congregation could be gathered thereby in a given locality and which could become the nucleus of a new church. Others, who felt diffident about attending the parish church or St Andrew's, where the congregation was wealthy, preferred the "mission hall" style of

[55] WM, 11 Aug 1874, p 4.
[56] CMG, 10 May 1867, p 5.
[57] CMG, 26 Oct 1866, p 5.
[58] CMG, 28 Aug 1869, p 5.
[59] CMG, 25 Jan 1868, p 5.
[60] CMG, 20 July 1866, p 5; 19 Aug 1871, p 5; Parish Magazine for June 1870.

service held at these places. From 1867 onwards such services were held at the Girls' Parochial School and at the new Cathays Schoolroom, which was "furnished" as a church at a cost of eighty pounds. When the Holy Communion was celebrated at the former school in the same year, a "goodly number" of communicants were gathered together, "many of whom had not attended any place of worship before."[61]

Such overflow congregations at these school services made it clear to Howell and others that a new church was needed in the Tredegarville area of the parish. A mission church had been established here for some years,[62] and in 1873 the St John's mission church choir gave a public concert to raise funds for a new building.[63] From 1869 Howell had been preoccupied with this question, although in that year a gift of land from Lord Tredegar had to be turned down as it was too near St Peter's Roman Catholic Church, and it had proved impossible to exchange this site for land owned by Lord Bute. But a church was desperately required which could seat between eight hundred and one thousand people. Its cost was estimated as being in the region of six to seven thousand pounds. In one of his stirring speeches to a meeting called for this purpose, Howell reminded his congregation that those who professed loyalty to the Church should give proof of their attachment by doing for her in their own day "what our forefathers did before us". As they were stewards who were required to give an account of their stewardship, he challenged them to use this opportunity of promoting the best and the highest and of leaving the Church in a better position than they found it. A new church in that district could become a centre from which could radiate "humanising and ameliorating influences" which would be a source of blessing to all classes, through schools, clothing clubs, mothers' meetings, penny banks, and such other societies for the temporal and spiritual welfare of the poor. Furthermore he was quite happy for this new church to form the basis of a new parish.[64]

[61] CMG, 22 May 1869, p 5; 15 Ap 1871, p 6.
[62] 18th *Report of the Llandaff Diocesan Church Extension Society*, 1869, p 8: it noted the need and voted £1,000 towards the cost.
[63] CMG, 31 May 1873, p 5.
[64] CMG, 20 Dec 1873, p 5.

The last point was not taken or remembered by one correspondent in the local paper, who expressed grave misgivings about Howell's plans. The new church would simply be a chapel of ease to St John's rather than a district church, argued *Anglican*. The work would over-tax Howell's energies and time, and would mean that a young and inexperienced curate would be in charge of it. They wanted more than that. Furthermore the same ceremonial - of lack of it - used in the other churches would be found here. The committee for the promotion of the new church comprised too many gentlemen who had "comfortable sittings" elsewhere, rather than local residents.[65] A reply made to this letter pointed out that a district church would require an endowment to be provided for its incumbent, and the question of patronage would have to be sorted out. The people of the area were anxious to have a suitable church building and retain the moderate church teaching provided by the clergy and curates of St John's, whose ministry was clearly appreciated and testified to by the fact that numerous people had to be turned away from the services through lack of room.[66]

Although a site, next to the National Schools in the Tredegarville area, had been given by Lord Tredegar, in 1873, it was not until Howell had left the parish that St James' Church was built, and contrary to expectations, as well as the desire of both Howell and his successor, it has remained in the parish of St John's ever since, rather than becoming a separate parish in its own right.[67]

In the last year of his Cardiff ministry Howell managed to establish a mission room at Blackweir. The building had formerly been a gunshed, and then a soldiers' reading room. The lay or Scripture reader, George Gatton, was responsible for this, and it was reported that for the Harvest of 1874 the place appeared like a rural church with its decorations, as well as being well lighted and comfortable.[68] In addition plans for a church in Cathays were

[65] WM, 23 Nov 1874, p 8.
[66] WM, 1 Dec 1874, p 6. He noted an understanding between the Cardiff churches that people attending churches outside their own parishes could receive "pastoral visitation" from the clergy of the church they attended. It seems that many crossed the parochial boundaries to attend the church of their choice, especially between Roath and Cardiff.
[67] CMG, 20 Dec 1873, p 4f; EC file, letters of 1877. It was originally proposed that the new church be dedicated to St Paul.
[68] WM, 1 Oct 1874, p 6. It was only recently closed as an Anglican church.

reasonably well advanced, Colonel Wood having given land near Woodville Terrace, and a small sum of money having been collected. This became the origin of St Teilo's Church.[69]

Thus Howell not only established a real and living witness in his parish, he also ensured that they were sufficient places of worship, even though it was not in his power to provide purpose built churches in every instance.

* * * *

It is hardly surprising that David Howell was deeply concerned about home and overseas missionary work, or that he endeavoured to promote this work within his parish.

Writing in his parish magazine for December 1872 Howell urged his people to support a day of prayer called by the bishops for the work of overseas mission, especially in the supply of "labourers" for it:

> I am deeply anxious that the day should be observed in our own Parish in such a manner as to bring down a rich and abiding blessing on our own souls, as well as on the great work for the furtherance of which the day is more especially set apart. It is my earnest desire that the SERVICES ... should not result in a mere transient excitement, afterwards calming down into spiritual deadness, and indifference; but that they should produce a deep and lasting impression on our hearts and consciences of our grave responsibilities in connection with the Missionary cause. There is a sense in which every Christian man and woman should be a Missionary. We should, each of us, feel that on us individually is laid the obligation to do something systematically for the propagation of the Gospel throughout the world.
>
> I suppose we all pray daily the prayer which Christ himself taught us; and we ought never to utter those petitions, "Thy kingdom come; Thy will be done in earth, as it is in heaven," without feeling that we are praying for Christian Missions, praying that it will please God to make His way known upon earth, His "saving health unto all nations." This is partly what is meant by those petitions of the Lord's Prayer. But we should not rest satisfied with doing this, for we should never fail to offer up a

---

[69] CMG, 15 Ap 1871, p 6.

> special prayer for a more abundant blessing from above upon Christian Missions at home and abroad. We should earnestly pray God of His mercy to send us more labourers, more ministers of Christ. We should beg Him to pour down more plentiful supplies of grace upon those who are already engaged in preaching His Word, to increase their earnestness, to support them in their trials, and to enable them to "endure to the end." Nor should we pray alone for the teachers of the truth; we ought to remember also those who hear, and to ask God to open their hearts, that they may receive the good seed sown, and make it effectual to the salvation of their souls.

Alas, there was a lack of financial support for the cause of mission, so that Howell, after noting that in spite of this the work already accomplished was great, continued:

> One and all we must awake and renew our Christian life and energy, as we would wish to see the Gospel of eternal life travel onward as it ought to do. We want the devotion of our wealth, but we want more than this; we want the devotion of ourselves, of our lives. Give as Christ gave! Give as His Apostles gave! What wonders they effected! St Paul spoke of the truth of the Gospel as being "in all the world" - "preached to every creature which is under heaven."

In the following year, on the day of intercession for mission, special services were held in each church, with services at 3.00pm and 7.00pm at St John's, while a prayer meeting was held at 8.15pm at Crockherbtown parochial schoolroom.[70]

Such was his concern. And this concern was shown above all in his work for the Church Missionary Society. Until his first year in the parish Howell had not been thoroughly acquainted with this society, but the local secretary, Dr James of Panteg, had warmed his heart by his description of CMS' work, and he was especially glad that the society had remained firm to its professedly evangelical principles. Nevertheless he felt that the £71 given by the Cardiff local association to the central funds was hardly the standard by which the Established Church was to be measured in Cardiff.[71] There was no missionary society more deserving of the

---

[70] *Parish Magazine*, Dec 1873.
[71] CMG, 6 May 1864, p 8.

warm support of churchmen, and he considered the Church indebted to the holy men who had founded this society.[72]

Commending the work of CMS, Howell noted its godly founders, Scott, Venn, Cecil and Romaine, and commented upon its sincere loyalty to the Reformed Church by its definite and distinctive principles. This was especially valuable when there was a tendency to ignore such principles for "a vague system of generalities, making a sincere and earnest life our apology for errors of faith."[73] By 1870 Howell was speaking at the CMS annual meeting at Exeter Hall in London. The work was having to be cut down because of a £15,000 deficit. Howell argued that this was a blessing in disguise, for it would drive men from human reliance to seek God's promises as they prayed he would continue to meet their financial needs. Without the presence of the Holy Spirit they were but "a galvanising and dead corpse", and thus he urged the society to trust the Holy Spirit so that it could continue to work "as the great mission handmaid of our reformed Church".[74]

The support of this society was thus continually placed before the church people of Cardiff. In 1869 the £75 collected by the local association was once again roundly condemned as utterly inadequate, even though Howell noted it was a time of depression in the town. But it was also a time when the Society had a deficiency in its income, and having to cut down its expenditure would cause discouragement to its missionaries in distant lands. In the light of the Lord's commission, of the many blessings Christians had received, they had a responsibility to do far more in the support of "so truly a blessed work". Not only would it impart civilisation with evangelisation to the non-Christian world, it would also bring blessing to the giving church.[75] Howell was also to be found supporting other missionary societies, often from the platform at a local meeting. Missions to the colonies,[76] the

---

[72] CMG, 19 May 1865, p 8.
[73] CMG, 18 May 1866, p 7.
[74] CMG, 7 May 1870, p 7.
[75] CMG, 5 June 1869, p 6. He was not alone in this feeling that Cardiff could do far better. Lewis Price, secretary of the local association, felt the same [CMG, 24 May 1873, p 8].
[76] WM, 29 Sept 1874, p 8.

Society for the Propagation of the Gospel (though reading between the lines it appears that some of his fellow-evangelicals didn't like this),[77] and even the Moravian missions benefited from his presence. This later meeting was chaired by that doughty Baptist, Dr William Edwards of Pontypool. Howell, in his address, admired the Moravian's concern for taking the Gospel to even the most inhospitable parts of the world, as well as their apostolic simplicity.[78] He stood too with Nonconformists on the platform of the British and Foreign Bible Society, but told them that finishing the meetings at ten o'clock was too late, as most of the servants attending them had to leave before they were able to give their contributions.[79] The Religious Tract Society also had a local auxiliary which Howell fully supported as he believed that healthy literature was needed to counteract "the pernicious influence of the great mass of cheap literature."[80] The then more local work of the Missions to Seamen, which had partly arisen out of Canon Morgan's work among the sailors in the Bristol Channel, also knew his concern,[81] while Howell's interest in home missions was equally well known.

There was no society to which he was more indebted than the Church Pastoral-Aid Society, Howell declared, for it gave him substantial grants towards the stipends of his curates. The St John's local association of the society collected £65 in 1869 in return for grants totalling £250, which Howell thought was a rather meagre return, especially when Canton under Vincent Saulez was able to return £45 from its smaller and poorer parish.[82] This society was concerned with home mission, as it still is, and Howell saw this society as one of the principal agencies in the work of evangelising his parish.

Another expression of Howell's social concern lay in the support given to local charities. Sermons and retiring collections were given annually to the Royal Infirmary, then supported by public charity. In 1872, for example, a sum of £16 each came from the two churches in the parish on "Hospital Sunday", when

[77] CMG, 14 Sept 1866, p 3.
[78] CMG, 5 May 1865, p 5.
[79] CMG, 24 June 1864, p 8; 13 June 1868, p 6; 19 June 1869, p 6.
[80] CMG, 14 Sept 1872, p 5.
[81] CMG, 13 Mar 1869, p 5; 8 Ap 1871, p 6; 27 Ap 1872, p 5.
[82] CMG, 6 Mar 1869, p 8.

the guest preacher was Henry Edwards, then vicar of Caernarvon.[83]

If Howell supported temperance work (meetings were held at St John's of the National Union for the Suppression of Intemperance,[84]) he was sufficiently realistic to know that alternatives to the public houses had to be provided. The Sunday School teachers were persuaded to arrange a series of "amusing social entertainments" with, it appears, literary and musical items. At the same time a series of sixpenny popular lectures were planned, possibly the St John's scientific lectures noted in 1867, while numerous concerts were organised and even a St John's Brass Band established. One of these "amusing and instructive" lectures was given by the Revd J Owen of Chelsea on the subject of mendacity, its claims and shams.[85] Obviously, these entertainments raised money for the schools and parochial activities, but they also served a valuable social purpose as well. The most valuable of these events was probably the annual Working Man's Flower Show held at the Drill Hall, which was deliberately designed to encourage healthful relaxation for such people. In this work Howell had the co-operation of the Marquess of Bute and his head gardener. In 1867 over two thousand attended, as did the artillery volunteers' band who played at it. A cottage flower show is mentioned in the following year.[86] Likewise he encouraged the local chapter of the Foresters, and believing in its aims of self-support, was glad to be enrolled amongst their number.[87]

Howell's involvement in the life of the community was impressive as well, and it is not surprising he became an outstanding figure in the life of Cardiff. An elected member of the School Board - even the Nonconformists wanted him elected,[88] he was also a member of the University College council, one of the secretaries of the Deaf and Dumb Institute in Llandaff, and contributed much to the work of the public library. His experience of its value later led Howell to join the movement to

[83] CMG, 27 Ap 1872, p 5; 21 Dec 1866, p 5.
[84] CMG, 23 Sept 1871, p 5.
[85] CMG, 18 Oct 1867, p 5; 21 Dec 1867, p 5; 15 May 1869, p 5; 7 Jan 1871, p 5.
[86] CMG, 28 June 1867, p 5; 15 Feb 1868, p 5.
[87] CMG, 5 Dec 1868, p 5.
[88] WM, 3 Feb 1875, p 8.

establish a free library in Wrexham, and his interest and good will to the Cardiff Library was seen in his bequest to it of his copy of the 1567 Welsh New Testament.[89] Although chosen to teach the young Marquess of Bute the Welsh language,[90] regretfully he was unable to lead that sad recluse to a living faith in Jesus Christ. Instead the marquess' interests in medievalism turned his head towards Roman Catholicism. Thus if H A Bruce wrote that Howell's "position in the Diocese is one utterly without influence",[91] he really meant that Howell had never sought, nor obtained, any diocesan sphere of work. In fact his parish work was far too extensive to allow this. But Howell had a quiet influence on the lives of many clergy, and his strong and significant work in Cardiff gave encouragement to many within the Church in Wales.

During these years there was one nasty personal attack made against his good name and reputation. Deeply concerned at Gladstone's Irish policy, by which Gladstone proposed and effected the disestablishment of the Irish Church, Howell became a member of the Conservative party. He thus proposed Mr Giffard as the prospective Tory candidate for the Cardiff seat, and in his speech he indicated the reason why he felt he had to support openly a political party: "Although he had not hitherto exercised his political privileges, he felt that, on an occasion such as this, with issues so grave before the country, political neutrality would be political cowardice". He had made personal enquiries respecting Mr Giffard because "he was no admirer of talent without character...", and he had discovered a man "whose private character was pure and stainless..., a churchman but no bigot...", and one who was "a true friend of religious liberty in the fullest sense of the word,... - of liberty for every one to worship God in their own way."[92]

This declaration of political support resulted in an attempt being made to discredit Howell and through him the Church of which he was a senior clergyman. He was charged with

---

[89] *Public Library Journal* [Cardiff], Mar 1903.
[90] David Hunter-Blair, *John Patrick, the Third Marquess of Bute* [Cardiff 1921], p 99.
[91] Bruce to Gladstone, 14 Jan 1870, GP 44086/78.
[92] CMG, 21 Nov 1868, p 7; cf 5 Sept 1868, pp 5 & 8. Howell also served on Gifford's election committee [CMG,, 14 Nov 1868, p 2].

inconsistency, while an article he had written before he was ordained, which contained "strong animadversions on supposed abuses in the Church", was translated from Welsh and printed for general circulation in an attempt to embarrass him. He wrote himself that when he had written that article he was but "an ardent, impulsive youth" only too ready to take for truth what he had read in print. He had thus taken an article in an English periodical, read it at face value, and incorporated it into an article he wrote for a Welsh periodical. He was now an older, and he hoped, a wiser man, and his experience of the so-called Liberalism of 1850 or 1851 had made him a Conservative in 1868. Political neutrality, he believed at that time of concern over the Irish Church, would mean "unfaithfulness to my responsibilities as a Christian citizen, and a minister of the Protestant Church." Howell saw the act of disestablishment as "an act of wanton spoliation, a breach of solemn National engagements, a betrayal of the best friends of the Throne and of the Commonwealth, a dangerous precedent in regard to the rights of property and the obligations of the Sovereign's oath, a fatal rejection of the Protestant Faith as the National recognition of Divine truth in an important branch of the empire". Furthermore Howell believed that as the Protestant Church in Ireland was weakened by the act, so would the Roman Church there increase in power and influence.[93]

This was a degree of candour, admitted the local paper, that "becomes him well". All he asked was that people should believe that he had had a change of opinion, and that, as the editor commented, persistence in holding opinions that a man sees to be wrong is not consistency but obstinacy. An admission of error, on the other hand, "is the mark of an intelligent and reasonable mind." The attack on Howell was also meant to damage the Conservative cause in Cardiff, of which he was an important and influential supporter.[94] The attack did no damage to either cause.

* * * *

[93] CMG, 14 Nov 1868, p 6, letter of Howell and from *A lover of truth*.
[94] CMG, 21 Nov 1868, p 5.

We have already noted that St John's parish was a parish which was rapidly expanding. The responsibilities placed on Howell to meet the needs of this expansion were substantial. New buildings were required for churches and schools, money had to be found for the stipends of curates, and funds for a whole variety of objects. Thus considerable sums of money had to be found year after year. This was the case for many parishes in Wales, and equally true that many incumbents were left to undertake the financial seeking and begging as well as the accounting thereof. This was true for Howell as well. Something of his exasperation at this state of affairs comes out in a letter he wrote to Lady Llanover in response to her comment that his successor at St John's, C J Thompson, was not continuing with the Welsh services. He wrote from Wrexham, accordingly, that he at least believed the new vicar's declaration that he had every intention of continuing with the Welsh services, but he (Howell) having just had to find £577 to pay off the schools' debts, added "I can only too fully sympathise with him in his apprehended difficulty of finding grants to work his parish. It is now, as in the days of old, hard to make bricks without straw."[95]

It is also clear that Howell felt that the wealthy people of the parish were not supporting the needs of the church as they should, especially with regard to the church schools. He considered it scandalous that in a town the size of Cardiff the infants' school had to be closed for a year from 1864, the subscriptions for that year amounting to but four guineas, and when reopened the following year by Howell its debts were still £220.[96] The excuse given by some for their refusal to contribute, namely that the Ecclesiastical Commission which was in receipt of the ecclesiastical revenues of the parish, did nothing for the promotion of its welfare, has already been noted, but this was clearly a sore point with the vestry as with Howell himself.[97]

The income of the parish came from several sources, although the main source in previous years, the church rate levied like any other rate on the property in the parish, had been discontinued through Nonconformist pressure shortly before Howell's

---

[95] Howell to Lady Llanover, 9 Sept 1875, NLW D Parry Jones papers, 1979 deposit.
[96] CMG, 10 Mar 1865, p 5.
[97] Howell to Ecclesiastical Commissioners, 11 Mar 1868, EC file.

appointment. Complaint was made at the adjourned 1865 vestry that many people who benefited from the church now gave nothing towards its upkeep, though previously they had been required to pay that church rate.[98] The only provision in church law for an offertory was at the communion service, and this was to be devoted to the poor. Nevertheless by the 1860s offertories for church expenses were being taken at other services, although many clergy resisted this move as being uncongenial to their congregations. But even the offertory could be avoided. In 1867 it was said that those who regularly sat in the free places would turn the other way when the plate was presented to them. In 1874 the total amount of offertories given at St John's was £421, and £326 at St Andrew's,[99] but these sums included the collections taken for specific purposes, and for which a special sermon had been preached. Voluntary collections or subscriptions in lieu of the church rate were still being collected in 1867, when they produced £173, the offertories for the poor (at the communion services) £112, special collections for societies £231, the curate's fund £98, and for church cleaning and repairs, £140.[100]

Another source of income was the pew rents. By law part of this income was reserved for the incumbent, and another part for the clerk, but the amount was subject to local arrangements. The pew rents in St Andrew's Church amounted in 1866 to £96, of which £40 was given to the incumbent, but the vestry in that year agreed to increase this to £60. The offertories for church expenses came to £84. The St John's pew rents amounted to £149 in the same year, an increase of £16 over the previous year, while a sum of £30 was received from the Taff Vale Railway Company in lieu of rates. In 1866, however, though the net income of St John's Church was £180, the expenses of the church came to a pound less, and this rather precarious situation remained true for most of Howell's ministry in the parish.[101] In 1871, for example, when considerable sums of money had to be spent on repair work to the parish church, its income from pew rents came to £122

[98] CMG, 19 May 1865, p 7.
[99] WM, 11 Aug 1874, p 4.
[100] The parish accounts for 1877.
[101] CMG, 6 Ap 1866, p 7. The vestry was also responsible for setting and collecting the secular rates. In 1861 the ratable value was £28,442, and in 1871 £49,756 [CMG, 6 Ap 1872, p 6].

with another £30 from the railway company, but expenditure came to £208, so there was an actual deficit of over £50.[102] But that was a bad year for pew rents, for some reason,[103] and in 1875 the sum obtained from this source was £187, which, with the Taff Vale money enabled the books to be balanced with an expenditure of £210.[104] The salary for the organist remained unpaid for some years, and there was some indignation at this at the 1868 Vestry, when parishioners were asked to find £40 to pay these arrears.[105] The organist's salary of £50 per annum came from voluntary subscriptions, and it appears that since Stacey had left, no-one had bothered to collect them, and Howell declined to collect debts accumulated two or three years before he was instituted to the parish. This and other matters caused a rather rowdy meeting to be adjourned.[106]

Unfair though it may seem, by law the incumbent was responsible for the payment of his assistant clergy. In a parish such as Cardiff, where the income was small and the responsibilities considerable, the parish endeavoured to assist him, as did various societies who gave grants, including the diocesan charities. The Ecclesiastical Commissioners, whose funds were equally limited, only gave annual renewable grants to parishes in mining districts. In 1866 there were two curates. The senior received £130 per annum, and the junior £100. A grant of £100 was given by the Church Pastoral-Aid Society, and £50 from the Llandaff Diocesan Extension Fund, but both required an annual collection to be given to their funds in return. But Howell was forced to find £80 out of his own pocket, to the apparent surprise of the vestry. In that year, however, it agreed to find £50 of this sum from an offertory which would be taken every third Sunday in the month.[107] By 1874 CPAS gave an additional grant of £80 for a Scripture reader. The combined grants from this source came to £280, though only £101 was returned to the parent

---

[102] CMG, 15 Ap 1871, p 6.
[103] It appears some refused to pay, though this did not apply to those pewholders who lived outside the parish, and others gave monies for church improvements instead, as did E P Richards and Mr Dalton in 1865 [CMG, 21 Ap 1865, p 8; 19 May 1865, p 7].
[104] *Parish accounts* 1875.
[105] CMG, 18 Ap 1868, p 7.
[106] CMG, 21 Ap 1865, p 8; 19 May 1865, p 7.
[107] CMG, 6 Ap 1866, p 7.

society.[108] This was a little better than 1870, when for the £250 received only £34 was returned. Howell then argued that the society deserved "a much enlarged liberality" from the parish in return for its three grants, and his message was heard and enacted.[109] In 1865 there was also a curate who served St Andrew's Church, and by the time Howell left there were five curates. The other curates were probably supported by the diocesan extension fund and from parochial funds, although Howell must always have had the worry that at the end of the day he was legally responsible for their stipends as incumbent.

Howell's own income was hardly commensurate with the size of his parish and the demands placed on him. In 1832 the living was valued at £254 according to the files of the Queen Anne's Bounty - a society which applied to poor parishes various revenues given to the church by that Queen. Of that sum £80 came from tithes, a charge of ten per-cent on certain agricultural products which was commuted to a money-payment in 1836, £51 from the Easter dues, which in 1778 was said to consist of a sum of one shilling per head on every parishioner over the age of twelve - but the difficulty of collection must have been immense - and £66 from the surplice fees from weddings and funerals. By Howell's day the Easter dues had been superseded by an Easter offertory given by the congregation, and the fees were to be much reduced due to the opening of the new cemetery and the subsequent restrictions placed on burials in the churchyard. When he arrived in 1864 the living was valued at £302 per annum. This sum consisted of £48 in commuted tithes, £92 surplice fees, Easter offerings £24, an agreed share of the pew rents £18, a share of the rectorial tithes originally given by the patrons of the living, the dean and chapter of Gloucester Cathedral, and termed the official stipend of the living, £52, a grant from the Ecclesiastical Commissioners of £20 - part of its policy to ensure that livings with a large population had a minimum value of £300, and an

---

[108] WM, 30 Mar 1874, p 8. Mr Gatton was this 'layreader', a former missionary who had served as a sergeant in the Rifle Brigade during the Indian Mutiny, and occasionally lectured on this subject [CMG, 14 July 1865, p 7; 9 Jan 1869, p 5; 2 Dec 1871, p 5]. Gatton preached a sermon on the death of his son in 1873, published as *The Faith of the Shunaminite*, dedicated to his wife, his co-partner in his mission work.

[109] *Parish Magazine*, Ap 1870.

annual gift from the Marquess of Bute of £30.[110] The vicarage was in such a bad state of repair that another house had to be found at an annual cost to the vicar's pocket of £40, which the commissioners' met with a grant of £20 and which sum is included in the above figures.[111] We have already noted that the vicar was responsible for the stipends of his assistant clergy, and in his early days this took at least £80 out of his pocket. His effectual income after such deductions was less than £200, and from this he still had to pay property tax on his tithe income.

Nevertheless, Howell's income increased steadily, even though one imagines that the parochial outgoings rose in proportion. By 1875 his share of the pew-rents from St Andrew's Church amounted to £152, a clear indication of his popularity, and the Easter offerings from the parish in 1865 were £152, which if Howell regarded as "tangible proof of the high opinion entertained for him by the congregations" of his two churches, was also an indication of their respect for a hard working pastor.[112] In 1870 Howell requested the commissioners, who had taken over the estates of the dean and chapter of Gloucester in his parish, to regard the tithe rent charge of £94 as a "local claim" which could be given in its entirety to the parish and thus augment what he termed its meagre income of roughly £300 per annum, less deductions. The care of such a parish required a larger income than he received, he added, but the commissioners were not prepared to accept his request. They needed the money as well.[113] Howell's successor, Thompson, was luckier, for he applied in the same way when he came to the parish in 1875, knowing that the lease on the chapter's tithe rent charge expired in that year. He requested that this tithe rent charge be added to the income of the benefice which he then said consisted of a population of 16-17,000, with five places of worship, five assistant clergy, eight schools, and a total income of £341. The income had declined as the parish churchyard had closed, and the Easter offerings were but £50, for his predecessor had been a very popular man and

---

[110] Contained in the dean and chapter of Gloucester records, Gloucester Record Office, D936 C/3.
[111] EC file, letter 4 May 1864.
[112] CMG, 14 July 1865, p 5.
[113] EC file for St John's, letters of Howell to the commissioners, 4 Oct and 2 Nov 1870.

"used to obtain much more". With such an increase in population and the closure of a lease, the commissioners were almost forced to grant his request, so that Thompson's income increased by £52 per annum. It was a hard-won achievement.[114]

The condition of the vicarage added to the difficulties Howell faced as he entered the parish. The old vicarage lay against the north-east side of the churchyard, facing the castle, and in 1781 consisted of two parlours, floored, ceiled and half-wainscoted, a kitchen, two pantries and brewhouse on the ground floor, and four rooms and a closet on the first, with two attics. A barn stood at a distance and there were three stalls for horses and an orchard.[115] His predecessor had allowed his curates to make use of the house, but in 1832, according to the files of the Ecclesiastical Commission, the then curate, Mr Graham, found the house too small for his family, and leased it to a local doctor, James Bird. The end result was that the house was in a deplorable condition when Howell moved into the parish. The surveyors had refused to tender for repairs because of its condition, and he, unable to obtain a temporary dwelling for his growing family in the parish, was forced to take a small cottage in the parish of Roath to his "great inconvenience" and at a cost of £40 per year.[116] But the expenses of his parish and the costs of this alternative dwelling proved so prohibitive that within a year or so he was forced to move to this vicarage. Its rooms had insufficient light as the windows were so small and the building was overshadowed by the church, consequently little sunlight entered its rooms; the kitchen was too small and some of the ground floor rooms were below street level and damp and offensive in smell. The rain came into the house whenever it rained so that the floors were rotten and there was a real fear that the children might fall through them. On one occasion the rain soaked the papers on his desk.[117] The result of these living conditions, and the habitual overwork which Howell undertook, hardly taking a single rest day in two years, resulted in a serious breakdown in his health in the

[114] Ibid, letter of Thompson, 17 Nov 1875.
[115] EC file on St John's, contained in correspondence of 1883-4.
[116] Howell to commissioners, 12 Ap 1864, EC file.
[117] Ibid, 13 Ap 1864, and Howell to Ollivant, 24 Jan 1868, EC file; CMG, 24 Oct 1868, p 7.

latter part of 1866, giving rise to "a great deal of anxiety in the town".[118] Letters to the local paper took his side. The house was quite unfit for one who depended on his health for the discharge of his parochial duties.[119] Dr Taylor testified to a parish vestry that the house was not a fit place for a gentleman in his position, especially when he had a family.[120] Once, when tempted to accept the bishop's offer of the parish of Gelligaer because of these conditions, some of his friends offered to lease a house for him in Crockherbtown until a new vicarage was built.[121]

All were agreed that a new vicarage was needed and should be built. The parish planned to sell the old vicarage to the town council for the purposes of street improvements, and a price of £500 had been agreed, although later a dispute developed as to the distance the street wall was to be from the wall of the church itself.[122] But there were two problems which prevented a new vicarage being built for the next five years. The first was obtaining a site within the parish itself, as required by ecclesiastical law, and the second was finding the money needed to build the house in accordance with the requirements laid down by the Ecclesiastical Commissioners.

The commissioners required a freehold site. Lord Bute, now a papist and the leading landowner in Cardiff, was only prepared to offer a leasehold site. He or his agent, E P Richard, a member of St Andrew's Church, had refused to offer or even sell a freehold site in such "a curt, abrupt and magisterial" manner that *Fair Play,* writing in the *Cardiff Times,* commented that "a kindly disposition and conciliatory spirit" would do more to serve the Bute interest in Cardiff "than all the lordly power which the Barons of Cardiff

---

[118] CMG, 14 Dec 1866, p 5. He noted that when he left the parish that his health had been badly affected by these conditions [*Weekly Mail,* 3 Ap 1875, p 4.] Howell at least learnt from this mistake, and thereafter took chaplaincies in Europe, Munich in 1872, Switzerland the following year [CMG, 3 Aug 1872, p 5; 13 Sept 1873, p 8].
[119] CMG, 10 Oct 1868, p 5.
[120] CMG, 3 Ap 1869, p 6.
[121] CMG, 24 Oct 1868, p 7. Howell was the right man in the right place at Cardiff, wrote a correspondent to the CMG [10 Oct 1868, p 5], while Gelligaer as a parish was hardly wide enough for a man of his labours and talents.
[122] CMG, 3 Ap 1869, p 6; 10 July 1869, p 5; 8 Mar 1873, p 5. The house itself was sold for £54 for demolition [CMG, 26 Ap 1873, p 5]. The two separate areas of garden belonging to the vicarage were sold in 1887 and 1890, after a long dispute with the Bute trustees who claimed one of the sites. A sum of £1,900 was obtained for them [QAB file].

Castle ever exercised."[123] It is hard to follow events, but by August 1869 Howell was mentioning that another site, with a sixty foot frontage in an "elegant street", was available on a 999 year lease with an annual rental of £22.10s, but alas, this was not acceptable to the commissioners.[124] This land appears to have been in the then highly fashionable Charles Street, and in the ownership of Mrs Hester Vachell. By 1871 it seems that some compromise had been reached allowing the freehold to be sold, but as the parish did not have the money to hand to purchase it, it hoped the commissioners would allow the vicar and wardens to pay the chief or ground rent for five to six years, and then purchase the freehold at the cost of twenty-five years rental. Bishop Ollivant also added his plea. The house was urgently needed, and the difficulties of obtaining a suitable freehold site had proved insurmountable. Some negotiations took place, to complicate matters, between the commissioners and the Bute trustees, about exchanging this site for a better one in the Bute ownership. These came to nothing. Eventually the parish was allowed to go ahead on the terms it had proposed to the commission. It had taken nearly six years of protracted debate and worry just to obtain a site for the new vicarage.[125]

As these matters were being negotiated, the wardens and Howell were endeavouring to find the monies required to build a house that would be suitable both as a vicarage and also to fit in with the then prestigious area of Charles Street. It was hoped that a benefaction could be obtained from the commissioners, by which the parish either received an outright grant on account of "local interests", namely the commission's financial interest in the parish, or alternatively a grant of money on condition an equal sum was found within the parish itself. But the churchwardens' promise of a benefaction of £1,000, half the estimated cost of the new vicarage, provided the commission met that sum with an equal grant, was not acceptable, and was rejected on three

---

[123] *Cardiff Times*, 17 July 1869, p 8, and p 5, which hinted that the Cardiff Conservatives were divided over the issue: "upon his [the Marquess] enthusiastic admirer, the worthy vicar, the blow must have fallen heavily." See also CMG, 10 July 1869, p 5.
[124] Howell's letters of 6 July, 11 Aug 1869, in EC file; CMG, 23 Ap 1870, p 8.
[125] Letters of Howell to the Commissioners, 25 May 1870 and 23 Feb 1871, EC file; letter of Ollivant, ibid, 29 Jan 1870.

separate occasions. There was uproar in Cardiff. Did not the commissioners benefit from the rectorial tithes of the parish? Did they not realise that the present vicarage had been certified as unfit for human habitation? Were they not aware that the vicar and his family suffered almost continual sickness as a result of its condition? When Ollivant at a public meeting suggested that the commission had turned down the application because the parish had not offered a benefaction against which it could offer a grant, the mayor of Cardiff rose and corrected him. It was not a want of liberality on their part. An embarrassed Ollivant must have pressed for the fourth application of late 1868 to be granted, for it was successful and the commissioners allowed a grant of £1,000 capital to meet the promised benefaction of the same amount. But the bishop noted that the delay had led to one unforeseen circumstance, the Marquess of Bute had turned papist, "and no one can tell what difficulty there may be in getting a site or any assistance from him."[126] This, as we have noted, proved to be the case. The parish share of the cost, £1,000, had only been promised, not found. At first it was argued that if poor Canton could raise £948 to provide a parsonage then St John's parish could easily find the £1,200 required.[127] By the time the wardens came to collect their share of the cost there was a trade depression, and as Howell mentioned, it was easier to collect £4,000 two years previously than a quarter of that money then. Luckily the commission extended its time limit for this money to be found, or else their offer would have lapsed.[128] The congregation, *A Dissenter* reported under the heading of *The Beggarly Establishment* in the letter columns of the local paper, had been driven to "its wits' end" to find the monies required, and in appealing for public help with this and for the church clock was simply showing its weakness. Let some Nonconformists take over the business, he challenged, and they would speedily provide a house for the vicar![129]

---

[126] Letters of 9 Nov 1864, 27 Nov 1867, 24 Jan 1868, 25 Nov 1868, 8 Mar 1869, in EC file.
[127] CMG, 24 Oct 1868, p 7.
[128] Howell to Commissioners, 25 May 1869, EC file.
[129] *Cardiff Times*, 10 Ap 1869, p 5.

The wardens' appeal was not unsuccessful. Lady Llanover gave ten pounds, as did the good bishop, while the Powell-Duffryn Steam Coal Company gave twenty-five.[130]

The money was eventually found, and after the perusal of the architect's plans by the commission's architect, requiring a kitchen door wide enough to take a maid carrying a dinner tray, the new vicarage was built and Howell moved in 1874. It cost £2,000, excluding the land, and took nine years of sustained effort to obtain. Howell only lived in it for a year, and when he left had to pay over twelve pounds in dilapidation charges. There was rust on the outside railings and on a cistern, a new socket was needed on the coal-house door, and cracks in the breakfast room ceiling needed to be repaired.[131] The house remained as the vicarage until 1933, and today is used by the Society of Friends.

* * * *

The *Western Mail* reported in February 1875 that rumours about Howell leaving the parish had been received incredulously, but it was true. Bishop Hughes of St Asaph, needing a good Welshman to take charge of the most substantial parish in his diocese, Wrexham, and finding none suitable in his own, had persuaded Howell to accept that living. The *Weekly Mail* reported:

> They, [the parishioners] we are persuaded, will share with us the unmixed regret with which we contemplate his secession from us. On the other hand, it cannot be doubted that Mr Howell has acted wisely in relinquishing the heavy duties of his present sphere of usefulness for the lighter work which the living of Wrexham will impose on him. It is well known that the labours which the vicar has undergone for many years, and which have been ceaselessly on the increase, have over-taxed his strength and energies, and that the time has at length arrived when no alternative remained but to make the unwilling acknowledgement that they were in excess of the powers of endurance. It is within our knowledge that Mr Howell has had more than one offer of preferment, more lucrative in its emoluments, and less onerous in its labour than that which he

[130] *Parish Magazine*, May 1870.
[131] QAB file for St John's Cardiff, 1875.

now holds, and that he has declined these simply because he has considered that duty bound him to Cardiff so long as he was able to discharge it. His recent illness has, however, we regret to say, affected him severely, though, we trust, not seriously, and his medical advisors have prescribed for him a season of rest, and a less energetic pursuit of his holy calling than that in which he has for so long been engaged. The Bishop of St Asaph, from the honourable and conscientious desire to fill the vacant church at Wrexham efficiently, has, in terms the kindness of which well accord with the excellence of his lordship's motive, offered this valuable living to Mr Howell; and we cannot doubt that it will greatly delight the parishioners of that historical town to know that so deserving and good a man has accepted it. That which Cardiff cannot but regard as a loss they will hail as a gain.[132]

A public meeting was convened at the town hall in order to try and persuade Howell to remain. This resulted in a petition signed by 1,700 people:

> We the undersigned, deeply sensible of the loss which the inhabitants of Cardiff in general, the poor and afflicted in the parish of St John's, in particular, will incur by your removal to another sphere of labour, respectfully request you to consider whether it is possible that any arrangements can now be made to induce you to continue your faithful ministrations amongst us.[133]

Howell replied thanking them for the gratifying proof of the esteem in which he was held. Though he was deeply affected by their kindness he felt unable to accede to their request, feeling that his ministry in Cardiff had come to a close. His letter to the chairman, Mr Bushell, after mentioning the extreme kindness he had always received from the people of Cardiff, continued:

> When the offer of Wrexham reached me, now more than two months ago, there were two things which weighed much with me in forming my conclusions. First, that the offer was a spontaneous one on the part of the Bishop of St Asaph, and not the result of any solicitation or desire on my part; and, secondly, that my health for more than eighteen months previously had been so uncertain,

---

[132] *Weekly Mail*, 6 Feb 1875, p 10.
[133] WM, 20 Mar 1875, p 8.

accompanied by a constant sense of fatigue and exhaustion, with a growing apprehension of an approaching breakdown, that a prospect of comparatively lighter duties came as a most welcome boon to me. I still feel the force of these considerations. Of nothing am I more deeply convinced than that the concurrent direction of circumstances is an indication of the will of God, and equally persuaded I am that no man is justified in clinging to a position, the duties of which he is no longer able efficiently to discharge.

There was another consideration: he had already accepted the living of Wrexham, and felt unable, as a person of honour, to withdraw, even though he added that his "inclinations are all on one side" and his "judgement and conscience on the other". He acknowledged, however, that "feeling .... is a poor guide in matters of duty". One thing had profoundly affected him, namely that those who had signed the memorial included the names of many leading Nonconformists and others "unconnected with the Established Church - a proof surely of the Christian brotherhood underlying our sectional differences; and also that Christian work earnestly undertaken seldom fails to command the hearty appreciation of all good men."[134] There was much regret at his decision, for as one editor put it, Howell had been closely identified with the town, and his work there had made him "an object of reverential affection to the vast body of Cardiff people, irrespective of sect and party."[135] But it remained to be seen whether Wrexham would be a "lighter sphere of labour" as all seemed to suggest. Parkinson's law operated in the case of Howell as well, even though it had not been promulgated at that time!

Howell's closing sermon, printed in full by the *Western Mail*, and subsequently as a pamphlet, began by mentioning the harmony he had had with his congregation: "I doubt if, in a single instance, we have been at variance during a pastorate of eleven years. At a time of much religious excitement, and of prevailing religious dissensions, we have been linked together in unbroken cordiality, and have laboured together in Christian quietude and peace". He continued:

[134] *Weekly Mail*, 3 Ap 1875, p 4.
[135] *Weekly Mail*, 6 Feb 1875, p 9 of supplement.

Now brethren, finally farewell. The word passes from my lips with a solemn sadness which no words of mine can well express. Farewell! My work is done; my mission ended; my message is delivered. Never again shall I enter this pulpit as my own; never again shall I address you as my spiritual charge; and never again shall we meet as we do at this moment until we meet for judgment before your Maker and mine. And oh, what a meeting - what a meeting, will that be! Shall it be a meeting of joy and gladness? shall it be a meeting of mutual rejoicing and God-praising, or the reverse? God only knows! The past, however, is irreversible. Not a single item in the record can be made otherwise than it is. All our backslidings and shortcomings, our wasted privileges and neglected opportunities, our broken vows and unfulfilled resolutions, our formal prayers, our heartless praises, our misspent Sabbaths, and our undevout communions - all, all are indelibly recorded in that Book of Remembrance which in a few moments will be closed, and never opened again until it shall be opened in the presence of God and of the assembled universe. The thought is an almost overwhelming one. Were it not for the assurance of God's mercy in Christ it would indeed be unendurable. Farewell, then, my brethren, until that day. Never, oh, never can I forget you. Deeply engraven on my heart and memory will ever be the recollection of your unbounded kindness. Forgive, I beseech you, my mistakes and imperfections. Forgive, I entreat you, my shortcomings and deficiencies. And if I may still add to the multitude of my obligations, it is to entreat a warm interest in your prayers for me and my work in the distant parish where my future lot is cast. Sustained as I have been by your prayers hitherto, I am deeply anxious to secure the same blessing elsewhere. Yes, my brethren, let us pray fervently for each other, until we reach that land of heavenly rest where prayers shall cease; where there shall be no more separations, no more partings, no more weepings, but where God will wipe away all tears from all eyes.[136]

As soon as it was realised that Howell was definitely leaving the parish, a testimonial fund was commenced. Significantly, at its inaugural meeting Fr Puller of Roath and Fr Jones of St Mary's were present on the platform, indicating perhaps their appreciation of Howell's ministry and his friendship with people with whom he had considerable doctrinal differences. The

---

[136] *In Memoriam*, pp 6-7.

attendance was said to be "numerous, influential, and ... enthusiastic." In losing Howell from Cardiff, said W D Bushell,[137] who presided, they were losing "the mainstay of the church in Cardiff". "They had found him early and late, day by day, and year by year, in the earnest and assiduous discharge of his duties." Howell's character, worth, intelligence, piety, earnestness and devotion were known to them all, and the sacrifices he had made for them in the discharge of his ministry had undermined his health to such an extent that he believed "it was through a providential interference that he was invited to depart from amongst them."[138] Although it was not stated publicly, it was also known that Howell had "involved himself in a considerable pecuniary obligation" regarding the church schools, and it was quietly arranged that these should be met by parishioners, so that Howell did not have to leave still burdened with these responsibilities.[139]

The eventual presentation consisted of a purse of gold containing eight hundred pounds, and a silver salver from the parish, to which all classes of the community, including many Nonconformists, had contributed, a drawing room clock from the St John's Sunday School, a gold lever clock by the ladies of Cardiff and a silver toast rack from the infants taught by Mrs Howell in the Sunday School. These presents, and others, were exhibited for a time in Mr Ingram's shop window.[140] There was another unexpected gift. A group of Irish girls working in the potato sheds at the docks came to his door in tears to present him with an inscribed silver salver as a tribute to his social work amongst themselves and their families.[141]

Howell responded with a letter from Wrexham. He would misconstrue the meaning of the gifts were he to see them in the light of personal merit. Rather, such tokens of goodwill "represent not my deservings, but your love to Him whose messenger and ambassador I have been to you for more than eleven years ..." These had been some of the best years of his life.

[137] He was chairman of the Taff Vale Railway. His son, William Dore Bushell, ordained in 1864, was an assistant master at Harrow, and owned Caldey Island as a summer retreat.
[138] WM, 12 Feb 1875, p 4.
[139] *Wrexham Guardian*, 13 Feb 1875, p 3.
[140] *Wrexham Guardian*, 20 Mar 1875 [quoting *Western Mail*], and 24 Ap, p 5.
[141] quoted in WM, 22 Jan 1903, p 6.

To be engaged in "active service" is always the highest ambition of the true defenders of our Queen and country. How much more ought it to be even the earnest desire of a soldier of the cross to be where the fight is hottest, and where self-denying service is most urgently needed? This has been my privilege; and though I retire from the field not without wounds and scars, I still hope to be able (D.V.) to do battle for the truth, and to do the same service to the cause with which Almighty God has specially connected his Divine glory.

He ended with the prayer that the spiritual progress of Cardiff should always keep pace with its material prosperity, and that all who held themselves Christians might "be led into the way of truth, and hold the faith in unity of spirit, the bond of peace, and in righteousness of life."[142] To suggest he was popular in his parish could not convey the nature of his relationship with his people: "love and affection would be more accurate terms", suggested an obituary writer in the *Western Mail*. He continued: when 'Vicar Howell', as he was still known, came many years later to preach for the Church Missionary Society at St John's Church, there was hardly enough room to contain the congregation, some even sat on the chancel steps.[143]

Over seventy candidates applied to take Howell's place. The papers of the dean and chapter of Gloucester indicate the names of some of them; possibly they formed a short list. They included D E Williams of Llanelli, John Gower of Trefriw, Lewis Price of Llywel, David Jones of Penmaenmawr, John Gauntlett, curate of Swansea, and Thomas Cunnick, the CPAS secretary for Wales. A number spoke Welsh, and one, E M Griffiths, offered the chapter clerk "a handsome acknowledgement ... if he could influence the appointment" in his favour. Archdeacon Blosse wrote suggesting that the bishop had hoped to make St Andrew's into a separate parish, but had found that the pew rents and offertories did not provide a sufficient stipend. One assumes the hint that the chapter could augment this was not taken. But Blosse went on, "I trust and pray that you may be led to appoint a man who may walk in the steps of his predecessor - he cannot do better than that."[144]

[142] WM, 8 May 1875, p 8.
[143] WM, 16 Jan 1903, p 3; 22 Jan 1903, p 6; 30 Mar 1897, p 4.
[144] Gloucester Record Office, D936 c/5.

The chapter discarded their shortlist. Instead they nominated Charles James Thompson, then the diocesan inspector of schools for Llandaff, to succeed Howell. This was an appointment which may have been influenced by Howell, for speaking to his last Easter vestry he made it clear that he considered it a good one, and that his successor would be able to carry forward the work he had only begun, "in a way that will leave this parish in a much more prosperous condition, in a spiritual sense, than it is at present."[145] This again is an indication of Howell's eirenic spirit, for Thompson was certainly not in the evangelical camp. It was Thompson who introduced the surplice into the pulpit at St John's, and followed it up with many other changes.[146]

In his first sermon to the congregation at St John's, Thompson gave what the papers described as a solemn charge. After noting the solemnity of the pastoral office, he argued it was even more solemn to assume the duty of a parish such as St John's:

> a parish in which souls - souls for whom Christ died - are to be counted by thousands; a parish in which, God be thanked, there is a large amount of spiritual life; a parish in which, though, alas! there must be many souls who are still slumbering unto death; there are, on the other hand, many hundreds who are awake to all the responsibility of life; many hundreds with softened hearts, with enlightened understandings, and with quickened conscience, - I say, my brethren, how solemn a thing it is to undertake the charge of such a work as this. I dared not have sought or even suggested myself for such a charge, and there is nothing during the thirteen years of my ministry which has at the same time humbled and yet cheered me more, - nothing which I feel sure will furnish me with more strength for the present, and with more hopefulness for the future, - than this, that I have been called and sent to succeed my devoted predecessor by no act or solicitation of my own.

As he dedicated his talents, strength and energy to the service of the parish, he prayed they would honour him with the same generous confidence with which they honoured Howell, and to continue to uphold his ministry in prayer.[147]

---

[145] *Wrexham Guardian*, 3 Ap 1875, p 3.
[146] *Llandaff Diocesan Conference Report*, 1896, p 107. He called it a musty old black gown, but the surplice was seen "as the thin edge of the wedge."
[147] WM, 1 Ap 1875, p 4; Parish Magazine, June 1875.

In 1868 when writing to the Ecclesiastical Commissioners who had declined to give him a grant for his proposed new vicarage, Howell described the condition of the parish when he entered it four years earlier:

> Called to succeed a nominalent [sic] incumbent of forty-three years, I have had everything to do. Arrears of all kinds to clear off, a parish overrun with Dissent, church accommodation for one tenth of the population, and schools small and mean built in 1818 - a byword to the Diocese, a vicarage house declared by architect and doctors to be unfit for habitation ...[148]

Such was the position then, and within eleven years it had changed completely. The four Sunday services in two buildings had been replaced by thirteen in four; the two schools had become six, with 1,755 pupils. A Sunday school had been commenced which in 1875 had 1,800 members aged between five and seventy, and which was clearly conducted on the Nonconformist-inspired "all age" principle. It was said he had collected over £30,000 for church purposes during his eleven years in Cardiff.[149] Clearly Howell's preaching had established a spiritually alive congregation. Instead a stranger to Cardiff had said that he had seen in St John's what he never expected to find, a church too small for its congregation.[150] But this preaching was backed by the prayer of his flock. And it brought into the church a vast number of former Nonconformists, as well as "infusing into it something of the freedom and energy which distinguish the Dissenting communions."[151]

It was this preaching, evangelical in tone and practical in detail, that drove his congregation to prayer, and to a holiness of life whose repercussions were worked out in the commercial and civic life of the town. This preaching stimulated the church to involve itself in evangelism, pastoral care and social action on behalf of the people living within the parish, and to a deep involvement in home and overseas mission. Concern for the poor led not only to the provision of winter meals and other comforts, but also to

---

[148] Howell to commissioners, 11 Mar 1868, EC file.
[149] From J V Morgan, *Welsh Religious Leaders*, p 106.
[150] Ibid, p 119.
[151] *Wrexham Guardian*, 13 Feb 1875, p 8, quoting the *Cardiff Times*.

evangelism so that lives could reflect God's glory. And such Gospel truths compelled Howell and his congregation to co-operate with Christians of other traditions whenever possible, especially within the field of social work. He was known, said the *Cardiff Times*, for exercising an influence over persons "who would hold themselves aloof from any other of the same cloth", while his conciliatory spirit gave him the sympathy of the Nonconformist churches, even though they despised his politics![152]

Clearly Howell was regarded as the leader of a movement, church inspired, which had revitalised Christian life in Cardiff, and his long term influence on the lives of individuals who came to positions of responsibility themselves in the community, can never be adequately measured. "The great want of the Church", said the *Weekly Mail*, is men of the stamp of the vicar of St John's.[153]

---

[152] Quoted in Wrexham Guardian, 13 Feb 1875, p 8. It also stated that many Nonconformist people became members of the Church as a result of his ministry.
[153] *Weekly Mail*, 6 Feb 1875, p 10.

The Wrexham Years

Canon George Cunliffe resigned the parish of Wrexham in 1875. He had been vicar since 1827, having followed Jonathan Shipley who had been instituted to the parish in 1770, in the patronage of his father, then bishop of St Asaph. Shipley was also dean of St Asaph, and was thus non-resident for most of his incumbency at Wrexham, but he had introduced Sunday evening services in the parish.[1] Wrexham was regarded as one of the most important parishes in north Wales, with its 18,000 population and its great parish church of St Giles, acclaimed as one of the wonders of Wales. The *Wrexham Directory* of 1886 boasted that Wrexham was "the largest and most populous town in North Wales".[2] However one country parson, Thomas Lloyd of Estyn, saw Wrexham as containing "a rich, well taught, educated, closely lying population", that is, an easy place in which to minister, as compared to a Welsh country parish where the resources and abilities of "a good brave, true shepherd of souls" would be tested to their full extent.[3]

The patronage of the parish was vested in Bishop Joshua Hughes, who had been appointed bishop of St Asaph by Gladstone in 1870 at the culmination of a long search for a man who was not only a fluent Welsh speaker, but also one eligible to take his place in the House of Lords. Gladstone is said to have been mortified when he discovered that Hughes' B.D. degree was of Lampeter, rather than of Cambridge as he supposed, but even if this was true for the social reasons suggested by this story, it speaks more of the English conception of episcopal office than of Hughes' real abilities. The appointment of Hughes had been widely welcomed in Wales, though not, it seems, by the English

---

[1] A W Palmer, *A History of the Parish Church of Wrexham* [Wrexham 1886], p 69.
[2] *The Wrexham Directory of 1886*, reprint of 1981, p 11.
[3] *Wrexham Guardian*, 6 Mar 1875, p 7.

gentry and Anglicised clergy of the diocese, who did not give him, as we shall see, an easy ride. Hughes' desire to give equality to the Welsh language within his diocese caused such people considerable offence. The new bishop was able to build on the administrative ability and work of his predecessor, Vowler Short, while he endeavoured to bring new spiritual life within his diocese. Short had concentrated on the building of schools, and his antipathy to the Welsh language had become notorious.[4]

Although Wrexham was an important parish, its spiritual life could hardly be described as encouraging to a new incumbent. In the 1850s Bishop Short was said to have been favourably impressed with this parish, and congratulated Cunliffe on his success in having seventy Easter communicants! By the time of Howell's appointment that number had crept up to one hundred and twenty-five, and there were three churches, two mission rooms, and nine Sunday services. A report on the spiritual life on Wrexham, part of a wider survey of the towns of Wales, signed by JBKJ, told a different story of Cunliffe's ministry. He wrote that he was the worst clergyman in the diocese, who had obtained his living by "cultivating" the bishop. Aristocratic, no preacher, isolated by his pride from the rest of mankind, he saw no reason why he should be "pestered" by the "vulgar people", and thus declined to call upon the poor or the stranger. He had not been known to spend a penny on charity. His curates were hardly better. One, Davies, had incurred the bishop's displeasure, and as a result had become lazy and indifferent. Another, Nixon, was of "the dullest mediocrity", and the curate of St Mark's Church, Roberts, had disgusted "all thoughtful people" with his ritualistic tendencies. The congregation numbered about five hundred and the writer added that a good clergyman would empty half the Nonconformist chapels. The report was written a few years before Howell became vicar of Wrexham.[5]

The town of Wrexham was regarded as an English enclave within a Welsh-speaking area. In 1886, for example, the *Wrexham*

---

[4] See my forthcoming book for fuller details, *In Pursuit of a Welsh Episcopate.*
[5] J V Morgan, *A Study in Nationality* [London 1911], p 258, quoting the *Report of the Royal Commission into the Church of England in Wales* [London 1911], V 127, 241f: and a cutting in the Wrexham parish file at Wrexham Public Library. The report by JBKJ is at the NLW, MS 4318B, cit Wrexham.

Directory recorded that of the fourteen Nonconformist chapels then in the town only six were Welsh-speaking causes. The church in Wrexham was equally regarded as forming an English domain. On three occasions its parishioners made clear that they preferred it this way. In 1837 the bishop was memorialised by many of the parishioners asking that the Welsh service held in the parish church on Sunday afternoons should be held only on alternative Sundays.[6] In the following year the vicar's brother, Sir Robert Cunliffe, persuaded the vestry, with two dissenting votes, to drop this service altogether.[7] A Welsh service was however resurrected some time later, so that a further memorial was presented to the bishop in 1853 by the "whole parish" - so it is said - praying that all the services at the parish church should be in English. It was argued that the afternoon Welsh service held on alternative Sundays at the parish church only attracted around thirty to fifty people, all of whom understood English and attended English services. The existence of this service was preventing some development in the work of the Sunday School. A counter-petition argued that this proposal had been passed at a select and unrepresentative vestry meeting, denied the statistics of their opponents, and pointed out that while every exertion was being made to translate the Scriptures into every known language it was inconsistent to suppress the only Welsh church service in the parish. In further correspondence Cunliffe pointed out to his bishop that while he thought it an "essential benefit" for the Welsh to attend English services as well, "as a means of their learning the English language with greater facility", he also accepted it was unfair that the Welsh "should be refused the privilege of continuing to worship in the Tabernacle that they have used for this purpose from their youth to old age and infirmity", especially as the English had seven full services each fortnight. If, however, the services in the parish church were all English services, he would be able to obtain a "better style of man" as curate, and wondered if a separate Welsh church might be the answer, although the vestry was much against such a proposal.

Sixteen years later, in 1871, some of the members of the daughter church, St Mark's, protested against a proposal made by

[6] Palmer, *The Parish Church*, p 181, cf pp 43f.
[7] A H Dodd, *A History of Wrexham* [Wrexham 1957], p 155.

the bishop to hold a Welsh evening service there. Claiming that the bishop had been misinformed as to the number of Welsh speakers in the parish (who, in any case, spoke English), the argument was made that English people had given generously to the building and endowment of their church on the assumption it would be used for English services. Although they accepted there was no evening service at St Mark's, this was a source of annoyance to them as well, and if there was to be a service, it should be an English one. Cunliffe too had his reservations. If such a Welsh evening service was held it would need to be taken by the licensed curate for that church, John Williams, who, as the evening lecturer at the parish church, had built up a congregation of over one thousand. On the whole he felt that the Welsh service would be a failure, and a good English service, well-attended, would be lost.[8] It appears that Cunliffe had endeavoured to maintain Welsh services in the parish, though he was probably not Welsh-speaking himself, and had met with the hostility of many of his parishioners. It appears that by 1875 he had ensured that a Welsh service was being held in the parish church every Sunday afternoon.[9]

Almost within a week of the announcement of Cunliffe's retirement,[10] Bishop Hughes had persuaded David Howell to accept his offer of the parish. He would have known him since Howell's days as the CPAS Welsh secretary. His choice was not surprising. Howell was one of the few clergy in Wales who had had experience of working a large and rapidly growing parish, and he had a good track record in building up parochial life and spiritual witness. Besides this he was also committed to the need to give equality to the Welsh language, and, what is more, he had a renowned preaching ministry. As a bonus, too, Howell, like Hughes, was an evangelical, although one with a greater

---

[8] NLW SA/MISC/1725-6, SA/LET/492, 498-9. There had been a proposal to establish a separate Welsh church at Wrexham in 1720, to enable those who absented themselves from church on pretence of not knowing English, to attend a church service. Instead many attended Nonconformist meeting-houses, or resorted to the alehouses, "to the great dishonour of Almighty God and to the endangering of the loss of their own souls" [SA/MISC/586].

[9] *Wrexham Guardian*, 1 May 1875, p 5. David Williams alleged later that Howell's name was suggested to Bishop Hughes by John Griffiths of Neath [*Geninen*, 22 [1904] 43].

[10] Announced in the *Wrexham Guardian*, 23 Jan 1875.

catholicity of spirit than most. Hughes thus saw him as a major acquisition to his diocese.[11] Howell was the man required, and Howell was willing. A strange note appears in the *Wrexham Guardian*, however, relating to his appointment. It suggested that "the state of his health renders it necessary and imperative that he should accept a change such as that likely to be afforded by the living of Wrexham".[12] But Howell would surely have known that in moving from Cardiff to Wrexham he was taking on even more responsibilities than he was leaving. The same issue of the paper, after quoting Howell's achievements at Cardiff, concluded by saying "we trust his parishioners in Wrexham will give him that hearty welcome to which he is so fully entitled." They may well have done so. The diocese was another matter.

Canon David Williams, a former proctor for the diocese, and rector of Castle Caereinion, though he did not refer to Howell's appointment by name, nevertheless had it much in mind when he wrote a letter to the *Wrexham Guardian* in its last edition of February:

> I maintain that a bishop holds his patronage in *trust for the clergy of his diocese*. This was also the view taken by the Bishop of Llandaff when asked to bestow one of his Flintshire livings on a clergyman officiating in that county. I have just been informed that Bishop Thirlwall took the same view of his responsibility when asked a short time ago by a friend of mine to appoint a Montgomeryshire clergyman to a vacant Montgomeryshire living.[13]

An anonymous layman quoted in the same paper suggested that his annoyance over Howell's appointment was part of a wider concern regarding Bishop Hughes' patronage. The bishops of St Asaph had a much greater amount of patronage in their diocese than was the case in most English dioceses. Describing himself as *A North Wales layman*, he continued, sarcastically:

> Bishop Hughes is a Southwalian, duly qualified for his important position at the renowned college of Lampeter, and he appears resolved to utilise the diocese over which he presides as a Southwalian colony, as he seems rarely to neglect an opportunity of promoting his Levitical brethren from that quarter.

[11] WM, 16 Jan 1903, p 5.
[12] *Wrexham Guardian*, 6 Feb 1875, p 4.
[13] Ibid, 27 Feb 1875, p 7.

David Howell, he continued,

> Although a literate, had [he] laboured in the diocese of St Asaph no one would have grudged him his promotion; but why the bishop, while rejecting literate candidates for holy orders, should have travelled so far from his own boundary in search of a literate as the only eligible person for his principal favours, is a question to which the clergy of the diocese have a perfect right to expect an answer.[14]

On the other hand, another writer argued that the appointment was probably a compliment to the clergy of the diocese in that Hughes had to go outside it to find a low churchman for Wrexham![15]

In fact this appointment raised such a controversy within the diocese that it was rumoured that an unofficial meeting of clergy had been called specifically to pass a vote disapproving of the bishop's conduct. This was denied on the authority of Walsham How, an influential cleric in the diocese and later bishop of Wakefield,[16] who nevertheless went on to accuse a number of clergy of considering themselves worthy of promotion to Wrexham. But he was accused in turn by Venables Williams of Llandrillo, of holding his own living, the wealthiest in the diocese, by purchase. Williams also added that he was proud to have proposed a vote of censure on the bishop at the Abergele Clerical Society on this matter.[17] Though the *Wrexham Guardian* supported Canon Williams' principle in general, it yet argued there were exceptions to the rule that a bishop exercised his patronage for the sake of his clergy:

> ... circumstances may demand that he should be a powerful preacher in more than one language; an active and zealous parish priest; a ready speaker on a platform; one able to comprehend the intricacies and the ever-growing demands of an ever-increasing population; conciliatory, but determined when resisting attacks upon the Church; combining a spirit of toleration with a firm resolve to expose and oppose the dangerous and destructive compromises demanded in its name ...

[14] Ibid.
[15] Letter of *Clericus Asaphensis* in ibid of 13 Mar 1875, p 7.
[16] *Wrexham Guardian*, 27 Feb 1875, p 7; 6 Mar, p 4.
[17] Ibid, 13 Mar 1875, p 7. His father had purchased the advowson of Whittington for him.

> It can be easily conceived that a small diocese ... may not be able to produce a man with these united qualities at a given time, and this is just one of those cases when a Bishop, without intending to cast a slur on his clergy, would be justified in our opinion in seeking a man elsewhere.

Wrexham, the editor argued, was a parish which required "peculiar treatment", and Howell, by his record, was the man most fitted to offer that treatment. It was unfair to censure the bishop for living up to his concern of establishing a bilingual and preaching ministry in his diocese in order to offset the advance of Dissent, though it thought it strange that the bishop should promote a literate to such an important living when he declined to ordain such men. It hoped that the bishop's conduct, in this appointment, "although somewhat bold and exceptional", would be successful.[18]

Others, such as F W Kittermaster of Ruabon, commended the bishop for regarding his patronage as a matter which concerned the parish and not simply the clergy of the diocese.[19] This opinion, wrote a *Wrexham Churchman* in the same paper, was one shared by the people of Wrexham. "I look round for many miles to seek a clergyman who would be acceptable to the people of Wrexham", he wrote, "and I fail to discern him." "As a rule", he continued, "the clergy of North Wales are easy going persons. They hold their services in a systematic manner because it is their duty, but any extraneous efforts on behalf of the Church are out of character with them." Howell's ministry, he believed, would be the revival of the church at Wrexham, and they had cause to be grateful to the bishop for so good a nomination.[20]

After all this controversy Howell's induction was an anti-climax, although it probably was typical of its time. It took place on a Saturday morning in late April. The ceremony was performed by the rural dean, W Davies, with the attendance of a curate, the churchwardens, and a few others. A short speech by

---

[18] Ibid, 6 Mar 1875, p 4, and cf p 7, and ibid, 13 Mar 1875, p 7.
[19] *Wrexham Guardian*, 13 Mar 1875, p 7.
[20] Ibid, 20 Mar 1875, p 7. Bishop Edwards alluded to this controversy during his own troubles of 1897 regarding patronage in his diocese as an example of the rebelliousness of a small part of the clergy of the diocese [*Church Times*, 23 Dec 1897, p 756].

Howell followed in which he expressed the hope that his "vicarate" would be productive of spiritual good to the parish, and spiritual prosperity to the families of the town. The following Sunday he "read himself in" at the parish church to a large congregation, amongst whom were many Nonconformists. Canon Cunliffe read the lessons. After Howell had read and given his assent to the Thirty-Nine Articles he informed his congregation that he hoped all would have "not a mere traditionary attachment" to the Church of England, but a "well-informed conviction of the Scriptural soundness of her doctrines and discipline." But this good doctrine needed to issue in holiness of life in order to be profitable.[21]

*   *   *   *

The parish of Wrexham was both a multi-church and also a bilingual parish. As Howell wrote to the Ecclesiastical Commissioners, requesting a renewal of the curates' grants, this meant a double ecclesiastical machinery and a proportionate increase of "ministerial agencies".[22] The parish was spread over 11,941 acres, comprising a number of townships, and was situated in the heart of the north Wales colliery district, so that there was continual immigration into the area as new mines were opened. Cunliffe, writing to the Ecclesiastical Commissioners in 1865 noted that the parish population was then estimated at 13,000, but the parish church could only hold 2,000. Though there were district churches at Brynbo, Minera and Drelincourt, and a National School at Bersham licensed for worship, the total church seating for this population was not more than 3,200. The growing districts of Ecclesham and below Erddig, with a population of 2,100, were totally neglected and the parish church was too distant from them.

Though a number of new parishes had been created from the old parish of Wrexham by the time of Howell's arrival, new immigration into the existing parish kept its population at 13,000

---

[21] *Wrexham Guardian*, 1 May 1875, p 4. Howell had read the prayers at a weekday evening service previously, at which Mr Jones of Dolgellau preached. There was a larger congregation than usual [*Wrexham Guardian*, 24 Ap 1875 p 5].

[22] Ecclesiastical Commission file on the parish of Wrexham, in the custody of the Representative Body of the Church in Wales.

and upwards. Even after Howell had seen two of the district churches created as new parishes by 1888 the now contracted parish still had the same population, which Howell calculated as one seventeenth of the population of the whole diocese. Two years later the population had grown by another thousand, and it was estimated that one third of the population was engaged in mining.[23]

St Giles parish church had been well restored in 1867. At the same time the pew rents were abolished and new seating installed. This brought the seating capacity of the church down to 1,350, all these being free seats.[24] Consequently Howell's ministry was not burdened with the cares of building and restoration work at the parish church, matters which normally resulted in a draining of spiritual time and resources for the poor incumbent.

Wrexham was also a Nonconformist town, as F W Dillistone makes clear in his biography of the Biblical commentator, C H Dodd, who was brought up in the town during the 1890s. Dodd wrote of this time:

> The bulk of the population was divided between the Established Church and Dissent. The two communities lived side by side, but apart. I do not remember that there was any active animosity, except perhaps at election time; for with us it was certainly true that the Church of England was the "Tory party at its prayers", and Dissent was solidly Liberal. Social distinctions too were involved. The Dissenters, who almost certainly outnumbered the "church people", included most of the shopkeepers, large and small, and the respectable artisans, with a fair quota of minor professional people. The Church held the gentry and the superior professional class and, at the other end of the scale, their immediate dependents and the "poor", who were more or less objects of charity.

They might have said of Howell, using a popular saying of the day noted by Dillistone, "he has left religion and gone to the Church".[25]

Three major issues faced Howell almost as soon as he arrived. He needed to obtain funds in order to pay for his curates, for the

---

[23] Ibid.
[24] Palmer, *Parish Church*, p 53-6; SA/MISC/134, indicates a cost of £4,351.
[25] F W Dillistone, *C H Dodd* [London 1977], pp 28f.

incumbent was still responsible for their stipends. His predecessor was a wealthy man, from an aristocratic family, and had resources of his own, but Howell had to rely at this date almost entirely upon his ecclesiastical income. Secondly there were the difficulties experienced at the Vicarage house. A new house became available, but soon gave rise to considerable legal and financial complications. Basically the house was too expensive for the income of the living, especially for a man with a large family. And thirdly, there was the expressed need to built up and strengthen the work amongst the Welsh-speaking churchpeople. All this, of course, was apart from the work of consolidating the spiritual foundations of the parish, of laying down an "ecclesiastical machinery" to work it properly, and of coping with the ever increasing population who moved into the town and into other areas of the parish where the church was ill-represented. We look at these three issues in turn before we note the parochial round and daily task.

If the parish was numerically large and the income of the vicar seemed to some to be in proportion to its size, the demands on his purse were equally heavy. In 1880 the value of the living was returned to the Ecclesiastical Commissioners as follows: tithe rent commutated £674 (two years previously it had been £732), ten acres of glebe land rented £50, dividends on stock £25 and surplice fees £79. There were no Easter offerings. This came to a total of £828. The annual value of the parsonage house was calculated at £130. The deductions required from this stipend were as follows: a mortgage charge on the vicarage house via Queen Anne's Bounty £70, costs of collecting the tithe £78, land tax £4, and stipends of curates £200. The net value of the parish was thus about £438. The tithe rent charge was uncertain, and the two parishes created out of the original parish had reduced the surplice fees, so that in 1889 Howell estimated his gross income to be £524. From this sum there were deductions of £179 plus £204 for curates' stipends and church expenses. His net income was therefore £140, although at that time he had an additional income of £350 from his St Asaph canonry. But as he was required to be in residence there for three months every year he employed another curate at £140 per annum from this income and thus at his own expense. In 1891 the local paper regarded the gross income of the vicarage as £380, mainly due to the decrease in the value of the tithe rent charge.[26]

It was obviously unfair that the incumbent of any parish of the size of Wrexham, where curates were essential for its running, should be required to pay for them from his own income, instead of his parishioners who benefited from their work. Indeed, it was only at this time that the "offertory movement" was beginning to make an impression on the church at large. The church rate, which had paid for the maintenance of the parish church, had ceased to be assessed after strong Nonconformist objections, and was effectively ended by parliamentary legislation in 1868. Voluntary rates never achieved the same amount of money, and while many parishes helped with a special "curates' fund", and para-church organisations and dioceses gave grants, the ultimate responsibility for ensuring the curates of a parish were paid fell onto the incumbent. In one respect Howell was lucky. His parish was in a mining area, and the Ecclesiastical Commissioners gave *annual* grants for curates in these areas, requiring an incumbent to raise half the stipend himself and lodge it with the commissioners, who would then pay the full stipend to the incumbent to pass onto his curate on a quarterly basis. Howell, in his initial application for a renewal of these grants, made it clear he was prepared to pay the stipend of two of the clergy from his own pocket.

Even before Howell's induction one of the curates of the parish, Davies, who was leaving for a first living, told the Easter vestry that the new vicar would need to draw upon the laity of the parish by some hundreds of pounds in order to pay his curates. If he believed that the congregation would respond to that appeal, indicating that the labourers were worthy of their hire, a writer in a local paper considered him presumptuous in telling the parishioners what the future would hold himself, rather than the new vicar. Indeed, he felt it was more "a bugbear to frighten the parishioners."[27] It was suggested in the next week's paper, however, that the vicar would need two or three more curates than his income would allow.[28]

---

[26] Ecclesiastical Commission file and *Wrexham Advertiser*, 28 Mar 1891, p 7.
[27] *Wrexham Guardian*, 10 Ap 1875, p 7.
[28] Ibid, 17 Ap 1875, p 4.

Howell ended one tradition so far as the clergy were concerned, and replaced it with something better. Until the time of his appointment the parish clergy took no part in the evening services. Instead a lecturer was appointed by a local committee, who also paid him £50 per annum, to take that service. He was normally a local incumbent. This was ended by Howell, and the parish clergy took the evening services, but the committee, one suspects, was retained and utilised to provide the finances for the assistant clergy.[29]

The main grants for his curates came from the Ecclesiastical Commissioners. In 1876 he appealed to their generally stony hearts for a grant for a curate at Esclusham, a hamlet then containing three collieries. Howell then argued that he was finding from his own pocket £200 - out of an income of £665 - for the support of his curates, and felt he could afford no more. He had to wait a year for that grant, and only after making it clear that the equal grant required to make up the full grant to £120 would have to come from his own pocket - that is, an extra £60 on top of his existing commitments. These grants were on an annual basis, and had to be applied for year by year, and there was no guarantee they would be renewed. Thus in 1878 Howell applied for the renewal of two grants of £60 each, without which, he argued, his parishioners would greatly suffer. In no other parish in north Wales did the population, a mining and a bilingual population, increase with the same rapidity, he wrote. It was hard on the clergy to have to face this worry year by year. When Esclusham became a separate parish in 1880 the commissioners withdrew one of the grants. Howell protested. Noting his income as £530 he argued that he still needed to employ another curate, so that from that year onwards he would have to find not £207 but £267 out of his income for this purpose. This was a source of considerable worry to him, so much so that in his reply his normal sense of rectitude left him: "I shall thus be seriously crippled in my efforts to extend the influence of the Church in a parish deplorably neglected during many years ..." In later years he was to point out that the tithe disturbances were seriously reducing his income, and argued that the "new people" coming to

---

[29] Palmer, *Parish Church*, pp 47f.

live in the mining townships of his parish were of a class "little able to provide for themselves".[30]

Of the four or five curates with him in the parish at any one time during his incumbency two seem to have been supported by these grants, with Howell paying from his own pocket the half amount required. Two, sometimes three, were supported by grants from the evangelical Church Pastoral-Aid Society. This society normally gave a grant equivalent to half the stipend required, but asked for a "return grant" for the parish, normally provided by a special collection at a particular service or from subscriptions. It was noted in 1881 that the parish received £180 from the society, but its return grant was but £29.12s..[31]

A letter written by Howell appeared in the annual report of the CPAS in 1885, although it was then stated as being from "the incumbent of a large parish in North Wales". It read:

> In returning the form of application for the renewal of the Society's grants, my first duty is to thank God, humbly and fervently, for his manifest blessings on the Society's operations in this parish; and next to thank the Committee for help, without which the work of the Church in this parish, instead of, as at present, covering the whole area, would have left at least one-third of the population unprovided for. When I came here, nine years ago, there were two churches and one mission-room. Now there are six churches and two mission rooms. Formerly there were *five* Sunday services - now there are within the same area *sixteen* Sunday services, with Bible Classes, week-day services, &c. Formerly there were *three* Sunday Schools, with an attendance of a little over 300; nor we have *ten* Sunday Schools, with an attendance of nearly 1,700. One district, formerly worked by a P.A.S. curate, is now a separate parish, having a church, parsonage, and an endowment of £300 per annum - mainly due to the Society's operations. The parish is the most populous in the six counties of North Wales, being the centre of the N.W. coal and mining district - and the new railways now about commencing will add greatly to the population and the commercial importance of the place. Without the Society's aid I should be helpless; and the services which are now so well appreciated would have to be withdrawn, for, in the present deeply

---

[30] Ecclesiastical Commission file.
[31] *Wrexham Guardian*, 2 Ap 1881, p 5. There was a special CPAS service at St Giles' church.

distressed condition of trade in the town and neighbourhood, it is with the utmost difficulty that I am able to provide for current expenses. With heartiest gratitude for past assistance, and begging a continuance of the Society's grants.[32]

It might be asked how much the parish assisted Howell in these charges. The parish finances were in a bad way, simply because at that time churchpeople were not used to giving money to the church, as Howell was quick to point out. John Bury, the parish churchwarden, wrote to the Easter vestry in 1886 to say that he was personally out of pocket to the sum of £90, having paid the church expenses from his own pocket for many years, finding that the parish funds were not sufficient to reimburse him. The offertories and collections which were made at specific services for church purposes, from 1879 at least, were not equal to the requisites, as he put it, and he noted that costly improvements were needed to the gas supply to the church and to its fabric, which they were unable to afford at that time. It could not have helped that the choristers were refusing to sing gratuitously any more![33] There had however been one stroke of good fortune. A legacy was received from the estate of Peter Walker of £500 for the curates' augmentation fund in 1882. But, we must conclude, with that single exception, Howell did not receive from his parishioners the support he should have had in this direction.

* * * *

The *Wrexham Advertiser* noted that when Howell first came to the parish he and his family had been forced to take apartments in the town while the vicarage was being put in good repair.[34] This house was subsequently to be known as the Old Vicarage. Here Howell and his family lived for two years, and he was "more than once requested by American visitors to be furnished with a relic of the historic building where Bishop Heber wrote the famous hymn."[35] Cunliffe had had to pay £457 in dilapidations for this

---

[32] Fiftieth Report of the Church Pastoral-Aid Society, 1885, p 58.
[33] Wrexham Parish Church Minute book, Clwyd County Record Office, Ruthin, PD/101/1/262.
[34] *Wrexham Guardian*, 24 Ap 1875, p 5.
[35] Newspaper cuttings at the Ruthin record office contained in the Wrexham file, PD/101/1/262.

property, so that the house might be put in order for the new incumbent. Perhaps the sum was so high because he had rented the old vicarage out during his incumbency, living instead in his own house. He also had to pay £230 for chancel repairs, and did so under considerable protest. He pointed out to the governors of Queen Anne's Bounty that these chancel repairs had not been charged for centuries to the vicar, and he had received nothing on his induction in 1826 from his predecessor: "Handing this sum over to my successor I find myself greatly embarrassed, being obliged to expend the whole of the nest egg I had laid by for my old age." He also noted, but would not plead, his handing over of his private property, Llwynisaf, to the governors for the benefit of future incumbents. Howell certified that £345 of this dilapidation money had been spent on putting the old vicarage in order, and the balance of £111 had been placed to the new vicarage account.

This new vicarage was the house mentioned above, which had formerly been the private home of Canon Cunliffe. He had purchased it in 1830 for the sum of £2,500, buying the freehold at a later date. It was a gift which gave much embarrassment to Howell and the church authorities for a number of years.

Llwynisaf with its extensive grounds of eight acres was therefore presented to the Governors of Queen Anne's Bounty, on certain conditions, in order that it might serve as the parsonage house of the parish. The grounds contained a conservatory, hot houses, stables, coach house, cowhouse, stables, piggery; and the house possessed three principal living rooms, the kitchen and the usual offices for a house of this size, five bedrooms and a bathroom on the first floor, and another six bedrooms on the second floor. Together with some cottages the house was valued at £12,000. The original conditions were that Mrs Cunliffe should have a life interest in the property, that Cunliffe should not be charged dilapidations on it, if that was legally possible, and that the governors would meet all the legal costs involved in the transfer. The original stipulation regarding the life interest was exchanged in 1880 for an annuity, paid from the vicarage (that is, parish) income, of £70 per annum, - this apparently was not simply a pension but also a means of avoiding legacy duty on this gift - and it was then agreed that the house should be secured to the living at once, on the understanding that the monies arising from the sale of the old vicarage would be applied to the repairs required on this property.

Howell had already moved into the house by the time this new agreement had been made, and the additional annual payment involved must have come as some surprise, if not annoyance to him, for he was initially obliged to borrow money to meet the first annuity payment. Bishop Hughes wrote that Howell had suffered materially by this exchange. He could have refused to accept the new house, and so rid himself of this additional liability, but he felt that this course would be a severe disadvantage to future incumbents as there could be no comparison between the old and the new houses regarding situation, general convenience and land. Hughes regretted that an agreement which had his full blessing should have entailed such a severe loss on a most deserving clergyman.[36]

Far worse was to come. The old vicarage house was sold for the sum of £1,300,[37] which sum, it had been agreed, would be spent on making Llwynisaf into an acceptable home. But the Ecclesiastical Commissioners, whose brief was to inspect the plans and make their requirements known, insisted that the sum required to make the house into a fit vicarage house was £3,458. This was because the house was found to be infested with dry rot. Cunliffe made it clear that he had already given the house and could offer no more. But this left a deficiency of £2,158. There was another problem. The property was still held by the Bounty governors, and could not be passed over to the Ecclesiastical Commissioners and annexed to the benefice because part of its land was held on lease - for five hundred years - and thus the property was not held in freehold possession. The commissioners made it clear that nothing could be done to the house without their sanction, but insisted that their sanction could only be given when the house had been properly secured to the living! But the Bounty people declined to do this until the whole of the land was freehold. The commissioners also declined to allow the expenditure on the property of any money in their hands arising from the sale of some of the glebe land of the parish, even though

[36] Ecclesiastical Commission file.
[37] The minute book of the parish church suggested £2,325.

the bishop of St Asaph had given permission for Howell to do this and then mortgage the benefice under Gilbert's Act to the Queen Anne's Bounty for that sum of £2,158. That act allowed a mortgage to be taken out on a sum equivalent to three times the annual value of the living.

For a long time it appeared that the whole matter was buried in the administrative procedures of the two authorities concerned. Howell and the churchwardens, understandably concerned at the substantial mortgage required, made alternative suggestions. Could not the house be demolished and a new one built in the grounds? Or could it be sold and the purchase money used to buy a new house and any monies left over made available to augment the benefice? The answer was no in both cases. It was not simply a matter of red tape, but the realisation that the commissioners' requirements for vicarage houses would ensure that the cost of a new vicarage would far exceed the cost of the repairs. "It was a burdensome gift", wrote Howell, for the cost of maintaining the property would be quite beyond the income of the benefice. Bishop Hughes said much the same thing. But the problem remained of providing a comfortable residence for the vicar, without unduly touching on his already too limited income. There was also another worry for Howell. Was he responsible in ecclesiastical law for the cost of dilapidations on this new vicarage? It was eventually settled in his favour after Bishop Hughes' urgent protests about "the anxiety caused to a most worthy and hard working incumbent of a very important parish by the state of uncertainty in which he is left."

Eventually common sense prevailed. The commissioners allowed some modifications in the plans which reduced the estimates significantly, so that the eventual cost of the repair work was £2,531. The small leasehold plot was purchased - though by whom it is not known - and three years after this correspondence had been started the Bounty governors annexed the house to the benefice. Howell was left with paying the bill for counsel's opinion, as well as the expenses of the commission's architect who came from London to inspect the building. By April 1881 the work was completed. The cost of £2,531 was met with the £1,300 realised from the sale of the old vicarage house - though Howell had to pay dilapidations of £110 on it, and a mortgage from Queen

Anne's Bounty of £1,190, the governors meeting the bishop's request that the term be as long as possible. The interest rate was four per cent, the annual installments were £24 on the principal sum and £13 interest, and the mortgage would foreclose in 1923. The incumbents were thus saddled with a mortgage of £1,190, but it was reduced a little when the legacy duty of £182 on part of this bequest was repaid to the Bounty authorities, and applied to this account on Howell's application. His request that an additional £41, still to be paid, should be paid to him, was also allowed, for as he put it, by ensuring that the annuity was paid to Cunliffe out of his own ecclesiastical income, this bequest had been secured for the church. Perhaps the authorities had a heart after all![38]

* * * *

Howell's views on the Welsh language were well known. Dissent had been caused, he believed, by the Church's failure to sympathise with Welsh feeling and to make use of the Welsh language in its ministrations. He also held that effective Welsh preaching within the Church would not only restore many people to it who had been lost to Dissent,[39] but also enable the Welsh language to survive. Though he accepted that many Welsh speakers also spoke English, he realised they still preferred to worship in their native tongue, finding it far more expressive in Christian terms than the thin language of English devotion. Though he offended many within the Church in Wales by publicly expressing these views, they were shared by Bishop Hughes, who obviously had this Welsh element in mind when he appointed Howell to Wrexham.

Although we have noted that Welsh services appear to have been held on Sunday afternoons in St Giles' church, this was simply paying lip service to this need, especially at a time when the number of Welsh speakers was growing in the parish through its

---

[38] Ecclesiastical Commission and Queen Anne's Bounty files. Full payment was made in 1910-11, not without the then vicar, David Davies, suggesting in a letter to QAB that their letters " were more like the communications of a Jewish money lender than the trustees of Church revenues."

[39] *Wrexham Guardian*, 17 July 1875, p 5, noted that many Dissenters attended Howell's preaching ministry, which was probably in English, and castigated those who walked out of a service when they found he was not the designated preacher.

rapid industrialisation. This provision, a second class one, was quite general in Wales at that time. Even in the cathedrals at St Asaph and Bangor the Welsh services were parochial ones, sung by a voluntary choir, rather than cathedral services. Welsh people noted these things. And Sunday afternoon was the time most working men wanted to have their after dinner slumber.[40]

It seems that Howell ended these Sunday afternoon services, and substituted two Sunday services at the Savings Bank - a sort of church institute, though managed by trustees - together with a weekday service and Bible classes. A monthly Welsh communion service was also held in the parish church at 8.00am, as well as a Welsh Sunday School class in the afternoon.[41] He was able to write to Lady Llanover in November 1875 that his Welsh congregation was slowly but steadily growing.[42]

These arrangements could only be temporary. The Welsh people deserved better. Cost was the prohibitive factor, not the will to undertake the work. To cater adequately for the Welsh people a church of their own was needed, plus their own curate. An abortive attempt is noted in 1883, when Howell offered £100 and the bishop £50 towards a site, but nothing came of it.[43] By 1888, with a steadily increasing Welsh congregation, a new church was a necessity. The institute was insufficient now to hold the numbers attending, and, as Howell pointed out, they were using the building only by the kindness of its trustees.

The permission of the Ecclesiastical Commissioners having been obtained, Howell offered part of the vicarage grounds as a site for the new Welsh church, so that the new church would be central and convenient to all. A printed and bilingual appeal for subscriptions suggested the cost of the new church would be £1,700.[44]

All seemed to be well, and then, as usual, problems occurred. This time they were caused by parishioners. Part of the money required for building the new Welsh church was to come from the sale of unconsecrated land, attached to St Mark's Church in the

[40] *North Wales Guardian*, 22 Feb 1890, p 2.
[41] Palmer, *Parish Church*, p 48: Wrexham Directory, 1886, p 11.
[42] Howell to Lady Llanover, 3 Nov 1875, in NLW D Parry-Jones Papers 1979 deposit.
[43] *Wrexham Guardian*, 20 Jan 1883, p 5.
[44] Ecclesiastical Commission file.

town, to the Wrexham, Mold and Connah's Quay Railway Company. The company was to build a new wall for the churchyard, and pay in addition a sum of £280. Bishop Hughes consented to the sale on the agreed stipulation that the money should be used for the benefit of the new Welsh church in Wrexham.

St Mark's Church had been built as a chapel-of-ease or daughter church in 1853 to meet the needs of a growing population. At that date the parish church sat over 2,700 people, so it was alleged, one third of the then population of the parish. But as many of its pews were appropriated or let to families, and those which were available for general use were tucked into obscure corners and galleries, many absented themselves from its services who might otherwise have attended, especially those of the poorer classes. It was argued, therefore, that a new church was required, one with free seating, which would be available for the working class inhabitants of that area. Sir Watkin Williams-Wynn gave the land, money was obtained by subscription, and a grant given by the Ecclesiastical Commissioners of £300 on the condition that all seats were free and that the church would seat eight hundred adults. This was later reduced to seating for 615 adults and 146 children. The final cost was over four thousand pounds.

The church, built for the poor, never achieved its projected parochial status, with the result that its congregation appears to have had a corporate inferiority complex about its position in the parish. Its congregation were no longer the poor for whom the church was designed, but the wealthy middle-class of the town. A letter written by a member of the church in the local paper relating to Howell's appointment possibly reveals this. The parish church people, he wrote, treated the St Mark's people as if they were not Christians or even Dissenters. He hoped that the new vicar would break through this prejudice and come to their services.[45]

This background helps us to explain the great row which developed over the use of this St Mark's money for the Welsh church, although another part of the problem lay in a lack of communication, the bishop being seriously ill at the time. The

---

[45] *Wrexham Guardian*, 27 Mar 1875, p 7.

good people of St Mark's could not see why this money was not allocated to them; after all it came from the sale of their land. And it was quite clear they needed it. Money was required for improving the lighting and heating of the church and for general improvements and repairs to the premises. The cost of the new lighting was £80, which Howell felt could be found by some effort on the part of the church members. They were reminded in the same letter that the bishop had only consented to the sale of the land on condition that the money should go towards the Welsh church. If the money was not used in this way it would be capitalised and the interest used to augment the income of the parish and thus the incumbent's stipend. There was no way in which St Mark's Church would get this money!

The people of St Mark's Church thought otherwise. The vicar's financial zeal was misplaced they argued, and his desire for a Welsh church greatly mistaken. If the Welsh needed a Church, let them build it themselves! There was no necessity for such a church in Wrexham. All the Welsh spoke English! The vicar was too rigid a dictator in parish matters; he only came to St Mark's three times in a year. They wanted a clergyman of their own, one who would take an interest in them! Instead the vicar was sending "young men, highly respectable young men", but they were sent "to try their prentice hands on that congregation". It was wrong that the older men of the congregation had to listen Sunday by Sunday to these young men. Perhaps Howell should have told them to follow their own reasoning and provide their own clergy at their own expense! He must have smiled when he left the parish and the St Mark's people complimented him on the excellent curates he had obtained for them.

All this controversy blew up at a vestry meeting in January 1889 at St Mark's. Howell was diplomatically absent, and none of the other clergy were present. In Howell's defence it was pointed out that many newcomers to Wrexham spoke Welsh and desired Welsh services. It was unfair that they had to worship in a room in which everything from vaccination to Dorcas meetings took place. There were a number of successful Welsh chapels in the town, while the number of those worshipping in the Savings Bank services were as numerous as those at St Mark's church. Neither could their church be regarded as a poor man's church any longer.

Although a minority at the meeting felt St Mark's church should assist the new Welsh church in this particular way, the majority were opposed to such a plan, and consequently petitioned the Ecclesiastical Commissioners for the money to be granted to them to be used for their own purposes. Their petition was refused. Thus in May 1890 the new Welsh church of St David was consecrated, the commission's architect certifying that it was sufficiently well built to be a parish church if that was ever required. It sat 224 on open benches and 26 in the choir.[46]

The whole episode illustrates the anti-Welsh feeling within the town and parish. It was suggested this was because Wrexham lay on the English side of Offa's Dyke. One may also note the resentment of a daughter church at its apparent neglect by the vicar of the parish. But St Mark's was but one of many churches in that parish, and Howell had to sort out his own priorities accordingly.

* * * *

The strength of Howell's ministry in Wrexham as in Cardiff lay in his preaching and direct pastoral work. St Giles' church would be filled, tradition relates, with 1,600 people, Sunday by Sunday, when he was preaching. To obtain a good seat one needed to be there an hour beforehand, and it was standing room only for those who arrived even half an hour later. His sermons were topical and direct. His New Year mottoes, distributed to every parishioner, were equally direct. The 1879 theme was about obligation, and in 1885 self examination in moral and spiritual life. The message ended with an expectation of the second coming of the Lord. The following year he offered three divine rules for daily life:

Do all to the glory of God: 1 Corinthians 10.31

Do all in the name of the Lord Jesus: Colossians.3.17

Do it heartily as unto the Lord: Colossians 3.23

These cards made it plain that he was available for spiritual counsel and instruction either at the close of each service or at the vestry, in his own home, or even in their own homes.[47]

---

[46] Letters in the Ecclesiastical Commission file: *Wrexham Advertiser*, 23 Mar 1891, p 6, and 26 Jan 1889, pp 5f.

[47] Material in the Wrexham Church file at Ruthin, PD/101/1.373.

Evidence for his spiritual concern for people is found in a number of related areas. One was to offer formal ways in which people could commit their lives to Christ. His preaching ministry declared Christ as the way, as a friend, and emphasised the need for repentance and the need for a Saviour. He could write of the watchnight services which he probably instituted, and which appear to have brought people into St Giles' church who hardly ever attended a place of worship, that these services had been more signally blessed than any other service in previous years. It was his prayer that in this year, it was 1882, as in previous years, people "would testify that their first turning to God was at this solemn service held at midnight."[48]

He could also write to the young people of the parish, as in March 1889 about the rite of confirmation:

> When rightly regarded, Confirmation is nothing else, and nothing less, than an act of voluntary and deliberate self-surrender and self-consecration to the service of God; and, however much abused or misused, in some instances, it is eminently useful as a public profession of faith, as a time of prayer for the outpouring of the Holy Spirit on young Christians, and as an opportunity for receiving systematic instruction from the Clergy of the Church. In this light do I commend the Rite to your devout consideration, and equally to the consideration of your parents and employers, from whom, I trust, you will receive every encouragement. Thousands in every age have found it a rich means of grace to their souls. From it many of the most eminent saints have dated their conversion to God. And what it has been to others, it may be to you; yea, it cannot fail to be to you if you will only come to it earnestly seeking and expecting the Divine blessing. Such an opportunity may never again offer itself to some of you. I would, therefore, "beseech you by the mercies of God" to consecrate yourselves to His service. That the merciful Lord may guide you aright in this matter - that He may richly bless you with the Confirming influences of his Holy Spirit, "to establish, strengthen, and settle you" in all that relates to the Christian character, is the heart's desire and prayer of
>
> Your faithful friend and pastor, David Howell.

---

[48] *North Wales Guardian*, 6 Jan 1883, p 8.

In Easter 1884 a mission was held to the parish. It was announced by a pastoral letter from Howell sent to every home in the parish on the previous New Year's day. In this letter he shows his directness and boldness about spiritual matters, a boldness which led to much individual spiritual blessing as well as to the upbuilding of the Church in his parish:

> As in thought, I survey the parish, and my mind passes from street to street, and house after house in each street, I am filled with anxious reflections, which I must take leave to unburden to you. Side by side with much that is gratifying and encouraging - families striving to live in the fear of God, and "working righteousness" - children carefully trained in their duty towards God and their neighbour - the Lord's Day devoutly observed - family worship reverently conducted - healthy literature in the parlour and kitchen - work for Christ cheerfully undertaken - the "battle of life" bravely fought from day to day in the strength of God - side by side with all this, and much besides, for which I thank God and take courage, there is much that fills my heart with most anxious concern for not a few of you. The contrast between the number of those who come to the House of God, and those who come to the Lord's Table, is such that I am often constrained to exclaim with the Prophet of old, "Who hath believed our report? and to whom is the arm of the Lord revealed?" "I have laboured in vain; I have spent my strength for nought, and in vain; yet surely my judgement is with the Lord, and my work with my God." Week after week am I privileged to proclaim God's message of mercy and love to perishing sinners, but with results which often fill my soul with sorrow. And the question continually occurs to me - Where does the fault lie? What is it that hinders? Especially is this the case at the beginning of the New Year, which almost to a certainty will be the last year to some whose eyes now rest on these words. Would that I could persuade each of you who have not yet surrendered your hearts to the Lord to put to yourselves the question, directly and pointedly, and to keep pressing it until you are able to answer it, Why am I what I am? Why am I not, in the full and true sense of the word, a *Christian*?

He asked various questions of such people in the hope that it might assist the "undecided and procrastinating" into surrendering their lives to Christ. He then addressed himself to the Christians of the parish:

> But there are others also among you who are often in my thoughts - soldiers and servants of Christ, children of the Church, bound by every obligation of duty, and of gratitude, to be active, self-denying, and wholehearted in God's service. As communicants, district visitors, Sunday School teachers, choir-members, and wardens of the Church, you are bound and pledged by as solemn a covenant as man can enter into with God, to give up yourselves to His service, and to walk before Him in holiness and righteousness from day to day. At the beginning of a New Year, you would do well to examine your relationship with God, and how far you are discharging your duties to Him by the devotion of your time, gifts, wealth, and influence to His service. "*Examine your selves, whether ye be in the faith: prove your own selves. Know ye not your own selves how that Jesus Christ is in you, except ye be reprobates?*" was an Apostolic exhortation to Apostolic converts. ... Moreover, some of the most eminent saints of God have found it helpful at the beginning of a New Year to make a formal fresh surrender of themselves to God, and to write out and sign a renewed covenant with Him. To do this is worse than useless if it be not done with the most whole-hearted sincerity, and the most solemn determination, with God's help, to carry it out. But it helps to give force and definiteness in one's good resolutions if they are shaped after something of this kind.
>
> "In the strength of the Lord" -
>
> 1. I consecrate myself unreservedly to Him who has redeemed me, that at all times He may appoint me my place and work, and that, attentive to the promptings of His Holy Spirit, I may cheerfully obey Him in all things.
>
> 2. Trusting in Jesus Christ as my personal Saviour, I will expect the more abundant life of love, the fullness of the Spirit, and the power from on high, which will enable me courageously, tenderly, and wisely to do my utmost to "win souls for Christ."
>
> 3. I will be a witness for Christ - viz: that His word is true. His atoning sacrifice and intercession availing for all that believe, and that His "service is perfect freedom."
>
> 4. I will frequently "wait upon the Lord" in the ordinances of His Church, and especially in the Sacrament of His Body and

Blood, that my strength may be renewed, my graces quickened, and that my spiritual nature may be kept full to overflowing.

5. Resting on the promise - "My word shall not return unto Me void" - I will daily search the Holy Scriptures, and meditate therein, that the word of Christ may dwell in me "richly in all wisdom".

6 I will "watch for souls," that, as I have opportunity, I may either speak, or write, to someone of Christ and His salvation, and of the duty and privilege of all who are on "the Lord's side" to be "workers together with Him."

For those who found this covenant too binding - though he suggested it should be binding on every Christian, he offered some rules which could be solemnly adopted at the beginning of a new year. However, Howell made it absolutely clear that rules

are only of use when there is unreserved heart loyalty to Christ, and an honest "endeavour to follow the blessed steps of His most holy life." Without this the best of rules will only make man a religious machine - a thing of attitudes and platitudes - without spiritual force, because without spiritual life. Be it never forgotten that Religion is the life of a saved man - not the efforts of an unsaved man to get saved. Work for God must be work from life - not for life; and salvation must be first of all received, possessed, and enjoyed, before it can be "worked out with fear and trembling."

Here are the rules:

1 To read a portion of Holy Scripture every day.
2 To pray morning and evening, and to make special mention of my Parish, Church, and Clergy.
3 To observe the Lord's Day strictly, and to attend Church morning and evening.
4 To attend Divine Worship as often as possible during the week.
5 To attend a Bible Class, or Sunday School, and do all I can to induce others to do so.
6 Never to neglect the Sacrament of the Lord's Supper.
7 To do some special work for Christ every week.

A *Return Card* has also survived from this mission. It requested people to sign if they wished to attend a confirmation class, become a communicant or Sunday school teacher, join a Bible class, mothers' meeting, or a number of other such organisations which were listed, or to speak on any of the above subjects to the vicar.[49]

Six years after its foundation by Wilson Carlile, the Church Army was invited to Wrexham by Howell. The new movement was regarded then with some suspicion in church circles. The Church Army captains were to play a significant role in parish life of Wrexham. By 1891 members of the Church Army ran the mission hall in Hill Street, and also held services at the Beast Market and at two other mission centres at 8.00pm each Sunday night.[50] The door to door pastoral visiting of the parish, the Bible classes and Sunday Schools, and even the day schools, were also seen by Howell as extending the mission of the Church into the community. And, of course, in much of this work Howell needed a trained laity to assist in these areas of parochial life.

Howell, when he arrived in the parish, found that there was a parochial organisation on which he could build. The Wrexham Clergy and Laity Visiting Association had been formed in the previous year. Its purpose was to visit in the parish, house by house, and enquire into circumstances, to read a portion of Scripture, and to give advice. The visitors met once a month to compare notes and to receive encouragement. This was a work which Howell extended and combined with temperance work. Indeed he was rather critical of the society in 1881, when in seven months 130 visitors had only managed to produce five temperance pledges.[51]

A Bible class was formed by 1878, and this was well attended by both church people as well as by Nonconformists, even though it was conducted by the clergy. By 1881 there were three each week in the parish church, including a Welsh one, and a Sunday afternoon class at St Mark's Church. Five years later the work had expanded considerably. St Giles had separate classes for men, women and children, while a prayer meeting was held after the Sunday evening services at the Savings Bank. In October of that year, 1886, Howell sent out a general invitation for people to join these classes, pointing out that:

---

[49] From material in the Wrexham Church file at Ruthin.
[50] *North Wales Guardian*, 15 Mar 1890, p 5.
[51] *Wrexham Guardian*, 13 Feb 1875, p 5: *Wrexham Advertiser*, 5 Mar 1881, p 5.

All classes are invited to attend; and those who have hitherto attended, are earnestly requested to do all in their power to secure the attendance of others. It involves no more labour to conduct a Class of one hundred than of one-fourth the number; and it is usually found that the larger the attendance, the greater is the interest excited. The importance of being grounded in the knowledge of God's Word - not simply of its historical facts but of the great principles which underlie and penetrate all Revelation - was never greater than in this our own day. At a time when religious restlessness and distraction so generally prevail - when Christians are so easily led astray by novelties and vagaries, self-assertion taking the place of authority, and speculation being mistaken for originality - it is surely a matter of the deepest importance that an intelligent and well-balanced faith in the only source of infallible truth should be diligently cultivated. Moreover, an intelligent knowledge of the Word of God is essential to a solid and enlightened Christian experience. Without such experience, what is there to sustain the soul in a time of fiery temptation, or of heavy affliction, in a season of mental perplexity, or of spiritual depression?

In the following extract from that same letter it is clear that Howell regarded these Bible classes as an essential part of his ministry:

I have no deeper conviction than that the almost incredible ignorance of Holy Scripture on the part of so many Christians, is one of the greatest, if not *the* greatest, of the evils and perils of the present day. As some remedy for this condition of things, Bible Classes have been found eminently useful. They offer a suitable opportunity for a simple and familiar exposition of the Scriptures of truth; as well as for clearing up apparent difficulties, for removing prejudices, and for setting forth the harmony there is between the teachings of God's Holy Word and the Articles and Offices of the Church. May I not add that to spend one hour in the week, in such an exercise, can hardly fail, under God, to strengthen and stimulate the spiritual energies of those who attend? But in order that a Bible Class may produce its full measure of good results, it is essential (1) that it should *take precedence of all other engagements*, and that nothing short of unavoidable necessity should justify absence from it: (2) that it should be distinctly regarded as a *"means of grace"* , and a blessing be prayerfully *expected* from it: and (3) that the portion of Scripture read be always carefully *digested*, so that it may take root in the memory, and be deeply impressed on the heart.[52]

The Victorian age was an age of Sunday schools, and it is not surprising that this institution flourished in Wrexham. By 1881 there were over 1,500 children attending the three Church Sunday schools, with an average attendance of 1,350. By 1885 there were ten Sunday schools in the parish, and in the combined procession of that year the number was so great that it took twenty minutes for the procession to pass a given spot. Two bands accompanied it. And of course there were the tea and sports thereafter. Catechising took place on the first Sunday afternoon in the month at St Mark's Church, and later on a quarterly basis at St Giles, and for this purpose Howell prepared a monthly syllabus for the pupils. This was given out at the monthly meeting of the Sunday school teachers, when, as one Dr Williams reported to the St Asaph Diocesan Conference, Howell "in the kindest manner possible" took them into his confidence and sought their advice.[53] This may seem to be a paragraph of statistics, but it is God alone who will judge this work of teaching and evangelising amongst the young in this way.

Bishop Hughes' predecessor in the see of St Asaph, Thomas Vowler Short, was the great pioneer of church schools not only in his diocese, but throughout the Church of England. He regarded them as the right arm of parochial life, particularly as they taught church doctrine and the catechism within their syllabus, and the local clergyman had open access to them. It was often a condition of entry that pupils should also attend the church service on Sunday. Many clergy rightly declined to impose this rule, although it was a requirement for a grant from the National Society for Educating the Poor in the Principles of the Church of England, to give the National Society its full title. Forster, of the 1870 Education Act, is said to have remarked that if all the dioceses had been as well provided with church schools as St Asaph, then his act which set up board or state schools would not have been necessary. This act allowed a "conscience clause" allowing pupils to opt out

---

[52] Drawn from material in the Wrexham Church file at Ruthin.
[53] *Wrexham Guardian*, 12 Feb 1881, p 5; 9 Ap 1881, p 5; Haul, 1885, p 254; *Report of the St Asaph Diocesan Conference*, 1881, pp 36-7.

of church attendance and teaching, for it accepted that in many areas the church school was the only school available for the children of churchpeople and Nonconformists alike. These National Schools cost money, and often that money came from the pockets of the clergy. Though there were grants from the National Society and government grants, the latter depended on meeting the inspectors' requirements regarding buildings and equipment, the provision of teachers and the number of pupils. After 1870 the state grant system became one characterised by the expression "payment by results".

There were a number of church schools in the parish of Wrexham when Howell arrived; one at least seems to have been a dual-purpose building, forming a place for worship on Sundays. By 1881 it was made clear that the continuation of state grant-aid depended on the provision of new buildings and equipment to replace the old National Schools with their 800 pupils. Although Howell advertised that the existence of these church schools saved the ratepayers of Wrexham considerable sums of money, his hope of receiving substantial subscriptions from the townspeople failed to materialise, and he had to organise an appeal for £4,000, of which £1,400 was already in hand, and to which he gave himself £100. Had he not raised this money the schools would have passed to the secular School Board and the distinctive church teaching they gave would have been lost.

Howell's appeal to his parishioners on this occasion was a characteristic one:

> The present supply of school accommodation in the town of Wrexham is deficient, and must forthwith be supplemented. We have no alternative. How this is to be done, is a question which may admit of differences of opinion; but I trust that I shall be able to point out to you the best way of doing it. We must not, however, for a single moment lose sight of the fact, to which I would again give emphatic prominence, and I therefore repeat it, that the thing is to be done, and must be done. If we do not do it ourselves, it will be done for us - in all probability less efficiently, and in all certainty at a far larger cost. The schools we now have, were erected a long time since - no less than 40 years ago - at a time when the views on educational matters, which are now universal, were held only by a very few. They are badly situated, and ill-adapted for the purpose to which they are applied. They have no class-

rooms, such are now held to be essential to the proper working of all public elementary schools. They have been condemned by inspector after inspector. The strain which the accommodation they supply is required to bear, is too great for their capacity; and in order to satisfy the requirements of the law, new and suitable school buildings must be erected. ...

Surely now is the moment for the proverbial "stitch in time." A comparatively slight effort will save them [the ratepayers] from the lasting and heavy expense which will inevitably be the result of allowing the deficiency in school accommodation to be made good by calling in the powers of the School Board, at present limited to enforcing attendances only. ...

The means by which the educational requirements of the town are now met, are, as you all know, acceptable to all the inhabitants. All the existing schools work together in perfect harmony, to the satisfaction of the community at large, with an entire absence of anything like irritation, and at a comparatively small expense. It would therefore be most deeply to be regretted if anything should occur to mar the existing harmony, or to increase the burden of local taxation. ...

If we wish to educate our children to the highest, the best, the only true sense of the term, then must we do our utmost to bring them up in the faith and fear of God. Mere secular knowledge is indeed a power; but it is one which, when divorced from religious principle, is far more likely to be enlisted on the side of evil than of good in that struggle which awaits every child amongst us who may live to become a man. ... The child of today is the man of the future; and the character of the next generation, the well-being of society, and it may be the fate of our country, will mainly depend on the success of the efforts we and others are now making to bring up children in the nurture of the Lord.

Four years later a new school was opened at Madeira Hill, at a cost of over £5,000, to replace the old schools in the Beast Market, which were sold, and £1,500 borrowed to meet the additional costs. By 1891 £482 of this loan was still outstanding, a considerable part of which, I believe, was owed to Howell.[54] As

---

[54] SA/DR/51, fol 101; *Report of the St Asaph Diocesan Conference,* 1881, p 39. The position of church schools in the town was complicated by the existence of the Wrexham School Board, on which the church party always managed to elect a number of church representatives: see G V Williams, "Wrexham School Board Elections, 1871-1901", *Denbighshire Historical Society Transactions,* 40 [1991] 43-59. A costume bazaar, in which people and stalls were dressed in national costumes and colours, took place to raise money for these projects [SA/DR/50, fol 143].

he was to state later, the greatest sacrifices of his life had been made for the church schools.⁵⁵

There were a number of other activities in the parish which fell into this broad category of mission. The Savings Bank has already been mentioned. Its name appears to have come from its use as a "penny bank", but its premises were also used by a wide variety of organisations, most connected with the parish, and for a number of years Welsh services were held there.

Mothers' meetings, unconnected with any formal organisation started by Mrs Sumner, were presumably established in the parish by Howell. Their brief was wider than that of the Mothers' Union. They were concerned with all kinds of domestic interests to enable the poor to be better housekeepers and parents, as well as having an evangelical imput at the same time. In 1891 there were five such meetings held on a weekly basis, meeting at the Savings Bank, the Mission Room and the Free School amongst other places.⁵⁶ There is notice of a pleasure trip arranged for the members in 1885. All proceeded to Wynnstay, where Sir Watkin looked after the beef and Lady Williams-Wynn the cups, as a report put it, and Howell took a service and gave an address.⁵⁷

In that same year of 1885 there is another report of the fifth annual bazaar and Christmas tree entertainment. It was hoped that £200 would be raised by it, partly to assist the parochial funds, and partly to provide warm clothing for the poor. A working party met throughout the year on Friday afternoons in order to prepare the necessary goods.

On a wider front Howell gave much energy to promoting the temperance movement. A branch of the Church of England Temperance Society met fortnightly at the Savings Bank, and Howell was instrumental in providing an alternative to the public houses of the town. This was the Bromfield Social, Reading and Recreational Club, which was held at the Central Coffee Palace in Wrexham. "It is good to see so many young men attending" it, said Howell in 1893, as he went on to note the evils of drink and

---

⁵⁵ *Record*, 23 Ap 1897, p 398.
⁵⁶ *Wrexham Advertiser*, 10 Sept 1881, p 8; Ecclesiastical commission files; Report on the Wrexham deanery, 1888, SA/RD/44. A Friday night school is also mentioned in the *Wrexham Guardian*, 19 Sept 1881, p 4.
⁵⁷ *Haul*, 1885, p 316.

to express the hope that power would be given to the new parish and district councils to establish similar alternatives to the public houses.[58] In his evidence to the Royal Commission on the Operation of the Sunday Closing (Wales) Act, 1881, which met in Wrexham in 1889, Howell noted that the act had given a decided improvement to the tone of Sunday in his parish, had led to an increased workforce on Mondays, a steady increase in depositors at the various savings banks and friendly societies, and had been of much advantage to the home life of many of his parishioners.[59] Another aspect of his concern for society is shown by his use of a legacy left him by a Mrs Ann Berry in 1876. It was used to provide a parochial nurse for the parish, who probably acted as a midwife as well as caring for the infirm and housebound amongst the poor who could not otherwise afford medical care.[60]

* * * *

As David Howell wrote his annual letter to the Ecclesiastical Commissioners in 1886, requesting the continuation of his curates' grants, he saw fit to provide them with a statement of what had been achieved over the past ten years. Obviously his intention was in part to illustrate that the grants they had given had been wisely and profitably used, and therefore should be continued without interruption. It was remarkable what had been achieved in those ten years, 1875-86, but when the figures quoted for 1891 are laid alongside these, the result is quite outstanding, and there can be no surprise that these figures were quoted over and over again in church defence meetings as an indication of the good work and progress of the Church in Wales. They will be summarised here in tabular form:

---

[58] *Wrexham Advertiser*, 1 Ap 1983, p 8.
[59] *Report of the Royal Commission on the Welsh Sunday Closing Act* [London 1890], pp 301-4.
[60] Dodd, *History of Wrexham*, pp 262f.

	1875	1888	1891
number of clergy	3	9	10
number of churches	2	7	9
number of mission rooms	2	3	5
number of Sunday services	7	19	21
number of monthly celebrations	5	14	22
number of Sunday Schools	5	15	14
number of Easter communicants	128	560	835

These figures took into account the three new parishes which had been taken from the original parish of Wrexham, during Howell's incumbency: Esclusham in 1879, Bwlchgwyn in 1880 and Rhosddu in 1886.

As he continued to write to the Commissioners, Howell mentioned the Bible Classes, the mothers' meetings, and other agencies to promote temperance, thrift, mission and education. All this, he asserted, was evidence of the renewed life of the Church in the Principality, and much of this was due, "under God, to the assistance so kindly and generously given me by your Board." Further figures were quoted in 1891. Since 1875, within the boundaries of the then parish, six churches had been built or restored, two vicarages built, six day or Sunday Schools built or restored, £2,637 collected for foreign mission, £7,742 for home mission, £6,136 for local causes and £4,121 for the parish schools. Indeed, it was later calculated that over £100,000 had been raised between those years for church purposes within the parish, although this must be qualified by remembering that the value of land given by local landowners, who often contributed handsomely to the cost of new buildings, is also included.[61] But even with this qualification it is an impressive figure.

* * * *

---

[61] Ecclesiastical Commission file; the report on the RD of Wrexham in NLW, SA/RD/44: *The Report of the Royal Commission into the Church of England in Wales*, V pp 241f; the cutting, "Church Extension in Wrexham 1875-1891" at Wrexham Public Library, parish file; and *Bye-gones*, Dec 1881, p 351, which noted a religious census in Wrexham of that year.

The parish of Wrexham must have been as demanding as Cardiff, but by 1881 Howell's work was being recognised. In that year he was offered a "valuable living" in the diocese of Lichfield by Mrs Heywood Lonsdale of Gredington. His health had broken down in that year, and he had been required to take a convalescing tour in the Mediterranean.[62] But when it was known that Howell had been offered this living, and was about to accept it, a petition "numerously signed by his parishioners" requested him to remain. And so he did, even though more battles had to be fought and labours given, as we have seen.[63]

Appointed rural dean of Wrexham in 1882, Howell made use of the deanery organisation to promote an active spirit of co-operation between clergy and laity. The minute book of the deanery association records debates on such subjects as the extension of the episcopate, the holding of daily services, the better observance of the Lord's Day, or the imperfect character of the Welsh Book of Common Prayer. A vigorous Sunday School teachers' association was already in existence, while deanery choral festivals were commenced. In this work he was ably assisted by a local barrister, Trevor Parkins, later to be his warden at Gresford.[64] Though this work must have added considerably to his burdens - for in addition he was away for three months of the year in residence at St Asaph - he obviously felt it extremely important. When he finally left the deanery he wrote in reply to its letter of good wishes upon his appointment to St Davids:

> I am, as you know, a strong advocate of anything that promotes intercourse and an exchange of opinion between clergy and laity, if only that it tends to correct the official habit of thought to which the clerical vocation renders us liable, besides that it helps to arrest that exclusiveness which is almost inseparable from isolation. I believe the Pulpit would often be more edifying if it only knew what was passing in the Pew, and if only regarded in this light, I have always felt that the Deanery Association has ground sufficient to justify its existence ...[65]

---

[62] *Wrexham Guardian*, 5 Nov 1881. p 5. His son preached for him.
[63] Ibid, 31 Dec 1881, p 5. It was probably the parish of Ightfield, worth £344 pa.
[64] The RD minute book is at the Ruthin Record Office, PD/100/1/253.
[65] Howell to Trevor Parkin, 23 Nov 1897, contained in the above.

In 1891, with his wife grievously ill, and knowing that the duties of his archdeaconry (to which he had been appointed in 1889) were interfering with his work as vicar of Wrexham, Howell accepted the smaller living of Gresford. An editorial in the local paper wrote that he would leave the parish with the most ungrudging good-will of all, having given it high and demanding standards. He had preserved good, indeed, cordial, relationships between church and chapel. It would be a hard task to follow such a man.[66] Howell, realising this, wrote to his parishioners, making it clear that not only had he been extremely happy in the parish, but also pointing out that "the advent of a new incumbent is calculated to call forth energies and interests, now, it may be, lying dormant." He continued: "A change of ministry has often brought into existence new activity, zeal and enterprise in many a parish." Regarding himself as a pioneer, Howell was able, with his profound sense of the providence of God arising from his calvinistic theology, to realise that "one man soweth, and another reapeth", thus clearing the way for a successor of higher gifts, as he put it.[67] Such was Howell's parting prayer for the parish which had been the scene of his labours for the previous sixteen years.

Years later, after Howell's death, his memory was still held in such regard that a window dedicated to his memory was unveiled at St Giles' church in 1904. This depicted the Sermon on the Mount. Canon Fletcher, his successor in the parish and later archdeacon, then gave what was reported as "an eloquent panegyric on the late dean". It included these words about his ministry in Wrexham:

> The ministry of Dean Howell ... in this town, was, to his mind, characterised by three great points. First of all there was his tremendous industry. That was seen, of course, in the Churches and schools that he built in that parish. But it was seen also in his indefatigable labours. He (the Vicar) had been told that the colliers as they went to work in early morning would often see the Vicar's gas lighted in his study, and know that he had begun to work for

[66] *Wrexham Advertiser*, 14 Mar 1891, p 14. Canon Richardson of Corwen had declined the living previously, ibid, 7 Mar 1891, p 5.
[67] Quoted in a newspaper cutting at Ruthin Record Office, PD/101/1/262; SA/DR/50, fol 142.

them, perhaps on his knees, before they went forth to their daily toil. Secondly, there was his pastoral visitation. There his deep earnestness, his true sympathy, his large heartedness, won for him a ready entrance into the homes, aye more, into the hearts of his parishioners which made them glad to come up to the House of God and listen to his message. And then, last of all, there was his preaching; above all his fervent eloquence drew thousands to the Saviour's side. None of them could forget the last occasion when he preached within those walls. The sight of that great crowd, and the remembrance of how hundreds were turned away from the Church's door, and the fervid earnestness and the flowing eloquence of the old man whose steps were nearing the grave, would live with them as long as life remained.

... It was clear that the really great man gave his service for his fellow creatures. He stepped out in their lives and was a revelation to them of what human nature could be; his very presence amongst them was a rebuke to all their meanness. He made them ashamed of themselves, and was a summons to them to rise out of their dead selves to higher things. He was the stimulus to loftier thought and action. A great man really served the world by his teachings. True greatness consisted not in anything outside us, but in ourselves; in what we really were in our characters, in our thoughts, in our motives, in our lives.

Others also spoke of Dean Howell in that same ceremony. Mr S Moss, M.P., said that "Churchmen and Nonconformists alike ... all revered and loved the late Dean Howell." Another wrote:

> His eloquence, earnestness and fervour as a preacher, and the charm of manner which made him almost the idol of all classes are characteristics which are well known. His sympathies and kindly actions were not alone for Church people - they were freely extended to all sections and classes. His lamented death, therefore, was not a loss to the Church alone, but to the community in general, by whom his memory will ever be cherished.[68]

* * * *

[68] Contained in *The Memorial Window to the late Very Revd David Howell in Wrexham Parish Church,* 1904, pp 6, 8f, 13.

Wrexham was to remember David Howell in many ways. There was the Howell who had built up the parish and given it a renewed spiritual life. As late as 1976 one Silin, writing a column in the local paper, asserted that he had increased the influence of the Church in the town to a degree unknown before and afterwards.[69] For many he had become a spiritual father, having pointed them to Christ as Lord and Saviour. There was the pastoral work as well, which, in the address of congratulation given him on being made archdeacon, was described in terms of "unwearied attention to his pastoral labours ..., his preaching gifts, his devotion to the work of the ministry ..., done with a cheerful energy and courage, and the single purpose of promoting for the spiritual and temporal welfare of his parishioners.[70] He would be remembered, too, for endeavouring to encourage laypeople to assist in the work of the church, both in his parish, with its numerous bands and group of lay workers, and within the deanery.[71] And they would remember too that he had suffered much - as all sensitive people must - from the bitterness his reforming zeal had caused within the parish. But if he was a spiritual leader, he was also a warm and human personality. This is clear from the tributes paid him after his death by those who remembered his ministry at Wrexham. *An Old Resident* wrote in the columns of the local newspaper of Howell's affable manner and facial smile which endeared him to all classes, especially the poorer brethren, into whose homes his presence and sympathy "have ever been warmly welcomed".[72] It comes out too in his love for his dog, Lion. When Lion died in 1889 Howell published a broadside in his memory. Lion would lead the servants into prayers each morning, and when Howell came home "at the close of a long day of exhausting duties, when jaded and depressed by the sight of miseries and sufferings which I could neither alleviate nor relieve, I have been met at my door with such a welcome as a prince might have envied." Writing to one, "my dear neighbour", who thought this was a bit much, he told him that his dog had

[69] *Wrexham Leader*, 10 Sept 1976, p 15.
[70] *North Wales Guardian*, 26 Ap 1890, p 5.
[71] W Roberts, vicar of Llangower, Bala, speaking at the 1887 St Asaph Diocesan Conference [Report, p 22], regarded Howell as the best organiser in Wales who was able to find work for anyone every day of the week.
[72] SA/DR/54, fol 330, a letter to the *North Wales Guardian*.

"more Christian qualities than many Christians he saw around him". Fifty years after his death they remembered Howell taking Lion into the pulpit of St Giles' church with him, and saying, "Everybody needs a friend. Lion is my friend." And then he went on to speak about Jesus Christ as the friend of all.[73] But it was this dog too that went courting on Sunday, and received his master's comment: "a parson's dog!".[74]

Howell's ministry at Wrexham challenged lives and led people to Christ. And then he challenged people to use the gifts they had to offer for the work of building up the Kingdom of God. Howell was not unique in this field, many other clergy were equally concerned about using the laity of the Church effectively, and all clergy, in theory at least, must be concerned about seeing people reborn to spiritual life. But this fact does not diminish Howell's achievement. It must not be forgotten that his parish was in one of the heartlands of militant Welsh Nonconformity, nor should we assume that this work was easy. Writing to his friend Nathan in 1884 he said, "I sometimes long for a post where I should have less work, or rather less worry, than is inescapable from the charge of 14,000 with numerous pecuniary responsibilities, and endless duties. I long for more rest for quiet thoughts, reading and devotion ..."[75]

If Howell thought that such time for rest and devotion was to be given him in his next parish of Gresford he was rudely shaken. For there he met what must have been the most difficult period of his life.

---

[73] Wrexham Library, file on the parish church: *'Lion', a Faithful Friend, died 10 July 1889*. The file also contains a cutting from the Leader of 10 Mar 1953 regarding the tombstone.
[74] Howell to Daniel Silvan Evans, 28 May 1883, NLW MS Cwrt Mawr 903B, fol 9.
[75] Howell to Nathan, 24 June 1884, NLW MS 987B, fol 97.

The Disestablishment Controversy

The campaign to disestablish the Anglican Church in Wales, which was formally started by the 1862 Swansea conference of the Liberation Society, reached a momentum by the 1880s. In the next chapter we describe one of the consequences of that campaign as it affected Howell. However, before we can relate that event, or understand his position, it is necessary to assess his views not only about the Church in Wales, but also with regard to this campaign to disestablish the Welsh Church.

Few doubted that David Howell was a convinced churchman. His obituary in the *Haul* said that while he held other Christian traditions in high esteem, yet his "magnanimous heart beat purely for his Church". An obituary writer in *Cymru*, Idriswyn (Edward Thomas), argued that the Established Church had no priest more faithful than Howell. "I claim", he quoted him as saying, "to be a true child of the Prayer Book. I shall not be moved a step nearer to Geneva or Rome; but I will shake hands warmly with the Roman Catholic and the Nonconformist with one foot on the Book of Common Prayer and the other on the Bible."[1]

Frequently describing himself as a genuine son of the Church, Howell proclaimed his love for its services, and declared that its formal liturgy gave him much spiritual satisfaction. He believed that the Nonconformist dislike of the Book of Common Prayer was more often caused by a callous reading of it by the clergy, than by its theological or liturgical content. Howell argued too that the means of grace provided by the Church were more helpful for spiritual life than that of the free churches. Canon Camber Williams, vicar of St Davids during Howell's time as dean there, said of him in a memorial sermon that Howell loved the Church's liturgical order, embraced its doctrines, was fond of its services, and nothing gave him more comfort and spiritual help than the

---

[1] *Cymru* (OME), 27 (1904) 73f.

daily offices and order of the Church's year. By this I suspect Williams meant that the liturgy gave him a framework for his spiritual life, in much the same way as the creeds provide a framework for Christian doctrine. It was said too of Howell that it was almost a sermon to hear him read the scriptures. Another obituary writer, David Williams, rector of Llandyrnog, argued that Howell represented the best Anglican spirit of his age, and stood alongside the class of Tait, Temple and Davidson.[2] This was not as flattering as it seems, and Howell would not have appreciated such a comparison, but the point is again made that Howell was seen by his contemporaries as a loyal and good Churchman. Clearly those early years of reading the best of the Anglican divines, such as Hooker, Jeremy Taylor and Waterland, made him the man he became.

* * * *

David Howell's joy in his Church may best be expressed by a quotation from a sermon he preached in 1895, within the context of the disestablishment debate:

> The advantages of the Church are great and manifold. She covers the entire Principality as nothing else does. She has, and will have, come what will, her incomparable parochial system. She has, and will have, for of this nothing can dispossess her, the historical prestige and traditions of nearly two millenniums, ever a wealth of influence with an ancient and patriotic people. She has, and ever will have, the moral beauties of her Services, her treasures of devotion, her stores of learning, her long roll of saints, and her broad and generous sympathies. All this she has, and much besides, and, rightly used, they may be of inestimable use to her. But all this will avail her little unless she is permeated through and through by the Spirit of Christ. Like her Lord, her mission too must be, not to be ministered unto, but to minister, to the lowest as to the highest, from the cradle to the grave. She must be the servant of all. She must conquer by love, even though the more abundantly she love the less she be loved. She must have no weapons of offence, except her abounding · charity, her power of patience, and her imperturbable peace.[3]

[2] *Geninen*, 21 (1903) 153.
[3] David Howell, *Sermon on Romans 12.18: Preached at Manchester Cathedral on the Eve of St David's Day 1895* [Bangor 1895] p 16.

His enthusiasm for the Church, almost that of a convert, did not mean that Howell forgot his Nonconformist background. He knew the strengths and weaknesses of Nonconformity as did few other churchmen of his generation. David Williams suggested that nothing annoyed him more than to hear people "blacking" the Welsh Nonconformists, while he argued that no one did as much as Howell in endeavouring to bring peace between the Church and the other denominations.[4] His regard for and love of Welsh Methodism, in particular, never faded. His father was a leading member of the Welsh Calvinistic Methodist Church, his brother a deacon, and his brother-in-law, David Saunders, one of its most celebrated ministers. Howell remained on terms of intimate friendship with him throughout his life.[5] He was on equal terms of friendship with many other leading Nonconformist ministers. Robert Ellis (Cynddelw), Baptist minister, theologian and eisteddodfodwr, died in 1875, and Howell wrote in a letter of sympathy to his family, "he was one of my best and oldest friends, one of five of us who were very intimately acquainted for about a dozen years ... He was a type of nonconformist not very frequently met with, charitable and appreciative of the views of others. I have rarely known a man who better understood and respected the convictions of churchmen ... a holy, ripe and universally beloved Christian."[6] Thomas Thomas, president of the Baptist college at Pontypool, was also remembered with affection, and Howell retained a friendship with his son, the artist, T H Thomas, for many years.[7] Thomas' successor as principal of that college, then transferred to Cardiff, Principal William Edwards - a firm proponent for disestablishment - gave a personal testimony to Howell's spiritual influence in an obituary note.[8] Howell could even write to Thomas Gee, regarded as the arch-foe of the Church in Wales, to note how a friend of his was deeply impressed by "your family worship".[9]

[4] David Williams in Geninen, 22 [St Davids 1904] 43. He added that Howell trembled for the future if matters did not change, for a day of recompense would surely come.
[5] W James and J M Jones, *Cofiant a Phregethau y Parchedig D Saunders* [Abertawe 1894], p xxvi.
[6] NLW MS 10274D, item 277.
[7] NLW MS 17345C, fol 22.
[8] WM, 17 Jan 1903, p 5; and also 19 Jan 1905, p 5.
[9] NLW MS 8306D, fol 108.

As Rhys J Huws remarks, Howell entered the ministry of the Church taking with him much of the spirit of Nonconformity, and with this spirit, and his numerous contacts within the other churches, he was able to appreciate the contribution made by Nonconformity to the life of the nation. "Let God's blessing rest on all those who call upon the name of the Lord" was his constant prayer. As such he became an apostle of peace between the Church and Nonconformity, an interpreter to each one of the others' values. This is a point taken up by David Davies, rector of Canton, in an Assize sermon at Carmarthen, a few days after Howell's death had been announced. The significance of his life, he said:

> consisted ... in his influence over Nonconformist opinion; he understood it, he appreciated its strong points, he was trusted by Nonconformists, and was able to bridge over the rift and to prevent the severance between Churchmen and Nonconformists from growing wider. When they remembered how much both sides suffered from misapprehension, as well as misrepresentation, they were better able to appreciate the value of Dean Howell's life. Anything that made for a better understanding between men who were actuated by the highest motives, but who differed as to the value to be attached to conclusions or to facts connected with religion, could not but be welcome to all of them.[10]

Nonconformists, declared the *Western Mail*, felt that in Howell they had a stake in the national Church. "His dignified presence in pulpit or on platform removed for the moment any prejudice or hostility which even political Dissenters entertained towards the Establishment,"[11] and gave him, suggested another writer, a great popularity with both Church and chapel folk.[12] This may be because Nonconformists knew that Howell not only appreciated their work, but fully accepted the reasons for their dissent. This, he argued, along with A J Johnes and other such writers, was due in part to the activities of the Anglo-Welsh episcopate, who failed to appreciate the spiritual, linguistic and cultural heritage of the

---

[10] WM, 22 Jan 1903, p 6. As a result the assize judge made reference to Howell's death and influence during the course of the Assizes.
[11] WM, 16 Jan 1903, p 4.
[12] See *Young Wales*, 3 [1897] 95.

Church in Wales, and consequently allowed it to lose its cutting edge and thus forfeit its heritage to Nonconformity.[13] Neither did Howell hesitate to declare that Nonconformity had been a great blessing to the Principality, and that its ministers were doing a great work for good which the clergy were not always able to do themselves.

Howell reflected these beliefs in his parochial ministry, declining to make any distinction between Church and Nonconformist people in his pastoral work. Writing to Lady Hills-Johnes of Dolaucothi (the sister of the correspondent of Bishop Thirlwall) he admitted that he acted in defiance of the ecclesiastical laws in admitting Nonconformists to partake of the Holy Communion: "I have several such in my parish [Gresford], and also some who now are confirmed under certain circumstances."[14]

It is not surprising, therefore, that David Howell disliked and distrusted the growing partisanship of Welsh religious life. This sentiment had been with him from the beginning of his ministry, as this extract from his sermon on the laying of the foundation stone of Alderman Davies' School in Neath during 1857 makes clear:

> I believe that this party spirit is one of the greatest curses of this present age. We are received into the world by a partisan midwife, we are baptised with a partisan minister, we are taken to a partisan place of worship, and in Sunday and day partisan schools we learn a partisan catechism: we support partisan literature; we make partisan relationships; buy in partisan shops; carry on a partisan trade; make a partisan marriage; we die under the wings of a partisan communion; we are buried in partisan cemeteries; a partisan funeral sermon is preached for us; a partisan obituary is written for us; this is printed in a partisan printing-house, and published in a partisan publication; and so from womb to tomb we breathe the unhealthy fumes of this partisan air ....[15]

During those early years as curate of Neath, he had laid down the principles on which he would act, and as to how he would deal

---

[13] *Abstract of the Report of the Annual Meeting of the Church Pastoral-Aid Society* [CPAS Abstract], 1877, pp 24f, cf ibid, 1861, p 12.
[14] NLW Dolaucothi MS, L7004, Howell to Lady Hills-Johnes, 15 May 1896.
[15] David Howell, *Araeth a Draddodwyd ar yr Achlysur o osod i lawr Gareg - Sylfaen Ysgol Alderman Davies* [Aberdare 1857], pp 7f. Translated.

with those who differed from him. These were laid out in a lecture given by him in 1856 and published under the title *The Duty of Charity and Mutual Forbearance in Matters of Religious Belief.* Instead of dispute, he wrote, let there be mutual freedom and respect regarding the "open questions" of Christian belief, such as questions of church order and the mode of baptism. Christians were not at liberty to reject those whom God had obviously accepted as his people. But this, alas, was not so at the present time:

> It can scarcely admit of a doubt that the acerbity of feeling thus encouraged among professing Christians, tends greatly to prevent their growth in grace; and it must also tend, by multiplying divisions, to render yet smaller those divisions into which the Church of Christ is unfortunately split! In humble dependence on Him who took the title Prince of Peace, and who bequeathed His peace as the greatest of all blessings to His church, we shall endeavour in this lecture to note some of the causes of the many schisms which exist among us; to point out a few of their disastrous results, and to direct your attention to certain plain and simple remedies; and may the great HEAD of the Church so aid us with His blessing, that the attempt may not be altogether made in vain.
>
> The Principality of Wales affords, unhappily, but too many opportunities of studying such a subject; for there is no portion of the British dominions where dissension prevails so much on religious topics, and where that dissension is exhibited with so much bigotry and intolerance.

While Howell accepted that part of the reason for this dissension was because few of the clergy were Welsh-speaking, he also felt it was because they did not preach "the truth that is in Jesus ... with that fullness necessary to its success." Thankfully these were matters which were being remedied. He also believed that the earnestness and zeal of the Welsh character was another pertinent factor.[16]

He laid down five principles of action as a means of addressing this dissension. Firstly, accepting that no two people would ever have the same opinions about religious topics. Secondly,

---

[16] David Howell, *A Lecture: the Duty of Charity and Mutual Forbearance in Matters of Religious Belief* [Newport 1856], pp 3f.

distinguishing between doctrines which were absolutely essential to salvation, and those which were subsidiary. Thirdly, by neither overrating nor underrating rites, ceremonies and discipline, but remembering that not even the sacraments were to be put in the place of Christ. Fourthly, by considering that Christians are expected to work together and care for one another, and, finally, by checking spiritual pride, and cherishing love between the brethren. He continued:

> If we would have the blessing of God in our souls, if we would bring down His favour upon our Church, if we would have His acknowledgement to our labours, if we desire union to prevail among Christians, if ever we desire our own peculiar views to become acceptable to others, we must learn to bear and forbear, to judge, not that we be not judged, to be pitiful, to be courteous, to make allowance for error and prejudice, and to strive against all temptations to arrogance and self-conceit. We are not strong enough to accomplish those things ourselves; but we are not left to our own power, or our own devices; and He who has laid upon us the obligation, has engaged to supply "grace to help us in every time of need."[17]

Howell spoke on many other occasions of this need for charity. Listen to his words at the 1884 St Asaph diocesan conference as he spoke in a debate about disestablishment, words which were greeted with much applause:

> .... there is the duty of carrying on this controversy in the spirit of an ungrudging and unwearying Christian charity. If we say bitter things of others because others may say bitter things of us, what are we better than they? No, no, my brethren, if this controversy is to be carried on, let it be carried on in the spirit of our master Christ, of whom it was said that "when He was reviled He reviled not again, when He suffered He threatened not, but committed himself to Him that judgeth righteously."[18]

For his willingness to put these principles into practice, Howell had to face much hostility and prejudice himself. This was often

---

[17] Howell, *A Lecture*, pp 22f.
[18] *Report of the St Asaph Diocesan Conference*, 1884, p 21.

petty in character, for example, the criticism he faced for sitting on the eisteddfod platform with Nonconformist ministers, or the strange accusation that he was more chapel than church. He was accused, too, of being too friendly with chapel people. At least one writer suggested that these prejudices stood in the way of his preferment within the Church.[19] But in spite of this hostility, Howell persevered in his desire and longing for a united Christian Church in Wales. This longing emerged, for example, in his lecture on Welsh hymnology, in which he expressed his hope that the common use of hymns by all denominations might breed unity between them.[20] Archdeacon Griffiths of Neath is said to have talked about this desire to the Independent minister, Hiraethog - William Rees - who replied that it would need another St David to accomplish it. We have him, replied Griffiths, in David Howell.[21]

It was possibly for this reason, apart from friendship, that he complied with Lady Llanover's request to draw up a liturgy for use in her interdenominational chapel at Llanover, and which has subsequently become known as "The Use of Abercarn". The Welsh scholar and churchman, Silvan Evans, and Howell's own brother-in-law, David Saunders, were also involved. Howell appears to have acted as the "middle-man" between the revisers, her ladyship, the printer, and the rather difficult minister of the church who, at the end of the day, had to use the liturgy. This man was not amused that two of the revisers were Anglicans. From the letters surviving it was a task more of diplomacy than of liturgy, especially when items were printed which had not been revised by one of the contributors. There was another long controversy as to whether the full psalter rather than a selection should be bound up with the book, Howell maintaining that too often Nonconformists would choose the shortest psalm or lesson, rather than the most appropriate. It is hard to believe that Howell was satisfied with the completed liturgy, for it dispensed with Saints days and termed the Holy Communion service *The Order for the Administration of the Lord's Supper*, but he probably agreed with the removal of the Athanasian Creed, and the omission of any

---

[19] *Cymru* [OME], 27 [1904] 73.
[20] *Geninen*, 15 [1897] 13f.
[21] J V Morgan, *Welsh Religious Leaders in the Victorian Era* [London 1905], p 92.

reference to baptismal regeneration in the baptismal service.[22] The *Use* was in Welsh, but it was never widely adopted.

It was perhaps in the wider field of personal relationships that Howell became a mediating influence between the Church and Welsh Nonconformity, as the *Dictionary of National Biography* puts it, rather than in the writing of liturgies or the ambiguities of ecclesiastical politics. It was as the result of these relationships that he pleaded again and again for a spirit of mutual concern and charity to be established in Wales. Speaking at the Manchester Church Congress of 1888, on the subject of the Church in Wales, he urged:

> The strength of the Church in Wales lies not in her social prestige and ecclesiastical traditions, precious though these may be; but rather in her love to all her children, yea, in her love to those who may not love her. Love is the all-conquering weapon of the Church. Controversy provokes controversy. A spirit of rivalry in us intensifies rivalry in others. But a deep, broad, generous, ungrudging, all-embracing charity, will assure us of the smile of God, and at least the sympathy of all good men.[23]

These sentiments were expressed, and lived up to, at the time of the disestablishment controversy, when church and chapel, English and Welsh, Conservative and Liberal, seemed to be fighting one another on many different fronts, social, linguistic, political, cultural as well as ecclesiastical. Nonconformity, reacting against a Church which had denied it equality and liberty, felt that the Church's connection with the State was crippling its own mission, and had made that Church an alien body in Wales. There was some truth in the Nonconformist assertion that the leaders of that Church were endeavouring to suppress the Welsh language, and equal truth that the Church was being propped up by the support it received from English institutions. If the Church were to be free of these shackles, able to appoint its own Welsh-speaking bishops, supported by the voluntary principle of giving, then it might again be a force for truth and righteousness in Wales.

---

[22] See D Parry-Jones, "The Use of Abercarn", *Impact*, May, Sept-Nov, 1972, and *Province*, vols 18-19 [1967-8], and NLW D Parry-Jones Papers, 1979 deposit.

[23] *Report of the Manchester Church Congress*, 1888, p 75.

Others argued that the endowments given to the Church were given in reality to the cause of religion in Wales, and as Nonconformity was statistically stronger than the Church, some of these endowments should either go to them or to such social concerns as hospitals and schools, for which they might have been originally intended. Of course there were many other factors involved in this complex debate which ranged over eighty and more years, and over thirty years of parliamentary action, culminating in the disestablishment, disendowment and dismemberment of the Church of England in Wales, in 1920.

By the 1880s, as Welsh Nonconformity realised that its connection with the Liberal party could ensure that its concerns about disestablishment, education, land and social reforms might receive legislative effect, the Church, in its own defence, found itself more and more allied with the Conservative party. Thus a general polarization and hardening of attitudes was taking place, and it is not an over-generalisation to suggest that in these years, by debate, lecture and the written word, some vociferous Nonconformist leaders managed to take their revenge upon a Church which they believed had endeavoured to repress them and make them second-class citizens. They were not alone in their bitterness. Church leaders, who had helped spread that bitterness by their attacks on dissent and their apostolic claims for the Church to be the only true Church, reacted to this bitterness in the same spirit. It was an unhealthy picture all round, although, on the local level, family relationships and loyalties mitigated the worst effects and enabled reasonable relationships to continue between church and chapel folk.[24]

Howell made it quite clear that he was opposed to this campaign to disestablish the Church, as we will note in more detail in the next chapter. Yet he deeply regretted the bitterness which prevailed on both sides, and the all too general assumption that loyalty to the Church should be interpreted as a badge of clericalism and Anglicisation, while Dissent was to be seen as part and parcel of the patriotic movement in Wales. Such matters, he argued, could only "... accentuate our unhappy divisions, and

---

[24] See, for example, my *Followers of Jeroboam* [Cardiff 1984].

perpetuate a sense of injustice, as injurious to social peace as to the spiritual interests of the principality."[25]

Unlike many others of the religious leaders of Wales at this time, Howell refused to appear on any political platform. There was only one occasion when he relented from this principle. This is when he spoke on behalf of the Armenian people during the Bulgarian massacres. His sense of outrage was so great that he felt the government ought to intervene: "if, as a Christian nation, we waited more on God and less on man in connection with this solemn subject, our perplexities might be less and the path of our duty made more clear to us."[26]

Bernard Lewis, a member of George Kenyon's election committee at Wrexham, wrote that he had once canvassed Howell on behalf of his Conservative candidate, "but did not do so specially, as Mr Howell's orthodox views on such matters were well known. I urged him to do all he could to oppose Mr Kenyon's opponent who had declared in favour of disestablishment. Mr Howell then told me that, although he should vote for Mr Kenyon, yet he would not drag the Church through the mire by interfering in politics beyond voting, as he considered that there was too much political partisanship shown by many of the teachers of religion throughout the Principality, and which was detrimental to the cause of religion." Such were Howell's principles.[27]

It is hardly surprising, therefore, that Howell was to find himself totally lacking in sympathy with the more modern line of church defence taken by Bishop Edwards and others by the early 1890s. He hated the political intrigue, the polemics and the personal abuse involved in this style of defence, and felt it was unworthy of the Church to descend to the tactics often displayed by the more militant and political Nonconformists, such as

---

[25] Quoted in J P Lewis, *Church Plunder-State Blunder* [London 1913], p 26.
[26] NLW MS 4878E, fol 33 [1890], Howell to an unknown correspondent, 18 Sept 1896.
[27] *Wrexham Advertiser*, 22 July 1893, p 6. K O Morgan in his *Rebirth of a Nation: Wales 1880-1980* [Oxford 1981, p 50] is clearly wrong when he writes that Howell was a staunch member of the Liberal party. He certainly was in his younger days, but his concern over the disestablishment of the Irish Church led him to change his allegiance. His son was a Conservative MP. However Howell, as the *Wrexham Advertiser* of 24 Jan 1903, p 7, put it, set an admirable example to the clergy in abstaining from any open involvement with party politics.

Thomas Gee and the recently deceased Henry Richard. David Lloyd George, in a speech at Oswestry on the Suspensory Bill of 1893, protested about the language used in one of Edwards' speeches, although we should allow for more than a little hyperbole on Lloyd George's part. Edwards, he complained, had "latinised the tirades of an enraged washerwoman", and had engaged in "squalid slang" in describing his opponents as "prejudiced and ill-informed", "dishonest or disinterested people", or "loud and troublesome insects". He had read out some of these quotations to respectable English Churchmen, "who could hardly credit the possibility of a bishop of their Church descending so low in controversy, and they unanimously expressed disgust and horror at the man who could have so far degraded his sacred office as thus to trail his robes in the gutter." The bishop, Lloyd George remarked, appeared to rush out "of his palace door like a common scold, brush in hand, to daub his neighbours" on every possible occasion.[28] Such attitudes would win no applause from David Howell; he found them unworthy and disturbing. He seemed to live on a far higher plane, for as David Davies, one of the leading Baptist writers and defenders of disestablishment, admitted, "Personally I never felt inclined to discuss disestablishment with him. The atmosphere around him admitted of no contention. He admitted the faults of his Church, but with all its faults he loved it still, and one had no heart to disturb that love."[29] Had others his spirit, suggested J V Morgan, the disestablishment campaign would have lost half its force.[30]

Thus Howell, though he let his distaste for disestablishment be known, refused to throw himself into the militant battle for Church defence, even though many of his colleagues accused him of a lack of courage and conviction. He believed the arguments used should be based on higher considerations, and that those who defended the Church were often insensitive to the real issues of the case. Likewise, he felt it wrong to disturb the peace of God's flock. In a sermon published under the title of its text,

---

[28] *Wrexham Advertiser*, 25 Feb 1893, p 5.
[29] David Davies, *Reminiscences of my Country and People* [London 1925], p 241. Nevertheless Howell organised meetings to protest against the Suspensory Bill, even arranging to use chapel vestries for this purpose [*Report of the Royal Commission into ... the Church of England in Wales*, II [1910] 307].
[30] Morgan, Religious Leaders, p 116.

Romans 12.18: *"Live Peaceably with all men"*, Howell argued that this text was binding even on such an issue as the disestablishment campaign. His full and mature reflection on the whole subject was given elsewhere, paradoxically in London, at St Margaret's Church, Westminster, in 1890. Entitled *The Welsh Church*, the published sermon was widely noted, translated into Welsh, and caused, as will be noted later, a rift between himself and his bishop. His arguments then, and at other times, need to be recorded.

Howell commenced this sermon by expressing his longing that the Church should be realistic as to the real reasons and causes of Nonconformity, so that it might learn from the lessons of the past. He recognised the Church's own contribution to the growth of Dissent through its former apathy and indifference to spiritual and cultural concerns. He argued, therefore, that the Church should never lose sight of the fact that Dissent had been caused by the neglect, apathy and worldliness of the Church, and that the Church could never cope on its own with the spiritual demands and needs of the population. One of his frequently quoted sayings was that "the fathers have eaten sour grapes, and the children's teeth are set on edge." The abuses of the Church would not be forgotten in a day. Howell's historical argument may have been uncritical, but this could not diminish his concern for the state of things he and his generation had inherited from the past:

> And what have been the causes which have brought about a condition of things so deeply to be deplored by all who have the welfare of the ancient British Church at heart? The causes have been many and various. Most have been removed, but some still remain. There has been for generations the mistaken policy of suppressing Welsh nationality by means of the Church, with the same results in Wales as in Ireland. There has been the neglect of the language and literature of Wales on the part of the gentry and higher clergy, with the result that the people have now a prolific literature of their own, which is anything but friendly to the existing order of things. There has been too often a haughty and exclusive spirit on the part of the clergy towards those who differed from them, in forgetfulness of their Ordination vow to "maintain and set forth quietness, peace and love among all Christian people." There has been the mistaken policy of working the Church in Wales on the same lines as the Church of England, ignoring the genius and

temperament of the Welsh people, and treating that as fanaticism which, if rightly directed, would have been a mighty power for good. There has been a too great readiness to pander to the wants and ways of the richer classes, sacrificing the welfare of the many to the convenience of the few. There has been the neglect of teaching the people the corporate life and fundamental principles of the Church, her historical claims, the merits of her Liturgy, and the Scripturalness of her Creeds. There has been a want of sympathy with the national aspirations and wants of the people, with the result that the Church is hardly taken into account in the national movements of the day. There has been a want of evangelistic enterprise where masses of men have suddenly congregated, the Church not infrequently coming last into the field, when others had well-nigh reaped the harvest. There has been a neglect of the preaching best adapted to impress a sympathetic and emotional people, and a sneering at that as "mannerism" which, when genuine, is the expression of a holy enthusiasm, and which has often been eminently honoured of God. Something may also be laid to the charge of our system of patronage, the autocracy of the clergy, the exclusion of the laity from participation by right in the administration of the Church, and the innate love of self-government always and everywhere characteristic of the Celtic race. But above all other causes, is the weakness of the Church in Wales due to the fact that so much of the best blood of the nation no longer runs in her veins. It is sheer folly to hide from ourselves the truth that the most vigorous life-blood of the Welsh people no longer wells forth from the heart of the Welsh Church. What is the exact proportion of the people to be found within and without the Church, is a matter of secondary importance. For more important is the fact that so large a portion of the vigour and enthusiasm of the Welsh people is in full activity outside the Church.

Howell noted that the Welsh Church, with its "English settlers and Anglicised Welshness", was still regarded as having an alien nature; that within the Church there were jealousies between north and south which hindered progress; and he expressed his sorrow at the Church's neglect of Welsh-speaking people living in the towns of England. In these areas the Church had four churches and six mission rooms, compared with the one hundred and thirty Welsh Nonconformist chapels. Howell claimed, as did others, that there had been a systematic policy of introducing the English language to replace the Welsh language as a means towards uniformity, and that the Welsh language had been deliberately identified with Dissent and political movements such as Chartism. Warning that the Welsh clergy would be driven to seek disestablishment as the only means of ending this policy of alienation, Howell advised that Welsh spiritual life and fervour depended on the use of the mother tongue. In such concerns he was at one with Dean Edwards, and frequently quoted his works in the extensive footnotes to the published version of his Westminster sermon.[31]

Pointing out that the real attack on the Church only came when the Church had begun to regain its energy and vitality, and the so called "Church Revival" had started,[32] he argued that unlike the Church of England, where those outside her body "consist largely of the careless and indifferent, those outside the Church in Wales are actively hostile to her as an Establishment, and are banded together to bring her to the ground."[33] Yet Howell was prepared to concede that many of the Nonconformist leaders were quite sincere in wanting the Church's disestablishment on spiritual grounds, and some even believed it would assist the work of reunification. He thus argued in his Westminster sermon:

> Nor must it be forgotten that in this crusade there is a very much larger proportion of religious as distinguished from political Nonconformity than is the case in England. They are men of unquestioned religious character. They are men whose lives bear witness to their piety and sincerity. Their influence on the side of social morality and public righteousness is as decided as our own. In unstinted liberality they are an example to us all. The contributions of only one Welsh Dissenting denomination in 1887 amounted to £168,948. Not only so, but in their doctrinal beliefs they hardly differ from the great mass of Churchmen. Most of them will repeat our Creeds without faltering; some of the highest eulogiums on our Book of Common Prayer have come from their

---

[31] David Howell, *The Welsh Church: A Sermon Preached at St Margaret's Church, Westminster* [London 1890], p 7-9. This sermon is also known by its subtitle, *The Patriot's Yearning for the Prosperity of Zion*. Dean Edwards' more notable writings on the subject of the Welsh Church and asking for a reappraisal of its Anglicising policy will be found in his *Wales and the Welsh Church* [London 1889]. David Jones, vicar of Penmaenmawr, continued Howell's and Dean Edwards' work in this respect: see his *The Welsh Church and Welsh Nationality* [London 1895].

[32] *Report of the Norwich Church Congress*, 1895, p 402-4.

[33] Howell, *The Welsh Church*, p 4, cf p 9.

lips. For not a few of the best hymns in our Church collections are we indebted to them. There is hardly a department of theological literature in which they do not hold their own. Such, unquestionably, are not a few of those who are alienated from the Church, and who desire her disestablishment. And it is simply unjust to lump together all opponents of an Established Church, as if all alike were enemies of God's truth, and as if all alike were influenced by the worst of motives. That there are among them men, whose jealously of the social and political privileges of the Church has perverted their better feelings, is quite possible. But there are others of an entirely different stamp - religious men, who believe in their heart of hearts that the Church, disestablished, would be a greater power for good than she is now; that what she might lose in prestige and position she could more than gain in spiritual usefulness, freedom of action, and the energy which comes of self-reliance; that the early Church never was so pure and prosperous as when she was not patronized by the State; that an Establishment is incompatible with a democratic system of government, and with so large a portion of the population in pronounced Dissent; that a disestablished Church would cease to attract to her ministry those who "crouch to her, saying, Put me, I pray thee, into one of the priests' offices, that I may eat a piece of bread;" and that the adherents of the Church would take a far keener interest in her welfare when they had to support her, than when, as now, they so largely depend on the benefactions of the past. These, and such as these, are the ideas which influence not a few in opposing the Church as an Establishment; and it is downright injustice to confound such men with the enemies of all religion, or to regard them as if they were opposed to the Church in her spiritual capacity as the handmaid of God. In dealing with such men, it becomes us to deal with them, not as enemies, but as friends - mistaken friends, if you will - but still as those whose Nonconformity is the fruit of honest conviction; in some instances, it may be, due to the apathy and neglect of the Church itself.[34]

It may be that Howell was thinking of Alfred George Edwards as he wrote these words. The consequences of this sermon are noted in the following chapter.

*   *   *   *

[34] Ibid, pp 9-11.

David Howell never disguised his belief that the best defence of the Church was not to be found in attacking or abusing one's opponents, but rather in working for the renewal of the Church's spiritual life. Speaking at a Church Pastoral-Aid Society's clergy conference at Penmaenmawr, he argued that their best defence against the attack being made on them was to ensure that the parish work was effectively done and a spiritual ministry pursued.[35] Bishop Joshua Hughes said much the same thing: it was not necessary, he argued, to have one hand at the work and another holding a weapon.[36] Furthermore Howell argued that the Church's trust should not reside in political settlements or in politicians, but in the power of the Lord himself. Jesse Jones, in his biography of William Evans of Rhymney, a close friend of Howell, recalled that both had told Archbishop Benson, at a time when the storm was at its height, that the Church should "turn her directions straight to the Sun of Righteousness", and that the Church needed to be, above all else, a spiritual body.[37]

There were good grounds for optimism in this area of Church renewal, as compared to the position after the First World War. Signs of grace and hope were to be seen, even though it might have seemed to be a day of small things. Indeed, Howell surprised the delegates at the Norwich Church Congress of 1895 by stating that they had been accustomed to hearing the Church in Wales described as a weak church, but in reality they needed the sympathy of the Welsh as much as the Welsh needed theirs, for the percentage of Easter communicants to population in England was 5.8 per cent, whereas in Wales, on average, it was 6.7 per cent, and in the archdeaconry of Cardigan, the most Welsh area of Wales, it was eleven per cent. Howell went on to speak of the renewal of life in the Church in Wales. In 1831 it had 683 clergy, in 1895 over a thousand. Enormous strides had been made in providing new churches and mission rooms, as well as schools. In the fifty years between 1840-91 two and a fifth million pounds had been spent on the building and restoration of churches, while between 1848-94 the Assistant Curates Society had given grants to Wales totalling £214,000 and the CPAS between 1840-95

[35] *Record*, 7 Sept 1894, p 874; cf CPAS *Abstract*, 1883, p 17.
[36] *Haul*, 1889, p 69.
[37] T J Jones, *William Evans of Rhymney* [Lampeter nd], p 36. Translation.

£217,000. This position was contrasted with the circumstances he himself remembered about the Church some fifty years earlier:

> ... nearly fifty years ago, the Church in Wales found herself beset by almost unexampled difficulties. Her cathedrals, if not in ruins, were in a state of deplorable dilapidation. Her parish churches by hundreds were only true pictures of her moral and spiritual decay. The wretched little deal communion tables were such as would hardly have found a place in the poorest cottages; while the dirty and moth-eaten altar cloths would have found a place in few, if any, human dwellings. Roofs full of holes, seats rotten, grass growing in the porches, shovels, spades, planks and biers exposed; common basins used for fonts; celebrations, such as they were, few and far between; the services irreverently gabbled over; no responses, except by the clerk, who was not always the most reputable person in the parish; often no singing; and the preaching, as a matter of course, in character with all else besides. All this have I personally seen and known in the latter years of the first part of this present century, and that when Welsh Nonconformity was in the full tide of its spiritual vigour, when it revelled in the gifts of some of the greatest preachers that Wales, or indeed any other country, has produced since Apostolic times, and when to be a Churchman was to bear a stigma and a reproach in many parishes throughout Wales.
>
> Is it any wonder than an intensely religious, emotional and enthusiastic people should have become alienated under such circumstances? But even then God did not leave Himself without witness in the old Mother Church of Wales. It would not be difficult to name a considerable number of clergy in North and South Wales who between 1820 and 1860, were men of eminent saintliness and rare devotedness, who still fed the sacred fire on the old altar, or, in otherwords, were the salt that kept the mass from putrefaction.[38]

Howell thus deeply regretted the bitterness of the disestablishment dispute, especially at a time when the Church was reviving and needing all her strength to continue her mission. He would have sympathised with Gladstone, who remarked to the

[38] *Report of the Norwich Church Congress*, 1895, pp 402, 404. The *Wrexham Advertiser* of 24 Jan 1907, p 7, mentioned that Howell felt that the church defence advocates were wrong in suggesting that there was church progress throughout Wales. There were still many dark spots.

then Dean Owen, after Archbishop Benson's speech at the Rhyl Church Congress, "I very much regret the Archbishop came to Rhyl to speak as if it were proposed to disestablish the Apostles' Creed!"[39] In this same spirit Howell thus preached before the University of Cambridge in 1893:

> I regard myself much in the light of one who has just come from the battlefield, to the scene where young recruits are disciplined and trained for the great warfare of life. I might, indeed, say that I have come from the battlefield in a less figurative sense, for my beloved Principality is just now the scene of the saddest of all strifes, religious strife, strife among brethren. The collision of opinions in regard to ecclesiastical affairs may be the unavoidable outcome of those changes of ideas, aims, interests and convictions which accompany an advanced civilisation. But to anyone who has the interests of religious peace, charity, and Christian brotherhood at heart, it is none the less sad, and deeply distressing to witness the best interests of spiritual religion so terribly injured, social life embittered, and that peculiar acerbity infused into political controversy which comes only from religious passions and prejudices. Hearty co-operation in support of social and philanthropic objects is becoming increasingly difficult, purely political questions are decided by extraneous considerations, and a highly religious and generous people are bitterly divided on the one subject which of all others ought to draw men closer together.[40]

Two years later, in his St David's day sermon at Manchester on Romans 12.18, "Live Peaceably with all Men", Howell returned to this same theme, asking why Christians who differed about such matters as church order and government, the shape of the ministry, the inspiration of Scripture, or the conditions of Christian fellowship, could not live peacably with each other "without sacrificing the interests of Christian charity and brotherly love". Howell felt that this could and should take place even amongst those who were on opposite sides regarding the disestablishment and disendowment of the Church. Regretfully, he concluded that on this particular question the harmony and

---

[39] E E Owen, *The Early Life of Bishop Owen* [Llandyssul 1958], p 119.
[40] David Howell, *Fitness for Service: A Sermon Preached before the University of Cambridge*, 1893, pp 1f.

charity had been "seriously jeopardised already". It was a heartrending spectacle, he argued,

> when children of the same Father are found denouncing each other, social life embittered, and that peculiar acerbity infused into political controversy which comes only from religious passions and prejudices....
>
> True, the rack and the stake are no longer in favour as means of grace; but the spirit of intolerance, exclusiveness, and religious antipathy is still alive; and seldom has there been a time when the duty enjoined in the text more needed to be pressed home on the hearts and consciences of Christian men, at least in Wales. Men, even religious men, have need to be reminded that no provocation, however exasperating, can justify retaliation; that no vindication of truth, no defence of right, no sense of political injustice can release us from an essential law of the Christian life, that of loving each other. The temptation may be great to use carnal weapons. The stinging retort, the smart repartee, the withering sarcasm, the crushing rejoinder, the skilful home thrust, the opportunity of dealing a deadly blow at an antagonist, the temptation to use such weapons may be great. But can they be used without grieving the Holy Spirit of God? Could they be used if the personal presence of Christ were realised? Could we ask the blessing of God on the use of them? ....

It was no wonder that the Church faced the "scoffs and sneers of unbelievers." As a result the various denominations were fast learning the truth

> that to carry out controversy in the spirit of the world, after the manner of the world, and with the weapons of the world, is treachery to Christ, and can only lead to disaster. In such a case, even victory would be a defeat. The Church's first line of defence is humiliation, fasting, prayer, and waiting upon God. A Church prostrate before God, bewailing her sins and short-comings, bowed to the dust in penitent submission to the will of the Great Supreme, is a Church invincible by any real evil than man can do to her. Seldom, I say again, has there been a time when the spirit of my text is more needed to be cultivated if the best interests of the Church are to be served, and if we are to convince the world of the reality of the faith of Jesus Christ.

Begging those engaged in the controversy to understand each other's motives, aims and opinions, Howell added his own protest about the way in which some churchmen attacked their so-called opponents:

> It is sad to see how little is known on either side of the inner life and convictions of their opponents. Such terms as "robbers of God," "political atheists," "profaners of Churches," "iniquitous spoliators," and the like, are as little credible to those who use them as they are cruel and unjust to many of the most religious men in Wales, men whose high Christian character and moral integrity need no defence from those who know them, whatever we may think of their views. And equally reprehensible are the epithets thrown at men who conscientiously believe that they are defending the heritage of God, the interests of national Christianity, the rights of the poor, and the inviolability of sacred trusts, numbering among them many who have ever been foremost in every good work, pronounced in their sentiments and sympathy with all that is liberal, generous, and progressive in social and political life, students of history, men who have rendered inestimable service to the cause of sacred learning, and some of them men who have suffered not a little for their principles and opinions. To apply to such men terms of opprobrium because of their attachment to the principle of an Establishment, is as unjust as it is humiliating to all who have the cause of truth and charity at heart; and often I have found the words of Cromwell to the General Assembly of the Church of Scotland rise to my lips, "I beseech you, my beloved brethren, I beseech you in the bowels of Christ, to believe that you may be mistaken."... [41]

Howell entered a further protest about the scare mongering tactics employed by the Church's defenders in this controversary:

> Constantly, are we told that Disestablishment would be the "ruin of the Church," the "destruction of the Church," the "collapse of the Church", and other stronger terms are used, thus confounding the Church with the accident of the Establishment. But by the Church

---

[41] Howell, *Sermon on Romans 12.18*, pp 6f, 9-11, 17. Dean Edwards said much the same about the need for charity in *Wales and the Welsh Church*, pp 186, 280. Viator Cambrensis in *The Rise and Decline of Welsh Nonconformity* [London 1912] argued in the same way from the Nonconformist camp, pp 76 82.

is surely meant the historic Church of England, the Church which existed in this country some centuries before the State existed as we now understand the term, Episcopal in government, Liturgical in worship, Primitive in her Creeds, catholic in her sympathies. Never let it be forgotten that if Disestablishment were to take place tomorrow, it would not, and could not affect the Church in any of her essential attributes. It would not affect the authority of her Ministry, or alter a single article in her Creeds, or a line in her Services, or one syllable in her Book of Common Prayer. In all that constitutes her spiritual prerogatives, traditions, powers, and privileges, she would be the same the day after as the day before her Disestablishment.[42]

His private letters said much the time. Writing to Lady Hills-Johnes in 1895 he argued that a "narrow, technical and defiant attitude is not calculated to serve a cause involving such vast issues as that now in question. We must not fight for God with the devil's weapons and in nothing do we more need to be careful as to 'what spirit we are of'." He noted too his concern about the poor translations made of the Church's defence literature: "such things provoke our countrymen's contempt. Cromwell used to speak "of a certain class of people in his day as 'the Lord's *foolish* people', and they have some descendants still ... Our countrymen are far more easily led than driven."[43]

The Church was called, therefore, to consider the way of suffering, the way of the Cross, rather than allow the present controversy to waste its resources and to cause a decline in spiritual religion. Thus in his sermon on Romans 12.18, Howell argued that it was now "admitted on all sides that spiritual religion is not the power in Wales which it used to be." This was because of the distractions of modern life, the exhaustion of the "great spiritual force" of the previous century, the pressure of free thought, the declining power of what people used to call "Holy Ghost" or experiential religion", and, above all, "the almost

---

[42] Howell, *Sermon on Romans 12.18*, p 12. Howell could have quoted Bishop Campbell of Bangor in his support. In his Charge to that diocese of 1884 [pp 24f] Campbell wrote that "We are Churchmen, not because the Church is *established*, and that thus temporal advantages accrue to ourselves, but because we believe it to be the true representative of the Apostles among us. ... Let it be disestablished and disendowed tomorrow, our allegiance and our love remain the same."
[43] NLW Dolaucothi MS, 7001, Howell to Lady Hills-Johnes, 4 May 1895.

unexampled political change of the last twenty years ..." In spite of this spiritual declension, Howell refused to be a pessimist, for he continued,

> As to the ultimate future of the Church in the Principality, faith in God forbids even the least misgiving. The strength of the Church lies in the truth of God enshined within her. The wealth of the Church lies in the faith, and zeal, and love of her children. The safety of the Church lies in her loyalty to her mission, and in the indwelling presence and power of God the Holy Ghost. Men can only take away what man has given.[44]

These thoughts and ideas Howell proclaimed fearlessly and prophetically at the various St Asaph diocesan conferences. His words for many must have come as a matter of encouragement. Come what may, God's providential care would still be with them. After suffering there would be glory. But the condition of such blessing was that they must be faithful to the things and ways of God. Thus Bishop Hughes and the conference heard him declare from the floor in 1884 that he and many other churchpeople had become familiar with the cry of the Church in danger for many and many a year, but they now saw the Church stronger in herself and stronger in her hold on the affections of the people than at any time in her history over the previous two hundred and fifty years. They therefore regarded such discussions on disestablishment and church defence with impatience, as likely to do more harm than good. He continued:

> Our first duty in regard to disestablishment I take to be this: it is not to fear it. In saying this, don't suppose that I think lightly of it. God forbid! But I do think that many churchmen are far too ready to get into a panic about it, as if disestablishment would be the ruin and very end of the Church. Nothing of the kind. Establishment is a mere political accident, its work of man; and what man has done he can undo. But no sacrilegious hand of man can touch the ark of God's truth. Despoil the Church, her endowments if you will, and what then? Why, don't we know that truth in poverty conquered the world? My lord, the Church has more things to fear than poverty. In the Word of God I find the Church warned against

[44] Howell, *Sermon on Romans 12.18*, pp 14-16.

covetousness, lukewarmness, error, and against trusting in the "arm of flesh", but never against poverty. If the worst comes to the worst, my lord, don't let us be afraid of it.

Consider, he asked the conference, what churches such as the Free Church of Scotland, the Roman Catholic Church, the Calvinistic Methodist Church of Wales, had done in spite of poverty. And when the delegates had taken this thought into their minds he went on:

> And shall we, who have behind us the larger portion of the wealth, the learning, and the piety of the English nation become hysterical because men threaten to reduce us to the condition of the Lord's Apostles when they undertook the conversion of the world? Shame upon us if we do! Another duty I take to be this - it is to have more faith in our mission, to lay greater stress on the spiritual, and less on the political claims of the Church. If we believe, as we do believe, that our Church, almost from apostolic days, has been the spiritual mother of the people of this country, and that both in her doctrines and discipline she is most in harmony with the Word of God; if we believe that she is at the same time the most Scriptural and the most catholic of churches, it is shame to us if we fear and tremble because men shake their fists at us. No, no, my lord, let us grasp our spiritual weapons the tighter - truth, charity, self-sacrifice, faith in God and love to man - and we shall then find that even our trials will be to us "blessings in disguise".

The Church, he concluded, was called to a greater activity and liberality in spiritual things, so that it might become "in a sense indispensable to the nation."[45]

Howell once more came to this theme when the diocesan conference of the following year considered the subject "The Special Wants of the Church in Wales at the Present Time":

> I must frankly confess that I have been greatly astonished at the tone of despondency with which so many Churchmen regard the attacks now being made on the Church, as if disestablishment and

---

[45] *Report of the Third St Asaph Diocesan Conference*, 1884, pp 20f. Howell also in this speech called for reform in the Church, mentioning the areas of patronage, episcopal appointments, the rights of laity, and the system of church discipline. Cf. an article probably written by him in *Y Cyfaill Eglwysig*, 3 [1869] 200, "Deddf yr Eglwys".

disendowment meant the extermination of the Church, root and branch. I beg you will not for one moment suppose that I think lightly of either disestablishment or disendowment. Far, very far from it. But you must forgive me for saying that I regard establishment and endowment, in relation to what constitutes the Church, only, so to speak, as the candlestick when compared with the candle. Most deeply should I regret losing the grand old golden candlestick, the heirloom of many generations, in which the candle of God's truth has burned so brightly for many and many an age in this Christian land. But would not that candle burn, though perhaps not so brightly, if held in a wooden or an earthenware candlestick, as indeed she did, in the purest and holiest age of the Church? My Lord, I challenge any man to tell me of any church destroyed, or even seriously injured, so long as that church remained loyal and faithful to the truth of God. I challenge any man to tell me of any church destroyed, in the very meridian of her spiritual prosperity, when every fibre of her frame was charged with buoyant life and spiritual energy. Churches are not destroyed from without, but only where there is a decay of faith, and love, and zeal within. I grant you that some of us may have to witness serious changes in the outward machinery of the Church, some of which we may well deprecate most deeply. But surely, if history teaches us anything, it teaches us this, that institutions sometimes need pruning and purging if they are to bring forth richer and riper fruit. It is possible that we clergy may have our autocracy somewhat limited, but I am not quite sure that this would be any harm to us, so long as it did not affect our spiritual independence. It is possible that the laity of the Church may acquire a larger share in the government of the Church than at present. But is there not a priesthood of the laity as well as a priesthood of the clergy? and shame upon us if we doubt their loyalty to the great verities of the Christian faith ... "If God be with us, who can be against us?"[46]

*   *   *   *

If the Church was to meet the needs of the hour and face the future with confidence, a change of attitude was needed. Thus in his celebrated Westminster sermon he suggested that reform and readjustment was required. But, he added, the steady progress of the Church during the previous twenty years was a token that God

---

[46] *Report of the Fourth St Asaph Diocesan Conference*, 1885, pp 17f.

had not deserted her, and that the fruit of her old age would far exceed that of her youth. The first change Howell felt was required in order to receive such blessing from God was a reversal of the policy of the past, that policy of "discouraging Welsh nationality, of seeking the extinction of the Welsh language, and ignoring the essential ethnic peculiarities of the people inhabiting the Principality of Wales .... Of nothing am I more deeply convinced than that we can render far greater and better service to both Church and State as patriotic Welshmen than as mongrel Englishmen ... Is it possible to estimate what the Welsh people might have been if the Church had been to them a wise, sympathetic, and forbearing mother?"... And he asked, if the colonial Church found it necessary to adapt itself to the wants and ways of people, in order to win souls to Christ, why should not the same principle apply in Wales?

The second change Howell found necessary was a different attitude by the Church to those outside its pale: "if the Church is to become once more the Church of the Welsh nation, she must become more forbearing and forgiving; more lowly in heart, and Christ-like in spirit; more of the mother and less of the monitor to the entire body of the people in Wales." He felt, however, that "while the supposed political ascendancy of the Church continues, home reunion in Wales can be nothing but a pious hope". And thus he appealed, to further this end:

> But surely loyalty to the Church does not demand that we depreciate the labours of men who have covered Wales with houses of prayer, and whose Sunday Schools have made the Welsh people the best instructed in the Word of God of any portion of the British race? Surely it is true that whenever we find the image of Christ, and the fruits of the Spirit, there have we incontrovertible evidence of the grace of God? May God forbid, then, that we should ever limit our sympathies to anything less than the Apostolic prayer, "Grace be with all them that love the Lord Jesus Christ in sincerity."[47]

[47] Howell, *The Welsh Church*, p 12-19. Speaking at the 1884 St Asaph Diocesan Conference [*Report*, p 20], Howell asked, "surely the time is come when we should dwell not quite so boastfully on what we have done in the building and restoration of churches, schools and parsonages during the last fifty years, as if others had not done as much, without our endowments, with but half of our wealth, and not a tithe of our social influence. From the bottom of my heart do I thank God for what has been done; but don't let us swagger as if all the activity and liberality had been on our side."

The third and most urgent need Howell emphasised was that the Church should be lifted up to a higher spiritual life. "I am ... convinced that our spiritual life, in the Church and out of it, is at present at far too low a temperature to make anything in the nature of reunion possible in any real sense. Nothing but a great wave of genuine spiritual revival, burying all our discords in its mighty overflow, will ever bring about the time when 'Ephraim shall not envy Judah, and Judah shall not vex Ephraim.'" The fulfillment of these needs would be brought about by "a devout and devoted clergy, men of strong convictions and broad sympathies, men living and labouring from the highest aims and motives." He thus issued this challenge to his Church:

> Nothing but an outpouring of the Holy Spirit can calm the tempest, and sanctify the nation's life. "Not by might, nor by power, but by my Spirit, says the Lord of Hosts." Anything short of this will leave us divided, distracted, and drifting further and further away from God. Two things are essential to a baptism of Divine power. There must be a deep and abiding penitence for the past, and there must be a continuous intercession on the part of God's faithful people.[48]

Howell wrote in much the same vein to the Bangor Church Lay Association in 1889. While he agreed that the Church had been much improved since the Association was founded in 1853, he felt there had not been a corresponding advance in spirituality and moral force, not least among the clergy. One of the dangers of the present time, he suggested, was to mistake ecclesiastical activity for spiritual life. Never was ecclesiastical life more flourishing in the Jewish church, he added, than when our Lord compared it to a whitewashed sepulchre.[49] One may note too his speech to the Church Pastoral-Aid Society's annual conference in 1889. There was much talk about the number of new churches, the increase in services and in other agencies of the Church. But what was needed was more spiritual life.[50] Buildings reflected wealth more than spiritual life and activity.

---

[48] Howell, *The Welsh Church*, pp 17-21.
[49] NLW MS Minor Deposit 909B, fol 48: Howell to Robert Isaac Jones, secretary of the Bangor Lay Association, 19 July 1889.
[50] Cymru Fydd, II [1889] 322.

If there was thus urgency and challenge, there were also signs of hope, as Howell maintained in that Westminster sermon:

> [N]ever was there a time when so strong a confidence in her mission so permeated every fibre of her frame. Never was there a time when the conviction was so widespread that she is yet destined, whether established or disestablished, to render greater services to the Cymric people than she has ever rendered before. Surely this buoyant hopefulness is prophetic of a brighter and better future yet to come.

He could not believe that a Church with "a pure, Apostolic and Scriptural Creed; a Church pre-eminent throughout the centuries for her jealously of the essential Deity of the Incarnate Lord, and the exclusive supremacy of the inspired Word" could "be seriously injured, far less uprooted and destroyed."[51]

This prophetic note that the Church in Wales needed to look to its own spiritual life before it did anything else was one which Howell constantly reiterated. Speaking to the St Asaph diocesan conference in 1890, on the tithe dispute, he concluded:

> if there was one lesson more than another which the events of the last four years ought to teach the clergy, it was that it was their duty, for their own safety, to look less to man and more to God - to think less of their own interests and more of their duties - and above all to vindicate their rights by the holiness of their lives and the devotedness of their services rather than by faith in politicians, no matter to what party they might belong.[52]

---

[51] Howell, *The Welsh Church*, pp 11f. W Ryle Davies in the Welsh Nonconformist periodical *Traethodydd* ["Yr Hybarch Archddiaion Howell yn St Margaret, Westminster, a'r Tra Pharchedig Esgob Llanelwy yn St Paul's", 45 [1890], pp 22-34] criticised Howell for this sermon in no uncertain terms, in that he spoke of Nonconformists more as enemies than as friends, and for his hope of the Church of England in Wales as being once more the mother church of Wales: "If this is the new policy of Churchmen, I say to my fellow countrymen, beware of false prophets." The writer also noted the Bishop of St Asaph's second-rate sermon that same Sunday at St Paul's Cathedral, and criticised both the bishop and Howell for neglecting the opportunities of preaching the Gospel, instead of defending the Church in Wales.

[52] *Report of the St Asaph Diocesan Conference, 1890*, p 9. In May 1889 Howell wrote to Archbishop Benson that more injury was being done to the Welsh Church by the delay in passing the tithe bill than had been done by the operations of the Liberation Society over the previous thirty years [Lambeth Palace Library, Benson Papers 78, item 345].

He reminded the delegates at the Norwich Church Congress that the future of the Church in Wales rested largely in her own hands:

> What Wales needs is not religious discussions, but a living Christianity; not criticism, but a dogmatic faith; not seeking after truth, but a bold faithful and unfaltering presentation of Him who is "the Truth." The contests of the future in Wales must not be "who shall be the greatest", but who shall dive deepest into the depths of human misery and sin, and who shall make the greatest sacrifices to win for Christ the 500,000 souls who are now "as sheep having no shepherd." The lowliest are ever the strongest; and the Church of the future in Wales will be the Church which will conquer by love, and which shall drink deepest into the Spirit of Him who said, "The Son of Man came not to be ministered unto, but to minister, and to give His life a ransom for many."[53]

What is needed in Wales, Howell said again to the 1889 annual meeting of the Church Pastoral-Aid Society, was "a spirit of self-forgetfulness among the clergy, a spirit of holy zeal pervading the laity, with the glory of God and the spiritual welfare of souls as the supreme motive power of all our aims. Filled with the presence and power of the Holy Ghost, whether established or disestablished, endowed or disendowed, I am convinced the Church in Wales will continue to represent the Apostolic Christianity of the primitive British Church of this realm."[54] In speaking on the same theme at the Manchester Church Congress of 1888 he urged his listeners to wrestle in prayer for his Church, so that whether it was established or disestablished, it might flourish again.[55] At the end of the day Howell was chiefly concerned with the spiritual life and witness of the Church and saw its establishment and endowment as points of minor importance compared to this supreme goal of giving glory to God. And his hope was not simply that his Church might flourish, but that it would be a united Church which would flourish. There was at that time little doctrinal difference between the Anglican Church and Dissent. The modernism which infected and poisoned Welsh Nonconformity and deprived it of its witness and

[53] Report of the Norwich Church Conference, 1895, p 408.
[54] Quoted in Cymru Fydd, II [1889] 322.
[55] Report of the Manchester Church Congress, 1888, p 76.

life was still to come, and the equal aberration of the Tractarian movement was at that time confined to a few churches in Wales and was rightly regarded as a denial of the true Reformation settlement. His desire that Nonconformity might return to "Yr Hen Fam" and thus strengthen the Christian life in Wales was not such an unrealistic one at the time. And to achieve this Howell hints, though he never actually states it, that he would be prepared to see all the uniting churches on an equal basis. And this would mean the disestablishment of his own.[56]

Had Howell's prophetic words been more heeded by the leaders of his own Church, and had that Church realised that there were more serious and urgent issues before it than fighting disestablishment in the ways proposed and adopted by Bishop Edwards, as will be noted in the next chapter, then what strength might the Church have had, and what blessing might it not have known from God and given to Wales?

---

[56] For a wider approach to Howell's partly pro-disestablishment views see my article, "Traitors and Compromisers: the Shadow side of the Church's Fight against Disestablishment", *Journal of Welsh Religious History*, 3 [1995] 35-53.

Archidiaconal Years

Those years at Wrexham saw a growing appreciation of the value and importance of Howell's work. It is not surprising that this was recognised from time to time. Archbishop Tait conferred on him the Lambeth degree of B.D. in 1877, thereby publicly recognising his many services to the Church in Wales. The award also indicated the Welsh Church's desire for its 'big preachers' to have equivalent degrees to those paraded by many of the Welsh Nonconformist preachers, whose transatlantic trips generally found a D.D. hood in their return baggage! Howell found the expenses of that degree rather prohibitive at seventy-one pounds![1] David Howell was rural dean of the extensive deanery of Wrexham from 1882-92, became examining chaplain to Bishop Hughes, and in 1885 was collated as prebendary of Meliden and Treasurer of St Asaph cathedral. This was in the gift of the bishop. This prebend required a period of three months residence at the cathedral. The chapter act book describes the ceremony by which he was installed into office. "After the first lesson the dean and canons and others moved to the chapter house, and agreed to proceed to installation, whereupon the procession returned into the cathedral in the same order, chanting the Te Deum, the Very Revd the Dean leading by the hand the Revd David Howell to his seat...."[2] It was all very Anglican! The prebend had a stipend of £350, although Howell, as we noted earlier, paid from this income the stipend of one of his Wrexham curates. Bishop Hughes, in

---

[1] Howell to D Silvan Evans, 17 June 1878, NLW Cwrt Mawr MS 903B, fol 9. Lambeth MS 1715 is a record of the various degrees granted by the Archbishops of Canterbury. Between 1850-65 a number of Welsh clerics received Lambeth MAs: David James, Evan Jenkins of Dowlais, Leigh Morgan, David Archard Williams, and Ebenezer Woodman of Walton West. In addition Archbishop Tait granted DDs to John Griffith of Llandeilo and Daniel Evans of Caernarfon, and BDs to John Griffiths of Neath in 1877 and to Howell in the following year. Benson was much more sparing in the granting of these Lambeth degrees.

[2] NLW SA/CR/4.

appointing Howell to this senior prebend was clearly following his stated policy of opening the cathedral to the Welsh-speaking part of his diocese. In 1880, for example, he had insisted that at least one Sunday service and one weekday evensong should be in the Welsh language.

The cathedral chapter had been described in 1878 by Mr Scott Banks of Northop, an influential layman of the diocese, as "Four or five of the most meritorious members of the church ... collected together at St Asaph for the purpose of listening to each other."[3] This was a little unfair, as Hughes hoped to make use of the chapter as a means of forwarding church life and progress throughout the diocese. But times were difficult, and the chapter did not find such a task at all easy. This was the period of the tithe disputes, when tithes were withheld, albeit from religious motives (for Nonconformist farmers objected to paying for the State Church), although in reality the real issue was the agricultural depression of the day. As the revenue of the cathedral came mainly from this tithe income, the chapter was put into great difficulties. At one period the minor canons had to face a reduction in salary and the tuning of the organ was discontinued. There had been tithe distraints at Gresford in 1888, before Howell's appointment, but these had been carried out on the instructions of the Ecclesiastical Commissioners who had taken over the tithe property in that parish once owned by the dean and chapter of Winchester. There is no record, however, of Howell having to face difficulties with his tithe income.[4] Howell took part in the decision which opened the cathedral for daily prayer, and in the long dispute over the chapter's refusal to allow the consistory court to meet in the cathedral. His name is not mentioned, however, in the chapter's protest against the Welsh Church Suspensory Bill of 1893, in the course of which it organised meetings throughout the diocese to oppose the measure. However, Howell organised his own meetings of protest as has been noted before. Howell's residence at the cathedral for

[3] *Report of the St Asaph Diocesan Conference*, 1881, p 27.
[4] *Wrexham Advertiser*, 20 Oct 1888, p 6. The Ecclesiastical Commission, as lay rector, was responsible for chancel repairs. However, Howell spoke on the sufferings of the clergy affected by this dispute, some of whom were reduced to living on £40 per year, at a meeting in Exeter Hall, London [SA/DR/49, fol 6].

three months each year was not without fruit. He held, at first in the chapter house, a Bible class for over eighty women, established temperance meetings in the city, and organised quiet days for the clergy of the diocese. At the *Haul* commented, he refused to rest any more in the cathedral than he did in his own parish.[5]

The first diocesan conference for the diocese of St Asaph was held in 1878. These conferences were an innovation within the Victorian church, designed to improve communication between bishop and clergy, as well as to allow some lay participation in the working and thinking of the diocese. The movement had started in the sister diocese of Bangor in 1865, and had proved an outstanding success. Howell was frequently called upon to address these meetings. In 1884 he spoke on the disestablishment campaign; in the following year on church extension; a paper on parochial missions was given in 1887, and he spoke on the tithe dispute in 1890. Although Bishop Edwards, who succeeded Hughes, used the conferences to whip up support and enthusiasm for his policies of church defence, it is quite clear that much useful work was done by them, with papers being given or discussions promoted on such topics as temperance, education, social life, family prayer, spirituality, and Christian socialism, to name but a few.

Bishop Hughes, shortly before his death in office, decided to establish a third archdeaconry in his diocese, under the name of the archdeaconry of Denbigh. The geographical spread of the new archdeaconry widened, and its title was consequently changed to that of Wrexham.[6] Five rural deaneries with a strength of seventy parishes were assigned to it, including some of the most populous ones in the diocese. For very obvious reasons Howell was appointed as the new archdeacon, although Bishop Hughes died before he could be installed. For two years, 1889-91, Howell combined the work of the archdeaconry with his parochial work at Wrexham, undertaking these new duties without any further remuneration or even expenses of office. He retained, of course,

---

[5] *Haul*, 1886, p 346; 1885, p 347; SA/DR/46, fol 553. Some came from Rhyl to these Bible classes, and the dean was urged to conduct one for men.
[6] Ibid, 1889, pp 255; *Bye-Gones*, 9 Ap 1890, pp 350f. This noted that an alternative suggestion for the title of the archdeaconry was Powys, but argued that some of the churchpeople of Wrexham moved to have it named after their town.

his prebend and its income (now united formally with the archdeaconry), but he could write to Silvan that his was an empty archdeaconry, high on duties and expenses but without any additional emoluments.[7] It is hardly surprising that Howell found it almost impossible to combine a busy parish with an extensive archdeaconry, especially with the illness of his wife, and in 1891 he probably accepted with some relief the offer by Bishop Edwards of the small but lucrative living of Gresford. It was vacant by the death of Edward Braithwaite Smith, who was the first incumbent to be appointed for many years on his own merits, rather than because of his relationship to one of the bishops. Heneage Horsley, a son of the bishop of that name, had held the living from 1803-47, together with another parish and a cathedral prebend, but preferred to reside at Edinburgh, where he was also dean of Brechin. Horsley received over £450 per annum from this parish alone, but paid but £30 to the curate who undertook the duty for him.[8] His successor was another example of episcopal nepotism. Robert Wickham was a brother-in-law of Bishop Short, an Englishman in a partly Welsh-speaking parish, and who was later to become archdeacon of St Asaph.[9] He died in 1880, and Howell probably soon realised that his Gresford parishioners regarded him more highly as a successful breeder of pigs than as a spiritual guide and pastor to his flock![10]

The tithe income of the parish was said to be £585 per annum, but the value of the commuted tithes had fallen during the 1880s and in 1891 was worth £443. In addition, 77 acres of glebe land were rented out, together with other lands and tenements, including the Griffin Inn at Gresford, for £186, and there was an estimated income of £30 from surplice fees. But of this £659 a

---

[7] Howell to D Silvan Evans, 11 May 1889, NLW Cwrt Mawr MS 903B, fol 36; cf *North Wales Guardian*, 12 Ap 1890, p 6; *Bye-Gones*, 9 Ap 1890, pp 350f; and Wrexham Parish Church Minute Book, Clwyd Record Office, Ruthin, PD/101/1/262, recording the 1890 vestry's appreciation of Howell's sacrifice of time and labour in undertaking this additional duty.

[8] A J Johnes, *On the Causes which have produced Dissent from the Established Church in the Principality of Wales* [3rd edn, London 1870], p 200.

[9] D R Thomas, *History of the Diocese of St Asaph* [3 vols, Oswestry 1908-13], I 249: R W Morgan, *The Church and its Episcopal Corruption in Wales* [2nd edn London 1856] pp 77-9. To be fair to Wickham, we need to realise that he restored the church at a cost of £4,000, built a new vicarage and also new schools, the latter as a memorial to Bishop Short.

[10] David Evans, *Adgofion* [Lampeter 1904], pp 148f.

sum of £141 needed to be deducted as expenses and outgoings, of which £62 consisted of rates and £33 was paid to the agent who collected the tithe. In his first year, for example, Howell paid a sum of £20.16s.7d. for first fruits, and £2.2s.8d. in tenths. The first sum represented the valuation of the benefice in 1535, and was paid to Queen Anne's Bounty as a sort of tax upon his entry, and the second was an annual payment to the same body.[11] This money was used for the augmentation of less wealthy parishes. The parishioners numbered three thousand, and consisted of, to use Howell's phrase, "hybrid borderers, remnants of the old cattle lifters, neither Welsh nor English".[12] Howell had reported on this parish in his 1888 visitation - as rural dean - of the deanery of Wrexham. It then had one curate, an average morning congregation of three hundred, an afternoon one of forty-five adults and one hundred and thirty children - presumably an all-age Sunday School, and an evening congregation of three hundred and fifty. There were about two hundred communicants with two celebrations a month, with an average of twenty-three communicants at the early celebration, and fifty-one at the mid-day one. The day school had two hundred and twenty-two children on its books and the Sunday School seven hundred and seventy-four.[13]

Although several Nonconformist writers, anxious to make as much political capital as they could from any hint of controversy, alleged that Howell had been transferred to an "outlying" and smaller parish on the English border as he had "paid too much attention to his spiritual duties and too little to the harrowing of Dissenters", or had been "found guilty of the high treason of loving his native land, and speaking kindly of its language, its traditions and its aspirations,"[14] the reality is that Howell accepted the parish in order to carry out more fully his onerous duties as archdeacon. This may be why it was said by a former incumbent of Gresford, the Revd Colin Semper, that Howell made little impression on the parish. Mr Semper points out that the parish

---

[11] Queen Anne Bounty file on the parish, in the custody of the Representative Body of the Church in Wales, described hereafter as QAB.
[12] Howell to D Silvan Evans, 23 Dec 1896, NLW MS 903B fol 146.
[13] NLW SA/RD/44.
[14] William C Thomas, *The Church in Wales: Shall we End it or Mend it?* [Birmingham 1893], p 9.

magazine, started in 1866, ceases with his incumbency, and he was one of the few incumbents who failed to make any entries of his own in the so-called "parish book". Nevertheless this book does indicate that Howell was active in the parish. A meeting with the churchwardens led to an agreement not to allow Christmas and Harvest decorations to be placed on the medieval screens, the pulpit and within the altar rails; the bottom of the tower was fitted up as a choir vestry; the parish church defence committee prepared two hundred handbills to announce a lecture by the prominent Church defender, W E Helm, purchased numerous copies of booklets for free distribution, such as one hundred copies of Nye's *Church History*, and obtained nearly seven hundred and fifty signatures for a petition against disestablishment. Significantly Howell also emphasised the League of Prayer, suggesting that the greatest weapon of church defence lay in that activity. This league had been formed by W Walsham How, a former incumbent in the diocese of St Asaph, who had become bishop of Wakefield. In this work of prayer, Howell wrote, they could all unite to do something daily for the Church.[15] The papers of the Ecclesiastical Commission for the parish also suggest that Howell was a faithful and diligent pastor. He performed services in a school-room three miles from the parish church, obtained land from the commissioners for the purpose of building a village institute, and persuaded them, as the lay rectors, to discontinue the alleged right of the Parsonage Farm tenants, on a change of tenure, to have sittings in the chancel, "where accommodation is greatly needed for the choir". All the other tenants of the commissioners sat in the body of the church, Howell noted, and there was ample room for these tenants to join the others there.[16] And we also learn that he had some connection with a female temperance society, if only because on his departure he was presented by its members with an armchair.[17] Perhaps it was a symbolic gesture to thank him for his hard work in the parish and community and an indication that he could now "take it easy".

[15] Clwyd Record Office, Ruthin, PD/34/1/227.
[16] Ecclesiastical Commission file for the parish, in the custody of the Representative Body of the Church in Wales.
[17] *Wrexham Advertiser*, 22 May 1897, p 7.

It appears that Howell came into some conflict with his Sunday morning congregation, which consisted mainly of the more aristocratic and gentry members of the community, as was then the custom, the evening service being for the servants and ordinary people. Many of the richer merchants and business people of Chester had built their homes in his parish, and when he first saw their fashionable parade into the house of God he was deeply offended. Tradition relates that he reminded his congregation, on his first Sunday, that they had come to worship the Lord God of Israel and not the gods of fashion. He built up a large evening congregation, and was perhaps a little concerned about seeing so many of his former parishioners either walking the six or seven miles from Wrexham or catching what was to become a crowded train, in order to listen to his "pulpit ministry".[18] On the occasions when he preached at that evening service the church would be crowded to excess.[19]

His first month in office at Gresford started on a sad note. His wife, who had been seriously ill with heart disease since 1890, and was too ill to be moved from Wrexham, died at the vicarage there in the early days of June 1891. Almost his first act as vicar of Gresford was to attend her funeral in the churchyard of his new parish. She was an unassuming and retiring person, suggested an obituary in the local paper, but her benevolence of heart and Christian simplicity of life gave her an influence over both poor and great. She visited the Union workhouse frequently, did much work in connection with the clothing clubs and the mothers' meeting, so that the poor in Wrexham would experience a great loss. "In the parish", the obituary noted, "she was of the greatest help to her husband, who relied on her not only to work for the welfare of the community, but also upon her wise and helpful suggestions...".[20] Howell's sister, Mrs Saunders, whose husband, a Welsh Calvinistic Methodist minister, died in 1892, eventually came to keep house for him.

"It seems to be my lot to inhabit vicarages and glebe property in a deplorable state of dilapidation", wrote Howell to Queen

---

[18] I owe this note to the Revd Colin Semper.
[19] *Wrexham Advertiser*, 15 May 1897, p 7.
[20] Ibid, 6 June 1891, p 5; *Bye-Gones*, 10 June 1891, p 103; SA/DR/47, fol 761, which notes that the cathedral made note of Mrs Howell's death by singing the hymn "Thy will be done".

Anne's Bounty on 22 July 1891. "At Cardiff, and at Wrexham, as you will remember and here again, it is hard to exaggerate the sad condition of the Vicarage and its possessions, through the neglect of my predecessor. To make the house decently habitable will mean an expenditure of nearly a year's income."

Gresford Vicarage was even larger than the new house at Wrexham. Its impressive arcaded porch led into a substantial hall, with three large living rooms leading off it. The 'offices' included a servants' hall, separate quarters for men and women servants, and a stable yard with coach house and stables. It had been built in 1850 at the then substantial cost of £2,359.[21]

The house was in a deplorable condition. It had not been painted for years, and the roof was in such a bad condition that water poured into every room but one, destroying the plaster and damaging the woodwork. The drainage and sewerage passed under the house itself, and the local architect attributed the ill health of the previous incumbent and his family throughout most of his incumbency - and presumably his death - to the defective water supply. Water had to be pumped from a great depth for all domestic purposes, involving the labour of two men at a cost of thirty shillings per week. But, as Howell suggested, the house could be linked to the water main and a bath provided.

Dilapidations of £472 were charged to the estate of the previous incumbent, a massive sum which nevertheless bears out Howell's statements about the condition of the property. For the Smith family it was an unexpected charge, and the executors had to sell some land in order to meet it. Incidentally Archdeacon Wickam's estate had to pay a similar charge, of £405, in 1881. In addition to this sum of money which had to be spent on the house, Howell inquired about a substantial loan from Queen Anne's Bounty in order to make other improvements which would not be covered by these dilapidation charges. A loan of around a thousand pounds was agreed with Queen Anne's Bounty, repayable over ten years at a charge of £195 per annum. The loan was not taken out, however, partly because of the delay which would be caused in securing it, and also as Howell assumed he would be at Gresford for the remainder of his life. In fact, when

[21] Thomas, *St Asaph*, III 245.

he vacated the parish on his appointment to the deanery of St Davids six years later, Howell expressed concern about the loss he would face of the amount he had paid for this work from his own pocket. He was advised that he should continue to hold Gresford for the statutory six months after his appointment to St Davids, providing he supplied locums to take the services, and thus recover some of these costs, which, had he taken this mortgage, would have been passed on to his successor. In the event he did not do so. Instead he asked his successor, Mr Fishbourne, if he would allow him some part of the amount still outstanding, calculated at £305, but Fishbourne was advised it would be a voluntary payment on his part. There is no evidence that he paid it, but on the other hand there is no evidence either that Howell was charged any dilapidations on the property when he left, which probably indicates that some compromise between them had been reached.[22]

*　*　*　*

When the chapter of St Asaph Cathedral formally met to elect Alfred George Edwards as the new bishop of St Asaph, Howell was absent. He was declared contumacious. There may have been a perfectly valid reason for his absence, for Howell acted as one of his chaplains at the enthronement, but there were many who positively disliked, and even feared, Edwards' appointment. Thomas Gee's comment that his chief qualifications for office were that he had written much to *The Times* and was anti-Nonconformist[23] achieved widespread support, even from within the Anglican fold. The new bishop had nailed his colours to the mast in respect of the disestablishment controversy then raging throughout Wales, and his assaults on Nonconformity had added an even more bitter feeling to the already hardening attitudes between church and chapel. Unlike his eldest brother, H T Edwards, a former dean of Bangor, whose open letter to Gladstone is said to have helped persuade Gladstone to appoint a native Welsh-speaker to the diocese of St Asaph in 1870, the new

---

[22] QAB papers.
[23] T G Jones, *Cofiant Thomas Gee* [Denbigh 1913], p 550.

bishop had little regard for his Welsh upbringing and little sympathy for the Welsh movement within the Church in Wales. He seems at times to have regarded 'Welsh' and 'Nonconformist' as synonymous terms. This was in spite of the fact that Edwards was but one generation removed from *gwerin* stock, his grandfather being a convert of Daniel Rowland. It was apparent too that Edwards was going to take a much more militant attitude towards Nonconformity, which he positively disliked, and had already made clear that he believed the defence of the Church against disestablishment and disendowment was best secured by the gathering of statistical evidence and by political manoeuvres and alliances. Too often his temper seemed to take these matters into the sphere of personal abuse. To him attack was the best form of defence. As a bishop he now possessed considerable authority for his viewpoint. He might even have claimed that his appointment was an endorsement by the Conservative party as well as by the Church of his position. A *Times* correspondent quoted a Welsh periodical, *Tyst a'r Dydd*, about him: it said that "His purpose is to serve the Church, and he cares not what means he uses to attain that end."[24]

If these were the methods he used, Edwards' underlying policy was equally questioned by many. For he brought into his episcopate his own understanding of church defence, by which he pinned his hopes on so stressing the connection between the Church of England and Wales that any talk of dismemberment, and consequently of disestablishment and disendowment, would be ruled out of court. This policy meant that Edwards came into direct conflict with those who wished to stress the indigenous nature of the Welsh Church. Not only was he aggressive in furthering this policy, he also made it clear that his clergy were to accept it under pain of being charged with disloyalty and of being over sympathetic to Nonconformity if they did not. This was known throughout Wales as the "St Asaph policy".[25]

This new stress was directly opposed to the then current wave of patriotism and nationalism being manifested in Wales. In fact it further magnified, and seemed to prove, the old taunt that the

---

[24] J E Vincent, *Letters from Wales* [London 1889], p 142.
[25] George Lerry, *Alfred George Edwards* [Oswestry 1939], p 37.

Church in Wales was simply an anglicising force bent on achieving complete harmony, linguistic and otherwise, with England itself. And this was at a time when the patriotic movement had reached the zenith of its influence, being displayed in the eisteddfod and Welsh literary and language groups, the Welsh press, the university and educational movements, by the Cymru Fydd group in politics, and by an influential though not organised movement within the Welsh Church which endeavoured to seek its reform and renewal. One of the leading figures in this Welsh Church movement was Dean Edwards, the bishop's brother, and whose tragic suicide in 1884, after a long period of depression, deprived it of the leadership it needed. Other influential figures in this movement were David Jones, later vicar of Penmaenmawr, whose many books and pamphlets ceaselessly proclaimed this nationalistic message, and Archdeacon Griffiths of Neath, Howell's mentor.[26] By following Bishop Edwards' policy the Church found itself out of step with one of the main movements in Welsh life of that day, described by David Howell in a speech on Welsh patriotism as "the most potent factor in the existence and in the morals of the Welsh people."[27] He cited the Welsh Sunday Closing Act as a result of this movement. This was the first piece of legislation in modern times which recognised Wales as a separate nation.

All Howell's sympathies lay with this movement. He saw the Welsh Church as a vehicle for his nation's spirituality, even though he knew that this vocation had to be shared with Nonconformity. He believed, as we have noted beforehand, that the best defence of the Church lay in stressing its pastoral and preaching ministry. His instincts as well as his Christian faith told him to live peaceably with all men, and to recognise and applaud all what was good and gracious in others. He thus feared that Edwards' policy would create yet more bitterness. A clash between the two was almost inevitable, particularly as Edwards made it quite clear that he would tolerate no compromise with those Nonconformist and Liberal leaders who pressed for the disestablishment of the Church. Howell was not alone in these feelings. They were

---

[26] See Emlyn Sherrington's contribution in D Smith [ed], *A People and a Proletariat* [London 1980], pp 127-47.
[27] *Wrexham Advertiser*, 25 Feb 1893, p 6.

shared by many in the dioceses of St Asaph and Bangor, as we discuss later.

Yet the dispute which emerged between Edwards and Howell was not simply a question about principles and methods to be used in the disestablishment campaign. It was also a matter of personalities. Howell felt the alienating and cold stare of his father-in-God as disturbing and hurtful. And Edwards retaliated with his usual hostility to anyone who dared to refute his St Asaph policy, especially to one who held such an important office in his diocese. The nature of this personal duel comes out clearly in a letter written by Howell to Thomas Darlington, a senior inspector of schools in Wales who had learnt Welsh in order to fulfil his duties more adequately. This letter was written in 1893, at the height of another controversy between the two men:

> The article in last weeks "Illustrated Church News" is either by the Bishop or inspired by him. I dare not tackle him just now, as I would make short work of his explanations. His statements as to the falling off of Welsh nonconformists has been repeatedly refuted, but he goes on reiterating the same things as if his figures had never been questioned. His mental idiosyncrasy is phenomenal, and such as I never met with before. He seems incapable of being convinced. Fancy a man repeating in 1893 that which he had withdrawn in 1890, as is the case with the Llandudno Association figures! In England his office and position give weight to statements which are quite discredited in Wales.[28]

There indeed was the rub: Edwards as a bishop was regarded by the English church leaders as able to pronounce almost *ex cathedra* in matters relating to the Welsh Church. Guarded as all Howell's letters were to his bishop, of necessity, here in this letter Howell reveals his distaste and concern for the man and his works.

*   *   *   *

There was something more, however, which must have influenced their distaste for one another. How far Howell was aware of this at

---

[28] Howell to Thomas Darlington, 23 Aug 1893, in NLW MS 1058C.

at the beginning of their argument is not known, but he must have been aware of it at some stage of their quarrel, although again it is hard to access how much it affected his judgment and assessment of Edwards. As that assessment was the same as, and sometimes more charitable than those of other people, it probably did not.

Howell, it was known in certain influential circles, had been an approved candidate in a number of the Welsh episcopal elections. His Lambeth B.D. may have been an indication of this position, for at least three of the Welsh clergy who received Lambeth divinity degrees were also regarded as episcopal candidates. There were many influential voices who supported his candidature on these occasions. If Lady Llanover's support stood more on the debit side, that of Bishops Ryle and Bickersteth were clearly on the credit side, while Thomas Gee's and Henry Richard's support would have carried weight with Gladstone at least. His appointment to a bishopric, said an obituary note, would have been extremely popular "with the great body of the Welsh people."[29] Howell's qualifications were as good, if not better, than Joshua Hughes' on the ecclesiastical front, for was not Howell the outstanding Welsh Church preacher of the day, and had he not successfully had charge of two of the largest parishes in Wales, and held high ecclesiastical office? His social antecedents may not have been as good as the English bishops of that time, but the social backgrounds of William Laud or Thomas Burgess, to give but two examples, were similar to his, and his family background, of an independent yeoman stock, was better than that of either Joshua Hughes or John Owen.

Bishop Ollivant of Llandaff mentioned two social disqualifications against Howell in 1870, though he regarded Howell as the equal of Joshua Hughes, who received the appointment to St Asaph in that year. The first was Howell's marriage. He doubted whether Mrs Howell could hold her own in the polite society expected of palace lawns and diocesan functions. The other was his lack of a university education, One of Gladstone's other advisors said this would make him "more timid, ... feeling ... he was at a disadvantage ..."[30] H A Bruce, later

[29] *Bye-Gones*, 28 Jan 1903, p 17.
[30] A Kinnaird to Gladstone, 8 Jan 1870, British Library, Gladstone Papers [GP] 44424, fol 30.

Lord Aberdare, an influential figure in Gladstone's administration, was horrified that Gladstone was even considering Howell's name, and it is clear Bruce spoke for many of the Welsh upper classes, who were equally horrified by Hughes' eventual appointment. Howell, he wrote, had the qualities which resembled the better class of Nonconformist preacher. In learning, social position, weight of character and in his capacity to deal with the clergy or administer the affairs of a diocese, Bruce judged Howell as gravely deficient.[31] Although at one stage Gladstone regarded Howell as "the likeliest looking" of all the candidates he had placed on his short list, one who would fulfil his expectation of a bishop who could outpreach Dissent and thus win back Nonconformity to the Church - an expectation which Bruce regarded with horror - he obviously decided that Howell was too young, and could wait his turn.[32] In this episode the great problem which beset prime ministers from the 1840s to the 1880s of finding native Welsh-speaking bishops for Wales is illustrated. There were simply no Welsh-speaking clergy who could come up to the expectations demanded of a candidate for the English bench, with regard to breeding, learning and the ability to act as a peer of the realm. A lowering of standards was required, but would not this have some effect upon the status of bishops in general, and the government of the Church in Wales in particular? It is a problem that does not go away!

Howell was again mentioned to Disraeli in 1874 when he was endeavouring to find, without too much trouble, a replacement for Bishop Thirlwall of St Davids. Ollivant was quoted by Lord Dynevor as saying that while Howell was not a university man there was no one else in his diocese whom he would prefer to see there. Dynevor himself, who had the distinction of being not only a landed proprietor in the vacant diocese, a member of the Conservative party in the Lords, but also a cleric in the diocese of Gloucester, also recommended him highly. He was, he wrote, a wonderful preacher, who drew crowded congregations, and whose appointment would be received with enthusiasm by the middle class. But his lordship must then have checked his

[31] H A Bruce to Gladstone, 8 11 & 13 Jan 1870, GP 44086, fols 70, 78, 84.
[32] As suggested by Kinnaird in his letter to Gladstone of 8 Jan 1870: GP 44424, fol 30.

Crockford - a thing which Disraeli never did - and as a result reconsidered the matter, arguing now that Howell's want of scholarship, like that of Bishop Hughes, would be a bar to his acceptability amongst the upper classes and senior clergy of the diocese.[33] However, Disraeli fulfilled expectations and appointed the 'hot favourite', Basil Jones, then archdeacon of York and also a landowner in the diocese of St Davids.

By 1882 Gladstone was back in office, endeavouring to find another Welsh-speaking bishop for the diocese of Llandaff. The Conservative *Western Mail* pressed the claims of Howell onto the Liberal prime minister,[34] and Richard Grosvenor, Gladstone's political secretary, was asked to sound out Howell's claims, even though his chief was not too impressed by Lady Llanover's recommendation of her favourite, nor with her argument that most of the "highest" Welsh clergy wished for his appointment. More was needed in a bishop than just preaching ability, Gladstone replied to one of her letters, indicating some change in his own views since 1870. Eventually, almost displaying his annoyance at her constant interference, he challenged her with the question, "what had Howell done to deserve a bishopric?" Her ladyship answered that one at length, but probably Gladstone never read the letter, only a summary of it made by a secretary.[35]

Nevertheless it is clear that Howell's name had been repeatedly mentioned, and his claims examined, on three separate occasions for a Welsh bishopric between 1870-82, and it is obvious that he could not have been unaware of this fact, knowing the small world of the Welsh church and the intense interest these episcopal elections created at that time.

* * * *

Amongst the Benson papers at Lambeth Palace Library is a sad correspondence initiated by Evan Jenkins, then rector of Manafon near Berriew, Montgomeryshire, during the period 1893. Jenkins,

---

[33] Dynevor to Barrington, 12 17 & 26 June 1874, Bodleian Library, Oxford, Disraeli Papers [Dep Hughenden] 157/4/271 281, 299; and Dynevor's memorandum regarding Ollivant to Barrington, 9/10 June 1874; ibid, fols 263, 265.
[34] WM, 23 Dec 1882, p 3; 26 Dec 1882, p 2; 1 Jan 1883, p 3.
[35] Lady Llanover to Gladstone, 16, 24, 26 Dec 1882, GP 44478, fols 112, 188, 232.

an Oxford graduate and then in his early sixties, had committed some misdemeanour, but, certified as insane, and with the consent of his relatives, had been consigned to various asylums in Bridgend and elsewhere between 1891 and early 1893. His parish had been sequestrated, and most of its income appropriated for the stipend of a curate appointed to take pastoral care of it. From 1893 onwards Jenkins appears to have drifted between his brother's home - Edward was rector of Llanmihangel near Cowbridge, Manafon and lodgings in London. Jenkins regarded Bishop Edwards as the source of all his troubles; he was paranoid about him, and made many startling statements about his personal life and the time of his headship at Llandovery, and especially about his feud with his rival headmaster, Lloyd of Brecon. Many of these statements are obviously untrue, but some can be verified by other means, and others have the ring of hearsay evidence about them.

In his letter to the archbishop of 30 January 1893 Jenkins wrote that he blamed himself that such a man as Edwards should have been appointed bishop. David Howell of Wrexham was to have been the man, but he had informed his Grace that David Howell's first son, Taliesin, was born a month after marriage, and that Archdeacon Griffiths of Neath both officiated at his marriage and baptised his child in the space of two months, and yet recommended him to enter the ministry of the Church. Through the insane cry for Welsh bishops Howell would have attained the mitre but for the intervention of the Queen herself. Jenkins, who was obviously aware of the local gossip in the small villages of the vale of Glamorgan, having been brought up in those parts, possibly as a near contemporary of Howell, had little liking for him. Having accepted a residential canonry at St Asaph worth £350 per annum Howell had, he claimed, ridiculed the recent attempt to establish daily services in the cathedral, arguing that a 'gospel sermon' alone was needed. Nevertheless Jenkins believed that Howell would have been a better bishop than Edwards, and would have been elevated to that dignity had it not been for his letter. Howell, he claimed, was a saint compared to the "reckless ruffian" who was now bishop![36]

---

[36] Evan Jenkins to Benson, 30 Jan & 15 July 1893, Lambeth Palace Library, Benson Papers [BP] 116, fols 296-304 & 306. His chronology was a little out. For Jenkins see my article in *Montgomeryshire Collections*, 83 [1995] 177-88.

How far was Jenkins' allegations correct about the 1889 election to St Asaph? There is sufficient reason to believe it was a reasonably truthful account, and was known to quite a number of people. A letter of Howell's son, Tudor, to T E Ellis, withdrawing his candidature for the post of secretary to the proposed commission on the Welsh Sunday Closing Act, contains this passage:

> My reason for so doing is certain knowledge which came to me at the latter end of last week. I may say at once that it is the conduct of the Clergy and some of the supporters of the present Govt. in the appointment of the new bishop of S. Asaph. When the see became vacant, I knew my father, being a man of broad views, would be keenly opposed, and when another was appointed, I was not surprised. I have only just, however, heard to what depths of violence and meanness my father's enemies had descended in their opposition. I could better explain this sometime when I can have a conversation with you. Suffice it to say that matters were such as to cause in me the most utter loathing of the Church and her supporters. This being so I concluded it would not be honest of me to accept a post at the hands of the present Govt., while actuated by motives of the bitterest opposition to their keenest allies, the Clergy, I should be holding myself out as a friend to those I hate. For right down, unflinching, unchristianity commend me to the clergy. I have seen enough behind the scenes to sicken me of ecclesiasticism for three lifetimes. Surely, if there is true faith, it must be something far above these creeds and Churches?[37]

It is Lady Llanover who supplies the connecting threads. The *Record* in its issue of 8 February 1889 suggested that two names had been submitted to the Queen for the vacant bishopric of St Asaph.[38] It understood that these names were those of Canon Howell and Archdeacon Watkins of Durham. This may well have been incorrect at that point in time, but according to Lady Llanover, Howell's name had been submitted to the Queen. But the Queen had received some information "which tended to injure his moral character", and she therefore refused to accept Lord

---

[37] W T Howell to T E Ellis, 3 Ap 1889, NLW T E Ellis MS 855.
[38] *Record*, 8 Feb 1889, p 123.

Salisbury's recommendation of him for the bishopric.[39] Lady Llanover did not mention the circumstances though she alleges the matter concerned something long since buried and which had occurred before he had become a Christian. The matter, she believed, had been brought up for an ulterior motive by those who wanted to prevent Howell's appointment. She had written previously to Archbishop Benson noting some objections to Howell, who was being "traduced at the highest level". This may have been a reference to the bishop of St Davids, who was recommending his secretary, A G Edwards, for the post.[40] Further confirmation of this scenario is provided by letters from Bishop Bickersteth of Exeter to Lord Salisbury. Having written an unsolicited letter advancing Howell's claims for the see, he had obviously been told 'the truth'. He replied, "I had not the faintest suspicion of any such bar sinister in the escutcheon of the Canon's past history. I deeply lament it, but feel how formidable, perhaps insuperable, an obstacle it is for his appointment ..."[41] Even the *Record* failed to realise the full story when it noted in Howell's obituary that the time had not yet come to tell the full story of his friends' failure to obtain the bishopric for him.[42] We do not know whether the information about Howell came from that unhappy man, Jenkins, or not, but it was clearly known to those in high places, who saw it as a major disqualification for episcopal honours.

The following year Bishop Campbell resigned the see of Bangor, and by this time Edwards was in full possession of the facts about Howell. Perhaps startled that Howell had nearly obtained his [Edwards'] bishopric for himself, he began to realise that Howell was projecting an independent approach to the disestablishment controversy which was fundamentally different from his own. Edwards thus saw Howell as a dangerous rival, one who would be even more so if he were to be elevated to the episcopate. An archdeacon carries little weight outside his own diocese, whereas

---

[39] Howell was presented to the Queen by Bishop Edwards on her visit to North Wales in August 1889. One wonders if she even recollected his name! [Bye-Gones, Supplement 1889-90, p 54]
[40] Lady Llanover to Salisbury, 5 Feb 1889, Papers of the Third Marquess of Salisbury, Hatfield House [SP]; Ibid to Benson, 5 Feb 1889, BP 55, fol 89.
[41] Bickersteth to Salisbury, 26 Jan 1889 [SP].
[42] *Record*, 23 Jan 1903, p 79.

a bishop had a ready-made platform in the House of Lords and Convocation. Edwards was thus seriously perplexed to learn that Howell was high on the list of candidates for the see of Bangor. Indeed, he appeared to believe that the bishopric was within Howell's grasp.

That strange but interesting and informative writer, J Vyrnwy Morgan, in his book, *Welsh Religious Leaders in the Victorian Era*, picks up this fact, but misinterprets it. Stating that Howell was nearly appointed, he adds that an anonymous letter to the Ecclesiastical Commissioners robbed him of that honour, but though he hints that he knows the name of the writer of it, he declines to give it.[43] This is clearly gossip, but Howell himself knew he was a strong candidate, though in a letter to his friend Silvan he makes it clear that he was aware of a 'conspiracy' designed to keep him out, and even hints at the moral charges laid against him:

> I belong to no "clique". If I had I should not be what I am. During the recent vacancy at Bangor, the Evangelical clique were as opposed to my appointment as the High Church; I am bold to say there is not a Welsh clergyman living who has suffered from *cliqueness* as I have. The most savage, brutal, and infernal means have been used, and used successfully, to butcher my reputation, and to brand me with infamy. If you but knew one tenth of what has taken place, it would make your hair stand on end.[44]

There certainly appears to have been substance in Edwards' claim that Howell was being seriously considered for Bangor. Although Bishop Ryle had recommended him, and then withdrawn when he was informed of that early "shadow" against his name,[45] Bishop Bickersteth wrote again to recommend his claims, pointing out that upon more mature consideration he could no longer consider Howell's youthful indiscretion as an absolute bar to his appointment. Surely, he had long lived down the sins of his early manhood?[46] Furthermore, Canon Mason, an influential figure within the Church and a close friend of Archbishop Benson, was recommending him, and there was a hint

---

[43] J V Morgan, *Welsh Religious Leaders in the Victorian Era*, [London 1905], pp 112f.
[44] Howell to D Silvan Evans, 12 July 1890, NLW Cwrt Mawr MS 903B, fol 41.
[45] Ryle to Salisbury, 4 Mar 1890 [SP].
[46] Bickersteth to Salisbury, 17 & 26 Mar 1890 [SP].

that he had persuaded Canon Liddon of St Paul's to endorse Howell's claims.[47] Edwards was probably unaware that Dean Vaughan of Llandaff had also suggested Howell's name to Randall Davidson, dean of Windsor and by then Benson's close advisor in matters ecclesiastical and his intermediary with Queen Victoria. Though Vaughan had noted that the appointment of any Welsh speaker would mean a bishop who would not be on "a level" with his English colleagues "in any shape", yet Howell's sermon at St Margaret's, Westminster, indicated that he had "such a view of the real faults and perils of the Church in Wales .. [that] he would be a man of mark on the bench." Vaughan feared the appointment of anyone hostile to Nonconformity.[48]

Had Edwards known this he would have shuddered even more, for even with his limited knowledge of events he feared Howell's claims might be successful. Consequently, Edwards wrote strong letters to Benson, and probably others, against Howell's claims, and seems to have persuaded his friends to do likewise. Being assured on the highest possible authority that Howell was being considered for Bangor, he begged Benson to intervene or else "calamity" would result. He realised that Benson knew all about that blot on Howell's moral character, but in fact there was another as well: "If this sin [of impurity] is to be permitted in our bishops, the effect will be morally disastrous." Howell is a man whom few trust, Edwards continued, and he is shunned and disliked by many of the Welsh clergy. Bishop Jayne of Chester, Edwards' brother-in-law, wrote to Davidson that Howell had neglected the interests of the Welsh worshippers in Wrexham, and had never been able to influence his own curates. Their anxiety to prevent the appointment is shown by the overwriting of Edwards' moral argument as applied to Howell, and the downright lies about Howell's work in Wrexham and his relationship with his staff. But these allegations were designed to be harmful, for a Welsh bishop was meant to be concerned about his Welsh flock and to be able to influence his clergy.[49] In fact

---

[47] Benson to Davidson, 16 Mar 1890, Lambeth Palace Library, Davidson Papers [DP], 28 fol 33.
[48] Vaughan to Davidson, 13 Mar 1890, DP 522, fol 95.
[49] Edwards to Benson, 14 Mar 1890, BP 82, fol 18; Jayne to Davidson, 14 Mar 1890: DP 28, fol 45.

Bickersteth had already written to Salisbury noting from his own personal experience Howell's influence over his brother clergy.[50]

The archbishop replied through Davidson, perhaps a little wearily to his unruly suffragans, that Howell was on his list of names "to beware of", and Lord Salisbury had said "when the Howell question was up before, that the facts rendered his appointment impossible." He thought Edwards must be mistaken in his assumption, but if not, the prime minister must be reminded and warned.[51] It may be that Salisbury was impressed by Bickersteth's change of heart, but in all probability Queen Victoria, who took a hearty interest in the appointment of bishops to *her* Church, would have remembered. In such cases there might be forgiveness, but not selection.

The same issues determined Howell's non-candidature in the election to St Davids of 1897, which Edwards secured for his young lieutenant, John Owen. The tale of Edwards' interference in these appointments lies elsewhere, but enough has been said to indicate that the bishop ran an extremely successful 'dirty-tricks' department which enabled him to "run" - to quote the jargon of the day - his own men for these offices. If the *Record* asked in 1897 about Howell, "why are his claims overlooked?", suggesting that if the election was left to the Welsh clergy, Howell would be elected by a large majority,[52] it was not aware of the real reasons or of Edwards' malevolence to Howell.

One has the impression that Edwards' character was sufficiently well known for many to recognise that had Howell been appointed, Edwards would have stirred the matter up in such a way that this "blemish", hitherto known only to a few, would be released for public consumption. There is no doubt about his ability or willingness to do such things. Take one example. Edwards had wanted Owen appointed to Bangor in 1890. He managed to get Howell out of the way by the means described above, but the person who was appointed was his old rival, Lewis

---

[50] Bickersteth to Salisbury, 24 Jan 1889, [SP]; and see Howell's testimonial for his former curate, T Lloyd Williams, in the Temple Papers, Lambeth Palace Library, 40 fol 29.
[51] Benson to Davidson, 13 Mar 1890, DP 28 fol 33; Salisbury to ibid, 14 Mar 1890, DP 28 fol 43.
[52] *Record*, 29 Jan 1897, p 101; 5 Feb 1897, p 138. The Record of 23 Jan 1903 [p 79] suggested that Howell was strongly backed by Archbishop Temple and Dean Vaughan, but made it clear that Edwards' influence obtained the appointment for Owen.

Lloyd, headmaster of Christ Church College, Brecon. There had been enmity between the two headmasters for many years. Edwards alleged that some material puffing up Lloyd as one who would be an outstanding bishop, and which had been published in the *Western Mail*, had been written by Lloyd himself, and what is more, he sent the actual manuscript of this to Benson, alleging it was in Lloyd's own handwriting! Substantial enquiries were made, and the allegations were found to be groundless. It caused enormous embarrassment to both Benson and also Davidson, who as dean of Windsor had to break the news to a very angry Queen, and later wrote back to Benson about this "irresponsible bishop". The full maliciousness of Edwards' action is apparent in the timing of his "exposure". It was after the public announcement of Lloyd's appointment had been made, but before his election by the chapter. Had the allegation been proved Lloyd would have been publicly and utterly disgraced.[53] Edwards might have been more successful had he possessed some other information, though he was guilty of the same offence himself. This information was that Lloyd's sister had acted as his "campaign manager" and had written to numerous influential people asking them to help her brother obtain the bishopric.[54]

I am quite certain that with this track record Edwards would have let Howell know that he aware of this moral failure of former years. Although this was probably not the origin of their dislike for one another it could only have increased Howell's distaste for his bishop. Edwards' rigorous morality, which Howell knew was double sided - not extending to every area of his life, together with Howell's inability to reply effectively and possibly with ambitions unrealised, meant that there must have been an underlying tension within their relationship. It could not have been easy for Edwards to see Howell, maybe, as a former rival for his own appointment, or as a future episcopal colleague, especially when his views on church defence were conciliatory rather than militant, charitable rather than denunciatory. And yet, at the same time, it is only fair to conclude that Edwards sincerely believed in his methods and principles of church defence, even though he

---

[53] For these and other references see my forthcoming book, *In Pursuit of a Welsh Episcopate*.
[54] S E Lloyd to H Tobit Evans, 5 Ap 1890, NLW MS 20962E.

seems to have taken the mistaken view that the end justified the means.

Thus David Howell never achieved episcopal office. If Rhys J Huws considered he would have found episcopal office unsuitable and uncongenial for himself, feeling it would diminish the preacher and the "Welshman" in him, lessening his opportunities to inspire and serve the Church,[55] Howell never seems to have actively sought such office, although accepting that if it came he could do good by it. Indeed in his earlier years he assumed such office would pass him by, for as he wrote to his friend Nathan in 1884: "A Welshman and an old fashioned Churchman like myself who is not a university man, and who has no political interest or ecclesiastical influence has no more prospect of being a Bishop than of being the Prime Minister. In the Church, as in most other things, 'kisses go by favour.' Nor do I in the least complain. I am absolutely satisfied with what I am as far as in love and position are concerned."[56] But all of us are mixed personalities and it must have been a disappointment to Howell when he realised that not only had been rejected, but it was for reasons which may have seemed unfair and partisan to him.

Many assumed that the reason Howell had not been offered such office was because he was prepared to speak out about the ills of the Church, rather than looking for some palliative remedy in Church reform. Like a physician he and many others wished to go to the centre of the problem and address themselves to that, rather than simply treat the symptoms. David Davies, a Baptist warrior but a good commentator on the contemporary Welsh scene, commented that "Dean Edwards, Dean Howell, Rector Griffith [of Merthyr], and Archdeacon Griffiths, the four men eloquent of the past generation, but who used their great gifts to rebuke and warn, instead of exclaiming 'peace' when there was no 'peace', had to suffer and remain comparatively in the shadow, when men who never reached their ankles, and who have never yet learned to discern the signs of the times, were promoted to high places."[57] An obituary note on Howell in the *Wrexham*

---

[55] *Geninen*, 21 [St Davids 1903] 4.
[56] Howell to Nathan, 24 June 1884, NLW MS 987B, fol 97. He hoped for a quieter post with less responsibility than his present parish.
[57] David Davies, *The Ancient Celtic Church of Wales* [London 1910], pp 176f.

Advertiser, a paper which always had a soft spot for him, argued that he would have been a popular choice for a Welsh bishopric. It also suggested that had he confined himself to the disestablishment controversy - rather than to a spiritual and parochial ministry - his services would have gained him a mitre.[58] The same kind of statement was made by Thomas Gee who said in 1889 that Howell had more qualifications to be a Welsh bishop than any other Welsh cleric. But he added, "he has not been known to fight publicly against the Nonconformists, and when he had the opportunity to immortalise himself at the last Church Congress at Manchester his subject instead was the excellence of the Nonconformist style of preaching."[59] Gee was also referring, of course, to the one who had been appointed to St Asaph. Another suggested that the reason for Howell's failure to achieve high office was because he had opposed "the sacerdotal administration of the Church in Wales",[60] but this was from a paper notorious for its dislike of the Church in any case. The nicest tribute in this direction came from an anonymous writer in *Y Drysorfa*. If his width of sympathy and liberality of spirit were a hindrance to the promotion Howell deserved, reigning on a bishop's chair was a small thing compared to reigning in the hearts of a nation of people.[61]

It would be an honest question to ask, and one which is unanswerable: would Howell have become a bishop, in spite of that youthful moral blemish, had he adopted the current tactics and beliefs of the St Asaph school of church defenders? One has the distinct impression that Howell was excluded from episcopal office not so much because of his moral lapse, for that could be readily excused and explained (and the moral lives of some other bishops might not have survived a similar investigation), but because he was on the wrong side of the camp from the 'in party' of church defenders who had the political clout to keep him out.

* * * *

[58] *Wrexham Advertiser*, 24 Jan 1903, pp 5 & 7.
[59] Jones, *Cofiant Thomas Gee*, p 550. Translated.
[60] CDH, 28 July 1893, p 7.
[61] *Y Dysorfa*, 73 [1903] 100.

In 1890 Howell preached his celebrated sermon on the Welsh Church at St Margaret's Church, Westminster. Bishop Edwards was present, having asked Howell to take his place on this occasion as he was due to preach at St Paul's Cathedral that evening.[62] Many believed that he had left the church, rather abruptly some thought, while Howell was still preaching, though this was denied.[63] This sermon, which is noted in the previous chapter, was widely and fully reported in the Welsh press, who saw it as a major statement by Howell as to the position and prospects of the Church in Wales. It was commended by Dean Vaughan in a personal letter to Davidson.[64] The sermon was even translated into Welsh for the readers of the *Geninen*. Howell argued in that sermon that the cause of the Welsh Church's weakness was her inability to adapt herself "to the genius and special requirements of the Welsh people". In thus criticising the policy which had guided the Church in Wales for the previous century and more, Howell insisted that there needed to be a deepening of spiritual life within the Church, and a reversal of her general policy, if she was to regain the affections of the Welsh people. Concern was expressed too that mutual toleration and co-operation should exist between the various denominations in Wales. Howell's views were expressed with much force and great eloquence, and his sermon then and thereafter made a deep impression. The *Western Mail*, for example, reporting on the published version of this sermon "by a true Son of the Church", suggested that no abler Church defence pamphlet had been published for a long time.[65]

The sermon had been preached within three months of Edwards' own election as bishop, and he regarded Howell's comments in it as an attack on his own policy as well as on the Church in Wales. In particular he resented the use made of the

[62] *News of the Week*, 22 July 1893, p 6. The sermon was in aid of the Welsh Church in London. Edwards' sermon that evening at St Paul's was reported as having failed to live up to expectations [NWG, 1 Feb 1890, p 8; *Yr Haul*, 1890, pp 280f; *Wrexham Advertiser*, 7 June 1890, p 2].
[63] *Wrexham Advertiser*, 29 July 1893, p 6: *Record*, 21 July 1893, p 706. Edwards was clearly annoyed in turn. His chaplain, E M Roderick, later wrote that as the bishop had asked Howell to preach on that occasion, his attack and "thinly veiled sneer" on him was therefore all the more repulsive [*News of the Week*, 2 Aug 1896, p 6].
[64] Vaughan to Davidson, 13 Mar 1890: DP 522, fol 95.
[65] WM, 3 Ap 1890, p 2.

sermon by the Liberation Society, which produced a pamphlet arguing for disestablishment based upon it. But as it was pointed out to Edwards, the Liberation Society had used the speeches of such good churchmen as Dean Edwards and Sir Thomas Phillips in exactly the same way,[66] and were to make similar use of some of Bishop Edwards' statements in the future as well.[67]

Howell received substantial support from the public press and from leading members of the Church for what he had said and argued in that sermon. Edwards, unable to distinguish between principles and personalities, saw it as a personal attack on himself. Frightened that the already known appointment of Howell to the archdeaconry of Wrexham would appear to add his imprimatur on Howell's arguments, Edwards endeavoured to display his resentment at what Howell had argued by cancelling the appointment as well as by abandoning the plans for the new archdeaconry. He told Howell this in a letter two years later, having concealed his annoyance from him throughout that period, but added, "I was informed that matters had gone too far. The formation of the new Archdeaconry, and your appointment to it, had been determined upon by my predecessor, and I do not hold myself responsible for either."[68] Did Edwards feel that Howell had used the sermon to vent his anger on the Church which had rejected his episcopal candidature?

A further dispute followed. In October 1890 the Bishop called to see Howell, who was then in residence at the Canonry. He read out to him a scheme for the disestablishment of the Church in Wales and a letter which he said reflected upon the bishops of the Church and those who took part in the defence of the Church in Wales. Edwards then accused Howell, known, as the *Manchester*

---

[66] *News of the Week*, 29 July 1893, p 6. G O Morgan in his pamphlet, *The Church of England and the People of Wales* [London 1895], had so used it, as did a newspaper columnist who in reporting the sermon argued that Howell would have spoken *ex cathedra*, weighing with the utmost care every word he uttered. He claimed that Howell did not see disestablishment as an unmixed evil, for it could offer the Church a freedom to which they might look forward with hope and confidence [SA/DR/54. fol 328].

[67] As Howell himself suggested in his letter of 2 May printed in the *Wrexham Advertiser* supplement of 8 July 1893.

[68] This dispute is chronicled in Lerry, *A G Edwards*, pp 37-42, while the correspondence between Howell and Edwards was printed in a special supplement of the *Wrexham Advertiser* in its issue of 8 July 1893. See also ibid, 15 July 1893, p 6; 24 July, p 6, and *News of the Week*, 22 July 1893, p 6; and 29 July 1893, p 6.

Guardian noted, as a Welsh preacher throughout Wales before Edwards had even taken orders, of having privately circulated a scheme of disestablishment and disendowment, while publicly allowing himself to be known as an uncompromising opponent of such schemes. "It is inconceivable", he added, "how one, who was a Canon of one of these Cathedrals, and in enjoyment of its revenues, could reconcile himself to circulate the scheme, without one single word or hint of condemnation, [of] such a proposal." Howell's protestation that if disestablishment depended on his vote, he would hold up both hands and two feet against it, was rudely dismissed.[69]

The bishop had eventually to concede that he had misjudged both the man and the event. The truth of the matter was established as follows. A Nonconformist minister, Eiddon Jones of Llanrug, who was the Liberal election agent in north Wales, had written to Howell about matters involving the temperance movement, in which both were involved. In his letter he enclosed two copies of a scheme he had devised for the disestablishment of the Church in Wales, which he believed to be a fair scheme, hoping to receive Howell's comments. Provided his name was not mentioned, Howell was at liberty to show it to others in order to see how far this scheme might be acceptable to churchmen. With this understanding Howell sent one copy to Colonel West, M.P., and the other to Stephen Gladstone, the prime minister's son and then rector of Hawarden, both of whom had corresponded with Howell regarding his Westminster sermon. Howell sent with the scheme a covering letter saying he felt they would be interested in seeing the scheme as an indication of the ideas entertained on the subject of disestablishment by a frank, fair minded and well informed Nonconformist minister, and possibly by other Welsh

---

[69] *News of the Week*, 29 July 1893, p 6. A number of other schemes also appeared. One was produced by Thomas Gee, and another was known as the Bangor Scheme. This was endorsed, if not produced, by Lloyd George, and a number of clergy and others in that city. The latter caused considerable annoyance to Edwards who did his best to discredit both the scheme and its authors, though the scheme was not dissimilar to the proposals for disestablishment contained in the 1914 Act: see K O Morgan, *Rebirth of a Nation: Wales 1880-1980* [Oxford 1981], p 115; ibid, *David Lloyd George* [Cardiff 1964], p 28; Neville Masterman, *The Forerunner* [Llandybie 1972], p 210; Henry Lewis, *Is Disestablishment Just?* [Conway 1914], p 49; and my article, "Traitors and Compromisers: The Shadow side of the Church's Fight against Disestablishment", in *Journal of Welsh Religious History*, 3 [1995] 41-3.

Nonconformists as well. His letter to Stephen Gladstone included the disclaimer that he was not himself an advocate of disestablishment, nor was he afraid of it. At no point had Howell commended the scheme or even expressed any approval of it, either to his two correspondents or to Eiddon Jones.

Colonel West, it appears, lent the correspondence to a friend, who then showed it to Edwards. The Bishop, Howell wrote to Eiddon Jones, brought the letters to him, and "I explained to him the circumstances under which the scheme came into my possession, and my motive in sending it to my correspondents, of course observing your request as to anonymity." Howell added to that letter that the bishop seemed satisfied with his explanation. Colonel West, however, claimed that the author of the scheme had shown it to so many members of parliament that by the time it had reached Howell it was "virtually public property". But as Howell observed in that same letter to Eiddon Jones, this made the bishop's conduct even more unjustifiable.[70]

The matter died down. The bishop pressed Howell to remain as an examining chaplain, and nominated him to read a paper at the Rhyl Church Congress in 1891, during which Archbishop Benson gave a rousing speech "from the throne of St Augustine" in favour of church defence and militancy. But even these appointments were the subject of some controversy. One report suggested that Edwards had asked Howell to retain that post and the archdeaconry in order to show consideration to one who had been "conspicuously named for the vacant see" which Edwards now occupied. This was put out by Edwards' friends in the diocese, but denied by Howell. However, Howell's son Tudor alleged that Edwards had refused to allow the committee arranging the Rhyl Church Congress to invite his father to speak on the subject of the Welsh Church. Instead he spoke on a devotional subject: "Aids to the Life of Godliness."[71]

Two years later the matter was revived when Howell became aware that various damaging rumours were circulating in the diocese about his "dual" attitude to disestablishment, and in particular regarding his involvement in the scheme devised by

---

[70] Howell to Eiddon Jones, 2 Nov 1892, in NLW MS 3292E.
[71] *News of the Week*, 22 July 1893, p 6, and 29 July 1893, p 6. See footnote 86 below.

Eiddon Jones. It was claimed that Howell had circulated the scheme as his own amongst members of parliament, while it was alleged that he was "acting the part of a concealed opponent of the Church" in endeavouring to promote disestablishment from within. Howell, in order to protect his good name, endeavoured to track down the source of these rumours, and asked Colonel West to let him know the names of the persons to whom he had shown the scheme, so that he might investigate the matter more fully. The Bishop, hearing this from West, wrote to Howell in January 1893 and told his archdeacon he seemed more concerned with protecting his own name than in repudiating his sentiments about disestablishment and disendowment. He added fuel to the fire by making public these comments about Howell at various meetings, called admittedly for other purposes, at Wrexham and Oswestry, and possibly elsewhere. Edwards even relayed a rumour that Gladstone, then prime minister, had asked Howell to prepare his own scheme of disestablishment![72]

A series of letters then passed between the bishop and Howell, indicating not only an almost complete breakdown of relationship between them, but also the bishop's paranoid attitude to church defence. In a vain hope of clearing the air Howell corresponded with Eiddon Jones, requesting him to write a letter indicating that he had not heard from Howell on the subject since the original correspondence, and asking if he could name him publicly as the author of the scheme, for "I have, it seems, given a handle to those from whom other and better things might have been expected, to do me an inconsiderate injury." Eiddon Jones obliged Howell in both respects. He hoped that his scheme in dealing liberally with the Church's buildings and recent endowments, although reserving the older endowments for the nation, might encourage "a calm and fair consideration of the subject", and thus enable a "satisfactory adjustment" to be made which would avoid much bickering. Howell replied with his thanks, and endeavoured to set Eiddon's mind at rest that he was in any way responsible for what

---

[72] Howell to Eiddon Jones, 2 Nov 1892, in NLW MS 3292E; and Howell's letter of 2 May in the *Wrexham Advertiser* supplement of 8 July 1893; *News of the Week*, 22 July 1893, p 6.

had occurred: "rather an unworthy and unjustifiable use has been made of that which was never intended to be so used."[73]

As this correspondence was going on, the letters between Howell and Edwards, which Howell had unwisely shown to a friend, had been passed on without his knowledge or consent to Isaac Foulkes, editor and proprietor of the periodical *Y Cymro*. Without even informing Howell he mentioned this controversy and printed these letters in his paper as a matter of public interest.[74] With the matter out in the open, Howell seems to have considered it right to allow the whole correspondence which had passed between him and Edwards to be published in a special supplement of the *Wrexham Advertiser* of 8 July 1893. It is hardly surprising that Howell had mixed feelings about this forced publication. He had previously thought of publishing this correspondence in an attempt to quell the rumours then circulating, but he had written to Edwards saying he would refrain from this step if the bishop would adopt some other means of contradicting them. Edwards declined to do this, and demanded that the if the letters were published the scheme should be printed with them as well.[75] This Howell declined to do, for as he wrote to Eiddon Jones, had the scheme been published with the letters then:

> the Bishop will at once attack the scheme, and by this means will direct the attention of the public from the real point of your correspondence, which is not the Scheme, but your connection with it .... Nothing would serve the Bishop better than anything that would *direct* attention *from* himself to the Scheme ... [76]

Howell's feelings about this publicity emerge from a letter, marked "private", written by him to Goronwy Evans on the day the letters were published in the local press:

---

[73] Howell to Eiddon Jones, 2 Nov 1892, in NLW MS 3292E. Both Jones' draft and Howell's reply are dated 4 Nov.

[74] Howell to Goronwy Evans, 18 July 1893, NLW MS 10852C, fol 3; though cf *News of the Week*, 29 July 1893, p 6, which suggested Howell had sent them deliberately to the *Cymro*, then, as it noted, under the control of T E Ellis, MP, "one of the leaders of uncompromising disestablishment and disendowment". This was denied by the editor of the *Cymro*, and noted in the *Wrexham Advertiser*, 5 Aug 1893, p 3.

[75] *News of the Week*, 22 July 1893, p 6.

[76] Howell to Eiddon Jones, 10, 19 July 1893, in NLW MS 3292E; cf *News of the Week*, 29 July 1893, p 6.

I enclose a current copy of the correspondence which Mr Foulkes published without my knowledge, or consent. For the last three years the Bishop's vindictiveness has been such as I can hardly care to describe. From a regard to the interests of Religion as well as the Church I have abstained from publishing other correspondence I have had with him - but I now find that publication is the only [thing] he fears. I have long been conscious of some malign influence working persistently to my injury, but until recently I had no idea as to the source of it. I have never concealed my opinions on the subject of Disestablishment, which are those held by Maurice, Kingsley, Stanley and others, but neither have I concealed my conviction that far greater evils may befall the Church than Disestablishment, nor has my view in the least degree affected my regard for those who advocate Disestablishment from religious motives, and in a religious spirit. It is my earnest desire than not a word shall pass from my lips, or flow from my pen which I would wish to withdraw.[77]

Howell was to add, in a letter to Eiddon Jones, a deeper concern:

I also entertain grave doubts as to whether the unhappy man is at all times accountable for his actions - but his vindictiveness is none the less dangerous. With the English public the Bishop's words go far ...[78]

* * * *

In his first letter of this published correspondence, dated 5 January 1893, Edwards claimed that Howell's covering letter to Colonel West was critical of the Welsh bishops. Howell wrote in his reply of 13 February:

You are pleased to say that I have not shown any anxiety to "modify my letter," to "repudiate it," or to "withdraw any single statement in it." My lord, my opinions are not formed to be changed, modified, or cast off at will; neither are they expressed to be withdrawn or repudiated within two years. My letter was by no means written with the intention of furnishing my correspondent

[77] Howell to Goronwy Evans, 8 July 1893, NLW MS 10852C, fol 3.
[78] Howell to Eiddon Jones, 9 July 1893, NLW MS 3295E. According to the *News of the Week* of 29 July 1893, p 6, Jones was stupid enough to publish some of Howell's private comments under his own name in a letter to the *Liverpool Daily Post*, for which the paper had subsequently to apologise.

with an exposition of my view on the questions dealt with in it, nor did I dream that it would ever have gone beyond the gentleman to whom I sent it. There is, at the same time, not a single sentence in it which I would wish to recall; whilst it must not be forgotten that there is not a word in it, beyond what is quoted above, which was intended to have any reference whatever to the "scheme". I am not in favour of disestablishment, but I am not deterred by my convictions on this question, from criticising the administration policy that has prevailed in the Welsh Church for the past 180 years; on the contrary, these convictions require that I should do so, as a reversal of that policy is imperatively demanded, if the Church, established or disestablished, is ever to recover the allegiance of the people in Wales. These are my convictions, and I have a right to express them, as they are, in my opinion, the key to the resumption by the Church in Wales of her rightful position and influence. But while I strongly insist that the infinitely most important defence of the Church in Wales is the strengthening of her hold upon the affections and convictions of the people, by an administrative policy that secures their confidence, and, above all, by quickening and deepening her spiritual life, and extending her spiritual agencies and influences, I do not the less grant the necessity of defending her against the attacks of her opponents. I have, however, always considered the defence of the temporalities of the Church to belong mainly to the laity, as it is more their question than that of the clergy. But others, and better men than myself, have thought differently. I only claim the right to act in obedience to my convictions, and consistently with my principles, as one who is loyal to the doctrine and discipline of the Church. Your lordship accuses me of assuming, at the time of your visitation at Wrexham, a dual attitude in this matter. Had you given heed to the facts, which must have been at that time within your knowledge, you could not have suspected me of such an attitude.

Howell refers to this matter again in another letter of 7 March:

You charge me with having severely reflected upon the Bishops in my letter to Col. West. I never mentioned the Bishops, nor did I particularly allude to them. But, surely, I may criticise what, rightly or wrongly, I believe to be the imperfections of a policy, without incurring the suspicion of disloyalty to the church, and with perfect respect both to the opinions and to the persons and offices of those who differ from me; just as I can credit with honourable motives those within and without the church who advocate her disestablishment, however much I may differ from them from my point of view; a point of view, let me say, which remains unaffected by what I consider to have been the ungenerous and unjust attacks repeatedly made upon me by my own Bishop, during a period in which I have undergone the sorest and severest trials of my life. [The reference is to his wife's death].

Howell defended himself against the accusation of holding a "dual attitude" in his first letter of 13 February:

> And yet ... you accuse me of assuming a "dual attitude." Now what are the grounds put forward in your lordship's letter for believing me to be an advocate of disestablishment, when reduced to simple facts? Merely that a scheme of disestablishment which had been sent me, wholly unsolicited and unexpected, by a Nonconformist minister, was privately forwarded by me to two correspondents, together with a letter of my own, in which I not only did not approve of a single clause or proposal in that scheme, but did not even discuss it. "Dual attitude!" A grave charge surely for a bishop to bring against one of his clergy on such grounds! "Dual attitude!" My Lord, what are we to say of your lordship, who admits to have publicly stated on two occasions, once pointedly, at solemn assemblies of your clergy, that I would hold up both hands against disestablishment, while, at the same time, you believed that I was circulating and approving of a scheme for that very purpose? You give as your reasons for publishing my views at Wrexham, and at Oswestry, that this "dual attitude", which you attribute to me, appeared so striking to you. If you had any misgiving as to the sincerity of my profession; if you thought, as you now appear to say you did, that I was circulating a scheme for disestablishment which had my approval, while, at the same time, I had declared to you my readiness to vote against it, one would have thought that, instead of leading you to make public my profession, this "inexplicable" attitude would have induced you either to treat it with "silent contempt", or to ask for some explanation, or to expose it with just severity. You must have intended to convey the impression to your clergy that you believed my testimony, otherwise why quote it at all? Whereas, it appears that now you regarded it as only one of the contradictory phrases of a "dual attitude". This, indeed, is "inexplicable".

Howell was also concerned that the bishop had allowed rumours to circulate for over two years about his alleged "dual attitude" to disestablishment, and had then publicly broadcast them as being true, without giving Howell a chance to hear them or reply to these allegations. He continued:

> You may say it is obviously open to me to repudiate that or any other scheme. You seem to be more concerned for my repudiation of the "scheme" than for the vindication of my character from the charge of "dual attitude" which you have attempted to fasten on me. It is open to me, I trust, to do both. I will only add that the nature of the charge your lordship has preferred against me, and the tone of your letter, are such that I could not have noticed were it not for the respect which I owe to your office as my Bishop.

Edwards, he wrote in another letter of 2 May, had "laboured hard to fasten upon me the charge of secretly abetting disestablishment" and of circulating a scheme for that end. "The issue between us is perfectly clear", he wrote, "You have implied that I was an advocate of disestablishment, and I denied this to you in 1890, and have done so repeatedly and unequivocally by this correspondence. You were bound by every honourable consideration either to accept my denial, or produce your proofs. You did neither, but strove to fasten upon me the serious charge of assuming a 'dual attitude.'" Edward's 'proof' of this charge was summed up in these words which he addressed to Howell in a letter of the 3 April:

> The fact remained, by your own admission, that you circulated a scheme for the Disestablishment and Disendowment of the Church in Wales, sent to you by the Liberationist agent in North Wales. Why should a Liberationist agent select you, a dignitary of the Church, to send you a scheme of disendowment, which would sell the cathedral of which you are a canon, unless he knew that you would not resent it?

Any reasonable man would have rejected such "evidence" as extremely weak, but Edwards, clearly losing his case, resurrected the former dispute over the Westminster sermon, which he brought forward with a measure of personal abuse and innuendo. He wrote as follows in that same letter:

> Recently I called your attention in the course of a correspondence, to the mis-statements against the Church in Wales contained in

your sermon at St Margaret's, Westminster, and published in a Liberationist leaflet, noting especially that your accusation against the Church of non-provision for the Welsh-speaking people, came with a singularly bad grace from one who, as vicar of Cardiff for eleven years, and afterwards at Wrexham for fourteen years, was conspicuous for confining his ministrations to the English people, and that without making any adequate provision for the Welsh-speaking-people.[79]

Howell's reply to this letter (of 2 May) was one of dignity, if not of sorrow. To introduce such matters into the debate, he wrote, "is only an attempt to create prejudice, and to divert attention from the real point at issue". He was concerned that the bishop was endeavouring to prevent clergy from expressing their opinions without "the risk of incurring the suspicion and animadversions of their Bishop, if those opinions should differ from his." "You have thought it not inconsistent with the rules of controversy to attack my work at Cardiff", he added, "nearly every day of which had been completed before you were in Orders, and my work at Wrexham, with most of which you had as little to do." And he reminded him that "men of double your experience, and opportunities of judging and knowing the condition of the Welsh Church, have formed a very different opinion" of his Westminster sermon. He continued:

> ...It is my duty to defend myself against personal misrepresentations, and that you have no right to misinterpret my action under the cover of defending the Church, whose interests are as near to my heart as they are to yours; and I may add that, though we may differ in details, it is surely permitted to neither of us, without ineffable arrogance, to set himself up as the concentrated essence of true churchmanship, or to claim a monopoly of friendliness to the Church, or to be an infallible authority on Church Defence, any deviation from which is to be treated with suspicion, or branded with disloyalty ... These charges and insinuations [made against me] I have denied and disproved seriatim, and yet you persist in repeating them as though I had never done so, and thereby you have refused to believe me on

---

[79] A number of letters appeared in the local papers stating that these allegations were totally without foundation, eg, *Wrexham Advertiser*, 5 Aug 1893, p 6.

matters where my testimony should be decisive. My lord, I submit that this is a conduct that does not usually obtain among gentlemen, not to say Christians. ... [T]his correspondence [when published] will serve at least one good purpose, by giving me an opportunity of definitely contradicting such rumours, and of publicly exposing the unreliableness of those who have so assiduously circulated them.

One is led to wonder at Edwards' attitude in persistently pressing charges which had so little foundation to them, and which Howell so clearly refuted as untrue and unworthy of himself. It might be that an unscrupulous man is unable to understand a person of high principles who felt he had to defend his good name and reputation against slanderous misrepresentation. On the other hand Howell's well known moderation; his friendship with Nonconformists; his willingness to treat them as spiritual equals; his refusal to be aggressive in the defence of his Church, or to resort to political or polemical weapons; his defence of the character of the Welsh Church - rather than the Church of England in Wales, together with the influence he was able to give to his views, posed a deep threat to the "St Asaph" policy, and resulted in such jealousy and bitterness on the bishop's part that his higher instincts and Christian calling were put to one side. Put simply, Edwards could not take criticism, even constructive criticism, and could only reply to it with malicious insinuations.

* * * *

A week after the publication of these letters Howell wrote to a correspondent about this dispute. Noting that there was little public opinion within the Church in Wales, for "a portion of the Clergy take their opinions from the Church Press, others take their cue from the Bishops", he continued:

> But if I am to judge of the opinion of the *laity* by the letters which reach me daily, from men holding a large variety of opinions, and influential positions, it is strongly *adverse* to the Bishop. As could it be well otherwise, for a Bishop: who would tyrannise over the Clergy, would, if he could, be of the same temper towards the laity. What the Church wants are men of eirenic temper and considerate

disposition ... If the whole truth were known I should be commended for the *moderation* of my replies to the Bishop.[80]

The published correspondence created an ecclesiastical sensation, although the matter had been rumoured and discussed for many months previously.[81] An editorial in the *Wrexham Advertiser* of the following week indicates why this was the case:

> ... rarely have letters been more eagerly read than those which have passed between the two gentlemen named. It would not be going too far to add also that never has a correspondence of so remarkable a kind ever been placed before the public for what it amounts to is that the Bishop has charged one of his archdeacons with deceit and its attendant failings ... The position taken by his Lordship is one quite an variance with the usage which might reasonably be expected from one in his position. He has departed from the common courtesies of controversy, and must now be content to hear the contempt which follows. The position is a pitiful one, and even those who cannot be called friends of the Bishop nor his ways, must feel regret that he has so strangely acted. As for the Venerable Archdeacon, no one, - except the Bishop, - doubts his word. He has a wise opinion upon the subject of Disestablishment and Disendowment. He is not in favour of it, much less does he advocate it, but he sees and knows that the success of a church does not depend upon its connection with the state, but upon the hold and affection of the people. And yet it was for expressing wise statesmanlike views that the Bishop tried to prevent him being made Archdeacon! Surely the Bishop has mistaken the century. One of the glories of the Church of England is its catholicity and freedom. Will the Bishop try and change this well established order by conclusively proving the narrowness of his mind and the pettiness of his hate.[82]

Edwards was almost universally condemned by the press. *The Manchester Guardian* noted that the correspondence was in accord with the "extraordinary policy which has characterised the Bishop's episcopate", and added that many of the best clergy in Wales entirely disagreed with the bishop's plan of campaign.

[80] Howell to Goronwy Evans, 15 July 1893, NLW MS 10852C, fol 4.
[81] Record, 14 July 1893, pp 681f.
[82] *Wrexham Advertiser*, 15 July 1893, pp 4f.

Other editors noted the contrast between the two individuals concerned: one who had had a time honoured career and gained universal love and respect throughout Wales, the other who as the *Daily Chronicle* put it, had been pitchforked by Lord Salisbury into his present position four years earlier, on the strength of a few vigorous pamphlets and letters about the defence of the Welsh Church. Edwards, said a correspondent in the *Daily Chronicle*, was an "infallible young autocrat who rules over the see", and he said, as did others later, that only those who held identical views to his on church defence would be promoted in his diocese. The same writer warned those English defenders of the Church who believed "that the Bishop of St Asaph is a pillar of strength to their cause in Wales" that such a belief was presumptuous.[83] The evangelical weekly, the *Record*, said of Howell that "his life is the best vindication of his position that could be given. Had he been a younger and less known man he might have suffered seriously, at least in ecclesiastical circles, from such an attack; but one who has so long been regarded as a 'pillar' of the Church in Wales, and whose work began before his comparatively juvenile bishop was in orders, requires no defender. But in truth the archdeacon has given no cause whatever of legitimate offence." *The Yorkshire Post*, with many other papers, noted that there was a strong feeling amongst some Welsh churchmen "which is antagonistic to the part the Bishop of St Asaph takes in the Welsh Church campaign. Their belief is that the fervid attack of the Bishop tends to throw the quieter Nonconformists into the hands of the disestablishing party."[84]

The *Record* also took a similar position, and noting the bitterness which appeared to characterise the bishop's public statements, its editor continued:

> And now it would seem that his Lordship does not hesitate to treat the Church's friends with marked hostility if they do not happen to agree with his personal view. His letters not merely breathe a spirit of suspicion and distrust: they abound in innuendoes, which are always more difficult to meet than direct charges, and are more proportionally damaging ...

[83] Quoted by ibid, 15 July 1893, p 6.
[84] Quoted in ibid, 29 June 1893, p 6; Record, 14 July 1893, pp 681f.

Its editor also alleged that while the bishop "threw" the responsibility of Howell's appointment to the archdeaconry onto his predecessor, his own friends "had never tired of praising the magnanimity and grace of Bishop Edwards in nominating one who was popularly regarded as a formidable rival for the Bishopric to so prominent a position."[85]

One paper, however, partly stood out against this pro-Howell sentiment. This was the *News of the Week*. It carried an article in its issue of 22 July which was extremely critical of Howell under the heading "The Case from the Bishop's Standpoint". It was said to have been communicated by a special correspondent, but there was some suggestion made that it might have been written by Edwards himself.[86] A devastating reply to this article was printed in the next week's issue. It was written by Howell's youngest son, Tudor. All the allegations made were answered point for point. Edwards was accused of episcopal tyranny, one who feared the ventilation of any views different from his own, whether they had been expressed in the press, within the diocese, or at the Rhyl Church Congress. Tudor Howell was incensed that the bishop had refused to accept his father's word, and added, "I personally have reason to know this from an insulting remark which the dignity of a bishop did not prevent him from flinging at me across a Church defence platform in England." Noting the bishop's "persistent unproved insinuations" against his father, such as "corrupting the press", he continued with a catalogue of epithets, "such gross misuse of terms, such misconstruction of words and actions, such disbelief of reiterated declarations, such offensive

---

[85] *Record*, 14 July 1893, pp 681f.
[86] The *News of the Week* [22 July 1893, p 6] accused Howell of reopening a matter in 1893 which had been closed in 1890, unless it was because of a rumour that Gladstone had asked him to prepare a scheme of Welsh disestablishment and disendowment. He had failed to justify the publishing of the correspondence without the scheme, as requested by Edwards, and thereby he had failed in his bishop's trust in him as examining chaplain, archdeacon, and being chosen to preach at Westminster. After the disloyalty shown to the Church in Wales in that sermon, the content of which had been published in a Liberationist pamphlet in support of disestablishment, the bishop had endeavoured to cancel his appointment as archdeacon, and in a case of "once bitten, twice shy", proposed that Howell should only speak on a devotional subject at the Rhyl Church Congress. As a consequence, there was "no attack upon the Church in Wales at the Rhyl Conference." The correspondent concluded: had Howell been appointed bishop of St Asaph, "how great a difference must such a step have made in the interests of disestablishment?"

introduction of irrelevant matters, and an all pervading spirit of suspicion and unfriendliness usually foreign to the intercourse of gentlemen." If Howell was accused by Edwards of finding "it necessary to scavenge in the dust-heap of Liberation abuses", his son replied that "he had, at any rate, the excellent example of his bishop to do so." And if Howell was permitted to read a devotional paper at the Rhyl conference, surely he was "fit to deal with the Church in Wales", rather than having all the other speakers on one side, namely that of the bishop of St Asaph.[87]

An interesting editorial note appeared in the *Wrexham Advertiser* of the 29 July. It said that the Bishop of St Asaph

> considers it very hard that those who hold various positions in the Church should be misunderstood. He asks pardon if he has made any blunders, from those he has endeavoured to defend. This is very gracious, and is somewhat encouraging as implying that the Bishop faintly recognises that there is a remote possibility that he might make a mistake. Equally refreshing is the announcement that he has never said a single word about those who differed from him that he wished to withdraw. Comment is needless.[88]

That the diocese of St Asaph did not share its bishop's views about Archdeacon Howell may be noted in the published *Charge* delivered to the clergy and churchwardens of the Archdeaconry of Wrexham in 1897 by William Trevor Parkins, "Vicar-General and Official Principal of the Lord Bishop of St Asaph." He said this of Howell, who had just left the archdeaconry to become dean of St Davids:

> It is a remarkable circumstance that the distinguished clergyman who was lately your Archdeacon, has filled with conspicuous ability important positions in each of the four dioceses of Wales. His merits, therefore, are widely known, and his appointment by the Crown to the Deanery of St David's has met everywhere with very great approval, and I am confident that your sincere good wishes and most cordial regards will follow him in the new sphere of usefulness he has been called upon to fill.[89]

[87] *News of the Week*, 29 July 1893, p 7.
[88] *Wrexham Advertiser*, 29 July 1893, p 6.
[89] W T Parkin, *A Charge delivered to the Clergy and Churchwardens of the Archdeaconry of Wrexham* [Oswestry 1897], p 3.

Indeed, the clergy seemed to go out of their way to show their appreciation of Howell's stand, and it must have been mortifying to the bishop that even during the diocesan conference after Howell had left the diocese, the clergy vigorously applauded his name every time it was mentioned by a speaker.[90]

But by that time further troubles had occurred, even though Howell had left the diocese for the quieter world of St Davids cathedral close. Another row broke out in the diocese, and Edwards did his best to drag Howell's name into it.

*   *   *   *

Ostensibly this row was about Bishop Edwards' disposal of his patronage. The bishops of St Asaph and Bangor had a greater amount of patronage available to them in their own dioceses than most English bishops possessed, and could thus exercise a stronger control over their clergy than was possible elsewhere. Grievances were expressed at a private meeting at the Grosvenor Hotel, Chester, attended by about twenty beneficed clergy. They complained about an element of favouritism in these appointments, that the diocesan curates had been ignored, and an excessive favour shown to men from other dioceses. They complained too of Edwards' "autocratic treatment of the clergy and the evident disposition he manifests to mark his displeasure upon those who incur it".[91]

A "highly respectful" memorial was eventually produced, signed by a number of clergy, though a covering letter indicated that those with large families and small incomes had not been asked to sign, while others had declined to sign feeling that such action would be injurious to their hopes of preferment. The memorial was eventually signed by seventy-five beneficed clergymen of the diocese, and included the names of Archdeacon D R Thomas of Montgomery - the historian of the diocese, the chancellor, four rural deans and one proctor. The memorial pointed out the dissatisfaction and concern within the diocese that senior men had been overlooked for "valuable livings" by

---

[90] *Record*, 6 Aug 1897, p 791; *Church Times*, 23 Dec 1897, p 756.
[91] CDH, 26 Nov 1897, p 7.

Edwards in favour of younger and inexperienced men. Furthermore it stated that clergymen had been appointed to livings for which they were disqualified having insufficient knowledge of the Welsh language.

Edwards declined to reply. Instead he called a public meeting at Wrexham in order to discuss the matter. The memorialists declined to attend, stating that it was improper to allow a tribunal to consider this subject, when it consisted of the bishop, the newly appointed incumbents, and the curates of the diocese whose future depended on their bishop's good pleasure, and who, for that reason, had not been asked to sign. One of the signatories suggested that the meeting should have been called at St Asaph, but Wrexham had been chosen because the clergy in the deaneries around it had had the fewest number of signatories to the memorial. If anything, this indicates the great suspicion of Edwards felt by many of his clergy.

The Wrexham meeting was attended by seventy out of two hundred incumbents in the diocese, but contrary to the bishop's clear statement beforehand, it was also attended by a number of the more influential lay people of the diocese and elsewhere, who came by the bishop's express invitation.[92] The duke of Westminster was one of these personages. He, looking around the meeting, felt that in view of its character they might take a vote of confidence in the bishop's administration of the diocese for granted.[93] It is perhaps not surprising that the memorialists and the press saw this meeting as one which had been "well whipped up and carefully packed" with "'the faithful laity' and the sycophants of the diocese", to quote W Venables Williams, one of the more respected senior clergymen of the diocese.[94] Even the *Liverpool Courier*, a Tory paper, agreed with the more radical

---

[92] Including Lords Powis, Mostyn, Penrhyn, Harlech and Llangattock, J D Llewelyn and Gen Hills-Johnes. See Cornwallis West's letter to the memorialists in CDH, 7 Jan 1898, p 7, and ibid, 4 Feb 1898, p 5.

[93] CDH, 17 Dec 1897, p 3; 24 Dec 1897, p6. The rector of Marchwiel, E Rhys James, declined to attend the meeting but sent a letter to the bishop stating that the only meeting he deserved at his hands was a thrashing with an ashstick. Edwards read out this letter to a sympathetic audience. The following Sunday the local landowner, Philip Yorke of Erddig, appeared at Marchwiel and endeavoured without success to prevent people worshipping there [*Record*, 30 Dec 1897, p 129].

[94] CDH, 21 Jan 1898, p 6.

Caernarvon and Denbigh Herald that the meeting was "little better than a mockery".[95]

The memorialists answered the bishop's defence at that meeting clause by clause. The paper which he had then read was "evasive, unsatisfactory and insufficient". His reply to those who expressed concern about his appointments of English speaking clergy to Welsh parishes was a case in point: "Am I to shut the door against all clergy who do not speak Welsh". This reply did not answer the problem they were addressing. They resented the bitter and unreconcilatory tones the bishop had assumed and the "unfortunate personalities indulged in on that occasion". Venables Williams later described the bishop as speaking "with the highly characteristic schoolmaster's birchrod in hand."[96] Archdeacon D R Thomas, publicly protested that Edwards had demanded his complete loyalty to him alone, pointing out that he also had a loyalty to the clergy of his archdeaconry - a fact that all archdeacons should do well to remember! Other clergy, such as the learned Grimaldi Davies of Welshpool (who had resigned his examining chaplaincy in protest at the way Edwards was using his patronage), wrote stating that the examples of patronage, given by Edwards, which had been offered to clergy but declined by them, were either not true or could not have been accepted for various reasons well known to the bishop at that time. The bishop's arguments that English men were entitled to the same treatment in Wales as Welsh clergy received in England, or that he held his patronage for the sake of the diocese rather than for individual clergy, were regarded as equally misleading and not answering the accusations made.[97]

One of the bishop's lieutenants, Archdeacon Wynne Jones, now entered the fray by endeavouring to involve Howell in this dispute. Wynne Jones was a target for the memorialists, for he was one of that select number in the diocese who appeared to be receiving the patronage which was being denied to others, or so it was claimed. A former barrister, he had been curate at Wrexham, when Edwards had told his startled vicar that he was making his

---

[95] Quoted in the CDH, 17 Dec 1897, pp 4f.
[96] CDH, 21 Jan 1898, p 6.
[97] The controversy will be found in Lerry, *A G Edwards*, pp 57-76, and CDH, 26 Nov 1897, p 6; 17 Dec 1897, p 6; 24 Dec 1897, p 6; 7 Jan 1898, p 7; 21 Jan 1898, p 6.

curate the new archdeacon![98] Wynne Jones claimed that a letter from Howell to Canon Roberts had been passed around a subsequent meeting of the memorialists. He alleged that it contained a phrase suggesting that the bishop's actions made him unfit for his post. Wynne Jones interpreted this to mean that Howell was referring to the office of bishop, whereas Howell had meant that Edwards was unfit to act as chairman of a meeting of the clergy when he was a party to the dispute. He absolutely denied Wynne Jones' accusation and added that he had not interfered in any way in the affairs of his former diocese. However, there does appear to have been a great deal of wriggling on the part of Roberts and Howell about this letter, Roberts for a time suggesting that the words in question were in a postscript to a letter written by a mutual friend, though without address or signature. And it was certainly unwise of Roberts to pass such a letter around which was capable of being seriously misunderstood, even though Howell might well have agreed with the interpretation placed upon it by Wynne Jones! Howell's protest was a fair one: he rightly protested that almost the first act of his successor as archdeacon was an attempt not only to "vilify and defame" him by accusing him of being "a spring of the disturbance", but was also an attempt "to divert public attention from the grievances of the St Asaph clergy by a virulent attack upon myself."[99]

The memorialists were now repeating their charges, and that in the public press. They pointed out, quite correctly, that it was

---

[98] Lerry, *A G Edwards*, p 74. Sir William Watkins-Wynn writing to Lord Salisbury suggested that Archdeacon Wynne Jones should be promoted to the deanery of St Asaph, then in the crown's gift due to the elevation of Dean Watkin Williams to the bishopric of Bangor [letter of 7 Jan 1899, SP]. Though his appointment as archdeacon had been severely criticised by many of the clergy, and especially during the recent disturbance, "he has won all over to his side by the energy, tact, justice and firmness he has shown." Besides, he added, his considerable private means would be needed in that office. The good baronet apparently believed that the possession of a private income was a *sine qua non* for such an appointment, as he had also recommended for the same reason, E Wood Edwards, an elder brother of the bishop, for that deanery in 1889, on the grounds that his wife's death had made his present parish an uncongenial sphere. On that occasion he wrongly believed that the appointment was in the hands of the prime minister [13 Feb 1889, SP].

[99] CDH, 7 Jan 1898, p 7. In Howell's obituary in WM [16 Jan 1903, p 5], reference is made to this letter, and possibly his earlier correspondence with Edwards, as material which it was "easy to misconstrue", containing "ill-advised utterances", although no one doubted Howell's consistent loyalty to the Church. This was an unfair statement, for in each case Howell was writing a private letter rather than issuing one for the public domain.

their right to memorialise their bishop and for him to answer them privately, rather than at a packed and public meeting. Had he done what they wished the matter would have remained private. The bishop had totally misrepresented their concern, and they now found it necessary to spell that out, with personal details. Of the young and inexperienced men who had received repeated appointments to important diocesan posts they cited John Owen, formerly dean of St Asaph and later bishop of St Davids; Watkin Williams, dean of St Asaph, and later bishop of Bangor, who had received five preferments in three years, although the term "young and inexperienced" could hardly apply to his grey hairs; Thomas Lloyd, later bishop of Maenan but in fact assistant bishop to Edwards, and Daniel Davies, later bishop of Bangor, four appointments in seven years after ten years in orders, amongst others. Eight men were noted as sharing twenty-four promotions between them, all of whom were under ten years in orders, compared to eighty-two clergy who had not been promoted but all of whom had been in orders for sixteen years or more. As to the bishop's policy of promoting English speakers to Welsh parishes the bishop's own brother, Dean Edwards, was quoted against him: "such appointments have done the Welsh Church deadly injury." The memorial, they concluded, was a church defence movement in the true sense of that term.[100]

Dean Watkin Williams endeavored to be the peace maker. Rightly alleging that much hurt was being done to the diocese by this controversy and to the cause of church defence, he eventually arranged a meeting between Edwards and the memorialists. This took place after the bishop had returned from a holiday abroad, recommended by his doctors because of his ill-health, having been taken ill at some meeting. His son, a Sandhurst cadet, was sent for.[101] At this meeting Edwards claimed that by the time he had returned the memorialists had made the matter public, and he endeavoured to prove that the memorialists had never asked for a private reply, but only one which would "remove all dissatisfaction and restore confidence and good feeling" among

---

[100] Ibid, 17 Dec 1897, pp 4f; 7 Jan 1898, p 7; *Record*, 21 Jan 1898, p 66; *Church Times*, 14 Jan 1898, pp 51f.
[101] CDH, 11 Feb 1898, p 6.

the clergy of the diocese. He may well have been right in this. The position, too, of the Welsh parishes was not as simple as the memorialists believed. The Welsh language was becoming a minority language in many parishes, and the interests of the Welsh people could be better served in a number of these parishes by the appointment of a Welsh-speaking curate rather than a Welsh incumbent. The bishop too claimed to exercise his patronage for the good of the Church in general, which included the laity, and not simply for the clergy of the diocese. But if this was a fair remark, his next move was to divide and rule - even in the tightest corners Edwards knew how to wriggle out of his difficulties - and he now made a distinction between those who had simply signed the memorial, and those who had organised it. The "purposes and methods" of the latter were well known to him and to the world in general, and he believed that the result would be that "an evil spirit had been unmasked and disabled for further mischief". It is obvious he did not mean that remark to be applied to himself![102]

More than one third of the diocesan incumbents signed the memorial; another third probably expressed some share of sympathy with Archdeacon Thomas' protest about the methods and system practised by Edwards. It was this system which was described as a "syndicate for working ecclesiastical promotion in Wales, and which is doing far more injury to the best and permanent interests of the Church than any amount of service rendered to her temporal interests can counter-balance."[103] It is statements such as this which give the lie to George Lerry's contention that those who were promoted by Edwards, and whose names have already been noted, were men of talent and excellence who rose to high positions in later life, and consequently Edwards simply recognised their ability and put it to effective use in his diocese.[104] In fact Edwards "milked the system" of episcopal and other appointments in Wales and generally got his own supporters into positions of influence within the Church, often at the expense of far abler and more moderate men. Many of these men owed their appointments more to Edwards' ability to intrigue in high

---

[102] Ibid, 21 Jan 1898, p 6, and 4 Feb 1898, p 5.
[103] Ibid, 21 Jan 1898, p 6.
[104] Lerry, *A G Edwards*, p 76.

places than to any additional merit they possessed over other candidates at that time. When Watkin Williams was about to be offered the diocese of Bangor, it was observed that if Edwards got another of his supporters into the see of Llandaff, then all Wales would become the diocese of St Asaph![105] Alas, a pastoral bishop such as Joshua Hughes had been replaced by a petty, vicious and unprincipled schoolmaster.

Though Edwards chose to describe the cause of this revolt as a matter of frustrated ambition, and though he suppressed it by recourse to what can only be described as personal intrigue, as well as by the dubious support of his leading and generally Conservative laity,[106] he could hardly have failed to discern the real issue behind it. Though it was ostensibly about the exercise of his patronage, that was simply a symptom of the real problem, which concerned Edwards' style of leadership in the diocese. Edwards took a militant stand on church defence, and, as Lerry notes, demanded that his clergy should follow that lead and imitate his aggressive attitude towards Nonconformity. He wanted a war.

But if Edwards wanted a war against Nonconformity, his clergy preferred peace. Some might have seen this in purely temporal terms, for they were well aware what could happen if Nonconformists replied to such provocation in kind. The tithe disturbances were still a recent memory. Many of the clergy, living in small communities, could not afford to be on unfriendly terms with their religious rivals; others thought it a question of Christian charity to live in peace with all men. Some, like Howell, had come from the ranks of Nonconformity, and still had friends and relatives who occupied positions of importance within it. Others realised that the Nonconformist agitation against the Church was a popular cause only because it was on the Liberal party programme, along with the issues of land legislation and educational matters. The controversy was thus stirred up by a few, rather than conspicuously accepted by the majority of ordinary chapel people. A number, like Howell, were able to see that some of the leaders of Nonconformity wished to have the

---

[105] CDH, 16 Sept 1898, p 7.
[106] One of Edwards' lay supporters, T A Wynne Edwards, suggested that the Church needed a discipline akin to that of the armed forces, "which puts down revolt with a high hand" [CDH, 7 Jan 1898, p 7].

Church disestablished for its own good, even though most churchfolk did not see it in this way. And churchmen knew too that there were a number within their own ranks who would be happy to see a church freed of its state ties.

These clergy felt that Edwards was simply trying to reply to the more noisy Nonconformist agitators in kind, and to give far better than he received. Though they disliked the idea of disestablishment as much as Edwards, though they would speak against it in gentle remonstrance, such men saw the anti-disestablishment campaign that Edwards was endeavouring to promote as one they would wish to avoid and which would detract from the spiritual work of the Church. Their model of controversy might have been the quietly effective campaign launched by Lord Powis to prevent the union of the two sees of Bangor and St Asaph during the 1840s. For a few that would still have been a living memory. The campaign succeeded by Parliamentary pressure backed by petitions and meetings, but it was a peaceable and quiet pressure which recognised the strength and moral position of those who opposed them. Edwards wanted something more aggressive, which seemed to them to be directly opposed to their spiritual concerns. And so their hearts shrunk from his demand. Perhaps better disestablishment on reasonable terms than an all-out war which could only diminish the effectiveness of spiritual life in Wales. Trevor Hughes of Bistre captured this mood exactly. He wrote that the body of the clergy were so discouraged by the policy of their bishop and still more by the measures recently passed that many had decided never to vote again for a Tory candidate. Instead they now saw that the only solution to their problems was disestablishment itself.[107]

If this agitation died down, another soon started regarding the appointment to the bishopric of Bangor, Lewis Lloyd having resigned that see in 1898. A small but influential group of clergy in the diocese of Bangor indicated the qualities they expected in their new bishop. He should have had experience of church work from the inside, and not be a former schoolmaster who had to learn his work on coming to the bench. This was a pointer to Lloyd, who had been a weak and ineffectual bishop. They wanted

[107] CDH, 5 Nov 1897, p 5.

a man whose age and experience could command the respect and confidence of clergy and people; one who had religious earnestness and clear transparent spirituality; no political exploiter, no diplomatic trickster. Everyone recognised the portrait they drew. It was Bishop Edwards. His policy was disliked and his way of dealing with the clergy condemned in wider areas than his own diocese. A spiritual bishop was required, not a political one.[108]

There was no wish, therefore, for the appointment to be decided by the St Asaph "clique", as part of its attempt to control the Welsh Church. The clergy of Bangor had no desire for the Church in Wales to be served by men who were forcing it into a political arena. Indeed, an Englishman would be preferred to a bishop of Edwards' stamp. They had no wish to be brought under a yoke which their clerical colleagues at St Asaph had already found intolerable.[109] As the *Record* commented, the needs of the Welsh Church made clear it was imperative that a bishop should be appointed who could secure the peace of the diocese and set an example of loyal obedience in letter and in spirit to the law of the Church.[110] It was yet another anti-Edwards statement.

A number of the clergy in that diocese organised a counter-memorial, protesting about the former and claiming its promoters were disturbing the peace of the diocese. But it failed to get one third of the support of the diocese's beneficed clergy, and less than one third of the curates signed it. And though the dean of Bangor, Evan Lewis, claimed that many clergy had signed the other memorial without understanding what they were signing, even he had to accept that the original petition had showed the strength of feeling in the diocese against a "St Asaph" appointment.[111] But Watkin Williams, dean of St Asaph, was appointed, and was clearly regarded as forming part of the St Asaph clique, though he displayed a courageous if stubborn independence on many issues thereafter. Upon the appointment of Williams to the see, a local newspaper suggested it was time for the dean and chapter to show that their agitation was not a farce. But it was not to be. Williams'

[108] Ibid, 7 Oct 1898, p 8; *Record,* 1898, p 986.
[109] CDH, 30 Sept 1898, pp 4, 7; 7 Oct 1898, p 4.
[110] *Record,* 14 Nov 1898, p 1005.
[111] CDH, 18 Nov 1898, p 4.

election by the chapter went through without a hitch, and the paper's prophecy that it feared "they were not made of martyr stuff" was shown to be absolutely true.[112]

* * * *

It may seem unfair to bring in this additional material when only a part of it concerns the life of David Howell. Perhaps there are incidents that should be forgotten, as no doubt Edwards felt when he burnt his private papers at the end of his long life. I believe, however, that these matters need to be remembered, not simply to remind us of good men whose reputation was unfairly tarnished, but to provide a warning. Woe to those, as Howell would no doubt have said, woe to those who try to retain a church's privileged status by the power of the sword, or the sarcasm of the tongue, or the biting revenge of one like Rehoboam in the Old Testament who preferred to listen to the warlike utterances of his young men rather than to the wisdom of the old and trusted counsellors. On the one hand we must be grateful that Edwards was stopped in mid-flight by the courage of Howell and other senior clergy in the diocese. It possibly modified his position, and forced him to proceed with more caution. But at the end of the day he won his battle, and those who opposed his policy and methods were simply forgotten and their protests buried in oblivion.

The historical myth of disestablishment has presented Edwards for too long as the doughty and brave warrior who endeavoured to save his Church against enormous odds, and then by ability and initiative managed to obtain far more advantageous terms for her than anyone thought possible. The latter part is true, but while the temporal gain is remembered the spiritual loss is forgotten. Had Edwards accepted that disestablishment was to come, and not feared it as he did - in itself a spiritual judgment upon him - he might have obtained terms which, though harder than those eventually obtained as a result of the 1919 Temporalities Act, would have enabled the church to have reconstructed itself at a much earlier date and under far better circumstances. By forcing

[112] Ibid, 16 Dec 1898, p 4.

the issue over the years, and by the bitterness of the resulting struggle, he deflected the Church from its real spiritual work, confused statistics with spiritual progress and life, and by forcing Nonconformity to play the same game reduced it to a pigmy version of the spiritual life it had once enjoyed and given to Wales. In other words Edwards brought out the worst on both sides, and those who laboured for righteousness found themselves cast out as unworthy of their calling. Politics replaced Christianity, to the distress of Christian life in Wales.

Howell had the vision to see these real issues. His last words longing for spiritual revival were an indication of his concern. Only God could save the Churches; certainly not those leading them. He was in the firing line, and though he won the initial battle, he, and those with him, lost the campaign. Edwards had too much influence on his side. He was too important a politician - understanding that word in its narrowest sense - to allow himself to be beaten within his own Church. Tudor Howell rightly divined the true position. Edwards was no gentleman. But those who opposed him did so on the assumption that bishops were still gentlemen and civilised people. And so they lost.

The net result, as R Tudur Jones reminds us, was that Edwards by refusing to allow any debate or check upon his policy forced the Church into a battle. By declining to allow this debate within the Church and possibly accepting a consensus policy, and by refusing any discussion with Nonconformity, which might have led to an agreed formula of disestablishment, Edwards permitted the politicians to enter and solve the problem between Church and Nonconformity, but on their own terms.[113] The claim of Lord Salisbury, who had appointed Edwards, that he had carefully examined the qualifications of all those clergymen whose names had been suggested for the vacant see of St Asaph, and was "convinced that there is none whose selection would be of so much advantage to the Church in Wales in its present difficult position" as Edwards,[114] has a rather hollow ring about it when confronted with this evidence.

We thus need to remember those who had the spiritual interests of their Church at heart, rather than political manoeuvring, who

[113] R T Jones, *Ffydd ac Argyfwng Cenedl* [Abertawe 1981], II 235-7.
[114] Lerry, *A G Edwards*, p 26.

because they failed to win their case have been forgotten. Alas, we ourselves have forgotten that there was another, and perhaps a better way, and that this way was advocated by brave and loyal churchmen too. They saw clearly what Lonsdale Ragg, a later warden of the Church Hostel, Bangor, realised in 1917, that the Church in Wales had lost some of its spirituality because of the way it had conducted the fight against disestablishment.[115]

[115] *Report of the Church in Wales Spiritual Influence Committee,* [1917] p 12.

Dean of St. David's

Dean Phillips of St Davids died in 1897, after only eighteen months in office. His death was a little inconvenient, for it occurred during an episcopal vacancy, and the new bishop could only be installed when a new dean had taken office.[1] The appointment of the new dean, generally in the hands of the bishop for a Welsh deanery, unlike English deaneries, thus fell into the hands of the Prime Minister. This was the Conservative Lord Salisbury. John Owen, the newly appointed bishop, wrote letters to Salisbury on an almost daily basis regarding the appointment to the deanery. He was obviously concerned, for the dean was generally regarded as the second in the diocesan hierarchy, next only to the bishop. The influence of a dean in the diocese of St Davids, confined to one remote part of it, however, could never be as substantial as the influence Owen was able to exert during his time as dean of St Asaph. Owen might well have hoped to have had the same working relationship with his dean as he had had with Bishop Edwards, but this never proved to be the case in the diocese of St Davids, mainly because of its extent and the difficulties of communication within it.

Owen suggested a number of names to Salisbury for appointment to the deanery, arguing that the appointment was important not only for the diocese but for himself as well. Owen made clear that his first choice was Archdeacon Bevan, vicar of Hay, and a doughty defender of the Church against disestablishment. Age was on his side, Owen claimed, for Bevan was seventy-two, and he had another important qualification besides his fine presence, namely ample private means, being a brother-in-law of Sir Joseph Bailey. But Owen knew, and was also informed, that Bevan had declined other such offers, including the deanery he had held himself, and would decline this too. Owen, however, wished that he should be given

[1] *Bye-Gones*, 31 Mar 1897, pp 65f.

the compliment of receiving such an offer, and was saddened that this was not done. Nevertheless he wrote that there would be other opportunities of showing his appreciation and respect for Bevan's character and services.

Failing Bevan, Owen wished to have Chancellor Davey, then vice-principal of St Davids College, and later to succeed C J Vaughan as dean of Llandaff. He relayed the information that Phillips' predecessor as dean, the ninety-four year old Dean Allen, told him that the late bishop, Basil Jones, would have appointed Davey as Phillips' successor, and he forwarded to Salisbury a letter from David Lewis, vicar of St Davids, claiming that Davey would also be the choice of the cathedral chapter. Davey, he claimed, would keep up the standard of the deanery, was certainly up to an English deanery, let alone a Welsh one, and was regarded as the most honoured clergyman, with the single exception of Dean Vaughan, in the Welsh Church. He was also a personal friend of the Bishop of Lincoln, the Tractarian Edward King. The bishop of Llandaff, Richard Lewis, also wrote supporting the claims of Davey for the deanery.

Owen also mentioned some other names of men he thought might be up to the standard required. These were Canon Lewis of St Davids; the suffragan Bishop of Swansea, John Lloyd; A J M Green, rector of Halkin, Flintshire, the father of Archbishop Green; and the rector of Narberth, John Morris. But he did not want the headmaster of Llandovery to be appointed. He needed Owen Evans to be near to him at the episcopal residence of Abergwili, and St Davids was too far away. Evans became archdeacon and vicar of Carmarthen in 1900.[2]

By early March Salisbury's secretary had suggested to Owen that David Howell might be appointed to the deanery. Owen did not like the idea. Howell, he wrote in reply, was only a Lambeth B.D. He had not studied at any university or college, which Owen felt was unacceptable in a post where a fair standard of learning was required: "This I venture to think, without entering upon any other aspect of the question, is an insurmountable objection for a deanery."[3] Strange that he should have said this about a man who

---

[2] Salisbury Correspondence, Hatfield House: John Owen to McDonnell, Salisbury's secretary, 5 Feb 1897, 8, 6, 10, 11, 23 March 1897; David Lewis to John Owen, 5 Mar 1897; Richard Lewis to Salisbury, 12 Mar 1897.
[3] Ibid: Owen to McDonnell, 11 Mar 1897.

had been nominated to preach before the University of Cambridge, but perhaps not so strange that a friend and colleague of Bishop Edwards should have entered in a barbed reference to another 'aspect' of Howell's life, about which Salisbury already knew.

After much speculation in the public press it was announced at the end of March that David Howell had been offered, and had accepted, the deanery. He was instituted at Lambeth Palace in the absence of a bishop.[4] Howell regarded the appointment as a great honour, and counted it a high privilege to worship on the same spot as had the 'old Fathers' of the Christian faith in Wales over many centuries. He also felt that the appointment would allow him to devote more time to the historical and other work he had long wished "to engage more thoroughly in."[5] Others saw it, however, as more a consolation prize for his failure to obtain a bishopric, and at least one person suggested it was more akin to "an exile". Howell himself saw the appointment "as marking the last stage of his ministerial work."[6] Possibly Salisbury offered the deanery to Howell in a gesture of reparation for the personal anguish Howell had suffered at the hands of Edwards, whom Salisbury had also appointed. The offer might also be seen as an endorsement by the prime minister of Howell's stand against the tactics adopted by Edwards in the disestablishment campaign. Salisbury, after all, was a gentleman, and considered that bishops and clergymen too should act in a gentlemanly and Christian way, however great the provocation. And possibly, by appointing Howell to St Davids, he was giving him a better platform from which to declare his desire for peace and brotherhood. But the appointment may also have been seen as a compliment to Howell's youngest son, Tudor, then the Conservative member for the Denbigh constituency. Salisbury was one of the last prime ministers to make use of his ecclesiastical patronage as a means of obliquely rewarding his political friends.[7] But it might be fairer to

---

[4] *Record*, 15 Ap 1897, p 378.
[5] *Bye-gones*, 31 Mar 1897, pp 65f.
[6] *The Record*, 23 Jan 1903, p 79; cutting in SA/DR/52, fol 729.
[7] See Lord Salisbury's patronage book at Hatfield House. Though K O Morgan considered Howell to be a stalwart Liberal [*Rebirth of a Nation* (Oxford 1981), p 50], he became a member of the Conservative party during his latter years at Cardiff. Eugene Stock, [*My Recollections* (London 1909) p 178] remarks that the evangelical clergy were inevitably Tories at this time.

see the appointment as a recognition of Howell's long years of hard and unremitting service to the Church and people of Wales. There were many who noted that Howell's appointment to the deanery was by the accident of a crown appointment, and wondered whether he, or anyone else who had expressed independence of thought or criticism about the then stance of church life and defence, would have been appointed to such a prestigious position by a Welsh bishop.[8]

Owen and his ecclesiastical friends might have felt uncomfortable at the prospect of Howell's preferment, but it was noted by the *Record* that his appointment had been welcomed by people of all shades of opinion, as recorded by the English and Welsh, Conservative and radical, Anglican and Nonconformist press.[9] Thomas C Evans (Cadrawd) of Llangynwyd, near Maesteg, an old friend of Howell, a blacksmith and a literary figure of some note in his day, greeted the news by having a door cut from his parlour into the garden, so that when Howell visited him and needed to make use of the privy at the end of the garden he would not be embarrassed by having to go to it via the kitchen.[10]

Howell would probably have been more embarrassed by the state of the deanery house. During his short tenure of the deanery Dean Phillips complained about this house to the Ecclesiastical Commissioners. Dean Lewellin had only resided in it for a few months of the year, and these were probably the summer months, as the dean was also principal of St David's College, Lampeter, as well as vicar of that place. His successor, Dean Allan, resided in the chancellor's house and continued to do so after he had retired from the deanery. Phillips found the deanery badly built; it even appears that the house had never been properly completed. The drains ran under the house and the drive was dangerous for carriages. The place was damp for most of the year. Having expended £634 of his own personal money on making necessary repairs Phillips obtained a mortgage of £324 from Queen Anne's

---

[8] J V Morgan, *Welsh Political and Education Leaders in the Victorian Era*, [London 1908], p 38.
[9] *Record*, 9 Ap 1897, p 344 (its issue of 26 Mar suggested his son-in-law, Protheroe, would be appointed); WM, 30 Mar 1897, p 4; CDH, 30 Mar 1897, p 6.
[10] M G Llewelyn, *Sand in the Grass* [London 1943], pp 100f.

Bounty.[11] On his appointment Howell requested that the money left by the late dean (presumably the dilapidation charges, which his family would have been required to pay from his estate), should be used on the improvement of the stables and coach-house, but not, he wrote specifically, on the coal cellar, which was already capable of taking twenty-six tons of coal. The water supply came from two fields, called Vackery fields, near St Nonn's well, and the various deans had rented these fields from a private individual. Howell purchased them for £240, letting the fields at an annual rent of eight guineas. On his death these fields were purchased by the Ecclesiastical Commissioners from his estate, who allowed the various deans the lease of one field at a charge of two guineas and the use of the water supply. The other field was sold.[12]

In spite of Bishop Owen's reservations about Howell's appointment, they seem to have worked harmoniously together, probably because Owen never forgot his deep "gwerin" roots and like Howell appreciated the power and strength of Welsh Nonconformity and tradition. It seems clear, too, that with a diocese of his own, Owen no longer needed to be dependent on Bishop Edwards, and began to exercise a modifying influence upon his former chief. At a dinner held soon after his own appointment had been announced, Howell spoke of the new bishop of St Davids. John Owen, he said, needed the co-operation of his clergy. He would be what his diocese was prepared to make him, though unfortunately Howell did not go on to suggest how this statement might have applied to the diocese of St Asaph! A church filled with the spirit of love - of ungrudging, uncalculating love - to all who love the Lord Jesus Christ with sincerity, cannot be other than the salt of the earth and the light of the world.[13] Such was Howell's prayer for his new bishop and the new diocese in which both were to serve.

Though he was past today's retiring age when he was appointed, Howell refused to regard the deanery as a sinecure.

---

[11] Dean Phillips to the Ecclesiastical Commission, 30 Dec 1895; The Representative Body of the Church in Wales, Cardiff, Ecclesiastical Commission [EC] file for St Davids, D360.
[12] EC file for St Davids.
[13] *Wrexham Advertiser*, 12 June 1897, p 7.

Welsh services were restored in the Cathedral itself. On St David's day he used a nave altar for the Welsh celebration,[14] and remarked afterwards about Bishop Barlow's desire to remove the cathedral to Carmarthen: "If ever I meet that Bishop Barlow in another world, he will not have a pleasant time of it."[15] Likewise Howell continued the work of restoring the cathedral begun by his predecessors as deans, and gave it a new and much needed impetus. He was thus able to complete the rebuilding of the Lady Chapel at the east end of the cathedral, which had stood in ruins for centuries.[16]

Much of his time was spent in raising money from his friends and others for this work of restoration. The *Western Mail* commented in his obituary that he was probably the only churchman in Wales at that time who had sufficient command of the public purse to be able to collect the necessary funds for this undertaking.[17] A number of examples of his ability in raising money may be quoted. "If you wish to be immortalised", he wrote to D Lleufer Thomas, a noted literary and judicial figure in Welsh circles, "we can still find some room for further expenditure". And he adds with a hint of the Howell we have noted from earlier days – a more carefree and relaxed man – "Why don't you make your pilgrimage to St Davids", in order to see the work going on in the Lady Chapel; "you shall have a bed and a house and fire and bread and cheese and meat and a hearty welcome from yours affectionately, David Howell."[18] There was a more sedate style for Archbishop Temple. The need was urgent. That part of the cathedral restored by "a former generation only serves to throw into prominent relief those portions that are still in so sad a state of dilapidation." The cathedral's ruined east and north sections was "a damning blot on the pretensions of modern British Christianity". A publicity brochure which accompanied this and probably other letters noted that the neglect of the past had given the cathedral "an air of desolation". Twelve thousand

---

[14] Ibid, 24 Jan 1903, p 7, suggested he later used the high altar - an almost unprecedented move.
[15] Ibid, 24 Jan 1903, p 7.
[16] *Bye-Gones*, 17 Aug 1898, p 448; 21 Aug 1901, p 168; 30 Oct, p 210; *Haul*, 1901, pp 512-4.
[17] WM, 16 Jan 1903, p 5.
[18] NLW MS 3636D, fols 42f.

pounds was needed for the repair of the eastern chapels and St Mary's College, and these would form a memorial to the earlier restorers of the cathedral, Bishop Basil Jones, Dean Allan and Dean Phillips. "[I]t becomes us", wrote Howell, "to make what ought to be one of the dearest spots on earth to British Christians all that its history and capabilities demand."[19]

Howell also approached the Ecclesiastical Commissioners for their assistance on the grounds of a local claim. This local claim was made on the assumption that the dean and chapter would have materially assisted this restoration out of the property and funds available to them, had these funds not been passed over by them to the commissioners. These local claims had almost the first call upon the commissioners' funding. St Davids Cathedral, Howell informed them, was one of only two cathedrals out of twenty-nine in England and Wales which was partly a ruin. On the one hand there was the architectural splendour of the cathedral and its need for restoration, on the other hand there was the high cost of the work involved and the exceptional poverty of the locality. The amount of money the chapter received from the commissioners for the maintenance of the services and the repair of the fabric was quite inadequate for these purposes, and the last contribution of £10,000 for the £24,000 cost of the previous work was not given as a final donation, but in proportion to the work then projected. Consequently, Howell and the chapter felt that the commission ought to allow them the same proportion of money for the costs of restoring the Lady Chapel. Their architect, J Oldrid Scott, had specified that £2,930 had already been spent, but £11,580 was still needed for the Lady Chapel and the other works. This was in July 1902. Alas the commissioners did not agree with Howell's arguments. Their grant in 1866 was given in return for the transfer to them of the capitular estate of the cathedral. There was no understanding regarding future expenditure. Instead they awarded a miserable grant of £500 as "a moderate contribution" from them as landowners in the diocese.[20]

---

[19] Lambeth Palace Library, Temple Papers, 11, fols 82, 84, of 16 Nov 1898. Temple subscribed £25.
[20] EC file.

The Lady Chapel, in a ruinous state since 1775, was rededicated in October 1901. The sermon was preached by Dr Ryle, bishop of Exeter, previously principal of St David's College, Lampeter. The *Haul* added an ironic note about the Welsh service held that evening in the chapel. The offertory had amounted to £33, which it regarded as extremely poor, and consequently wished that more rich laymen had been present.[21] A fund, opened after his death to provide a suitable memorial to Howell, sponsored by Sir W T Lewis, George Kenyon, Sir Alfred Thomas, O M Edwards and John Ballinger, amongst others, raised sufficient monies to pay for two thirds of the cost of the restoration of St Nicholas' chapel.[22] The restoration of St Mary's College had to wait another fifty years. Howell was saddened, we know, that so few Welsh people took an interest in their mother church. Most of those who made the difficult journey to see the cathedral - seventeen miles from the nearest railway station - were foreigners.[23]

An attempt was also made to persuade the Ecclesiastical Commissioners to allow a house they owned in the cathedral precincts, Penyffoes, whose tenant, Hannah Sinnet, had just died, to become a home of rest for the poorer clergy in the diocese. Visitors, wrote Howell, the prime mover in this, could have the advantage of sea-air and sea-bathing, the privileges of the cathedral services and library, in as restful a spot as could be found anywhere. The house could not be used for a better purpose. A lay vicar could look after the house with the assistance of a housekeeper. Alas the commissioners could not entertain such a desirable object save at a fair and thus prohibitive rent, and the scheme fell to the ground, another victim of the mercenary interests of the Church's civil establishment.[24]

By this time Howell was well engrossed in the work of the cathedral. Camber Williams, canon missioner of the diocese, in his memorial sermon to Howell, noted his faithfulness to the duties of his office and his love for the cathedral, as well as the comfort he found in the liturgy of the Church. Unless there was good reason he never missed a service, and he could never

[21] *Haul*, 1901, p 514.
[22] NLW SD/Admin/1978 fol 2: WM, 22 Jan 1903, p 6. A projected scholarship never materialised.
[23] Howell to David Samuel, 19 Mar 1901, in NLW MS 2826D. Translated.
[24] EC file.

remember him being late. There was the unassuming simplicity of his conduct. He was absolutely free from vanity or ostentation, perfectly natural and simple in all his ways; they all knew that he lightly bore the signs and marks of his office, and as a result he was one of the most approachable of men. Williams also gave two pictures of Howell as dean. One was at the Saturday afternoon intercessory prayer service he had instituted, and which followed the main cathedral service. Here the needs of the whole world as well as local events were remembered. And he recalled the impressiveness of Howell's last sermon in that cathedral, when he preached on Christ as the light of the world. He breathed, he recalled, the atmosphere of heaven.[25] Another glimpse of his ministry is given by a surviving leaflet he wrote for the cathedral worshippers. Described as leaflet number seventeen it related to Holy Week and Easter Day, 1901. Wondering how men could question and quibble, reason and argue, on the subject of the "sacrifice, oblation, and satisfaction" of the cross, he wrote "all we can do, and should do, is to stand still and gaze with adoring wonder." He continued:

> And here let me say, from my own observation of ministerial results during what is now becoming a long life, that in proportion as this great truth of Redemption through the vicarious death of Christ has formed the very life-blood of a ministry, permeating it through and through, has that ministry been fruitful in spiritual results - in changed lives, strong convictions, devout experiences, and in moral power for both conversion and edification. ... Certain it is that there may be much Church activity, multiplied organisations, an impressive ritual, with abounding energy and zeal, while spiritual as distinguished from merely ecclesiastical life may remain languid and languishing. It is the Gospel of the 'precious blood' that rightly gives vitality and force to a ministry; and never can we have a right conception of sin, of the holiness of God, of the demands of His moral government, of the principles involved in the restoration of fallen humanity, or rightly understood the way of salvation, or the purposes of the Incarnation, except in and through the Great Propitiation; for be it never forgotten that Reconciliation is not by the Incarnation, but by the Propitiation.

---

[25] *Haul*, 1903, pp 57-61; WM, 22 Jan 1903, p 6.

It is by the blood of Christ, he asserted, that we have peace with God, "boldness to enter into the holiest", redemption, and forgiveness of sins "according to the richness of His grace." "Blessed truth! Glorious Gospel!", he exclaimed. And such was his ministry in the cathedral of St Davids, proclaiming the truth and glory of the Gospel.

Apart from his cathedral ministry Howell "occupied a large place in the work of the city".[26] For example, he acted as chairman of the committee which opened the new County School in the city, persuading many parents to send their children to it, thus ensuring its success and viability.[27] It is not surprising that he soon became regarded as the centre of spiritual power and influence within the surrounding area, or that, because his duties at the cathedral were comparatively light, he was able to lecture and preach extensively far and near. His lectures on St Davids and its cathedral - probably a fund raising exercise, and on Welsh hymnology, both achieved considerable popularity,[28] in an age when the public lecture was one of the principal means of entertainment. Did not that likable rascal, Dr Gomer Lewis of Swansea, give his lecture on "The Glory of Variety" three hundred and fifty times?[29]

A personal reminiscence of Howell's time at St Davids is given in the memoirs of John Miles Thomas. He was a cathedral choirboy during Howell's time as dean, and frequently called at the deanery where he helped the dean's daughter brush and comb her dog. There was a staff of a cook and four maids, and probably a coachman as Howell kept a carriage, although Thomas notes that he often walked around the place, unlike the other clergy. It was at the deanery that Howell held an annual party for the choirboys, during which they played the clothes basket game, and each received on leaving an orange, then regarded as a great luxury. On New Year's day each chorister received a gift of a book, such as the life of Field Marshall Roberts or Baden Powell. In return, the choirboys had to repeat for him each Saturday afternoon the collect for the next Sunday, and these he would "mark" with one

---

[26] WM, 21 Jan 1903, p 4.
[27] A W James, *St Davids and Dewisland* [Cardiff 1981], p 157.
[28] WM, 19 Jan 1899, p 3; 16 Jan 1903, p 5; *Bye-Gones,* 28 Jan 1903, pp 16f.
[29] Morgan, *Welsh Political and Education Leaders,* p 711.

of several replies, "Fair, you must do better", "good, but you can improve", "very good, well done, Admirable, admirable", which he pronounced in nautical terms. On these occasions he would tell them all sorts of odd things, such as not to clean their ears with pointed instruments, or about Martin Luther's remark that if all his thoughts were written on a board before his eyes he would run away. He once impressed them much by reading a letter from his soldier son who was serving in the South African campaign. What intrigued them most was not the warfare but that he slept under a wagon by night. On the day of the dean's death, Thomas' mother wept and told him that were it not for good men like the dean, God would surely destroy this wicked world. She had reason to be grateful too. When the organist complained about her son's corduroy trousers, it was Howell, knowing the real reason, who went out and bought her son two good suits.[30]

* * * *

David Howell died after a five day illness on the 15 January 1903. His last words were, "Its all right". He had suffered from heart disease for some time,[31] yet the previous Sunday he had preached at the cathedral. He was spared, as he desired to be, the experience of outliving his capacity for useful work. His family obtained the permission of the Privy Council for his body to be buried in the St Nicholas chapel. This chapel was later restored as his memorial. His funeral was simple, in accordance with his known wishes: "I detest public Funerals and my *aversion* to Funeral Sermons is unutterable", he had written to Silvan Evans years before.[32] Nevertheless the service was impressive, even though many who would have wished to be there were prevented by the remoteness of the cathedral. The pulpit and lectern were

---

[30] J M Thomas, *Looking Back* [Carmarthen 1979], pp 32-5.
[31] Obituary note, *Wrexham Advertiser*, 17 Jan 1903, p 3.
[32] Howell to D Silvan Evans, 13 Ap 1888, NLW MS Cwrt Mawr 903B, fol 33 (1888). He wanted a private funeral, at 10.00am, three days after his death, in utmost privacy, with no allusions made about him, not even in the press. One writer assumed it was his wish to be buried with his wife at Gresford [*Geninen*, 22 [1904] 43]. The consent of the Privy Council was required under the terms of the 1855 Burial Act as burials had been discontinued in the cathedral since 1881 [NLW SD/Ch/Misc/330].

draped in purple cloth, and the wreaths covered the steps of the sanctuary. The funeral procession was long, containing many clergymen and the local Nonconformist ministers. An audible sigh is said to have occurred as the bishop passed, for David Howell was no longer in front of him as usual. Sir John Goss' anthem, "O Saviour of the World" was sung, said to be his favourite anthem, and Howell's own hymn, "O fy Arglwydd! O fy Mhrynwr!" concluded the service. A memorial service followed the funeral service that evening, during which there were two sermons, one in English by Chancellor Allan Smith, who followed Howell as dean, and the other by Canon Williams, in Welsh, which has already been noted.[33]

The tributes to his memory poured in and were extensively reported in most of the Welsh language papers and periodicals. *Y Goleuad* said that his death left Wales poorer, weaker and emptier. He was not a party or a denominational man, but a man of nation and Church in general, and above all, a man of God. The *Llan* described him as one of Wales' most talented sons, and the *Western Mail* remarked that Howell was one of the leading lights of the Church in Wales in his generation, and that he had thrown himself into the stream of national life.[34] The Anglican scholar, W H Griffith Thomas, wrote in the *Record* that he had "loved him as a Son loves his Father" and never expected to see his like again. As a young man he had been much influenced by Howell in his Wrexham days.[35] Howell had sponsored him for ordination. Canon Christopher, of St Aldgate's Oxford, whose curate Thomas became, wrote to Thomas while he was staying with Howell at "the hospitable, genial, spiritually healthy Deanery of St Davids".[36] Talbot Rice, a son of the Lord Dynevor who had suggested Howell's name for a Welsh bishopric, and vicar of Swansea, noted in his parish magazine Howell's "devotion to his Master", his eloquence, largeness of heart, faithful and hard work, in which he had done much "for the great cause of Christ's Kingdom that is wider than any Church."[37] Gresford Church was deep in

---

[33] WM, 22 Jan 1903, p 6.
[34] Quoted in *Geninen* 21 [St Davids 1903] 10-13; *Record*, 30 Jan 1903, p 103.
[35] *Record*, 23 Jan 1903, p 79; WM, 16 Jan 1903, p 5; *Bye-Gones*, 28 Jan 1903, pp 16f.
[36] J S Reynolds, Canon Christopher [Abingdon 1967], p 294.
[37] *Swansea Parish Magazine*, 1903, p 27.

mourning for its own memorial service, when its vicar, Edward Fishbourne, reminded the congregation as to how Howell had loved to preach Christ crucified, and how, recently and enfeebled, he had preached at Wrexham repeating the phrase, "Come to Christ, love Christ". The *Wrexham Advertiser* which noted this also included part of Howell's last letter to his old Wrexham friend and executor, John Bury, with whom he corresponded weekly. Noting the death of the rather fiery rector of Marchwiel, Howell added, "it was a saying of the unhappy Lord Byron that, if there were to be no hereafter, the Christian gets more out of this life than others; but if there be a hereafter, then his prospect only is worth coveting. The bedrock of God's promises have stood and will stand, all the possible mysteries of the future. May God increase our faith ..."[38] Clearly, Howell was prepared for the act of dying, and in death his faith in his Saviour was not wanting. His last message to the Welsh people was read almost as his body was laid in the grave. It summed up his prayer of fifteen years and more that there might be a powerful and universal religious revival, and it ended with these words:

> Mark well. If I knew that this was my last message to my fellow-countrymen throughout the length and breadth of Wales, before I am summoned to judgement, and the light of eternity already breaking upon me, it would be this and none other: namely, that the primary need of my country and my beloved nation at this moment is a *spiritual revival through a special outpouring of the Holy Spirit.*[39]

Howell's will was proved at £10,160 gross, £7,592 net. Bequests were left to the Church Missionary Society, the British and Foreign Bible Society, and the Church Pastoral-Aid Society. Part of his library went to the library of St Davids cathedral; his copy of Salesbury's New Testament of 1567 was bequeathed to the Cardiff Free Library; the Spanish clock and silver crucifix given him by Arthur Seymour Jones went to his son-in-law,

---

[38] *Wrexham Advertiser*, 24 Jan 1903, p 7. *Cochfarf,* another old friend and then mayor of Cardiff, noted in the WM of 19 Jan 1903, p 6, Howell's New Year's letter to his friends. It contained the well known lines attributed to Stephen Grellet, "I expect to pass through this life but once ..."

[39] Quoted by the *Record,* 30 Jan 1903, p 103. It appeared first in *Y Cyfaill Eglwysig.*

Archdeacon Protheroe, a fairly high-churchman, and his son John was left his papers and manuscripts, with strict instructions not to publish any of his sermons and addresses.[40]

*   *   *   *

Little is known of Howell's personal and family life. His wife, Anne Powell of Pencoed, died at Wrexham Vicarage in 1891, aged fifty-six, and was buried at Gresford, the funeral being one of Howell's first engagements as vicar of that parish. There are a few allusions to her in his letters, but all reveal their deep love for one another. If he could write to Silvan from the St Asaph canonry, "my wife is here for the day from Wrexham, and like all women full of fuss and much serving",[41] her early death after a long illness shattered him. The letter conveying the news of her death to Silvan is the only letter written in Welsh in their whole correspondence, apart from the letter which mentioned the inscription he had placed on her grave. They had been married for forty years: "often did my dear one mention your departed wife in her last days of great suffering". The customary funeral card bore that verse from Proverbs 31.28: "Her children rise up and call her blessed, and her husband also, and he praiseth her." The card is still to be found contained in his letter to Lady Hills-Johnes. He writes to her of the real shock of his wife's death:

> Alas since I saw you I have had the greatest loss that could well happen to any human being in this world in the death of my dear wife. She was almost *everything* to me and few men ever depended on a woman as I did on her. Her strength of will and force of character made her truly invaluable to me. She was self-forgetfulness to a fault and I am fully convinced that her life was sacrificed to her devotion to others. How to face the *future* without her I know not, but God does, and that is enough. I know how true are the words, 'Submit Thyself to God and Thou shalt find God fights the battles of the will resigned." but I find submission and resignation are not the same. God knows it is my

---

[40] *Record*, 20 Feb and 27 Mar 1903, pp 179, 298. Howell's father had left him £3,000. See also *Bye-Gones*, 4 Mar 1903, p 41.

[41] Howell to D Silvan Evans, 20 Aug 1888, 5 May 1891, 4 Ap 1898, NLW MS 903B, fols 31, 42 and 51. In the latter he recorded the inscription on his wife's grave in Welsh.

honest desire to resign myself to His dealings, but alas, I do so so imperfectly.[42]

Declining an invitation to visit Dolaucothi in April of the next year, which seems to have been an annual visit, he apologised saying that

> since then my whole life has changed, and what had been, I am bold to say, one of the *happiest* of lives, has since become one of dismal darkness, loneliness and desolation. One of the brightest homes that any human being has been blessed with has since become a mere lodging house as a place to eat and sleep in, and I seem to have lost all interest in everything ... My youngest daughter, Dorothy, promises to be an interesting child, but she is at school. My other daughter, who keeps house for me, is exceedingly delicate, and I have to care for her, rather than she for me. I have also had other troubles, that have added bitterness to my cure, but my bereavement seems to shallion [sic] all the rest. I dare not say that "all these things are against me!" Nothing God permits can eventually be against us, and Old Chrysostom was right when he used to explain his darkest days of exile and distress - "Glory be to God for *all* that happens!" Of the same spirit was the motto of the old Princes of Glamorgan - "a ddioddefws a orfu" - "He who suffered, conquered". But I am such a poor mean creature, that mental suffering seems to make my very soul sink ... Martyrdom is not a pleasant experience. Do forgive me for troubling you with my miseries. It is a selfish relief. My faith in God, and his *goodness* has *never* turned, never, but I have such a terrible heartache when I think of her, that I can hardly control myself. She had such kindness - such a well balanced *judgement,* and such an almost supernatural *discernment* of *character* that without her I feel like a shipwrecked mariner ready to be driven anywhere.[43]

Howell's own obituary note described his great sorrow at her death: "who by her rare tact, unerring judgment, and devoted loyalty had nobly and faithfully sustained her husband in the arduous labours and anxieties of his ministerial life."[44] Anne

---

[42] Howell to Lady Hills-Johnes, 15 Oct 1891, NLW Dolaucothi MS, L6999. Howell and Lady Hills-Johnes seem to have been correspondents over many years. Howell's letter to her on her engagement to General Hills-Johnes received her husband's inscription, "decidedly doleful congratulations."
[43] Ibid, of 18 Ap 1892, L7000.
[44] *Record,* 23 Jan 1903, p 79.

Powell was sixteen when they married, and Howell knew how much he owed her for those sacrificial years when he was training for the ministry. It is not surprising in another way that he felt her death so deeply. His passionate nature, his sensitivity, so clearly seen in his pulpit ministry, were also reflections of his own character. Loving God with all ones strength too means that human relationships also reflect part of that love. Perhaps of all that we know of Howell, these letters to Dolaucothi show the strengths that were his. Had his wife survived might she have been a moderating force in his years of attrition with Edwards?

David and Anne Howell had four sons and four daughters. Their eldest son, Taliesin, born in 1852, was still in Cardiff in 1873,[45] but seems to have settled in Australia after that. He was not at either of his parents' funerals and only an oblique reference was made to him in the obituaries, though he received an equal share in his father's will as his brothers. An oral tradition within the family is that when Howell was in residence at St Asaph a rather nondescript person was brought in to him dressed in a common seaman's garb. It was Taliesin. The second son, born in early 1853, was John Aneurin Howell, MA. He was vicar of Penmaenmawr in the 1880s and later of St Bede's, Toxteth Park, Liverpool, until his early death in 1909. We know a little more about his third son, Arthur Anthony, as he is recorded in *Who's Who*, and is mentioned in a number of his father's letters. These indicate that if Howell felt rather disappointed in his children, he also expected too much of them. In 1883 Arthur failed his medical examinations, and this, combined with John's third class in schools, having been four years at Shrewsbury School "at £140 per annum", made Howell despair of both. "What have we done that our children", he wrote to Silvan, "should be such a burden and reproach to us? It seems to me that everybody's children except mine do something to justify the expenditure bestowed upon them. In many years I was cheered by the hope that my children would at 21 and 22 become self-supporting and that my wife and myself could enjoy a few quiet years of freedom from anxiety before the final separation. So far from this, every year

---

[45] CMG, 4 Jan 1873, p 5. At his mother's funeral he was confused by some with the Revd Jonathan Howell, a distant cousin of Howell's, who had served for some years as his curate in Wrexham.

increases our burdens." Even worse was his cry of despair which ended the letter, "If it were not for the mystery of the future I should often wish to be out of the present."[46]

Arthur later passed his physician's examinations in 1887, but went down with brain fever, due, it transpired, to overwork, sleeplessness and miserable lodgings, and probably through a father's over-expectations. "May God visit us in mercy and spare our boy if it's his will", wrote Howell at this time. The following year Arthur collapsed with the same problem before his final examinations. "I am not without hope that he will pull through, if it be the will of God", wrote Howell, "but I hope with trembling."[47] Arthur served Queen and country in the South African War as a medical officer, and later served in the army, becoming eventually a temporary Brigadier General at the time of his death in January 1918.

His youngest son has already been mentioned. William Tudor, born in 1863, educated at Shrewsbury and New College, was a barrister, and between 1895-1900 was member of parliament for the Denbigh Boroughs in the Conservative interest, but then declined to seek re-election. His subsequent career is not known, though he died in Canada in 1911.[48]

The eldest daughter Kate (Catherine Morfydd) married one of Howell's former Cardiff curates in 1873, James Howard Protheroe, who was then vicar of Mountain Ash and later became vicar of Aberystwyth and archdeacon of Cardigan from 1893. Tragically Protheroe died a few months after his father-in-law. His widow later moved to Walton on Thames. Dorothy married a person who served in the Indian Civil Service and lived in Bombay. It was said that her departure to India was a contributory factor to Howell's death.[49] A daughter, Mary, born in 1859, appears to have lived with her father at St Davids and looked after him, taking over from his sister, Mrs Saunders, who

---

[46] Howell to D Silvan Evans, 20 July 1883: NLW Cwrt Mawr MS 903B, fol 12.
[47] Ibid, of 24 Ap 1887 and 10 Ap 1888, fols 25 and 30.
[48] *Bye-Gones*, 11 Oct 1911, p 143: William Tudor Howell was prominent in London Welsh circles, see ibid, 2 Mar 1892, pp 271f. A speech of his, indicating his interest in the social gospel, is found in the *Report of the St Asaph Diocesan Conference*, 1890, p 27.
[49] *Bye-Gones*, 28 Jan 1903, pp 16f.

came to keep house for him at Gresford.[50] Mary appears to have remained in St Davids after his death. The last child, Gwenllian, married a Mr Thomas, and had two sons, one of whom lived until recently at Ipswich. In addition Howell left a brother, Alderman William Howell of Pencoed, a prominent figure in Glamorgan Methodism.

---

[50] Howell said of her, "she's worth all the family put together, more of sense and grace than all ..." [Howell to David Samuel, 19 Mar 1901, in NLW MS 2826. Translated]. Her son, the Revd John Saunders, was an influential figure during the 1904-05 revival.

Nationality and Patriotism

Every obituary of David Howell stressed his love and concern for his nation, its language and its Church. His devotion and service meant that few Welshmen became better known than he did to his fellow-countrymen, or were more able to command their respect and admiration.

One of the major ways in which Howell expressed his concern for Wales and its language was through the eisteddfodic movement. Here he forged friendships with people of different religious traditions, and he obviously hoped that the eisteddfod movement would not only encourage the survival and use of the Welsh language, but be a unifying force in the life of the nation. On the platform he was more generally known by his bardic name, Llawdden. This was the name of a fifteenth century bard. The name may have come to Howell's attention through the elegy on him contained in the *Iolo Manuscripts*, edited by Taliesin Williams of Merthyr Tydfil, and published in 1848, although Taliesin had used the name Llawdden as his own bardic signature at the Cardiff eisteddfod of 1834.[1]

At quite an early age Howell is found competing in local eisteddfodau, and contributing poetry to many of the Welsh periodicals of his day, irrespective of their denominational allegiance. Regarded even then as more of a literary man's poet than a popular one, his poetic interest had diminished by his later days. It may be that he heeded his father's advice as noted earlier. Writing in 1887 to Mrs Ceiriog Hughes, regarding a pension for her husband, the poet, he added, "Yes, in my young and foolish days I was known as Llawdden, but the stern realities of life have long ago driven all poetry and sentiment out of me. I am now a very prosaic old Parson, whose only source of happiness at present

---

[1] *Awenyddion Gwent a Dyfed ... Eisteddfod Caerdydd 1834* [Cardiff 1834] pp 1, 29.

is in poor and puny efforts to leave the world better than he found it."² The muse was not entirely forgotten, for writing some years earlier to Dewi Haran, David Evans, an auctioneer and bard of Llanharan, he drew attention to their days together as pupils of Myfyr, Evan Davies the watchmaker and druid of Pontypridd, who had acted as their 'Gamaliel'. Writing that though he had forsaken literature for the Church, Howell added, "as now I descend toward the vale and the greyness of evening spreads over me, I am as though intending to fall in love again with the *awen* and end my life as I began it, if God wills it."³ Apart from some outstanding hymns, Howell never fulfilled this intention, so that an obituary writer could simply note his poetical work with the comment that "the present generation knows but little" of it.⁴

Thereafter Howell was better known as an eisteddfodic figure and adjudicator. He had started with the smaller and local eisteddfodau, often acting with J Ceiriog Hughes. He clearly learnt much from him, for writing from Cardiff he told Ceiriog that having frequently acted as an adjudicator over the previous ten years, he had had the remarkable experience of never having his judgment questioned. "I ascribe it solely", he wrote, "to the fact that I have always acted on the principles you propose". However he did complain of the amount of work his adjudications required when set against a busy parochial life.⁵ Howell's career as an adjudicator at the National Eisteddfod began in 1875. Replying to that invitation Howell wrote that he had made up his mind to have nothing more to do with these adjudications, "but I have so many pleasing associations connected with Pwllheli that I feel constrained to say yes to your request". This Pwllheli eisteddfod was accompanied by tragedy, for Howell's fellow adjudicator, Robert Ellis (Cynddelw), died before they could announce their agreed adjudication: "a dear friend of mine for a quarter of a century and one of the most perfect characters I have ever known."⁶ Howell went on to adjudicate at

---

[2] Howell to Mrs J Ceiriog Hughes, 27 Sept 1887, NLW Ceiriog MS, 10183D, fol 60.
[3] Howell to David Evans, 11 Dec 1883, in NLW MS 6245B. Translated.
[4] WM, 16 Jan 1903, p 5.
[5] Howell to J Ceiriog Hughes, no date: NLW MS 10183D, fols 63-6.
[6] NLW MS 18345C, Correspondence regarding the Pwllheli National Eisteddfod 1875.

the 1876, 1880, 1881, 1884 and 1888 national eisteddfodau.[7] On these platforms Howell's great wit and biting, though not unfair, sarcasm, had full play.

His real contribution to the eisteddfodic movement lay in a different direction, as a helper and encourager, even as a father figure. He was one of that small group of men who had brought order into the whole movement, and had seen their policy triumph at the great Aberdare eisteddfod of 1861. His comrades in arms included such churchmen as Archdeacon D R Thomas, Dean John Pryce of Bangor, D Silvan Evans and Archdeacon John Griffiths. Nonconformists were few and far between at that time in that movement, for, as Howell wrote, this was a time "when it was almost as much as a minister's character was worth to be known as a bard, or to be seen on the platform of an Eisteddvod."[8] It must not be forgotten that the eisteddfod movement owed much to the Welsh literary clergy during its earlier days.

Howell was still concerned with the character of the eisteddfod during the 1890s. Writing to W J Roberts (Gwilym Cowlyd) of Llanrwst in 1896, in a letter expressing his hope that a royal charter could be obtained, he observed that "in the absence of such a Charter, we have no means of preventing any local body of speculators, simply as a commercial enterprise, without the least interest in Welsh literature, or even knowing our language, from getting up an eisteddfod, utterly regardless of long custom, usage and antiquity. This *has* been done repeatedly, and is being done now, while the literate of Wales look on helplessly without redress." A royal charter would enable the eisteddfod to be a recognised institutional body in which property could be vested, and help might be obtained from imperial sources. Alas, the eisteddfod movement was regretfully divided between the adherents of the Gorsedd and the Eisteddfod Association.[9] His feelings about the

[7] *Cymru*, 21 [1901] 48f. His adjudication at the Caernarfon eisteddfod is in *Y Traethodydd*, 80 [1925] 245f. See also NLW MS 10183D fols 67-70 [letters to J Ceiriog Hughes], and *Bye-Gones*, 12 Sept 1888, p 229.
[8] D Howell, "Welsh Nationality", *Liverpool Welsh National Society Transactions*, 1891-2, p 81.
[9] Howell to G Roberts, 21 Jan 1896, NLW MS 9224C fol 20. This was written in English with a concluding paragraph in Welsh noting that he used English as it was a more appropriate language for legal and commercial reasons, rather than the old language of emotion. See also *Haul* 1896, p 315. Howell was also involved in a campaign to have a Welsh symbol placed on the royal arms [NLW MS 17345C fol 22, Howell to T H Thomas, 10 July 1893].

Gorsedd were already known. It was not a necessary part of the eisteddfod. Many of its best friends and advocates were not members of it, and it rather resembled freemasonry.[10]

Howell argued the case for the continued existence of the movement in a speech at the Wrexham eisteddfod of 1877. Surely it was sufficient justification that it brought together an assembly of many thousands, mainly of the working population, Welshmen of all creeds and classes, religions and politics, to unite in one common effort for the common good of their common country. Furthermore it helped retain the use of the Welsh language. Perhaps, he queried, Wales had become drunk on an Anglicisation policy. But if he learnt English was there any need for the Welshman to forget his Welsh? There was a Glamorgan saying that two is better than one for everything except eating bread when it is scarce! Is it not an advantage to a soldier to have two arrows to his bow and two instruments to hand? It is no light thing to destroy one of the most ancient languages of the world, a language in which the Gospel was brought to Wales and one used by Daniel Rowland and Williams Pantycelyn.[11]

Howell's warm Welsh and kind face, open hearted manner, and voice half speaking, half preaching, always made a powerful impression at these gatherings. This was so from his earliest days, for Watcyn Wyn remembered him at the 1851 Pontypridd eisteddfod, dressed as a comfortable farmer of the period, full of life and vigour. When Howell spoke in the eisteddfod tent people would rush in to hear him, as in the same way members of parliament would rush into the chamber whenever it was known that Gladstone was on his feet to speak. At the Wrexham eisteddfod of 1888 Howell is said to have outdistanced Gladstone himself - who had spoken beforehand - in oratory. This was said to have been Howell's most celebrated speech. Speaking first in English and then in Welsh he praised the eisteddfod movement and declared his unfaltering faith in the Welsh language. The special correspondent of the *Western Mail* then recorded:

> He ascended the platform, and then took place one of the most thrilling episodes which I have ever witnessed at any eisteddfod,

---

[10] "The National Eisteddfod for 1876 at Wrexham", *Cymmrodor*, I [1877] 50f.
[11] Ibid, pp 49-52. Translated.

and I have attended all the important ones held in and out of the Principality within the last twenty-one years. Picture [him] ... ascending the platform, carrying a folded programme in his hand. His sturdy figure is dressed in clerical black, and he wears the white stock. His abundance of white hair is parted at the side. He wears his hair something after the manner in which the hair is shown in the 'Williams Pantycelyn' portrait. The rev. canon commenced in English, and his elocution was perfect. He gradually warmed up, and the audience grew excited. Suddenly he broke forth into Glamorganshire Welsh, something after the fashion of old Siencyn Harry did when he attempted to preach in English to the Misses Leigh at St Fagan's. But there was this difference between the two - Siencyn Harry had forgotten his English; Canon Howell's Cambrian spirit took higher flights than the English tongue could afford wings strong enough to follow. The effect of bursting thus into the higher atmosphere of Cymric eloquence was magical. The whole audience seemed enchanted, and the thunderous applause which followed told of a nation whose heart had been touched, and that deeply, by a master of the tribune. He descended again into English, and spoke well. But suddenly he darted up again into the higher region of Welsh sentiment. I am not using the language of exaggeration when I say that the canon seemed now the very impersonation of the old Welsh pulpit oratory which in the early days of the present century carried the nation after it. I have never heard such emotional eloquence as I did coming from the tongue of Canon Howell. He personified the Welsh language. He spoke of her age of more than 2,000 years; he referred to her anticipated death. He then referred to the religious character of the people who spoke it, and then the climax was reached with the genuine 'hwyl,' - 'hwyl' coming from the heart, and expressed in musical cadences such as only a Welsh orator can use when uttering the vernacular - spoke of her dying, if dying she must, in the pulpit, at a prayer meeting, or on her knees! Then he took another tack - she was not likely to die. Nay, he believed when the Judge appeared on the white clouds on the last day some Welshmen would be heard greeting him in the words of the poet of Pantycelyn, namely:-

> "Wele'n dyfod ar y cwmwl
> Rhwn fu farw ar y pren;
> Mil miliynau o angylion
> Sy'n amgylchu'r orsedd wen!
> Haleluia!
> Iesu a deyrnasa byth."

It would be impossible for the pen of the most gifted writer the world ever saw to describe the scene which now took place. I am sure that I am not exaggerating when I say that thousands were in tears, and even the monoglot English present seemed labouring under a very deep emotion.[12]

Rhys J Huws felt that there was no one like Howell in the eisteddfod. There he had a national pulpit. There he represented the complete nation. And there, he added, he frequently hit 'the nail on the head' as regards the real needs of the country. It is clear that Howell regarded the eisteddfod platform and movement as a means of encouraging the Welsh language and its literature, and of developing a concern and feeling for patriotism in Wales. This was clearly seen by him as a counter-balance to his belief that there had been an unseen but nevertheless real policy of suppressing the indigenous life of Wales over the previous five centuries.[13]

Howell, said Rhys J Huws in that same *Geninen* obituary, counted the happiness and sufferings of his own nation as his own personal property. But his was not a narrow or nationalistic view of his nation, but rather one which recognised his country's ideals and aspirations, sought to enlarge and extend them, and place them within a wider context. It was this view which Howell expressed on the eisteddfod platform, and defined in a popular lecture on Welsh nationalism which he gave on many different occasions, and which was eventually published in 1892:

> *Cymru Fu* holds an honourable position in the past history of nations. It is our wish, and our desire, and it shall be our effort, that it should not lose its individuality; and it is our aim that *Cymru Fydd* should not allow itself to be merged into other nationalities, but retain its old fire, its old love of learning, its old industry, and its old patriotism. I would not utter one syllable that could be

---

[12] WM, 16 Jan 1903, p 5. See also Grey-Edwards, *Reminiscences of an Unknown Man* [Cardiff 1940], p 104. M E Thomas, in *The Welsh Spirit of Gwent* [Cardiff 1988] p 21, notes Howell's speech at the 1897 Newport Eisteddfod as being one of its principal highlights. During the 1888 Wrexham eisteddfod Howell said that it was the great Welsh music festival, and he was thankful that "Welshmen of all classes and creeds could meet on one platform without being prejudiced with their crockets and fads." [*Bye-Gones*, 12 Sept 1888, p 220].

[13] The obituary by Rhys J Huws in *Geninen*, 21 [St Davids 1903] 5f.

construed into an advocacy of a suicidal nationalism - a nationalism that would madly seek to separate our interests from those of the great and grand Empire whose destinies it is our privilege to share. I am as far as possible from aiming at anything of this kind. The laws of Hywel Dda are merged in the laws of England; our Prince of Wales is the Heir-Apparent to the British Crown; the blood of the sons of Gwalia has mingled with that of the Saxon in cementing an Empire on which the sun never sets; the wisdom of the Cymro has contributed its share in erecting a Constitution which is the envy and admiration of the world. England's glory is our heritage and our birthright, as much as least as any other national element of which our Empire is made up. .... We are true as steel to what is now an old alliance, but we have not lost our national individuality, and we do not mean to lose it ... There is no antagonism between true patriotism and that feeling of friendliness and goodwill which we should feel and cultivate towards men of other nations. There is no conflict of interests between the Welshman's love of his beloved Wales, and his loyalty to the institutions of that greater Britain of which he forms the base. Any other feeling would be but a spurious patriotism, a contentious, suicidal selfishness, which every true Cymro will be the first to denounce. No, no, my brethren, we do not love England less because we love Cymru, ein hannwyl Gymru, more.[14]

The emergence of a national identity delighted Howell. He was happy to identify himself with the educational movements, the Sunday Closing Act for Wales, the Welsh press and literary activities, all of these being outward manifestations of this national movement.[15] But he was painfully aware that this identity depended to a large extent on the retention of the Welsh language. Speaking in that same lecture noted above Howell enlarged on this point, arguing that the first aspect of the mission of Welsh nationality would be:

> The cultivation of the language which Divine Providence has so graciously preserved to us, and which is still the language of thought and feeling to two-thirds of the inhabitants of Wales. Will

---

[14] "Welsh Nationality", 91f; Cymru Fydd was a national movement allied to the Welsh Liberal party, but Howell is not using the term in that narrower sense, but rather in its literal sense, "Wales tomorrow".
[15] See, for example, another essay on a similar theme, "Gwladgarwch y Cymry", *Geninen*, 10 [1892] 145-8.

it be said that it would be better for Wales if there was but one language, and that the language of law, of science, of commerce, and of the richest literature in the world? Such a question proceeds on the assumption that a knowledge of Welsh is essentially antagonistic to the knowledge of English, and that those who desire the cultivation of Welsh desire the exclusion of English. Against such an assumption, it is humiliating to have to protest. I contend that the knowledge of two living languages, side by side, is quite compatible with the due cultivation of both ... It is stated on high authority that the bilingual nations of Europe are among the most intelligence, enterprising, and progressive, and that when a people retain their own language, their morals are superior to the morals of those who have become amalgamated with other nations. ... Besides, it must not be forgotten that language is not a mere vehicle of thought, or an instrument of trade. It is in a sense the embodiment of a nation's mental history, and the expression of national characteristics. Therefore, for a nation to lose its language is to lose that which is an important part of itself.[16]

There was a close connection, Howell argued, between the Welsh language and the spirituality of the Welsh people. This was why he was so concerned for the defence of the Welsh language, and why he endeavoured to ensure that the Welsh language was not forgotten by his Church. "A nation's language", he wrote, "is the language of the heart of its people and the national temperament survives the extinction of the national language. Hence the importance of a clergy in full sympathy with the religious instincts of their countrymen. This is peculiarly the case in the Principality just now, when the Welsh people are evidently in a transition state, the great spiritual force of the last century having well-nigh spent itself."[17] The Church, he felt, had for too long "sneered disdainfully" at this Welsh movement, "if only because it called in question the anglicising policy which, for more than a century and a half, had done its utmost to smother the national life, and the most cherished traditions of the Welsh nation."[18] On this subject Howell expressed himself very fully at the Manchester Church Congress of 1888:

---

[16] "Welsh Nationality", p 86f.
[17] *Report of the Manchester Church Congress*, 1888, p 74.
[18] "Welsh Nationality", p 81.

Of late years, the Church in Wales has produced few, if any, truly great Welsh preachers - hardly a single man of intense force and commanding power over the people. Many able men and popular preachers, in the ordinary sense of the term, has she produced; but not a single Griffiths of Nevern, or Jones of Llangan, or Rowlands of Llangeitho. How can we account for this dearth of great preachers in the Welsh Church? It is partly because Welsh preaching, in its higher and more grander forms, has not been encouraged in the Church. It is also because the Church has not sought out, taken by the hand, and brought forth men whose strongest recommendations were the gifts and graces with which God had endowed them. It is also because the expense of preparation has practically placed admission to holy orders beyond the reach of the great mass of my countrymen. Still more has it been because the rulers of the Church in the past did not understand, and still less did they sympathise with, the special needs and peculiarities of the Welsh people. Too often have men been honoured, caressed, and promoted in proportion as they were aliens in language, sympathy, and heart from the Welsh people; while, on the other hand, the very qualities which are most attractive to the people, seemed to be the very reason why their possessors found no favour in the eyes of the rulers of the Church. That this has notoriously been the case in many instances during the first seventy years of the present century is well known throughout Wales. To be eminent as a Welsh preacher, or writer, was almost a sure and certain reason for being ignored by the heads of the Church. How to account for so perverse a prejudice, is a problem not easy to solve. Some will have it that it was because the cultivation of Welsh preaching was supposed to prolong the existence of the Welsh language. Others that good Welsh preaching was supposed to savour of dissent, and was calculated to promote a type of piety not approved of by the bishops of former days. Others, less charitable, will have it that proficiency in the use of the vernacular excited the jealously of those who were ignorant of it, and was therefore regarded as a reflection upon them. Certain it is that the Anglo-Welsh bishops of days gone by acted as if excellence in Welsh preaching were quite incompatible with pastoral efficiency. To be zealous in the promotion of education, and active in the discharge of certain pastoral duties, were considered to be the high road, if not the only road, to Episcopal favour ... Never, at least during the last 180 years, has the Welsh language been so great a power in Wales, or had so great an influence over the Welsh people, as at the present day. Never was Welsh literature, whatever

> may be said as to its quality, so abundantly produced, or so eagerly devoured by the rising generation of Welshmen, as at the present day. It surely follows, as a matter of course, that the Welsh clergy, from the bishops to the youngest curate, ought to be masters of the Welsh language - not speaking it nervously, stiffly, awkwardly, but fluently and with power - thinking, speaking, and writing the limpid idiomatic Welsh of the common people. Without this, the great mass of the Welsh speaking people of Wales will, I fear, continue to regard the clergy as alien in thought and sympathy .. I go even further, and say that nothing but native Welsh - not English thoughts clothed in Welsh words, but idiomatic, native-born, home-spun Welsh - is capable of influencing the Welsh-speaking people of Wales to any great extent. There are few things which my countrymen are less tolerant of than what is known in Wales as *llediaith,* which means Welsh spoken with an English accent.[19]

He thus pleaded for Welsh itinerant preachers to be appointed by the Church in each diocese in order to quicken life and uplift both clergy and laity to a higher level of spiritual life.

Howell's deep concern that his Church should be involved in the provision of Welsh language publications came out in his speech to the St Asaph Diocesan Conference in 1885:

> That the Church has shamefully neglected the Welsh press is equally true. Among not a few Churchmen the duty of supporting the Welsh press is only very languidly acknowledged. Some regard it as the means of perpetuating the Welsh language, which they would be glad to see dead and buried to-morrow. Others regard the Welsh press as the taproot of Welsh Radicalism, as if Radicalism were unknown, wherever the English language prevailed. Altogether the Welsh Church press has had a hard life of it between the lukewarmness of its friends and the hostility of its foes. And yet it is certain if the Welsh Church is to reach tens of thousands of the Welsh people, it can only be through the Welsh press for at least a generation to come.[20]

Compared to the record of Nonconformity, the Church's commitment to Welsh literature was almost non-existent.

---

[19] *Report of the Manchester Church Congress,* pp 72f. Bishop Thirwall's attempt to eliminate the Welsh clerical preaching meetings is a case in point.
[20] *Report of the St Asaph Diocesan Conference,* 1885, p 17.

Howell's commitment was more than a paper one, for he had founded in 1861 with William Spurrell, the Carmarthen printer, and materially assisted, one of the few Welsh Church periodicals of his day, *Y Cyfaill Eglwysig*. Although his great friend from his Merthyr days, Canon Evans of Rhymney, took over the task of editing, Howell contributed to it some of his best articles, including series on the parables of Jesus and on the festivals of the Church which appeared in the closing years of his life.[21] He also undertook to write the life of Dr James of Panteg, which was never accomplished,[22] but a flowery article on the Gwent coal miner and bard, Peredur, appeared in 1899, and an appreciation of his friend Nathan two years later.[23]

Howell's commitment to the Welsh language also emerges through his close involvement with Daniel Silvan Evans' Welsh dictionary, although his main work was as a confidential advisor and go-between between Evans and his patron, Lady Llanover. It was not an easy relationship, for while Lady Llanover had offered assistance to pay for the publication of the dictionary, she interfered in the editorial policy a little too much for the comfort of Silvan Evans and his colleagues. As Howell wrote, she was rather like his grandmother's cow, "A splendid milker, - but she had the nasty habit of following the pail, of sending it flying with the contents. I hoped she was the last of the species". He equally hoped too she would not put soot in the stew ["huddugl yn y cawl"].[24]

At first Humphreys of Caernarfon had been suggested as the printer, and he had agreed provided that Silvan paid him £250 and her Ladyship £1,250 as a guarantee against loss, although he himself would gain the proceeds of the sale of two thousand copies. Howell thought this arrangement appalling, even though it appears to have been Lady Llanover's choice, especially as Howell was aware that the Clarendon Press had offered to publish the

---

[21] WM, 16 Jan 1903, p 5; CDH, 28 July 1893, p 7; T J Jones, *Cofiant Canon Evans Rhymni* [Lampeter, nd], p 31f cf pp 5 and 20f; *Cyfaill Eglwysig*, 1885, p 195 [in which it is said he was the father of the paper], 1903, p 30, and 1913, p 147.
[22] *Bye-Gones*, 28 Nov 1888, p 277.
[23] *Geninen*, 17 [1899] 184f, 19 [1901] 177-80.
[24] Howell to Silvan Evans, 28 May 1883, NLW Cwrt Mawr MS 903B, fol 9, of 1883. A close friendship existed between the two, see the above MS generally and esp fol 38 [ibid, 2 Sept 1889].

Dictionary at its own risk, "and in a style, and with more expenditure, such as Humphreys is hardly capable of." This was in July 1883. By the following October it appears that Spurrell of Carmarthen had been chosen: "there is peace between Ephraim and Judah" was Howell's stark comment. February 1884 came, and Howell was regretting that Spurrell had been given the contract, especially as he would not allow the use of a Clarendon typeface, only a "bastard one". The work would be published in half a crown or five shilling parts, as much for Spurrell's sake as for that of the public: "Taffy is a small creature and likes to do things by degrees, as the man did who was sent to cut off a dog's tail and who cut off a small bit daily so as not to hurt him." By May of the following year Howell's fears were justified. Spurrell had written stating he had no wish to proceed with the work. When he first undertook to publish it he had assumed it would be in two volumes of 1,200 pages each, but now it would be more like four volumes. He had accepted a subsidy of £600 on this understanding and the selling price had been based on a two volume work. It would have been hard to sell the dictionary at the original price of three guineas. But to sell at the higher price now required by the extent of the work would be even more difficult. He had expended £200 on it already, and the resulting difficulties were having an adverse effect on his health. Howell told Silvan to answer him explicitly point for point, to do so as if he was making an affidavit for a court of law, and to show it to a solicitor before he sent it, for his letter might be used if the matter came to arbitration. My great concern, he wrote later to Silvan, is that you should not be worried or disturbed in your work.

The first part of the dictionary appeared in 1887, but the first volume was not completed until 1893. In 1889 Howell's skill as an intermediary was required for he had to inform Lady Llanover that she was a year in arrears to Silvan: "Rarely in my life have I witnessed a more painful scene. I said as little as I possibly could, as I saw it was useless beginning and could only repeat I was a stranger to the actual document which alone could decide the dispute." The project was never completed.[25] Howell later helped

---

[25] NLW Cwrt Mawr MS 903B, fols 10, 13, 15, 16, 19, 21, 22, 34 [Howell to Silvan Evans, 30 June 1883, 21 July 1883, 14 Dec 1883, 23 Feb 1884, 23 June 1884, 28 May 1885, 30 May 1885, 13 Ap 1889 - from which the quotation is taken].

in obtaining a civil list pension for Silvan, though he hinted that her ladyship had put some difficulties in the way. Instead Howell wrote to Mr Balfour to put matters straight so that his "dear old friend of thirty-four years" would receive all that the government could bestow upon him.[26]

Another way in which Howell exhibited his concern for the nation lay in his educational work and interest. It has been noted already that he actively promoted the work of education in every parish in which he served. He also helped in a wider connection, for he gave much assistance to George Thomas Kenyon with regard to his ill-fated bill of 1889 for intermediate education in Wales.[27] But he was not happy with the Welsh university colleges, especially after a scheme to establish a Welsh University based on St David's College, Lampeter and the Aberystwyth College failed, of which Howell was one of the promoters, along with David Williams, Vicar of Llanelli, John Griffith of Merthyr Tydfil, Evans of Rhymney and Dean Edwards of Bangor.[28] Writing in 1883 to Silvan Howell said he had never admired these colleges, not given or promised a farthing towards them. "It is simply a form of endowing dissent. The dissenting colleges will henceforth be theological seminaries, the preliminary training having been done at the expense of the State. If I were a Dissenter I should do precisely as our dissenting countrymen have done in this matter."[29] This attitude was in stark contrast to that of his mentor, Archdeacon John Griffiths, whose support for these colleges and the university movement was substantial. Nevertheless Howell later changed his attitude, and as dean of St Davids he joined the council of University College, Cardiff.[30] Howell's support for St David's College was more realistic. Noting its appeal for ten

---

[26] Ibid, 31 Jan 1898: fol 54. He was later concerned regarding Lady Llanover's spiritual health, see Howell to Lady Hills-Johnes, 18 Ap 1892, 5 Feb 1896: NLW Dolaucothi MSS L7000 and L7003.
[27] *Cymru Fydd*, II [1889] 42 & 308-18 for background; Howell to Marchant Williams, 13 Oct 1889, in NLW MS 20962E, and Record 26 Mar 1897, p 306. This notes a speech on the Intermediate Education Scheme at Liverpool when Howell warned that education was not an end in itself, and hoped that technical education could be taught.
[28] *Wrexham Guardian*, 15 Jan 1881, p 5.
[29] Howell to Silvan Evans, 14 Dec 1883; NLW Cwrt Mawr MS 903B, fol 15.
[30] Tribute by Lewis Williams in WM, 16 Jan 1903, p 5; and see *Bye-Gones*, 12 Sept 1888, p 232. This concerned the commencement of a guild of Welsh students at English and other universities, which Howell supported in the hope that it would break down isolation and provide a moral and social backbone to these students.

thousand pounds in 1885 he emphasised that this amount was far too low, compared to the amount that Nonconformist colleges would obtain from a similar appeal. Instead, he wished to "inflict a very pious punishment on the Board, by compelling them to accept at least twice the amount now asked for."[31]

If, on the one hand, Howell felt that definite religious instruction, based on the Bible, rather than denominational tenets, should be provided in every school in Wales, he was also concerned that the National or Church schools should not be too narrow or sectarian in their definition of religion. This was at a time when these schools were regarded as the "right arm" of the Church, and openly used for proselytising purposes. As to the first area of concern, he spoke at the Norwich Church Congress in this way:

> And here let me say, that to my mind it is hardly possible to overestimate the importance of religious instruction in our voluntary schools in Wales at the present time ... I should be false to my convictions if I did not declare that I can hardly conceive a graver calamity to a country than 50 school boards from whose schools the Word of God is excluded. In this I have reason to believe that I am expressing the sentiments of an increasing number of Nonconformists, who feel that, at a time when nearly one-third of the total population of the Principality is said to be outside all religious ministrations, there are far greater issues involved, to the welfare of society and the future of Wales, than the differences of Church and Dissent.[32]

It was Howell's claim that in over forty years of service as a manager of National or Church schools, during which time he had to deal with the children of Jews, Roman Catholics, and Welsh Dissenters of various types, he had never had any problems with the so-called "religious difficulty" about religious teaching in these schools.[33] The probable reason for this laudatory state of

---

[31] *St Asaph Diocesan Conference Report*, 1885, p 23.
[32] *Report of the Norwich Church Congress*, 1895, pp 403f.
[33] *Bye-Gones*, 28 Jan 1903, p 17; David Jones, quoting *Y Faner*, 26 Aug 1896, in *The Moral and Religious Condition of Wales* [Bangor 1906], pp 54f. T G Jones, *Cofiant Thomas Gee* [Dinbych 1913], p 547, notes that Howell had never experienced this religious difficulty before he became dean, and added, it was easy to believe this of a man who was so wide in his opinions.

affairs is explained in an address he gave at the laying of the foundation stone of the National School in Neath. In this address he explained that the policy of his vicar there, Archdeacon Griffiths, was that there would be no obligation for a child of Nonconformist parents to read or learn one word of the Catechism, articles or doctrines of the Church of England, nor to go within the walls of the church building if its parents were against it.[34] This was a policy Howell adopted for himself, but many clergy believed otherwise, following the lead of the National Society itself, and insisted that all those educated in church schools were taught the principles of the Church in school time and attended the church services on Sunday. Nevertheless Howell believed that a church school should be "pervaded by a religious spirit, and the application of healthy moral motives to the conduct of life", and that these ideals should have the first place in the training of the children.[35]

Howell's patriotism was thus wide, extending into many areas of the life of his nation, into the work of education, the life of the Church, the language of his people, and the cultural arena of the eisteddfod.

---

[34] David Howell, *Araeth a Draddodwyd ar yr Achlysur o osod i lawr Gareg - Sylfaen Ysgol Alderman Davies* [Aberdar 1857]. 3

[35] *Church Times*, 14 Ap 1897, p 450. He had made the greatest sacrifices of his life for the church voluntary schools.

The Evangelical Churchman

Howell's deep love of the Church and her liturgy and mission must be clear already from what has been written in previous chapters. It is equally clear he was in the mainstream of the evangelical life of his time, sharing with men from Simeon to Ryle a deep affection and reverence for the Church of England, and seeing it as the means of evangelising the nation. But his sympathy and spirituality could never be confined to one church, however much he loved it, or be contained within one tradition of his own Church. His churchmanship was much broader than most evangelicals, and this was true for his younger as well as his older days. Ollivant observed his independence of character.[1] Gladstone noted his kindly and charitable view of church matters,[2] and he quoted with favour Howell's words of reply when he was given an illuminated address by the Chester and North Wales Commercial Travellers' Association on his leaving north Wales. In this Howell quoted the seventeenth century Puritan, Philip Henry: "In all things in which all the people of God are agreed, I will spend my zeal, and wherein men differ, I will endeavour to walk according to the lights which God has given me, and charitably believe that others do so too."[3] A Wrexham paper on his appointment to that parish described his broad catholicity "by which his views were distinguished".[4] And obituary notes, though considering that Howell himself adhered more to those theological beliefs common to Welsh Churchmen and Nonconformists at the beginning of the nineteenth century, added "he was not the narrow minded and prejudiced evangelical whom we know today." Another wrote that if to some his churchmanship appeared

---

[1] Ollivant to Gladstone, 31 Jan 1870, BL Gladstone Papers 44424 fol 214.
[2] *Record*, 23 June 1897, p 734.
[3] Ibid, 27 Aug 1897, p 858.
[4] *Wrexham Guardian*, 6 Feb 1875, p 8.

to lack sharpness of definition, it was a forgivable lack, as Howell in his public work "knew no distinctions of class or politics or creed". Indeed, he worshipped freely in high, low and broad churches.[5]

That his churchmanship was broader than most evangelicals was well known to his contemporaries, some of whom despised him for it. Writing to Lady Hills-Johnes in 1896 he acknowledged this: "I am, alas, for my own poor reputation, far too broad, as I am often made to feel. I now measure my sympathies to my convictions."[6] During the 1890 election to the see of Bangor Howell wrote to his friend Silvan Evans, noting that the evangelical "clique" were as opposed to his appointment as the high church party: "I am bold to say, that there is not a Welsh clergyman living who has suffered from *cliqueness* as I have."[7]

This was possibly more a problem for Howell in Welsh than in English evangelical circles. It is clear that Howell was well known and much appreciated within the English evangelical world, which was perhaps more sympathetic towards his broad evangelical stance than his fellow countrymen. With Handley Moule and other prominent English evangelicals he was a council member of the Protestant Churchmen's Alliance,[8] although his main links were with the Church Pastoral-Aid Society, having acted as its Welsh secretary in his younger days. Always grateful for the Society's support to him personally in his parochial ministry, he was also deeply appreciative of its concern for the Welsh language, and he continued to plead its cause, and the cause of the Church in Wales, at its public meetings in London and throughout Wales. In 1861 he emphasised the evangelical nature of the society, "for wherever it extends its operations, Christianity, pure and undefiled, is preserved". And in 1877, on the same platform of Exeter Hall, he noted Wales' debt to the society, though pointing out that England also owed much to Wales, especially for the origin of the Bible Society.[9] In 1895 he argued, "If the principles and operation of the ... Society had been multiplied fifty-fold, or even twenty-fold, throughout Wales during the last quarter of a

---

[5] WM, 16 Jan 1903, p 5; *Record*, 23 Jan 1903, p 79; *Wrexham Advertiser*, 20 Jan 1903, p 7; cutting in SA/DR/52. fol 729.
[6] Howell to Lady Hills-Johnes, 15 May 1896, NLW Dolaucothi MS L7004.
[7] Howell to D Silvan Evans, 12 July 1890, NLW Cwrt Mawr MS 903B, fol 41.
[8] *Guide to the Church Congress at Cardiff* [London 1889] p 122.
[9] *CPAS Abstract and Report of Speeches*, 1861, p 13 and 1877, pp 23-6.

century, though the cry for Disestablishment might still have been raised, it would have been raised under widely different circumstances".[10] In the annual sermon of 1898 he poured forth shame on Christian England, wealthy England, the richest Church in Christendom, for the decrease in the society's income.[11] None who heard him on the Society's platform in Exeter Hall, wrote one after his death, will ever forget his fervent invocation of the Holy Spirit that he would descend upon the Church in Wales.[12]

This broad evangelical churchmanship of Howell's which was disliked in Wales, but more readily accepted by English evangelicals, owed as much to his reading during his earlier years as to the moderation of his temper. It may also have gained a little from his liking for an amount of tradition and ceremony. Indeed, he may have modelled himself on Henry Venn, who also disliked ecclesiastical controversy, refused to act as a party man, and had a wider vision and broader sympathy than most of the evangelicals of his day.[13]

Though Howell was prepared to work with all men in whom the Spirit of God was obviously working, and who were concerned with the spiritual life of Wales, he feared, nevertheless, the sacerdotal element, as he put it, within the Tractarian movement. He believed its misplaced attractiveness and charm, its over elaborate pomp and unnecessary ritual, would lead many astray, and cause difficulties with the encouragement of lay work within the Church, as well as a decline in the concern for evangelism.[14] In particular Howell feared that disestablishment would bring this sacerdotal system into the Welsh Church, and make it an aggressive power in its own interest.[15] Thus he disliked the use of such words as *altar* and *offeren*, expressed his concern that the altar was too often elevated at the expense of the pulpit, and denounced the teaching that only the episcopal office could confer grace as a denial of the work of the Holy Spirit.

---

[10] *Church and People*, 7 [1895] 58, cf 9 [1897] 41.
[11] *Church and People*, 10 [1898], pp 29-37.
[12] *CPAS Report*, 1904, p 38.
[13] cf Michael Hennell, *Sons of the Prophets* [London 1979] p 90.
[14] See *Cymru*, 27 [1904] 74, and J V Morgan, *The Church in Wales* [London 1918], p 159.
[15] David Howell, *Sermon Preached at Manchester Cathedral on the Eve of St Davids Day 1895 : Romans 12.18* [Bangor 1895], p 13.

Nevertheless he remained friendly with many ritualists, including Edward King, the saintly bishop of Lincoln,[16] and he once said, with a smile, about one church he had preached in, that they had "even sent some little boys to light me to the pulpit".[17] Howell would have accepted the symbolism of that! At the end of his life he was reading Bishop Gore's books with much interest.[18]

On a more positive note he insisted that every Christian had the right to a personal assurance of faith, and in his preaching he emphasised reconciliation with God through the imputed righteousness of the death of Jesus Christ, justification by faith alone in the atoning merits of the death of Jesus Christ, his resurrection and ascension, and the personal work of the Holy Spirit, together with the supremacy of the Word of God. "[T]hese doctrines", he argued, "are still the passport to the hearts of the Welsh people, and ... the full and fervent preaching [of them], ... with the power and unction of the Holy Ghost, is at present the most urgent and pre-eminent want of the Church in the Principality of Wales."[19] Howell feared the day when these truths would be questioned:

> O, my friends, that the day should ever have dawned, when men in the Christian ministry call in question every fundamental truth, and refuse to hold any principle, however well established, as sacred, but insist that all shall be put to the test anew; when men who have signed the creeds and articles and formularies of the Church of England say, that miracles are impossibilities, and that the prophecies of the Old Testament were not predictive of events in the New Testament; that the facts of Jewish history are only facts of a general providence; that the different books of Scripture simply contain an embodiment of the religious thought and life of the periods in which they were written; when men who profess to believe in the Bible dare to assert that moral consciousness is the criterion of truth; that imputed righteousness is imputed nonsense, and who in fact would reduce religion to a vague, misty, and sentimental subjective experience, and who sacrifice the vital and

---

[16] They had met at Hawarden as guests of Gladstone [*Record*, 23 Jan 1903, p 79].
[17] *Wrexham Advertiser*, 24 Jan 1903, p 7.
[18] *Geninen*, 21 [1903] 155.
[19] CPAS *Abstract and Report of Speeches*, 1877, p 26; see Howell's *St David's Cathedral Leaflet no 17: Holy Week and Easter Day 1901*, for his conservative evangelical views about the cross.

essential doctrines of revealed religion on the altar of a cold sceptical rationalism.[20]

Howell's faith was thus a robust, experimental and evangelical one, although he diverged from many evangelicals in his belief in the intermediate state.[21]

The backbone of his theology, it was said, was Bishop Pearson's work on the Creed,[22] in itself the very essence of an Anglican text, while it was argued that his sacramental theology was one hewn from Hooker and Jeremy Taylor.[23] This made him, as he frequently claimed, a child of the Prayer Book. In the *Use of Abercarn*, which he and others devised for Lady Llanover's chapel, he refused to allow any hint of baptismal regeneration to be introduced into the baptismal rite, although, by contrast, Canon Williams in an obituary note in the *Haul* suggested Howell placed more emphasis than was usual on what was received in baptism rather than upon the subsequent confirming of the baptismal vows.[24] Neither could Howell accept any idea of an objective presence in the Communion, writing as follows:

> I love them [the sacraments] as the means ordained by Christ to sustain spiritual life, but they are not Christ himself, nor the real presence itself .... The Incarnate God is not present in anything except faith, and faith, not lips, eat and drink the body and blood of the Son of Man. God is a spiritual being and his presence in the communion is spiritual. If this were not so then the martyrs and others suffered martyrdom by mistake.[25]

There was no wish, therefore, on Howell's part to elevate the sacraments above the power of the Word of God. As an evangelical he accepted that the sacraments derived their efficiency from the Word, and should not be over-emphasised above that Word. But in another sense it is not surprising that he

---

[20] Ibid, 1861, p 13.
[21] *Haul*, 1903, pp 57f.
[22] *Record*, 23 Jan 1903, p 79, quoting the *Times* obituary.
[23] *Geninen*, 21 [1903] 154. Howell acknowledged the influence of J B Mozley in his thought [J V Morgan, *Welsh Religious Leaders in the Victorian Era* [London 1905], p 125].
[24] *Haul*, 1903, pp 56-61.
[25] *Geninen*, 21 [1903] 154. Translated.

should have believed this, for his eloquence was outstanding, and preaching was his supreme gift as a Christian minister. Nevertheless, it was recorded that his careful reading of the Scriptures was in itself a sermon. He normally read the text in its original language in the course of his preparation.[26]

Many regarded him as one of the greatest preachers in the Church in Wales of his day, in both languages,[27] although Howell himself, in writing to Silvan, told him "it is as a preaching parson I stand for judgment, though with a poor chance of a favourable verdict in that respect."[28] His achievement was immense, for, until his Cardiff ministry, he habitually preached in Welsh. And yet within weeks of the start of that ministry, he had established himself as a fine preacher in his adopted tongue.[29]

Even Lloyd George added his testimony to Howell as a preacher in the House of Commons during 1912, proclaiming "All the great preachers in Wales are Nonconformists, with the exception of Dean Howell; everyone of the great preachers whose names are household words there are Nonconformists."[30] Dr John Thomas of Liverpool, a prominent Welsh Nonconformist preacher, however, had his joke at Howell's expense. At some disestablishment rally he argued that the Welsh Church had no great preachers. "It is said", he continued, "that Mr Howell is a good preacher, but who knows anything about him outside his own neighbourhood. I see by your silence you have never heard of him. 'I'll tell you who he is, he is the brother in law of Mr David Saunders.' This statement was followed by cheers. There, Dr Thomas concluded, 'I thought you would know him if I tied him to the tail of a Methodist preacher.'"[31]

Speaking to the Manchester Church Congress about Welsh preaching, Howell possibly described his own style:

---

[26] *Geninen*, 21 [1903] 153f.
[27] Ll J Wallis-Jones, *Welsh Characteristics* [London 1898] p 116: cf *Cymru*, 27 [1904] 73.
[28] Howell to D Silvan Evans, 23 Dec 1891, NLW Cwrt Mawr MS 903B, fol 46.
[29] D Williams in *Geninen*, 22 [St David 1904] 42. It is clear that Howell preached in English at Pwllheli and probably as a CPAS secretary, so that Williams possibly means an exclusive English ministry.
[30] *Hansard*, 25 April 1912, col 1275.
[31] Quoted R H Morgan, *The Disestablishment of the Church in Wales* [Wrexham 1888], p 36n.

Wales is the land of preaching. Like all Celtic peoples, the Welsh love oratory. They are naturally fluent, fervid and enthusiastic. They love intellectual excitement ... A great preacher is a Welshman's highest conception of a great man. .. It has been said that "he who would exchange his pulpit for a throne is not worthy of a pulpit", and this is very much the Welsh people's idea of a preacher's vocation - they look upon him much in the light of the prophets of old, as a special gift of God, and as a direct messenger from God. Strange as it may appear to those who regard a ten minutes' sermonette as a happy development of nineteenth-century Christianity, it is nevertheless strictly true that a Welshman's highest conception of terrestrial felicity is to revel in a couple of day's preaching, with three or four services each day, and at least two sermons at each service. Welsh preaching ... deals rather with the emotional, and the higher spiritual elements in human nature, than with the purely ethical and intellectual. It is, therefore, no wonder that it sometimes produces strong outward manifestations of feeling. I have myself repeatedly seen many thousands at a great open-air gathering swayed like the waving of a ripe cornfield under the commanding power of a great Welsh preacher. I have known a sudden change in the cadence of a preacher's voice produce an awful stillness among a huge mass of men and women; and another change produce an equally sudden outburst of spiritual rapture, as if the great multitude had been moved by one electric impulse. Among the leading characteristics of Welsh preaching are its vividness, descriptiveness, intense earnestness, strong grasp of first principles, and its direct dealing with the human conscience. Welsh preaching is noted for its musical eloquence. It has the sound of a melodious chant, and the close of a sermon usually takes the form of a fervid intonation. This feature is known in Wales as the '*hwyl*', - a term taken from a ship under full sail.[32]

To many Howell was "the silver tongued orator of the Welsh Church", a man who had been greatly used by God for the revival

---

[32] *Report of the Manchester Church Congress*, 1888, p 71. An observation of Howell's is noted by one D Griffith in *Y Dysgedydd* [1908, p 498] which seemed to capture his own style. The old preacher, he said, had a way of giving out one of Prys' psalms with a special seriousness which riveted the ear and touched the heart in a way which cannot easily be forgotten. In an article in the *Traethodydd* [158 [1896] 404] Howell urged that every sermon should have a clear and pastoral application: "The Welsh enjoy quite a vigorous flogging from the pulpit. They have no time for small sermons where sin and salvation have little place. How can a six to ten minute sermon feed the intellect, educate the conscience, or produce a conviction of sin, truth and righteousness." [Translated].

of that Church through his ministry of preaching and encouragement. It was claimed for him that he had preached on special occasions in more churches in Wales, and had been called more often to fill English pulpits, than any other Welsh clergyman, though no one ever disputed his claim that he had ever neglected his parish to do so.[33] He had preached at Canterbury for a fortnight in 1887,[34] and Talbot Rice, who often heard him preach on such occasions, remarked: "It was a feast to the eye and ear to listen to his preaching..."[35] His power, argued David Davies of Penarth in his *Reminiscences,* came from his voice, his fine personality and evident sincerity, which gave great force to his arguments and appeals.[36] J V Morgan suggested that he spoke as a man who had tasted and handled the word of life, and had broken away from the commonplaces of the church pulpit. He was distinctive, practical and highly spiritual, he argued, and his preaching was characterised by a depth of thought, intensity of feeling, and universal sympathy.[37] Those who heard him, Morgan said elsewhere, soon realised he lived in a higher world.[38] His obituary in the *Geneinen* stated that he never got angry or shouted, but allowed his voice to raise naturally until "people were completely melted". Even English-speaking people, who could not understand his Welsh preaching, were moved to weep as they heard him. After another of his sermons, David Parry of Llywel, one of the other great Anglican preachers of Wales, failed, through emotion, to give out the hymn at the end of the service, and many of the younger clergy had to go outside into the churchyard and weep.[39] His last sermon, wrote Canon Williams, was on Christ as the light of the world, and few would forget his description of the nature and work of Christ, the love of the Father for the Son, and the peace which follows believing.[40] Crowds flocked to hear him, wrote his godson, Grey-Edwards, and they would come from the hayfields at the height of harvest

[33] *Record*, 2 Ap 1897, p 321.
[34] *Haul*, 1887, p 93.
[35] *Swansea Parish Magazine*, 1903, p 41 [cf 1902, p 137].
[36] David Davies, *Reminiscences of my Country and People* [London 1925] p 240.
[37] J V Morgan, *Welsh Religious Leaders in the Victorian Era* [London 1905], 124f.
[38] J V Morgan, *The Church in Wales*, p 160.
[39] *Geninen*, 1903, pp 152f.
[40] *Haul*, 1903, pp 58-61.

to hear him preach at mid-day in the parish church.[41] J Morgan Jones suggested that on him had fallen the mantle of Jones of Llangan, for he was a true son of those Methodists who had roused the Principality from its sleep at the beginning of the nineteenth century.[42] Rhys J Hughes recalled too his great humour in preaching.[43]

His parochial preaching was described in 1874 as one which reminded his congregation of "their shortcomings in a way to which they had been unaccustomed". The reporter, from a local Cardiff newspaper, continued:

> The solemn verities of our most holy religion were clearly unfolded. The punishment which awaits sin was faithfully pointed out. But while the preacher did not scruple to unmask "the terrors of the law", his more congenial duty was to dwell on the doctrine of the Atonement, and to commend that grace which the New Testament so freely offers. Here was an anxious, earnest, man, deeply impressed with a sense of his own responsibility, and affectionately solicitous of the interests of those he addressed. His pleadings were as though he pleaded for life - "with tears, with pathetic gestures, and burning words."...
>
> In the pulpit the Vicar loves to contemplate the tranquil beauty of a Christian life.... His discourses seem peopled with images of sweetness, and gentleness, and benevolence - the spiritual graces of a Christian life. With him religion is a loving principle that leads with the silken cords of tender tolerance, nor seeks to drive with a thong of harsh polemical disputation.... Where, in others, that charm is sometimes borrowed, with him a vivid impression of reality is conveyed, which wins him hearts, and clinches affection to himself, which thousands angle for with clever unreality in vain.
> .... He is liberal to a degree. He draws a distinction between the spiritual revelation of saving truth, and the intellectual revelation of theological truth - warns those of over-zealous piety that zeal should at all times be tempered with love and influenced by wisdom, and urges the argument in his own tolerant words: "We must endeavour, by gentleness and zeal, tempered with discretion,

---

[41] A M Grey-Edwards, *Reminiscences of an Unknown Man* [1940], pp 103. This was also said by W Hay Aitkin, quoted by CDH, 28 July 1893, p 7. And see *Report of the Norwich Church Congress*, 1895, p 407.
[42] J Morgan Jones in WM, 16 Jan 1903, p 5.
[43] *Geninen*, 21 [St David 1903] 1f.

to bring those who differ from us on religious topics to a sense of their errors as we believe them."⁴⁴

It was Howell's earnest longing that the Church would re-establish the power of preaching. He held that it depended too often on pastoral care and scholarship rather than following the apostolic injunction of preaching the Word of God in order to lead people to Christ. Effective preaching, he continually stated, was the key to the Welshman's heart.⁴⁵ The power of the pulpit, he wrote to Bishop Joshua Hughes, was the agency which had emptied our churches and filled the chapels. He was persuaded that the same power, with the blessing of the Holy Spirit, would be the principal means of restoring the people to the Church. The Church needed, he wrote, to fight God's battles with God's weapons, "with a conscious and acknowledged dependence on his strength."⁴⁶ It is hardly surprising, therefore, that Howell deeply regretted that the Welsh Church had produced so few preachers of note, "hardly a single man of intense force and commanding power over the people."⁴⁷ He himself believed so much in the power and dignity of preaching that he would only preach one sermon per Sunday, and arranged his curates' work on a similar pattern.⁴⁸

By the time of Howell's death it was claimed that his style of preaching was a style rapidly falling into disuse. The style of which he was an acknowledged master seemed to be "ponderous and grandiose, too wordy and too expansive" in those days of "direct, unaffected talk from the pulpit".⁴⁹ Howell would have disputed that suggestion. His was the style of preaching which God has blessed down the years, which had built up Christians and empowered them for the evangelisation of their nation. It was a revival of this kind of preaching which was needed, which elevated, uplifted and instructed, rather than the kind of talking

---

⁴⁴ *Wrexham Guardian*, 6 Feb 1875, p 8, quoting in part the *Western Mail* of 9 Nov 1874, p 10. See Howell's sermon "The Corn of Wheat Dying" in J Cynddylan Jones [ed], *The Welsh Pulpit of Today* [London 1885] 214-23.
⁴⁵ *Report of the Norwich Church Congress*, 1895, p 407. Few of Howell's sermons were published. One, an Advent sermon in Welsh, about the "fullness of time", is contained in a collection of "Church" sermons, *Pregethau ar Suliau a Phrif Wyliau yr Eglwys* [Caerfryddin 1898].
⁴⁶ Howell to Bishop Hughes, 7 May 1886, Lambeth Library, Benson Papers 39 fol 200.
⁴⁷ *Report of the Manchester Church Congress*, 1888, p 72.
⁴⁸ Canon Lloyd in *Haul*, 1932, p 114.
⁴⁹ Cutting in NLW SA/DR/52, fol 729.

which should be done in the home. Such godly preaching had been found in the old-style clerical meetings, as he told the 1895 Norwich Church Congress:

> And here let me say, that I should be glad to see a revival of the old clerical meetings, which for more than a century were a great institution in the Church in Wales, and often greatly blessed to both clergy and people. By clerical meetings is not meant meetings of clergy only, as the term is understood in England, but meetings of clergy and laity, sometimes for mutual conference, but more frequently for a succession of sermons, beginning in the evening of one day, and continued morning, afternoon and evening of the next day, with two sermons at each service. And on these occasions, let me tell you, sermons meant sermons. They were none of your English sermonettes. .... [M]y countrymen love to have "strong meat" from the pulpit; and if the Church in Wales is as wise as she should be, she will leave nothing undone to raise the standard of efficiency among her clergy, and to make her pulpit both a spiritual and an intellectual power throughout my native land.

Such preaching as this, suggested Howell, needed to be grounded in the truth, and that truth had to be established in prayer; corporate, family and private prayer. That was the secret of the old-style preaching, it was to people who knew their theology, and it was undertaken in a spirit of prayer. Grounding in the truth was best achieved by catechising:

> We also want a revival of the ancient ordinance of catechizing in the primitive sense, to include, if possible - and why not possible? - all ages and all classes. It is hardly credible the ignorance of Holy Scripture, and of the great distinctive truths of Christianity, which not seldom exists among those who have been familiar with the services of the Church from their childhood; and this is true of what are called the upper as much as the lower classes. At a time when the tide of secularism, materialism, worldliness, and scepticism is coming in like a flood upon us, nothing but intelligent, definite, well-grounded convictions can withstand and overcome it; and for this there is no instrument like the ancient order of catechising. Is it too much to say that the Welsh revival of the last century would, humanly speaking, hardly have been possible if it had not been for the catechizing labours of that most illustrious Welsh Churchman of the eighteenth century, Griffith Jones of

Llanddowror, whose great work on the Church Catechism will bear comparison with any work of the kind in any age of the world ....[50]

Such truth needed to be established in and by prayer. It is clear that all Howell's work was undergirded with prayer, while he organised intercessory prayer meetings in every parish under his charge. One of his papers has as its title, *Prayer as an Aid to the Life of Godliness*. This had been given at the Rhyl Church Congress and later produced as a pamphlet by *Home Words*. Within it Howell suggests that the daily service of the Church was also the daily parochial prayer meeting. And he goes onto say:

> I am deeply convinced that we do not make anything like the use we ought to make of our churches, and that the power of united prayer is a truth which the Church has yet but imperfectly learnt. At present, though she would hardly own it, she seems to regard our Lord's emphatic assurances on this point as almost savouring of exaggeration. Here are His own words, as fresh and warm and unqualified as when they came from His Divine lips nearly nineteen centuries ago: "If two of you shall agree on earth as touching anything they shall ask, it shall be done for them of My Father which is in heaven." Now have these words still a real meaning? If not in the literal, in what sense are they to be understood? To what extent are they intended to be an actuating principle in the life of the Church? Are they an obsolete statute, or a still living law, and an active spiritual force in the moral government of God? I say again that the Church has yet to learn the power of united prayer; and is it not to our shame that God's sanctuaries are not day by day resounding with the united importunate pleadings of His covenanted people?

A warning note is sounded:

> But public prayer, in order to be an effectual spiritual force, must be the outcome of habitual private prayer; and such prayer must consist of something more than mere periodical acts of prayer, however reverently performed. Still less does it consist in a traditional habit, in which "the mind dreams its way through a dialect of dead words, and floats on the current of a stereotyped phraseology." The essence of true prayer lies more in condition

---

[50] *Report of the Norwich Church Congress*, 1895, pp 407-8.

than in action, more in the habitual attitude of the soul than in acts of devotion. Power in prayer can only be acquired by one who himself lives in prayer. The efficacy of prayer depends largely on the spirituality of him who prays. An unspiritual man cannot really pray, for he is out of sympathy with God. A sudden transition from a cold, carnal, world-conforming attitude to power in prayer, or power in preaching, is impossible. It can only come from an habitual consecration of the soul to God. "In the Christian life", said Origen, "is one continuous prayer". "No man is likely to make much of prayer", said Philip Henry, "who does not make a constant business of it." ..... Certain it is, that there is no other way to spiritual power; it can only come as the result of a life of prayer ... So true it is that no man has ever wielded great spiritual influence who was not often, and long, alone with God.[51]

To this concern for private prayer undergirding all the public prayer of the Church, Howell added:

> What I contend for is, that private prayer is as absolute a necessity to the soul as breathing is to the body - that nothing should be made an excuse for neglecting it, or a substitute for it - that such prayer, to be efficacious, must be regular, reverent, deliberate, specific, and expectant - and that a perfunctory observance of it invites certain retribution in shallowness, feebleness, dryness, and deadness of soul. "The breath of prayer comes from the life of faith"; and never do we need prayer so much as when we are least inclined to pray. Of one thing we may be certain, that no time can be more profitably spent than in close, confiding, "heart-deep" communion with God in prayer: and is not God pleading for more time from all of us? We all know the saying that "to work is to pray", but not work as a substitute for prayer, but only work in the spirit, and as the outcome of prayer. Bernard of Clairvaux tells us, that "He found on the days when he spent most time in prayer, and in study of the Scriptures, his letters were most rapidly written and were most persuasive, his active work was most quickly and successfully accomplished, and his own schemes were widened or lost in the greater purposes of God, anxiety was allayed, and the power of the Holy Ghost, to which he had opened his heart, was felt in every word he spoke, and in his presence and look."[52]

---

[51] David Howell, *Prayer as an Aid to the Life of Godliness* [London 1891] pp 9-10. The paper was the one given at the Rhyl Church Congress, see *Report*, 1891, pp 323-9.
[52] Ibid, pp 14-15.

And Howell concluded:

> Is it so? Is it so? Then to our knees, my brethren of the clergy! To your knees, my brethren of the laity! Many, great, and urgent are our Church's needs; but this, above all others - men mighty in prayer, men of giant faith in intercessory prayer, men instinct with the omnipotent energy of God the Holy Ghost, men pleading God's promises as living realities, and saying with the Patriarch of old, "We will not let Thee go, unless Thou bless us." "Ye that are the Lord's remembrancers, take ye no rest, and give Him no rest, till He establish, and till He make Jerusalem a praise in the earth." "Whatsoever ye shall ask in My Name, that will I do."[53]

Throughout his active ministerial life Howell commended what the Welsh call 'family duty'. Where there is family worship, he suggested, then there is mutual love, sympathy and loving kindness. What was essential to a peaceful home? Howell asked, and answered, "Orderliness, family discipline, Sabbath keeping, and family worship". Howell regarded 'Sabbath keeping' as one of the foundations of Welsh life, and believed it was a religious essential for the day of rest to be sanctified and set apart for reading and worship. There is no more beautiful sight, he declared, than the Sabbath of old; its quiet, peace and stillness, the church bells greeting the day, like the sound of angels' wings making music in the breeze. And yet, he argued, however good this 'Sabbath' worship might be, on its own it would impoverish the soul and grieve the Holy Spirit. A family without an altar to God is like a house without a roof. Public worship can be attended from habit, or duty, but family worship is a sign of spiritual life. In that paper, already quoted, *Prayer as an aid to the Life of Godliness*, Howell had this to say about family worship:

> Family prayer, especially if joined with family praise, will make every Christian home a very Bethel. Piety at home is one of the most urgent needs of our day. If the home piety be weak, it will affect the prayers of the congregation, and the preaching of the pulpit; for a man's piety really is - be he layman or clergyman - what he is at home. *Crefydd yr Aelwyd* has always been a marked

---
[53] Ibid, p 18.

characteristic of our own beloved Wales, and long may it continue such; for family religion is the tap-root of all national religion.[54]

* * * *

In the last year of his life David Howell returned to the same theme when he was called upon to address the St David's Diocesan Conference on the subject of Religion in the Home. After noting that Griffith Jones had built up his great spiritual work on two twin pillars, family worship and diligent catechising, Howell warned against the decay of family worship, which "betrays an anemic condition, which can hardly fail to develop other ailments". He continued:

> ... I regard family worship .. as an indispensable element in the Religion of the Home. That parents, children, and servants, professing allegiance to God, should live under the same roof, and not meet together for daily worship, passes my comprehension. Even the heathen have their family deities, as well as their temple gods. That our Mother Church expects her children to engage in daily public worship, whenever practicable, we all know. But we also know that in many Parishes it is impracticable to assemble any considerable number for daily public worship at the Parish Church, most desirable as I think it to be. And even if it were practicable, what about the servants in farm-houses, and what about the poor, the infirm, and the aged? To me it is quite evident that if daily united worship is to be generally observed, it can only be in the home.
>
> And here let me give expression to a conviction which has been growing upon me, namely, that family worship, to be really edifying, should be conducted far more reverently and orderly than is now too generally the case. It should be held with undeviating regularity, never too long, and never hurried. If the prayer be extempore, care should be taken that it be humbly devout, and really supplicatory ... Where it is practicable, the singing of Bishop Ken's morning and evening Hymns will add much to the impressiveness of the Service. "He who prays in his family," said the saintly Matthew Henry, "does well. He who reads the Scriptures and prays, does better. But he who reads the Scriptures, prays, and sings, does best of all." Such a service will oil the wheels

[54] Ibid, pp 8-9.

of domestic life, and help to maintain harmony in the home. It will tend to restrain inconsistencies of tongue and temper, and to draw the various members of a household nearer together and to God. I am, of course, assuming that the praying and living of the conductor of the service are in harmony, or else better, I think, no worship at all ...

But Religion in the Home means more than this. It means more than acts of religion. It means the spirit pervading the whole life of the home. It means that tone and temper, difficult to describe, but none the less real, which is as the very air we breathe, difficult to analyse, but essential to life. Visit two homes, both equally pronounced in their religious profession, and how quickly do we become conscious of a marked difference between them! Were I asked to give in one sentence the secret of Religion in the Home, it would be in the words of an embossed card which I have seen in many houses - "Christ is the head of this house; the unseen guest at every meal; the silent listener to every conversation." In other words, the secret of Religion in the Home is a practical realisation of the presence of our Lord as a living fact. And so far from this affecting the brightness and joyfulness of home-life, it will ever make it sweeter and happier. To confound pious gloom with the religion of Christ, whether in the home or out of it, is to libel Christianity, and to slander the Blessed One.

He ended his talk with these words to the clergy:

Another word, and I close. It is this. If you want to estimate the real usefulness of your Ministry, you may safely measure it by its influence on the home life of your people. A hundred things may contribute to the apparent prosperity of a congregation, such as an impressive ritual, attractive preaching, party zeal, organization, eclectic sympathies, and the like. But these things may exist, and sometimes do exist, where the home life of the people is deeply depressed. But if you would know whether your preaching reaches the roots of your people's hearts and lives, then follow them to their homes, listen to their talk by the way, and mark the effect of your preaching on the testy temper, the censorious speech, or the cutting criticism. My brethren, of this you may rest assured, that men and women really are what they are at home. And if you can influence their home life, you may be sure that, by the power of the Holy Ghost, you are training them for that home above, whose music is the seraph's song, and whose light is the smile of God.[55]

[55] David Howell, *Religion in the Home* [1902] pp 4-5, 7. This was reprinted from the Diocesan Conference Report.

The home was important. And so was the Sunday School. Speaking to a mass gathering of Sunday School teachers at Exeter Hall, London, in 1891, Howell stressed the responsibility of their work. Like many of his other English speeches, he translated it into Welsh and had it published in *Traethodydd*. Store the minds and memories of your children with good hymns and substantial teaching, he urged them, teaching in which God's love, Christ's blood and the Holy Spirit's grace were given a prominent place. As a preacher he envied the teachers' direct contact and personal touch with their pupils. Their aim was to draw the baptised church children to a personal conscious relationship to Christ and to awaken within them a living consciousness of spiritual truths, so that sin and salvation, God's love and Christ's redemption, and the work of the Holy Spirit were not dry and unnecessary shibboleths, but substantial and living truths. The teachers themselves needed a personal relationship to Christ, for it was the teacher, not so much the teaching, which was influential. The Word of God too must have first place in their teaching, which needed to be accompanied with love, sympathy and expectancy. Wrestle in prayer day by day, he urged, and expect a blessing thereby.[56]

*   *   *   *

Another theme in Howell's spirituality was hymnology. Hymns, he believed, had an immense influence in the formation of people's spiritual lives, as they had been in his. The older I get, he wrote in 1891, the more I find myself influenced by the texts of the good old Welsh hymns that were taught me at my grandmother's knee.[57] He was concerned that children's hymns were often too shallow and emotional, especially as children were generally more influenced by these hymns than by any other spiritual agency.[58] Welsh spirituality had been enriched by the doctrinal, scriptural and experimental character of Welsh hymns, he noted, especially those hymns which emphasised the

---

[56] *Traethodydd*, XLVI [1897] 258-62. Children, said Howell, required good hymns, not the florid and emotional collections of hymns generally provided for them [*Cardiff Times*, 9 Ap 1898, p 8].
[57] *Wrexham Advertiser*, 16 May 1891, p 6.
[58] *Record*, 7 Ap 1897, p 326.

atonement and the working of the Holy Spirit in the life of the believer. These hymns, he frequently argued, were far deeper and more spiritual than most English ones. In a speech to the London Church Congress of 1899, illustrated by a well-trained London choir, Howell said:

> [T]he hymns of Wales form the very backbone of the religious life of the Principality as nowhere else within my knowledge. But it may be asked, why should it be so in Wales more than in England? For one thing, there is the innate love of the Welsh people for poetry and music. There is also the fact .. that hymns formed a prominent feature in the religious movement of the last century, and the traditions of the movement are still a power in Wales. But more than this is the place occupied by hymns in the religious life of Wales due to the character of the hymns themselves. They are Scriptural, doctrinal, and experimental to an exceptional degree. They have not lost their effect with the wave of religious enthusiasm which gave many of them birth; but they are eminently adapted for all ages of the Church, and all conditions of men. They are not light and sensational, as many of the English revivalist hymns are; on the contrary, they are sober, solid, and profoundly spiritual - bold in their reiteration of the cardinal verities of Redemption - unvarying in the prominence given to the offices of the Holy Spirit - vivid, realistic, and intense, full of a buoyant and exultant faith, and eminently adapted to ground those who use them in the great fundamental truths of the Christian creed. Is it, therefore, any wonder, that hymns hold so prominent a place in the religious life of Wales? Moreover, something may be said as to the custom of learning by heart most of the hymns used in public worship which prevailed up to about thirty years ago. The congregations were expected to know by heart the hymns then generally used .... To take a hymn book to church was a thing almost unknown in my younger days; and those who did so were regarded as cultivating English pride ... and as making light of the tradition of the elders. And here let me just refer to a custom which the habit of storing the memory with hymns made it easy to observe, which prevailed, and still prevails in parts of South Wales. I refer to the custom of singing hymns during the celebration of the Holy Communion. After the first railful, those who had communicated retired to the body of the church, and there sang sacramental hymns while the service proceeded, until, at the close, the entire body of communicants joined in one united Eucharistic song of adoration and praise. ...

But for Welsh worship - to move Welsh hearts with a holy enthusiasm - give me a native Welsh hymn. However it may be explained, it is a patent fact, that there is, not a mere charm, but a mysterious power in a Welsh hymn which seems to open the Welsh heart as nothing else does.[59]

Give me a Welsh hymn, suggested Howell on another occasion, to raise a Welsh congregation to "heart heat". For there was a hidden power in a Welsh hymn which opened up the Welsh heart like a key opens up a lock, even though, as he said in the same lecture, Welsh hymns had less theology and artistic form than the older Latin hymns.[60]

Hymnology was "the highest expression of the religious life", wrote Howell to a correspondent, for it was "practically a *Union* of Christian hearts however we may differ in our spiritual beliefs". At this point all Christians could meet. This must have been an additional attraction to such an eirenic spirit as Howell.[61] It is not surprising that Howell wrote many Welsh hymns and translated others. One of his best known may almost sum up his spirituality. It is given here in its original and in a translation by Robert Ellis:

> O fy Arglwydd! O fy Mhrynwr!
> O fy Ngheidwad! O fy Nuw!
> Ti, fy Iesu, yw fy nghwbl,
> Ar dy haeddiant 'rwyf yn byw;
> Ffrwyth dy boen, a gwerth dy aberth
> Rhinwedd iawnol dwyfol waed,
> Dyna wraidd fy holl orfoledd,
> Dyma'r graig sydd dan fy nhraed.

> O my Lord, my redeemer
> O my keeper, O my God!
> Thou, O Jesus, art my all
> On thy victory I live.
> The fruit of thy pain, the worth of thy sacrifice.
> The atoning merit of thy precious blood,
> This is the root of all my exaltation,
> This is the rock which is under my feet.

---

[59] David Howell, *Welsh Hymnology* [1899] pp 4f; *Bye-Gones*, 18 Oct 1899, p 224; and see Howell's letters to Emlyn Evans on this subject, 1893-9 in NLW MS 8032B, fols 27-32. The original was a two hour lecture.

[60] David Howell, "Emynyddiaeth Gymreig", *Geninen*, 15 [1897] 10-14.

[61] Howell to Emlyn Evans, 27 Dec 1893, NLW MS 8032B, fol 28. And see the *Geninen* reference above, pp 13f.

Neither is it surprising in view of Howell's concern about the shallowness and emotionalism of the Welsh religious scene of his day that he wished to bring out a series of Welsh books of devotion similar to those published in the previous century. This never materialised.[62] Had he done so he might have redressed Lewis Williams' later criticism that he did not add much to Welsh theology save through his popular sermons.[63]

* * * *

Throughout his ministerial life Howell had a deep concern for the dignity and importance of the work of the ministry. His own influence came not simply through his preaching, but also because of his pastoral ministry. In this he acted in the tradition of Richard Baxter. His pastoral ministry was an extension of his pulpit ministry, by which Howell applied his message to individual hearts. It was said of his parochial ministry in Cardiff that he displayed an immense love of parochial labour, and devoted such attention and unwearied application to it that "it is a surprise to everybody but himself". The writer went on to say:

> Mr Howell has contributed less, perhaps, to pulpit literature than some of his more philosophic compeers have done; but he has contributed much more to parochial happiness than many; and while others have been content to let the cold light of their intelligence glimmer from the reading-desk for the benefit of those alone who could go thither and were able to understand it, the Vicar of St John's has taken the light in his hand, and, hastening away, has borne it through the dark places and the dismal passages of parochial life; throwing light and warmth where light and warmth were not, and, pouring out the indwelling emotions of his own loving and unselfish nature, has awakened the tearful gratitude of the poor, and drawn to himself the perfect affection of all.[64]

An obituary note in the evangelical *Record* added that "[t]hough widely known as an eloquent and impressive preacher, Dean

---

[62] Howell to Nathan, 24 June 1884, NLW MS 987B. fol 97.
[63] "Diwinyddiaeth yng Nghrymu o Ddr. Lewis Edwards hyd Heddiw", in *Y Traethodydd*, 82 [1927] 85.
[64] *Weekly Mail*, 7 Nov 1874, p 10. A similar tribute was given about his Wrexham ministry [SA/DR/54, fol 330].

Howell did not unduly exalt the place and influence of the sermon. He believed profoundly in the parochial system and in systematic pastoral visitation. To this, indeed, he was accustomed to devise whatever degree of influence or usefulness he had attained."[65]

The spiritual life of a minister was the clue to the success or failure of a ministry. So Howell believed. In a paper delivered to the Liverpool Clerical Society during the 1890s, *Ministerial Life in the Light of I Cor. IX,* he argued that the good name of a minister is precious far beyond his own immediate pastoral charge. "It is the man whose fidelity to conscience and to God is unswerving, who commands the respect of so-called 'men of the world' in the hour of sorrow or in the prospect of death", whom God will use, he maintained. He urged his clerical colleagues to continue with their study and reading: "the unread books of a Minister's Library will be no pleasant witnesses to meet at the great day of account." And he warned, using the example of Judas:

> [M]ay it not have been to teach the Ministers of every age how possible it is to be officially in frequent contact with Christ, to be the medium of power from Him, even to work miracles in His Name, to bear a high commission in His service, to be well versed in His teaching, and intimate with His ways, and yet to be in heart a stranger to the saving grace of God? Such a warning at such a cost would surely never have been left ringing in the ears of the Ministry from age to age, if the danger had not been one to which we are peculiarly liable. Nor can there be any doubt on this point, seeing that we have from our Lord himself words as solemn as ever came from His Divine lips. "Many will say to me in that day, Lord, Lord, have we not prophesied in Thy Name? and in Thy Name cast out devils? And in Thy Name done many wonderful works? And then will I profess unto them, I never knew you; depart from me, ye that work iniquity."...
>
> We further learn from the Apostle's experience that the Ministry has its peculiar dangers, and that no amount of religious attainments can relieve us of the duty of self-discipline. It is evidently implied that the very abundance of the Apostle's labours for others made him peculiarly liable to overlook himself. And is

---

[65] *Record*, 23 Jan 1903, p 79 [quoting the *Times*]; cf cutting in SA/DR/52, fol 729, which states Howell regarded his pastoral ministry as the foundation of all his success.

not this equally true of us? Is there no danger in a life which is "always on the run, seldom on the knees - a sentence without stops - an everlasting running round the circumference, while missing the centre?" Is there no danger of self-sufficiency from apparent success? Are we in no danger from love of power, love of success, love of ease, love of approbation, love of work for its own sake?...

We live in a halo of official sanctity, and therefore in danger of assuming that we are moved by spiritual motives because we act in the name and service of God. To us, Clergy, above all others, there is the snare of discharging the highest duties from secondary motives, and of habitually using religious phraseology, with no conscious insincerity, but without realising the terms and truths so familiar to our lips. In this way we are in danger of becoming mere functionaries, and of drifting into a duality of life and character, offensive to Him who requireth "truth in the inward parts."...

Granting that our private devotions may be more limp and languid than they should be, that the old pious periods are becoming stale and soul-less, and that such phrases as agonising in prayer, striving in prayer, and wrestling with God, need considerable discounting to make them quite suitable to our case, what then? Have we not large and attached congregations, well-ordered Services, an impressive ritual, frequent Communions, well trained Choirs, flourishing offertories, and multiplied organisations, and surely these things go for something? Granting that such old-fashioned experiences as conviction of sin, conversion, repentance, contrition of heart, and self-abasement before God, are rather traditional than actual experiences among our people - granting that not all our hearers are Communicants, and that but a small proportion of the sinning and dying men, women and children around us, whom we are called to baptise, marry and bury with the most spiritual Services to be found in the Liturgy of any Church, give any signs of grace, or are ever seen in the house of God, even if there was room for them, what then? "It is not given to mortals to command success." "We are doing our best, and who can do more?" Ah, my brethren, here is the point at issue. The question which may well come home to us with a searching urgency is, are we doing our best in the best way? Are we doing our best in God's way? If we are to be used of God, then it is certain it must be in His way, through His Spirit, and supremely for His glory. Our life must not be an occasional act of self-consecration, not only when, on bended knee, "we offer and present unto Thee, O Lord, ourselves, our souls and bodies, to be a reasonable, holy and lively sacrifice unto Thee", but there must be the abiding consciousness of being committed and given over to the absolute use and sovereign disposal of the Holy Spirit as a staff in his hand, standing or moving as only that hand is upon us. The "grace of ordination" must be a perpetual grace - not an act but a life - not a transaction in the past, but the ever-continued operation of the Triune Deity. Love of God and of souls, detached from every other aim and consideration, must be the motive-power of a God-approved Ministry, the work desired and done for its own sake - the Sermon, the Service, the visit, the prayer, containing and carrying with it its own motive, and its own reward, the promise and presence of God. And where this is the case, then will it follow that with the decline of youthful enthusiasm, and the vigour of manhood, and even with the decay of mental and physical power, there will be a concurrent growth of the spiritual life, a strengthening of old convictions, a deeper insight into the mysteries of Divine love, a firmer grasp of fundamental truths, and a fuller enjoyment of the Divine promises.

Quoting an American minister, Howell concluded:

"Dear brethren, our office is no ordinary one. We are ambassadors from the King of Kings to a revolted world. No work ever undertaken by mortals was ever so important, so solemn, or connected with such amazing consequences. Among all the thousands to whom we preach, not one but will take an impression from us that will never wear out. The fate of millions, through succeeding generations, depends on our faithfulness. Heaven and hell will for ever ring with recited memorials of our Ministry."[66]

Speaking to the Manchester Clerical Society during the 1890s on the subject of some of the dangers of ministerial life, Howell referred to the pressures placed on the ministry. There was the ceaseless table serving, the organisation concerned with schools, choirs, charities, buildings, clubs, trips and bazaars, and the endless machinery necessary to keep parochial life functioning. Are not, he asked, "many excellent lives ... handicapped and many strong minds ... spoiled of their strength through this ceaseless striving?" In all these matters the parson was expected to take the

---

[66] David Howell, *Ministerial Life in the Light of I Cor. IX* [Bangor, nd], pp 21f, 24 27 29-32.

lead. It was not the spiritual duties, not the study, not the presence in the sickroom nor the preparation for the pulpit, but the perpetual begging for money which wore out the individual life and adversely affected the temper: "Men have persevered, year after year, until all the moral sap of their nature has dried up, their spiritual strength dissipated, and they and their parishes suffering God knows how much." A readiness on the part of people to give from plenty not need was required, so that such financial requirements would be readily met, as nonconformity already did. He spoke too of the minister's prayer becoming a tradition rather than an act of conscious communion with God: "I know of nothing harder than spending a whole hour on my knees in true wrestling with God, personal pleading with a personal God." The want of personal application of the Christian faith to the lives of people, both in sermons and pastorally, distressed him, and he longed for good expository preaching. There were men who had dried up, who were better at forty than fifty, or better at fifty than sixty, and who slip from year to year until they are saved "only as through fire". Such men were mental and spiritual fossils, relics of the past, rather than a present spiritual power. Many of them were still living towards a high aim but living beneath it. And the remedy? To see God's face every day before man's; care not for the length of your worship, Howell warned, but be careful that your worship is holy between your soul and God.[67]

This theme of ministerial duty and renewal haunted Howell to the end of his days. In another sermon, the annual CPAS sermon of 1898, he lamented that a lack of power in the ministry of the Church was at the root of much of what was undesirable in the Church's life: "Earnestness, diligence, application, enterprise, learning, we have; but thirst for souls, absolute self renunciation, and an overwhelming sense of the importance of our position as standing between the living and the dead - are not these essential and indispensable conditions of power in the ministry?" And these qualities were lacking, at the very time when "large masses of our population are becoming more and more estranged from

---

[67] *Y Traethodydd*, XLVII [1896] 401-8 [Translated]. Writing to Professor Powel of Cardiff, Howell replied, "I have not had a more persuasive begging letter. Had you been a parson, your gift would have been a treasure to you." [Howell to Powel, 7 Aug 1890, in NLW MS 8541B]

the saving influence of Christianity ..." The conscience of the Church, he hoped, would be "awakened to the stupendous issues at stake."⁶⁸

*   *   *   *

It is clear that Howell felt that his own high expectation of the ministry of the Church contrasted poorly with his actual training for it, and he thus longed to see a better preparation provided for ordinands. In 1895 he expressed the hope that there might be an evangelical theological college, similar to Ridley or Wycliffe, founded in Wales. It was intended to counteract the influence of the Anglo-Catholic foundation at Aberdare, St Michael's College, which, however, he acknowledged as doing "a great work". Nothing came of his hope.⁶⁹ In advance of many he suggested that St David's College, Lampeter, should become purely a theological college, available for men who had taken their degrees at the various colleges of the University of Wales. This suggestion was still around in the 1940s!⁷⁰ But Howell's concern was not about the survival of that college so much as the provision of an adequate and through pastoral and spiritual preparation for Holy Orders. Writing to Bishop Hughes he urged that quiet days and retreats should be established in this college, conducted by men of known saintliness of life and character. He also urged that there should be a probationary year at the end of the college course, and that the new clergy should have much more contact with their bishops.⁷¹

Again, going back to his own experience of training, he urged in a speech at a St Asaph Diocesan Conference that the cost of training should be greatly reduced and, unless a candidate possessed adequate means, he should be able to secure financial help from some public society. As it was, a man without private means stood little chance of admission into the ministry of the Church of England, even though he might possess the combined gifts of the whole college of apostles! He continued:

---

⁶⁸ Sermon of 1898 to CPAS, in *CPAS Report*, 1898, pp 34 & 36.
⁶⁹ *Church and People*, 7 [1895] 57.
⁷⁰ D T W Price, *A History of St David's University College* [Cardiff 1990], II 102f, 108.
⁷¹ Howell to Bishop Hughes, 7 May 1886, BP 39, fol 200

> "Why, my lord, ours, I believe, is the only church in Christendom that has practically no voice in the primary selection of those who are to be trained to minister at her altars ...[or a] ... direct hand in the preparation of those who are destined for her priesthood. ... I venture to submit, my lord, that one of the most urgent needs of our own church just now, in connection with this subject for the training of candidates for holy orders, is a more devout observance of the Ember seasons, in the letter and still more in the spirit. The entire Church of England upon her knees, in every parish throughout England and Wales, during the twelve days of the four Ember seasons, would be a Church clothed with Pentecostal power and a Church omnipotent for good both at home and abroad."[72]

Howell also had another concern about the work of the ministry: it needed to be involved in alleviating the social conditions of that day. Speaking to the St David's Diocesan Conference he spoke about the conditions of the poor, and added,

> By all means, preach to them, as I am sure you do, the blessed Gospel of the love of God in Christ. But I beseech you, to preach also the Gospel of sanitation, of ventilation, of light, of pure air, and sober living; and sure I am that God will bless the one Gospel as well as the other. I have a deep conviction that there is a religion of the body as well as of the soul; and never should it be forgotten that our Lord is the Redeemer of the body as of the soul, and that the Christian body is the temple of the Holy Ghost. Not the least of the dangers of Wales is that of disconnecting religion from practical philanthropy. A man is taken to be religious because he repeats the phrases of Christian belief and experience, while living, or causing others to live, in utter neglect of physical laws, which are as much the laws of God as the Ten Commandments."[73]

Perhaps Howell over-stressed his point, and gave the impression that the two "gospels" were equally valid in a spiritual sense, but he was obviously concerned that the practical obligations of

---

[72] *St Asaph Diocesan Conference Report*, 1885, p 23.
[73] Howell, *Religion in the Home*, p 6. Speaking to a crowded audience of working men at the Exmouth Church Congress of 1894, Howell honoured them for their defence of their rights as workmen and citizens. He hoped they would fight equally against such abuses as sweated labour and poor housing, and asked them to catechise those who would solicit their vote about their policies regarding "drink" [*Record*, 12 Oct 1894, cutting in SA/DR/56. fol 487.

Christian truth should be lived out in his own and other's lives. It is hardly surprising, therefore, considering the conditions of his own age, that he became a well-known temperance advocate, putting "his strong shoulder to the wheel with all his heart and soul" as an obituary writer commented.[74] At one of the annual meetings of the Church of England Temperance Society at Exeter Hall, London, he spoke of his longing that more bishops and statesmen should give their support to "this noble work ... and righteous cause." He never forgot the time when the first bishop became a total abstainer: "if a bishop had been to a racecourse it could hardly have made a profounder sensation".[75] Howell also lectured extensively in favour of the Welsh Sunday Closing Act, giving evidence in its favour before the House of Lord's Select Committee. Such an act, he believed, would end, once for all, "the dark and dismal tide of intemperance and scenes of degradation in Wrexham that should fill anyone with a sense of shame." And, preaching before the Institute of Journalists in Llandaff Cathedral he emphasised the responsibility of the press to give a moral tone to the nation.[76]

*   *   *   *

It is thus hardly surprising that Howell had a deep concern for the reform of the Church, especially his own Church in Wales, so that it might proclaim the truth of the Gospel more effectively and testify to that truth in its own inner life. For too many years, he wrote to Bishop Hughes, the movement for reform within the Church had concentrated on legislative reforms regarding its organisation and the "outward equipments of clergy and churches". Rather it needed to concentrate on "pastoral and ministerial holiness".[77]

Combined with this there was a concern for the clergy of the Church. Bishops should be closer to their parochial clergy, he felt, and be able to help them to remove their despondency,

---

[74] WM, 16 Jan 1903, p 5. See also his speech in *Report of the St Asaph Diocesan Conference*, 1889, pp 12f, in which he argued that the cause of temperance was not being treated in a wholehearted and enthusiastic way by the Church.
[75] *North Wales Guardian*, 10 May 1890, p 3.
[76] *Record*, 3 Sept 1897, p 882.
[77] Howell to Bishop Hughes, 7 May 1886, BP 39, fol 200.

lukewarmness and isolation, thus enabling them to regain their spiritual tone. A quickening of the spiritual life of the clergy could equally result from a united pastoral letter from the four Welsh bishops. If they could be induced to issue one, with every sentence steeped in prayer, asking the whole body of the clergy to take Lent as a time of humiliation and intercession, "It is hardly possible to exaggerate the effect it would have in Wales, far more so than anything of the kind in England," claimed Howell. Equally, he wished to see more retreats provided for clergy and ordinands, as we will note later. In a letter written to Archbishop Benson's Tait missioner, John Cullin, during September 1887, Howell said that having a larger staff of Welsh curates than any other incumbent in the Principality for many years past, he was alarmed to find "how raw, unshaped and unspiritual many of the younger Welsh clergy are". He also felt that the cathedral residentiary canons could be used more for educational and evangelistic work, thus assisting the clergy in their parishes. The Church, he considered, would be made or broken in the parishes; where she would "be regarded simply in the light in which she is represented by her ministers - their moderation, their consistency, their charity, their spirituality, their efficiency and zeal as pastors and preachers, and above all by the degree in which their living and teaching reflect each other." This was spoken to the special meetings of the Llandaff Diocesan Church Extension Society held in 1879.

He hoped too that the Church in Wales would be more sympathetic to the national life of the country. He longed for the day when clergy would be more open to Welsh traditions and evangelical life, thus making it more the Church of the Welsh people than that of "the aristocracy and English settlers". More substantial Welsh press work was urgently required, and "short, pithy and striking Welsh tracts" produced. Howell's concern resulted in a Welsh committee being appointed by the SPCK. Because many of the problems of the Welsh Church in the past had been aggravated by a wrong use of patronage, generally by the appointment of monoglot Englishmen to Welsh-speaking parishes, and more recently the problems caused by Anglo-Catholic appointments to evangelical parishes, Howell urged there should be a reform in patronage. It should be administered by a board of assessors, with the bishop having a veto. He also urged that the

Welsh language should be encouraged, the services shortened but given an evangelical bias, the Holy Communion made as "eucharistical" as possible - with hymns before and after, prayer meetings held with extempore prayer and public catechising be revived, and annual deanery festivals for Sunday Schools introduced.

If these reforms were carried out with energy, faith and enthusiasm, the Church would soon regain the sympathies and recover the attachment of the warmhearted people of Wales, he wrote to Bishop Hughes. Perhaps Howell was over-optimistic, for many items on his "reform-list" only came in after his death, but each proceeded from his concern for the Church, in which he was at one with many other churchmen of all traditions.[78]

The mission work done throughout Wales by Archbishop Benson's missioners during the late 1880s, under the leadership of the Tait Missioner, gave Howell much encouragement.[79] Howell's concern with parochial missions stemmed from his involvement in the 1859 revival, and he held missions in both his Cardiff and Wrexham parishes, so that his eventual involvement in these so-called Welsh missions was at once practical and valuable. John Cullin, then Tait missioner, as well as Canon Mason, later Lady Margaret Professor at Cambridge, who was also involved in this mission work, both regarded Howell as one of the most active and influential of the Welsh clergy, and made much use of him.[80]

These missions arose from Archbishop Benson's concern for the Welsh Church, then facing the onslaught of the disestablishment controversy. Benson was alarmed by the state of the Welsh clergy who were frequently demoralised by the difficult and demanding pastoral situations they faced, as well as by the pressures placed on them by the growing antagonism caused by the campaign for disestablishment. The missions were parochially based, and were

---

[78] Shown in such speeches and letters as: *Speech to CPAS, Abstract of Reports and Speeches*, 1861, p 12; *Report of Speeches delivered at the Annual General Meeting of the Llandaff Diocesan Church Extension Society*, 1879, p 17; Howell to Bishop Hughes, 7 May 1887, BP 39, fol 200; Howell to Benson, 4 Dec 1886, 27 May 1887 and 8 Dec 1887 and memos etc, BP 51, fols 123, 125, 127, 138, 146, 148, 189; Howell to Cullin, 25 Sept 1887, BP 170, fol 83.

[79] See my monograph, *Reviving the Clergy, Renewing the Laity: Archbishop Benson's Mission in Wales* [Welshpool 1994].

[80] Cullin to Benson, 24 May 1886, BP 39, fol 225; and see BP 63, fol 17.

also used to train Welsh clergy in mission work,[81] although it is very clear from the reports sent back to Benson that one of their primary aspects was to provide spiritual help and encouragement to these parochial clergy.

There was thus a spiritual work amongst the clergy with conferences, quiet days and retreats, led by such men as Canon Mason, John Cullin and his deputy Herbert Sprigg; missions to a locality, the so-called flying missions when a missioner came to a parish and stayed a few days, meeting, teaching and encouraging clergy and lay leaders, and various itinerant missions to rural areas, which Howell regarded as most important.[82]

It is not surprising that Howell took a lead in this work within his own diocese, especially as Cullin felt that the official functionary appointed by Bishop Hughes for this work, Dean Herbert James, was totally unsuitable for the job. Cullin felt too that Howell was limited in his involvement in this work by this appointment.[83] Canon Mason had arranged a number of quiet days during 1887-8 for clergy throughout the diocese, which Howell wrote had been much appreciated, but there had been one unfortunate *contretemps* with Bishop Hughes. The bishop regarded Canon Mason, who was coming to Wrexham and Denbigh to lead these days, as an Anglo-Catholic, and not only objected to his coming, but refused him permission to speak. Howell, who regarded him as a fine spiritual teacher, was "overwhelmed with misery", for it indicated to him the lukewarmness of the Welsh bishops to this work. Nothing could be better balanced, judicious and edifying than Canon Mason's previous addresses during the spring, he wrote, with which no-one could find fault. Was not the bishop prejudiced and one-sided, and unjust to a man God had honoured as his own instrument for good in helping the clergy? Few things had more grieved him during the thirty years of his ministry.[84] Eventually Cullin's deputy, Herbert Sprigg, had to come in as a substitute, and he

---

[81] Canon Evans of Rhymney, David Edwards of Cefn, and Evan Davies of Brynamman, were amongst many involved.
[82] Howell to Cullin, 1 Oct 1886, BP 170, fol 113.
[83] Cullin to Benson, BP 63, fol 17.
[84] Howell to Benson, 8 and 28 Dec 1887, BP 51, fols 189, 201; J Cullin to Benson, 30 Dec 1897, BP 50, fol 241.

and he reported to the archbishop that he had spent two days each at Oswestry, Wrexham and Mold, preaching at each place to large numbers of lay-workers and holding conferences for the clergy. He thought the Church was gaining ground in the diocese and compared favourably to many districts in England. Howell, however, wrote that he felt Sprigg had been over-optimistic. The clergy of north Wales wanted a spiritual upheaval, "a breaking-up of the hard crust of easy-going complacency."[85]

The event became a means whereby Howell vented his frustrations at the apathy and timidity of the two north Wales bishops and their clergy, which "drive some of us well nigh to despair". Whether the Church was to remain established or not it still needed men of true faith, generous sympathy, and holiness, and this, he hinted, was all too often lacking. The Welsh clergy's reluctance against the mission scheme only ceased when they were informed it had the archbishop's blessing and approval, but many rural deans were still opposed to it. Nothing less than the presence of the bishop himself would persuade the clergy who most needed the help provided by the quiet days to attend them! But alas, where the bishops should have offered "spiritual aggressiveness", all they gave was some "mere official approval" by letter, rather than by putting the mission in the forefront of their work. They were holding back in "timid imitation of their English brethren" and by their dread of compromising their dignity. Alas, this stand was paralysing their influence. Unless the bishops were men of apostolic enthusiasm and self-forgetfulness, "we are done for".[86]

In spite of these reflections and these set-backs, Howell was greatly encouraged by the archbishop's interest in the Welsh Church. His interest had released him from despair, and given him a sanguine hope about the future. He noted also the quickening of spiritual interest all over Wales during the previous six months as a result of the archbishop's initiative, "a thing not known in Wales before for at least fifty years." He was thus

---

[85] Bishop Hughes to Howell, 20 Dec 1889, BP 51, fol 203; Howell to Benson, 6 Ap, 28 Dec 1888, 6 & 12 Jan 1889, BP 63, fol 40; and 51, fols 189, 201, 205-9; Spragg's report, BP 63, fol 34.
[86] Howell to Cullin, 25 Sept 1887, BP 170, fol 83; Howell to Benson, 9 Dec 1886, 26 May 1887, 6 & 12 Jan 1888, BP 39, fol 272; and 51, fols 146, 205, 209.

grateful that "the welfare of our long neglected Church" had so high a place in the archbishop's "thoughts and sympathies", and equally grateful for his choice of Canon Mason as one of the missioners, "just the man for Wales."[87]

Although Howell had been known as a preacher, and had taken part in the 1859 revival, he does not appear to have taken a leading role in mission work previous to this initiative. He may well have been one of the clergy who was encouraged by the archbishop's missioners to undertake such work. He is noted as the preacher at a fortnight's mission at Canterbury during 1887,[88] and thereafter took many missions "in our great towns",[89] including one, towards the end of his life, in the Maesteg area.[90] Speaking about this work in 1887 to the St Asaph Diocesan Conference, he not only endeavoured to commend this new movement, but also testified to his own spiritual indebtedness to it:

> I myself know one, whom I know more intimately than any other can, who, next to the grace of his ordination, owes to a mission, under God, almost all that he is.

His paper gave practical details as to how to prepare for, and organise a parochial mission. What are the symptoms that indicate a need for mission, Howell asked?

> I answer, that they are found in the prevalence of spiritual lukewarmness - of spiritual deadness. There is the barrenness of believers, the fewness of conversions, the want of personal devotedness and personal holiness among christians, the neglect of holy communion and the worldliness of communicants, a lack of zeal for the interests of the Church and the welfare of souls, and the want of liberality in supporting Church agencies at home and abroad. These, wherever they exist, are unmistakable proofs that a parish is not in a healthy condition, and that a well conducted mission is greatly needed.

---

[87] Howell to Benson, 9 Dec 1886, 26 May & 4 Dec 1887, BP 39, fol 272; and 51, fols 123, 149.
[88] *Haul*, 1887, p 93.
[89] CDH, 23 July 1893, p 7.
[90] Brinley Richards, *History of the Llynfi Valley* [Cowbridge 1982], p 252.

He urged that all those who were thinking of a mission or planning one should "look absolutely and exclusively to God the Holy Ghost for that power without which a mission is a mere religious effervescence, a carnal excitement, a strange fire on God's altar." And he warned of the dangers "of mistaking emotional impressions for spiritual conversion, and the still greater danger of regarding conversion as the end and not as the beginning of a new and higher life ... Above all there is the danger of a mission being regarded as an end, and not as a means to an end, that end being a higher level of Christian living, a more entire consecration of the soul to God, a closer reproduction of the life of Christ, a more faithful and whole-hearted service to the Church, and a more aggressive zeal for the welfare of souls."[91] Some years later he begged for an evangelistic agency to serve within the Church in Wales.[92]

* * * *

Seven years after its foundation in 1882 the work of the Church Army was reviewed by the archbishop of Canterbury, who appears to have requested Howell to offer his opinion. Howell expressed his concern that many of the candidates accepted for training were not churchmen, and that there was a want of church teaching in the army itself. He suggested that the probationary period for new officers should be longer and more thorough for "it is easier to keep a weak man out that to get him out once he is in." That training should include "the outlines of church controversy" regarding the Plymouth Brethren, Baptists and Romanists, and new officers should not be sent out without a service of dedication, addressed by a bishop or a suffragan bishop. He feared an over-optimism in its work: better to serve a few stations well than many badly. The work needed to be periodically inspected, and each officer should be required to spend some days in retreat every year, "though it would be as well to call it by another name".[93] In another letter Howell noted the good work

---

[91] *Report of the St Asaph Diocesan Conference*, 1887, pp 19-20.
[92] *Report of the Norwich Church Congress*, 1895, p 406.
[93] Howell to Benson: BP 70, fols 3, 34. It appears that in 1889 Prebendary Carlile requested the archbishop of Canterbury and the bishop of London to become patrons of the work.

done by the Church Army in his own neighbourhood and parish, though he felt it required a re-organisation or else it would "run into seed".[94]

Foreign mission also engaged Howell's concern, and he was especially worried at the lack of support given to it in Wales. Speaking at the St David's Diocesan Conference on this subject, he declared that the Church's principal reason for existence was the evangelisation of the world, but that less than one third of humanity was even remotely Christian. He feared that the demands of home mission were providing an excuse for not supporting this work. Those parishes who gave nothing to this cause showed considerable spiritual apathy in this and probably other matters as well. It is "hardly conceivable", he declared, that "the head of a parish, a pastor of souls, a steward of Christ, and a commissioned officer of a Church which prays daily 'Thy Kingdom come', can be held excusable for denying his people the privilege and opportunity of being 'workers together with God' in the salvation of mankind." This work must be seen at the forefront of Church life, and the voluntary contributions to its work should be in due proportion to the inherited endowments of the Church.[95] In a similar way, addressing the Church of England Zenana Missionary Society, he uttered a challenge, that the command to "go into all the world and preach the Gospel to every creature" was as valid a command as the Ten Commandments. He cannot, wrote Howell, "be a loyal subject of the Kingdom of Christ, who recognises no obligation beyond what serves his own personal safety". He continued: "every healthy Christian life is, of necessity, a missionary life".[96]

Any spiritual work which would forward the work of the Christian gospel in Wales received Howell's active support. In the summer of 1902 he was consulted by Mrs Penn Lewis, a lady influential in Keswick circles. He encouraged her to establish a convention for spiritual life in Wales, and entered into all the detailed arrangements with her about it. He may have been one

---

[94] Howell to Benson, 6 Ap 1888, BP 63, fol 40.
[95] David Howell, "Foreign Mission", *Report of the St Davids Diocesan Conference*, 1897, pp 27-30. Howell also spoke at CMS meetings in London, see E Stock, *The History of the Church Missionary Society* [London 1899] II 304, III 302. He also had a junior branch of SPG in one of his churches [*Wrexham Guardian*, 20 Dec 1885, p 8].
[96] David Howell, *Women and Missions* [1900], pp 2-4.

of those thirteen clergy and lay people who since the Keswick Conference of 1896 had held a prayer meeting for Wales. He wished to establish a meeting similar to Keswick for Wales, in order to deepen the spiritual life.[97] This need was continually on his mind. Howell's godson, Grey Edwards, remembered an expression he was fond of using was "'Mark you'; 'Mark the words - Greater works than these shall ye do.' His patriarchal appearance, and gracious fervid greetings with both hands were so natural and inspiring that he filled one with elation. I feel the pressure of both his hands as he held mine in offering up a prayer in the vestry before entering the Church, that 'the Holy Ghost might be with us in all the Power of his might, to direct, guide, and sanctify us.' The last time I met the dear man was at Whitland Junction, in Carmarthenshire, and his last conversation with me was about the Holy Spirit: 'Had he left us?'"[98]

Howell's concern for spiritual renewal for his Church and nation led him to write an article for the magazine he had founded many years before, *Y Cyfaill Eglwysig*. This he entitled his New Year's epistle to Wales. It appeared in the December 1902 issue. Eifion Evans in his book on the history of the 1904-5 revival provides a translation:

> The preaching, it is said, is able, scholarly, interesting and instructive; it is however accompanied with but little unction and anointing - there is no smiting of the conscience; no laying bare the condition of the soul as in times past. The terminology of former ages, such as conviction, conversion, repentance, adoption, mortification of sin, self-loathing, and such like, have become to a great extent foreign and meaningless ... The authority of the Bible and the fundamental truths of Christianity are being weighed in the balance of reason and criticism, as though they were nothing more than human opinions. A steadfast faith in the invisible, the miraculous, and the supernatural is regarded as open to question.... But what of the remedy? ... A Holy Spirit religion is the only cure for the moral and spiritual disease of Wales at this time... Take note: if it were known that this was my last message to my fellow-

---

[97] D Jenkins, *The Agricultural Community in South-West Wales* [Cardiff 1971] pp 221; J Penn Lewis, *The Awakening in Wales* [London 1905] p 29.

[98] Grey-Edwards, *Reminiscences*, pp 103f; cf Howell's thoughts for Lent in *Home Words*, Feb 1903, p 34: "do it in the power of the Holy Spirit."

countrymen throughout the length and breadth of Wales, before being summoned to judgment, the light of eternity already breaking over me, it would be, that the principal need of my country and dear nation at present is still spiritual revival through a special outpouring of the Holy Spirit."

This had been his constant prayer for the previous fifteen years.[100] It was his last message. He died as it was being read. This message helped create a deep sense of urgency about prayer, and many used the words of the prophet Isaiah he so often used for himself, "O that thou wouldst rend the heavens and come down". God answered this and the similar prayers of many. In that subsequent revival of 1904-5 many of the Welsh Anglican churches were deeply affected, and Bishop Owen of St Davids called upon the services of Timothy Rees, later bishop of Llandaff, to act as a special missioner during that period. But many of the clergy and ministers feared the revival movement, disliking its enthusiasm and freedom of worship, with the result that the leadership went into other less experienced hands, and the revival went off-beam and degenerated at times into mass emotionalism. It lacked a sense of theology which would have made it more objective and pointed more to Christ than to self. It may well be that the seeds of this lay in the Keswick movement, whose themes were those of holiness and consecration, rather than the themes more prevalent in Welsh spirituality, namely redemption and assurance. Alas, the end result was that the churches could not contain the revival, whose vitality passed outside the mainstream of traditional Welsh life.

But this is not to under-estimate the work of the revival, nor the contribution given to it, under God, of David Howell. His prophetic judgment, given at the end of his life, was a fitting conclusion to a life of evangelical fervour and Christian interest. As Robert Ellis suggests, his life was a little pool of spirituality upon the dry shores of the Church.[101]

---

[99] Eifion Evans, *The Welsh Revival of 1904* [Port Talbot 1969] pp 46f.
[100] *Record*, 30 Jan 1903, p 103.
[101] Robert Ellis, *Living Echoes* [Cardiff 1950], p. 90.

Conclusion

David Howell has been described as a builder of bridges: between the Welsh and the English elements in his nation; between Church and Nonconformity; within the Church itself, and as a priest, pastor and preacher between people and God. How well did this man of immense personal charm and charisma, simplicity of life and conversation, almost childlikeness, of humour, fellow-sympathy, good temper and faithfulness to duty[1] succeed as a bridge builder?

Clearly his spiritual life sustained him under "more fiery trials of which the world outside knew but little", as one writer noted, adding that his influence in Wales came not so much from his great gifts and natural instincts, but derived from his spiritual power.[2] It may well be that the moral lapse of his younger days made him more sympathetic and charitable to others. Howell said these words in a new year's sermon which might almost be said to sum up that part of his life, "let God ... sprinkle the record of this year's existence with the blood of atonement, that he could purge away every blemish, and write across the dark record the name of Jesus Christ."[3] If he knew this bridge-building in his own life, how well did he succeed for others?

His was a familiar name to many church families in England, especially evangelical households; his sermons and addresses at Church Congresses, the various society meetings at London's Exeter Hall, the provincial meetings held at Liverpool, Manchester and Birmingham, and his participation in the Lower House of Convocation, made this possible. He was thus able to act as a bridge between England and Wales. So he used his powerful oratory to declare the needs of Wales and the Welsh

---

[1] *Record*, 23 & 30 Jan 1903, pp 79, 103.
[2] *Record*, 9 Ap 1897, p 344.
[3] *North Wales Guardian*, 4 Jan 1890, p 5.

Church and to interpret Wales and its culture and spirituality to English ears, even though today some of his historicity may appear to us to be one sided and confused. Nevertheless his advocacy may well have assisted the Welsh Church's recognition as an indigenous church, entitled to Welsh-speaking bishops and clergy in bilingual parishes, although he was but one voice of a much wider movement. In a more direct way Howell's advocacy was able to persuade the many English societies such as CPAS and SPCK to give active support to the Welsh language in their policy statements. Within the nation itself Howell probably brought about some deeper understanding of the feelings of the Welsh Church people regarding the Anglicisation policy of the Church, and his voice, with that of others, undoubtedly helped the Church of England in Wales to recognise these claims as just and reasonable.

Howell's desire to act as a bridge between Church and Nonconformity was misunderstood. He may well have been far too idealistic in assuming that good preaching would cause Nonconformists, particularly the Welsh Calvinistic Methodists, to return to the Church of their fathers. Too much water had gone under the bridge for that to be an effective policy, however ceaselessly he and others proclaimed it; sufficient even for Gladstone to accept its validity. He was successful in reminding the Church that Nonconformists were still Christians, in spite of the disestablishment controversy, even though he disagreed with the methods some of them used to achieve that aim. Unfortunately his sense of moderation and goodwill was discomforted by the aggressiveness of Bishop A G Edwards and his team of 'young turks'. Had Howell's policy been accepted a compromise solution to the disestablishment controversy might have been found acceptable. Instead a policy of open warfare was allowed to fester on both sides and harmony and good-will lost. Had Howell achieved episcopal office he might have been able to establish a fair solution - for much of the Nonconformist demands during the 1890s were, I read, bluff, and given simply to persuade the Church to come to terms, but that was not to be. Lord Aberdare, on the grounds of misplaced snobbery (a man, he wrote of Howell, having those qualities which resemble the better class of Dissenting ministers), and Bishop Edwards, on more personal grounds, prevented his appointment. The loss was not Howell's. It was the Church's. For Howell could have warmed its heart and soul, although the cost to him might have been substantial, for his appointment would have antagonised the comfortable middle class leadership of the Church in Wales.

Within the Anglican Church, Howell endeavoured to act as a bridge between the various parties and groups within it. Endeavouring to see good in all men, his motto being "grace to all them that love the Lord Jesus Christ in sincerity",[4] he tried to interpret one to the other, arguing that one should "[b]e firm and definite in your appreciation of Evangelical truth, ... but be broad in your sympathies."[5] But such catholicity, in its truest sense, was his undoing. His fellow evangelicals mistrusted him, and even those whom he had personally befriended "when they greatly needed befriending" later turned against him, pursuing him with "malignancy".[6] The result was that at the end of his life, in ecclesiological terms, he was an isolated figure ploughing "a somewhat lonely field".[7] In this respect we need to say that Howell was a man ahead of his times, and even today many of his fellow evangelicals need to learn from him in this respect.

Howell's greatest service to Wales, however, was not so much in his concern for the reform and indigenousness of his Church, nor for the building up of large and successful parishes, though these proved that his methods worked and his spiritual emphasis was in the right place, but rather in his quiet and deep spiritual work within the lives of people, especially his fellow clergy. Yet many of the clergy feared him, as a bigoted report in *Cymru Fydd* noted:

> But the Welsh clergy don't care overmuch about the Canon. He can preach, and they cannot; he believes in the power of the Gospel, they believe in the charm of ritual; he yearns after spiritual life, too many of them are content with the convulsive movements produced by ecclesiastical magnetism; he inclines towards Disestablishment, while they regard it as the modern "abomination of desolation" .....[8]

[4] Letter of March 1871 in NLW Edward Hall purchase.
[5] *Record*, 23 Jan 1903, p 79.
[6] Ibid.
[7] *Wrexham Advertiser*, 24 Jan 1903, p 7: a man "left .... somewhat detached", quoted the *Record* [23 Jan 1903, p 79] from the Times.
[8] *Cymru Fydd*, II [1889] 322f.

Howell could be forthright, sometimes, about the lack of spiritual life within the clerical profession. Yet many noted the wide influence he exercised over many of his fellow clergy, including Bishop Bickersteth of Exeter,⁹ and W H Griffith Thomas, a well-known evangelical leader and writer of his day, for many years principal of Wycliffe Hall, Oxford. Thomas, who had come under Howell's influence during his Wrexham ministry, regarded Howell as his spiritual father.¹⁰

Howell's concern for mission, within his own parishes and throughout the Church in Wales, his pioneering work in breaking down barriers, his challenge for people to be involved in ministry, his directness in preaching, his pastoral work amongst individuals, produced a work and influence which can only be measured out of time. But may it not be argued that his spiritual work, often unseen and unheard, helped produce a new mood in Wales and enabled the Welsh Church to retain an inner spiritual feel, which helped it to prepare for the problems disestablishment would bring? And his insistence on prayer and revival was one of the human leads that led to the 1904-5 religious revival, even though its cause went disastrously wrong.

His was a life well-lived, of great significance and influence in his own day, though as Griffith Thomas remarked, that influence could have been much greater and far more significant: "His was an influence that would have proved of incalculable service to the cause of truth and love and peace, if he had been allowed to exercise it where it might and ought to have been exercised."¹¹ Alas, the history of the Church in Wales almost turned on the election of one man to power! The world which Howell had known almost died overnight eleven and a half years after his death in 1903, yet that new world still needed the Gospel he proclaimed. As his contemporaries noted at the time of his death, he left no successor, "no one who enjoys in anything like the same degree the respect, the confidence, and the affections of all the Welsh people of all creeds and classes."¹² But Howell's concern

---

⁹ Bickersteth to Lord Salisbury, 24 Jan 1889, Hatfield House, Salisbury Papers.
¹⁰ *Record*, 23 Jan 1903, p 79; J S Reynolds, *Canon Christopher* [Abington 1967], pp 255, 285, 294.
¹¹ *Record*, 23 Jan 1903, p 79.
¹² Ibid.

for ecclesiastical co-operation, peace and goodwill amongst Christians, for spiritual life in the Church rather than institutional order, evangelical harmony and mutual understanding, are still with us today. The life he lived can still offer us some clues about our future.

Index

Aberaeron 29
Abercarn, use of 164f 276
Aberdare, Lord, see Bruce H A
Aberdare, St Michael's College 296
Abergavenny, Divinity School 14-17
Aberystwyth 29 269
Aitkin, Robert 84
   W Hay 84
Allen, James 240 242 245
Armenian people 167
Assistant Curates' Society 53 173

Ballinger, John 246
Benson, Edward White 173 175 201-2
   204-8 214 304f
   mission to Wales 299-303
Bevan, William Latham 239f
Bickersteth, E H 204f 207 311
Blosse, Archdeacon 114
British and Foreign Bible Society 96
Bruce, H A (Lord Aberdare) 8 17 70
   81 98 199f 309
Brutus (David Owen) 15
Bunsen, Baron 20
Bury, John 251
Bushell, W D 113
Bute, 2nd marquess of 45 49 51f
   3rd marquess of 56 98 104 106
   108

Campbell, James Colquhoun 31 36
   39 52 204
Capel, Bury 61
Cardiff 39 41-117 221 269
   All Saints' Church 52 63
   appointment to parish 1875 114f
   Blackweir Church 92
   Canton 96 108
   Eglwys Dewi Sant 65
   mission to town 83-7
   Roath 55f 85
   St Andrew's Church 50 71f 74 77f
      85f 90 101 103f 106 114
   St James' Church 91f

   St Mary's Church 43 49 51-61 63
      68 75 85
   St John's Church 43-50 63f 68 75f
      78 85-7 101 116
   St Paul's Free Church 58f
   St Peter's RC Church 63
   St Stephen's Church 59f
   St Teilo's Church 93
   schools at 87-90 100
   Tractarians at 56-63
   vicarages 105-9 194
   Welsh Church 63f
Carlile, Wilson 144
Catechising 282f
Cefn y Coed 14f
Christopher, A M W 250
Church Army 144 304f
Church Association 58 62
Church Missionary Society 94f 251
Church of England Defence Association
   66
Church Pastoral-Aid Society 24 26-31
   46 53 74 96 102f 114 121 130f
   173 183 185 251 273 309
Church rates 66f 100f 128
Clapp, Thomas 55
Clerical meetings 29 282
Copleston, Edward 45
Cory, Richard 60
Cowbridge 14
Cullin, John 299-301
Cunliffe, George 118-21 125 131f
Cunnick, Thomas 114
Curates' Aid Society 53
Curates stipends and grants 96 102f
   126-31

Darlington, Thomas 198
Davey, William Harrison 240
Davidson, Randall Thomas 158 206-8
   211
Davies, Daniel 231
Davies, David (Canton) 160
Davies, David (Penarth) 168 209 279
Davies, Evan (Myfyr) 258

313

Davis, David Grimaldi 229
Diocesan conferences 189
Disestablishment of Church in Wales 3 65f 165-86 188 192 195-8 212-22 232-4 236-8 273f 309f
Disestablishment of Irish Church 65 98f
Disraeli, Benjamin 200f
Dynevor, Lord 200 250

Ecclesiastical Commissioners 102-5 116 127-9 133f 150 188 192 242f 245
Edwards, A M Grey 279f 306
Edwards, Alfred George 3f 11 124n 172 190 195 202 204 206-9 239 241 309f
  & Church Defence 167f 189 195-8 232-4 236-8
  Dispute with Howell 198 211-27 229f
  his promotion syndicate 232f 235
  patronage row 227-36
Edwards, E Wood 230n
Edwards, Henry Thomas 97 171 195 197 209 212 231 269
Edwards, Owen Morgan 246
Edwards, Dr William 41 96 159
Eisteddfodau 8 19 164 257-62
Ellis, Robert (Cynddelw) 20 159 258
Ellis, Thomas Edward 203
Episcopate, the Anglo-Welsh 160f
Escusham 125 129 151
Evangelicals in Welsh Church 26f
Evans, D Silvan 164 205 249 252 259 267-9 273
Evans, Archdeacon David 29f
Evans, David (Dewi Haran) 258
Evans, Goronwy 216
Evans, Owen 240
Evans, Thomas (Cadrawd) 242
Evans, William (Rhymni) 38 85 173 267 269
Evans, William (Tonyrefail) 10

Ffestiniog 29
Finances, parochial 100-5 126-31 151 190f
Fishbourne, Edward Alexander 195 251
Fletcher, William Henry 2

Free Church of England, The 58f
Furse, Charles Wellington 84f

Gatton, George 92 103n
Gaun, Mr 77f
Gauntlett, John 114
Gee, Thomas 159 168 195 210
Gelligaer 106
George, David Lloyd 168 213n 277
Gladstone, Stephen 213f
Gladstone, William Ewart 8f 11 20 64 70 118 175 195 199f 215 225n 260
Gore, Charles 275
Gower, John 114
Goyne, Richard 63f
Graham, Henry Elliott 45
Green, A J M 240
Gresford 153 188 250f
Griffith, John (Merthyr Tydfil) 26 61f 209 269
Griffiths, E M 114
Griffiths, Archdeacon John 2 10-14 22 24-8 61 85 164 197 209 259 269 271
Griffiths, John (Llandeilo) 26
Griffiths, John (Machynlleth) 85
Grosvenor, Richard 201

Hall, Sir Benjamin and Lady, see Llanover
Haslam, William 85
Hawkins, Edward 61
Heber, Reginald 131
Hills-Johnes, Lady 161 178 252f 273
Horsley, Heneage 190
How, William Walsham 123 192
Howell, Ann (wife of David Howell) 10 70f 81 113 153 190 193 199 252-4
Howell, David
  Anglo-Welsh position of Church, his comments on 169-178 218f 264-6
  Archdeacon of Wrexham 189f 212 223
  bardic name, Llawdden 19 257
  Benson's mission to clergy, his involvement in 298-303
  birth and early days 5-10
  bishoprics, recommended for 8f 70 199-210 273

children of 11 16 202f 214 225f 241 252-6
Church Army work 304f
Church, commitment to, 157-9 165 179-81 184 272 276f
community involvement 96-8 149f 248 297f
CPAS representative for Wales 26-30 39
death 249-52
disestablishment, his position regarding 65-7 166-86 188 192 195-8 212-22 237-8 273f 309f
dispute with Bishop Edwards 198 211-27 229f
education 14-17 21 37f
evaluation of work 2f 29 116f 153-6 164 187 250 308-12
evangelical churchman, an 272-7 310
foreign mission, devotion to 93-6 305
higher education, involvement in 269f
homes in which he lived 31f 105-9 127 131-5 193-5 242f
hymnology, interest in 288-91
income of his benefices 103-5 127f 190f
lay involvement, concern for 152 156
Lion, his dog 155f
literary & eisteddfodic interests 18-22 38 99 257-62 267 290
marriage 10-12 202
memorial fund 246
ministry at Cardiff 39f 41 66-117 221
    Gresford 153 190-5
    Neath 22-6
    Pwllheli 30-40
    St Asaph Cathedral 187-9
    St Davids 239-49
    Wrexham 109-111 118-56 206f
ministry, concern for 291-8 299
nonconformity, his relationship with 10 25 34 96 111 116f 126 144 154 157 159-65 169 171f 175-8 182 232f 243 270-3 308-10
opposition to 203 205-7 273 310
ordination, desire for 12f 22f

parochial missions, involvement in 83-7 141-4 303f
pastoral ministry, his 33-5 39 78-83 112f 139f 144f 153f 191-3 242-9 282-7 291
patriotism for Wales 262-4
political interests 98f 167
prayer and family worship, concern for 283-7
preaching ability 28-30 32f 35 71-5 112 116f 139f 193 247f 251 277-83 291f
reform in Church, concern for 181-6 211 298-300
reunion, his interest in 2 164f 185
& revival of 1859 29f
& revival of 1904-5 251 306f 311
rural dean of Wrexham 152 187
schools, his work for 87-90 100 146-9 270f
spiritual life 33 39 295
Sunday schools, interest in 90 113 146 152 288 300
temperance interests 97 149f
Tractarianism, distaste of 62f 186 274f 296 299 310
Welsh Church, concern for a 265f 306f
Welsh language, concern for 260-2 266 299
Welsh services, promotion of 24f 33f 63-5 135-9 170f 188 206 221 244 299f
Welsh preaching, desire for 281f
Howell, John (father of David) 7-9 13f 22 159
Howell, Tudor (son of David) 203 214 225f 241 255
Howell, William (brother of David) 9 256
Hughes, John (Ceiriog) 72 258
Mrs, 257
Hughes, Joshua 20 26 109f 118f 121 133-6 173 179 187-9 199 233 281 296 298 300-2
protest at his patronage 121-4
Hughes, Trevor 234
Hymns, Welsh 288-91

Jackson, J A 34
James, David (Panteg) 20 61 94 167

315

James, Herbert 301
Jayne, Francis John 206
Jenkins, David (Aberdare) 56
Jenkins, David (Manafon) 201-4
Jenkins, Evan 85
Jenkyn, Richard 14
Johnes, Arthur James 160
Jones, Basil 201 204 240 245
Jones, Charles 64
Jones, Daniel (Pwllheli) 40
Jones, David (Llangan) 6f 280
Jones, David (Penmaenmawr) 114 197
Jones, Eiddon 213 215f
Jones, Griffith Arthur 56-61 112
Jones, Henry 36
Jones, John (Talysarn) 10
Jones, J Morgan 280
Jones, Robert Isaac (Alltud Eifion) 28
Jones, Thomas (Pwllheli) 31f
Jones, Wynne 229f 230n

Kenyon, George 167 246 269
Keswick in Wales 305f
King, Edward 240 275
Kittermaster, F W 124
Knight, Bruce 8
Knight, Charles R 46

Lampeter 29
Lampeter, St David's College 15 37 269f 296
Law, Henry 69
Lay work 152
Leigh, David W 6
Lewellin, Llewelyn 242
Lewis, Bernard 167
Lewis, Evan 235
Lewis, Dr Gomer 248
Lewis, Mrs Penn 305
Lewis, Richard 240
Lewis, Sir William Thomas 246
Liberation Society 212
Liddon, Henry Parry 206
Llanbeblig 29
Llandaff Diocesan Choral Association 61
Llandeilo 29
Llangan 6
Llanover, Lord (Benjamin Hall) 8 18
Llanover, Lady 8 20 23 64f 69f 100 109 136 164 199 201 203 267f 276

Llanrhystud 30
Lloyd, John 240
Lloyd, Lewis 202 207f 234f
Lloyd, Thomas 231

Malcolmson, James 85f
Mason, Arthur James 205 300-3
Matthews, Edward 10
Merthyr Tydfil 17f
Ministry of the Church 291-8
Missions, parish 83-7 141-4 303f
Missions, to clergy 298-304
Missions to Seamen 53 96
Morgan, Benjamin 31
Morgan, D Parker 56
Morgan, John Vyrnwy 205 279
Morgan, William (Ystradyfodwg) 16
Morgan, William Leigh 52-6 58 63 68 96

Nathan, see Reynolds, Jonathan
Neath 12 22-6 161f 271
Nonconformist attack on Church 25 108
(see disestablishment)
Norton, Philip 59

Ollivant, Alfred 11f 14f 23 26 57 59 64 70f 107-9 199f
Osman, J W 57
Owen, John 175 199 207 231 239f 243 307

Parkins, William Trevor 152 226
Parry, David (Llywel) 26 279
Parsonages 31f 105-9 127 131-5 193-5
Patronage, protests regarding 121-4 227-36
reform of 299f
Pencoed 7
Penrhyndeudraeth 28
Pew rents 48f 101f 104
Phillips, Evan Owen 239f 242 245
Phillips, Sir Thomas 212
Pierpoint, Mr 69-71
Powis, 2nd earl of 234
Prayer 283-7
Preaching, Welsh 277f
Price, Lewis 114
Price, Thomas (Carnhuanawc) 19
Protestant Churchmen's Alliance 273

Protheroe, John Howard 252 255
Pryce, John 259
Puller, Frederick William 112
Pwllheli 30-6 39f 72f

Queen Anne's Bounty 32 103 127 132-5 191 193f

Ragg, Lonsdale 238
Rees, Henry 10
Rees, Timothy 307
Rees, Dr William 2 164
Religious Tract Society 96
Revival of 1859 29f
    of 1904-5 251 306f 311
Reynolds, Jonathan (Nathan Dyfed) 17-23 156 209 267
Rice, William Talbot 250 279
Richard, E P 106
Richard, Henry 168
Richards, Richard (Caerwys) 26
Roberts, Hugh 230
Roberts W J (Gwilym Cowlyd) 259
Rowland, Daniel 196
Ryle, Herbert Edward 246
Ryle, John Charles 199 205

St Asaph Cathedral 187-9
St Davids 239-49
    restoration of Cathedral 244-6
St Mary Hill 10 12
Salisbury, third marquess of 203f 207 224 230n 237 239-41
Saulez, Vincent 83 96
Saunders, David 7 159 164 277
    Mrs (David Howell's sister) 193 255f
Schools, church 87-90 100 146-9 270f
Scott, J Oldrid 245
Shipley, Jonathan 118
Short, Thomas Vowler 119 146 190
Signini, Father 63
Smith, Allan 250
Smith, Edward Braithwaite 190
Society for Promoting Christian Knowledge 299 309
Society for the Propagation of the Gospel 96
Sprigg, Herbert 301f
Spurrell, William 267f
Squire, Edward Burnard 63

Stacey, Thomas 45 51 63 75 102
Stephens, Thomas 16 20f
Sunday Schools 90 146 152 288 300

Temperance 97 149f 298
Temple, Frederick 244
Theological training 14-17 296f
Thirlwall, Connop 19 29 37 122 161 200
Thomas, Sir Alfred 246
Thomas, D Lleufer 244
Thomas, David Richard 227 229 232 259
Thomas, Ebenezer (Eben Fardd) 19
Thomas, Edward (Idriswyn) 157
Thomas, Dr John 277
Thomas, Owen 10
Thomas, Thomas (Caernarfon) 29
Thomas, Thomas (Pontypool) 159
Thomas, W H Griffith 250 311
Thompson, Charles James 65 100 104f 115
Tilly, Alfred 42 83
Twigg, Richard 85

University movement in Wales 269f

Vaughan, Charles John 206 211 240
Vaynor 14
Victoria, Queen 11 202f 206-8
Vincent, James Crawley 36

Walters, Thomas 16 26
Watkins, Henry William 203
Webb, John 43-5 52 69
Welsh Church press 299
Welsh Church "revival" 173f
Welsh Dictionary 267-9
Welsh services 24f 33f 63-5 120f 135-9 170f 188 244 300
West, Colonel 213-5 217
Westminster, duke of 228
Wickham, Robert 190 194
Williams, Camber 157 246 250 276 279
Williams, David (Castle Caereinion) 122
Williams, David (Llandyrnog) 158f
Williams, David (Llanelli) 269
Williams, David Edward 114
Williams, Eliezer 36
Williams, Hugh 61

Williams, John (Ab Ithel) 20f
Williams, Morris (Nicander) 36
Williams, Robert (Llanfaelog) 36
Williams, Rowland 37f
Williams, Taliesin 257
Williams W H (Watcyn Wyn) 1 18f
Williams, Watkin 230n 231-3 235f
Williams, William Venables 123f 228f

Wrenford, J Tinson 61f 85
Wrexham 109-11 118-56 206-7
  St Giles' Church 126 139
  St Mark's Church 136-9
  Schools 146-9
  Vicarage 131-5 194
  Welsh Church 135-9